D0789137

WITHDRAWN
UTSA LIBRARIES

The Maoist
Educational Revolution

WITHDRAWN
UTSA LIBRARIES

Theodore Hsi-en Chen

The Praeger Special Studies program—utilizing the most modern and efficient book production techniques and a selective worldwide distribution network—makes available to the academic, government, and business communities significant, timely research in U.S. and international economic, social, and political development.

The Maoist Educational Revolution

PRAEGER SPECIAL STUDIES IN INTERNATIONAL ECONOMICS AND DEVELOPMENT

Praeger Publishers New York Washington London

Library of Congress Cataloging in Publication Data

Ch'ên, Hsi-ên, 1902-
    The Maoist educational revolution.

    (Praeger special studies in international economics
and development)
    Includes bibliographical references.
    1. Education—China (People's Republic of China,
1949-   )—History.   2. Mao, Tsê-tung, 1893-
I. Title.
LA1131.C376   370'. 951   72-89643

PRAEGER PUBLISHERS
111 Fourth Avenue, New York, N.Y. 10003, U.S.A.
5, Cromwell Place, London SW7 2JL, England

Published in the United States of America in 1974
by Praeger Publishers, Inc.

All rights reserved

© 1974 by Praeger Publishers, Inc.

Printed in the United States of America

The study of Maoist education is essential to a full understanding of the Communist revolution in China because the aim of the revolution is not only to reshape the political structure and the economic system but to establish a new society, to be brought about and perpetuated by a "new type of man." Education is the means by which the "new man" is produced. What are the attributes of the new man? How are they different from the kind of man that, say, American education strives to produce? A profile of the new man would help visualize the kind of "proletarian society" that the Communist revolution aims to achieve.

The study of Maoist education is of interest to the West from another point of view. Western education has been subjected to severe criticism by educators who are dissatisfied with traditional education, by students who demand a "relevant" program more closely related to their needs, by social reformers who want education to play a direct role in social change, and by the public at large. Some of the criticisms made by Western educators and intellectuals sound strikingly similar to Maoist attacks on bourgeois education. They, too, have pinpointed such shortcomings as the dominance of the profit motive in capitalistic society, an educational system that reflects the profit-making and self-seeking motive of life, and extended periods of schooling that keep young people apart from the active social scene. In their research for alternatives, some Western critics have been fascinated by reports of revolutionary approaches in Maoist education. They see parallels between Maoist innovations and some of the reforms they have advocated and experimented with.

In the United States, suggestions have been made to remove barriers that prevent the underprivileged from admission into higher schools, to experiment with "open admission," to devise new programs that help young people to prepare for careers and at the same time enable them to acquire work experience and to take part in social movements of significance, to shorten the period of schooling, and to introduce other types of curricula than the traditional academic education. Those who propose such changes believe that much may be learned by a careful examination of Maoist innovations such as the abolition of academic entrance requirements, the combination of work and study, and the establishment of close links between school and society to make sure that the school, the home, the factories and communes, and various community groups coordinate their efforts to work toward the same goals. They want to know how well the Maoist system actually works and what evidence there is that Maoist education is producing "new men" to carry on the proletarian revolution.

Visitors to China have been impressed by the sight of people working hard and with apparent enthusiasm. They work collectively to dig canals, to reap harvests, to boost factory production, to maintain their cities. To what extent is this collective activity an expression of identification with the public cause? To what extent is this "work ethic" the result of education? If education can engender such devotion to the common good, it must certainly be recognized as a powerful force for the building of a new social order.

Students of comparative education are interested in any attempts to develop indigenous programs of education, those that go beyond the imitation of foreign models. Since the adoption of modern schools at the beginning of the century, China has followed one foreign model after another, but Maoist education rejects all foreign models and attempts to develop a program specifically designed to meet the needs of the Chinese proletarian revolution as visualized by Mao Tse-tung and his followers. Educators in all countries will watch with keen interest the course of this attempt.

This study of Maoist education is concerned mainly with developments since the Great Proletarian Cultural Revolution, or what is known specifically as the educational revolution. Although the Cultural Revolution has officially been terminated, the struggles have continued and the guiding principles of the educational revolution remain in effect. On October 1, 1972, celebrating the twenty-third anniversary of the founding of the People's Republic of China, a joint editorial of the Peking People's Daily, the Red Flag journal, and the People's Liberation Army Daily—the major mouthpieces of the Communist Party— repeated a call for doing "a good job in the revolution of education." This call was again repeated by Chou En-lai in his report to the Tenth National Congress of the Chinese Communist Party on August 24, 1973. The educational revolution that gathered momentum during the Cultural Revolution continues without essential change, and a careful study of the educational revolution is essential to an understanding of Chinese contemporary education.

Except when it is necessary to understand the background of the educational revolution, the educational developments in earlier periods will not be discussed. The Chinese Communists usually speak of education and culture in the same breath, but this study deals specifically with education in and outside the schools; it does not include culture— drama, literature, art, music.

The basic data have been gathered from Chinese Communist publications. Reports of foreign visitors to China have been freely consulted. The major documents and articles from Chinese sources appear in the appendixes. In citing Chinese-language publications, the reader may be confused by the difference between the romanization system in current use in China and the Wade-Giles system commonly used by Western sinologists. A few examples follow:

Chinese Communist system	Wade-Giles system	English translation
Renmin Ribao	Jen-min Jih-pao	People's Daily
Hongqi	Hung-ch'i	Red Flag
Jiefangjun Bao	Chieh-fang-chün Pao	People's Liberation Army Daily
Guoji Shudian	Kuo-chi Shu-dien	International Bookstore
Tonji University	T'ung-chi University	

The Wade-Giles romanization is used throughout the text.

The documents in the appendixes have not been edited, except for some deletions. What remains appears as it does in the sources indicated; the wording, spellings, and punctuation marks are left unchanged even though they differ from the style in the text. Direct quotations in the text are also unedited.

The term "Party" with a capital P always refers to the Chinese Communist Party. Another word of explanation may be appropriate regarding recurrent references to certain basic concepts, teaching methods, and teaching materials. The major works of Marx, Engels, Lenin, and Mao Tse-tung are named again and again because they are required reading not only in classes but also in all forms of ideological-political study in schools and outside. The class struggle, the struggle between two opposing lines, class education through the study of the "three histories" or "four histories," and the method of "recalling the miserable past and contrasting it with the happy present" are recurrent themes in virtually all educational writings. And the same familiar quotations from Chairman Mao are cited in all educational reports and discussions.

It is difficult to cite from the original sources without much repetition of the same words. The author has tried to reduce the repetitiousness found in the original sources, but some repetition seems unavoidable. Readers are requested to bear with the recurrent use of the same phrases and same clichés, and to remember that this repetitiousness is a method used by the Chinese Communists to present simple ideas and concepts and drill them into the consciousness of the people.

The terms "class origin" and "poor peasants" are used repeatedly; they are based on Mao Tse-tung's analysis of the classes in Chinese society, which divides the population into (1) the landlord and the compradore class, (2) the bourgeoisie, (3) the petty bourgeoisie, (4) the peasantry, and (5) the proletariat. The rural population is divided into landlords, rich peasants, middle peasants, poor peasants, and farm laborers. The "class status" of each person is determined on the basis of his birth and his former ownership of land and property.

The author wishes to acknowledge his indebtedness to Dean Irving R. Melbo of the School of Education, University of Southern California, for his encouragement and provision of facilities for research and writing. And to his wife Wen-Hui Chen, a scholar in her own right, for help in countless ways.

CONTENTS

Page

PREFACE   v

Chapter

1   THE BACKGROUND OF THE EDUCATIONAL
    REVOLUTION   1

        Continued Revolution   1
        The Cultural Revolution and Education   3
        Starting Afresh   4
        Prelude to Educational Revolution   6
        Educational Experimentation in Yenan   7
            The Kang Ta   8
            Mass Education   10
            Unfulfilled Promise   12
        Educational Reform after 1949   14
            Early Changes   14
            Achievement and Dissatisfaction   16
        Notes   18

2   THE EDUCATIONAL REVOLUTION   20

        Modern Chinese Education   20
        The Kuomintang Program   21
        The Soviet Model   24
        Bourgeois Intellectuals   25
        The Maoist Educational Line   29
        The Socialist Education Movement   31
        The Opposing Lines   34
        Notes   36

3   THE SCHOOLS   38

        The School System   38
        The Reopening of Schools   40
        The Draft Program   42
        Preschool Education   47

Chapter   Page

              The Goal of Universal Education   48
              Secondary Education   51
              The Curriculum   53
              Teaching Materials   55
              Notes   57

4   POLITICS AND IDEOLOGY   59

              Forms of Political Education   61
              Line Education   63
              Ideology in Curriculum and Extracur-
                ricular Activities   67
              Youth Organizations   70
              The New Man   73
              Adult Education   75
              Spare-Time Education   78
              Labor and Production   80
              The Role of the Military   82
              Notes   84

5   PROLETARIAN LEADERSHIP VERSUS
      DOMINATION BY INTELLECTUALS   87

              Dethroning the Intellectuals   87
              Mao Tse-tung Propaganda Teams   89
                 How The Teams Function   90
                 Problems   92
              Reeducation of Intellectuals   94
              Life in the Countryside   97
                 Planning   101
                 Results   104
                 Problems   106
              Notes   109

6   REMOLDING OF CADRES AND INTEL-
      LECTUALS   112

              The May 7 Cadre Schools   112
                 Life in the May 7 Schools   116
                 Results   118
                 Problems   120
              Other May 7 Approaches   120
              Reform of Intellectuals   121

Transformation of Teachers   129
    Teacher Training   131
    Problems   132
Notes   134

7   HIGHER EDUCATION   137

Reform Under the Revisionists   137
The Program After Reopening   138
Science and Engineering   141
The Liberal Arts Colleges   145
Nationwide Reform   149
Medical Education   149
Ideological Remolding   151
The New Higher Education   154
Notes   157

8   AN OVERVIEW   159

Accomplishments   161
Problems   163
Maoism and Formalism   165
The Problems of Youth   172
Fresh Air, Cool Breezes   175
Basic Studies   177
A Zigzag Course   181
Notes   185

9   A CRITIQUE   187

Positive Gains   188
The Method of Repetition   190
The Thinking Process   191
The Limits to Remolding   192
Party Control   196
The Question of Standards   199
Anti-Intellectualism   201
The Faucet Syndrome   205
Conclusions   206
Prospects After Mao   210
Notes   214

APPENDIX

GROUP A: Early Expressions of Mao's Educational
            Thinking

    1. Mao on Nature of Knowledge
       (February 8, 1942)   216
    2. Mao's Instruction on the Question
       of "Redness and Expertness"
       (January 31, 1958)   218
    3. Mao's Instruction on Part-Work,
       Part-Study (February 1958)   219
    4. Instructions Given at the Spring
       Festival Concerning Educational
       Work (February 13, 1964)   220
    5. Mao's Talk with the Nepalese
       Educational Delegation on
       Educational Problems (1964)   222

GROUP B: Escalating Demands for School Reform

    6. Peking Students Write to Party
       Central Committee and Chairman
       Mao Strongly Urging Abolition of
       Old College Entrance Examination
       System (June 6, 1966)   225
    7. Decision of CCP Central Committee
       and State Council on Reform of
       Entrance Examination and Enroll-
       ment in Higher Educational Insti-
       tutions (June 13, 1966)   229
    8. Students Propose New Educational
       System in Arts Faculties (July 12,
       1966)   231
    9. The "May 7 Directive" (May 7, 1966)   233
   10. The "16-Point Decision" (August 9,
       1966)   234

GROUP C: Reopening of Schools After Closure

   11. Reopen School to Make Revolution—
       To Primary School Revolutionary
       Teachers and Students (February
       18, 1967)   238

APPENDIX   Page

      12. Middle and Primary Schools
         Reopen Classes and Make Revo-
         lution (March 7, 1967)   239
      13. Circular of the CCP Central Com-
         mittee of the State Council, the
         Central Military Commission and
         the Central Cultural Revolution
         Group Concerning the Resumption
         of Classes and Revolution of Uni-
         versities, Secondary and Primary
         Schools (October 14, 1967)   240

GROUP D: School Programs After Reopening

      14. CCP Central Committee's Notifi-
         cation (Draft) Concerning the
         Great Proletarian Cultural Revo-
         lution in Primary Schools (for
         Discussion and Trial Enforcement)
         (February 4, 1967)   242
      15. Mao's "March 7 Directive" Concern-
         ing the Great Strategic Plan for the
         Great Proletarian Cultural Revolu-
         tion (March 7, 1967)   243
      16. Draft Program for Primary and
         Middle Schools in Chinese Country-
         side (May 13, 1969)   244
      17. Put Mao Tse-tung Thought in Com-
         mand of Cultural Courses (Sep-
         tember 25, 1970)   251
      18. The "May 7" Cadre School (May 12,
         1972)   255

GROUP E: Proletarian Leadership in Education: Mao
            Thought Propaganda Teams

      19. Mao's Directive on Working Class
         Leadership (August 30, 1968)   260
      20. The Working Class Must Exercise
         Leadership in Everything (August
         30, 1968)   260

APPENDIX   Page

    21. It Is Essential to Rely on the Poor
        and Lower-Middle Peasants in
        the Educational Revolution in the
        Countryside (1968)   263
    22. Promote Diligence, Frugality and
        Economy, Oppose Putting Undue
        Emphasis on Bigness and Mod-
        ernness (October 6, 1970)   268
    23. The Worker-Peasant-Soldier Teach-
        ers Are a Most Dynamic Revolu-
        tionary Force: Chairman Mao
        Tells Us to Mount the University
        Rostrum (December 28, 1970)   270

GROUP F: Reeducation of Intellectuals

    24. Mao's Directive on Reeducation of
        Intellectuals (December 6, 1968)   273
    25. Mao's "Latest Instruction" on Re-
        education (December 22, 1968)   273
    26. On the Reeducation of Intellectuals
        (September 12, 1968)   273
    27. Hooligans and Teddy Boys Are Not
        Allowed to Disrupt farm Produc-
        tion (August 4, 1968)   275
    28. Wipe out All Vermin (August 4, 1968)   276

GROUP G: New Programs in Higher Education

    29. Mao's Instruction Given on an
        Inspection Tour of Tientsin Uni-
        versity (August 13, 1958)   278
    30. Some Tentative Programmes for
        Revolutionizing Education
        (November 17, 1967)   278
    31. Tongji University's Programme
        for Revolutionizing Education:
        Six Months' Practice (May 17,
        1968)   279
    32. The Road for Training Engineering
        and Technical Personnel Indicated
        by the Shanghai Machine Tools
        Plant (July 22, 1968)   282

APPENDIX   Page

33. Chairman Mao Tse-tung's Latest
    Directive (August 2, 1968)   283
34. The Wishes of Workers, Peasants
    and Soldiers in Their Hundreds
    of Millions Have Come True !—
    Hailing the Workers, Peasants
    and Soldiers Entering the New-
    Type Socialist Universities
    (September 30, 1970)   284
35. Taking All Society as Their
    Factory (February 2, 1973)   287

ABOUT THE AUTHOR   296

The Maoist
Educational Revolution

1

THE BACKGROUND OF
THE EDUCATIONAL REVOLUTION

> In order to guarantee that our Party and country do not
> change their color, we must not only have a correct line
> and correct policies but must train and bring up millions
> of successors who will carry on the cause of proletarian
> revolution.
>
> From our highest organizations down to the grass-
> roots, we must everywhere give constant attention to the
> training and upbringing of successors to the revolutionary
> cause.[1]

In this quotation Mao Tse-tung says in effect that the success
of the Communist revolution hinges upon millions of young and old
who will dedicate themselves to the revolutionary cause and, since
the only way of rearing them is the process of education, the development of education must be a major concern of the Communist Party
and the state it directs. No leader could express more strongly his
faith in education and his belief that the destiny of his cause will be
determined by education. It follows that the primary task of education
must be to bring up a generation of faithful followers of the proletarian
ideology firmly committed to the proletarian revolution.

Continued Revolution

China is a land of revolution. Revolution, according to Mao, is
not a passing phase; his concept of continued revolution calls for constant vigilance and periodic "rectification" and "remolding" campaigns
to keep the revolutionary spirit at a high peak. Emotions must be
engendered to support the various campaigns and to sustain intensive

effort. Thought and ideas must be guided in such a way that the people will actively support whatever the leaders project in the name of the revolution. All this is to be accomplished by means of education.

This task goes far beyond what the schools can do. Everything that produces an impact on the human heart and mind outside the schools is an integral part of the educational program. It is significant that Mao Tse-tung and other Communist leaders have always talked about culture and education in the same breath. Culture, in the Communist terminology, includes drama, opera, dance, museums, radio, motion pictures, newspapers, all forms of literature, and the entire range of mass media that brings information and exhortation to the people in the village and the hamlet as well as the city and the home. It includes recreational and entertainment activities, all of which have an "educational" function to perform. All culture and education are directed toward the same goals of the proletarian revolution.

Therefore, when Mao speaks of education, he means far more than the schools. Much of what he considers as education has very little to do with classroom instruction. Indeed, in the view of the Chinese Communist leaders, the whole society educates and all social processes and social-political-economic institutions must consciously plan to discharge their educational responsibilities. This concept of education is much broader than what is understood as education in other countries. Such a broad program of education would be revolutionary even when applied to a conservative society; when it is linked to a bold social experiment, it must be reckoned as an unusually powerful force.

In terms of its broad scope and its ambitious aim of building a new revolutionary society by transforming the loyalties, the ideas, the emotions, and the habits of 700 to 800 million people, Mao's educational program has no parallel in the history of education. Educational theorists in the West who dreamed vaguely of education as a force for remaking society never conceived of such a daring experiment on such a gigantic scale. Even from the limited standpoint of academic theory, students of comparative education will find Maoist education a fascinating subject of study. But as the chief vehicle for bringing about a revolutionary proletarian society radically different from any other social order, past or present, Maoist education is a matter of far more than academic interest to the world. Moreover, this educational program, designed to produce the new man for a new society, provides a major key to understanding the aims of the Communist revolution and the nature of the proletarian society it aims to establish.

The word "people" was a word to conjure with when the Communists took control of the country in 1949. The regime was called the People's Republic of China, the form of government was called the people's democracy, the central government was named the Central

2

People's Government, the army the People's Liberation Army, the new currency the People's Currency (jen-min pi), and so on. The workers, peasants, national bourgeoisie, and petty bourgeoisie were the four classes of "people" who were supposed to have rallied to support the "people's democratic dictatorship." Those who opposed were chastised as "enemies of the people."

By the second decade of the regime, the word "revolution" appeared again and again in official pronouncements and ideological exhortations just as the word "people" appeared repeatedly in the early years. Despite the apparent success of the first decade in political consolidation and economic reorganization, Mao Tse-tung feared for the long-range future of his revolutionary cause. He was alarmed by signs of decline of the revolutionary spirit: the failure of the young generation to appreciate the importance of bitter struggle, the tendency of cadres and Communist Party members to rest satisfied with victory and to become corrupted by bureaucratic power, and the threat of revisionist ideas challenging his brand of Marxism-Leninism. To invigorate the revolutionary spirit and heighten ideological fervor, he refurbished the Marxist concept of "permanent revolution" and made it one of the central tenets of ideological indoctrination. Never forget the class struggle, he warned. The revolution has not yet succeeded; it must continue for a long time to come. There are enemies within and without constantly plotting for the revival of capitalism and the old social order. They must be attacked and prevented from carrying out their plots against the revolution.

The Cultural Revolution and Education

The constant theme of revolution was clearly reflected in the Great Proletarian Cultural Revolution of the mid-1960s (hereafter referred to as, simply, the Cultural Revolution). Apart from a fierce power struggle that reasserted Mao's supremacy against some close associates who had questioned his policies and ideological positions, the Cultural Revolution was a sweeping attack upon the thought and behavior of the past in order to clear the way for the appearance of the new revolutionary man. Repeating Mao's dictum that destruction was an essential phase of the revolution and following literally his instruction to "dare to destroy," the Red Guards posed as the embodiment of the revolutionary spirit; their slogan was to destroy the Four Old—old habits, old customs, old ideas, and old culture—and establish the Four New.

In the first decade of the regime, the Communist leaders concentrated on the political revolution and the economic revolution; the former was concerned with the consolidation of power and the latter with land reform, the five-year plans, and the advance to the socialist system of production and ownership. The Cultural Revolution that came to the fore in the second decade was much broader in scope than either the political or the economic. It was, indeed, the most revolutionary and most fundamental of the various revolutions.

At the heart of the Cultural Revolution is the educational revolution. To the outside world, the accomplishments of the political and economic revolutions were substantial and impressive. But in Mao Tse-tung's view, the revolution would fail without valiant fighters who would not flinch from hardship and difficulties. Dilution of ideological fervor goes with the decline of revolutionary valor, and the "pragmatic" policies advocated by some high-level Communist leaders could only lead to the spread of revisionism and the revival of capitalism. Individualism, personal ambition, desire for material gain and comfort, and the inclination of some leaders to cater to such unworthy bourgeois desires and motives would eventually turn the revolution away from the course Mao had charted. Besides the urgent task of eliminating these "revisionist" leaders, a long-range revolutionary program of engendering a fiery revolutionary spirit and a firm ideological conviction was indispensable in order to produce a generation of "revolutionary successors" thoroughly dedicated to a continuation of the revolution according to the blueprint outlined in Mao's writings and speeches. In other words, it was not enough to establish new political and economic institutions and systems; it was necessary to produce the "new man" who would safeguard the institutions and make the new systems work. This must be the work of education. Nothing short of a thorough educational revolution could guarantee the success of the proletarian revolution.[2]

Starting Afresh

Moderate reform would no longer suffice. Patchwork changes could not produce a program specifically designed to serve the needs of the proletarian revolution. To prepare for a fresh start, the Maoists adopted in 1966 the drastic measure of closing all schools and universities in order "to effect a thorough reform of the educational system" (see Appendix 7). Although the closure order specifically mentioned the senior middle schools, colleges, and universities, schools at all levels were closed after the summer of 1966. The schools were to be closed for "half a year" and effort was made to reopen them in 1967. The documents in Appendix Group C show the slow response to repeated orders to reopen the schools. The resumption of classes was sparse and sporadic through 1967 and 1968, and it was not until the autumn of 1970, after four years of academic inactivity, that some colleges and universities admitted the first class of students.[3]

4

There were no clear guidelines for the reopened schools. Each school was to experiment with programs in line with Mao's educational ideas and directives (for some of Mao's ideas on educational reform, see Appendixes 1-5). It took time for a general pattern to emerge and a system to be developed. What finally became the general practice of the land was indeed a revolutionary program of education radically different from what existed before 1949, or even before the Cultural Revolution. Take, for example, Tsinghua University, which, since it resumed classes in 1970, has been hailed as a model of the new type of university in science and technology.

Students in the first class admitted to Tsinghua University in 1970 were very different from the college students of pre-Cultural Revolution days. They were older and they did not look like an "academic" group. Most were workers, peasants, and soldiers who had been selected for higher study on the basis of their records in production and revolutionary work. They had not taken or passed entrance examinations. They were not asked to present credentials of previous schooling. They had not come for academic degrees. They had no intention of becoming scholars or pursuing academic careers.

These new college students came with their "shovels, hoes and sickles," and some brought "hair-cutting instruments and needle-and-thread boxes in their knapsacks" (see Appendix 34). The spirit and purpose of their entrance into the university was clearly expressed in the pledge one contingent of students made in a rally prior to entering the university. Carrying red banners and with packs on their backs, these students held high their red-covered copies of Quotations from Chairman Mao Tse-tung.[4] Facing a huge portrait of Mao, they pledged:

> Chairman Mao, dear Chairman Mao! We 221 workers,
> peasants, and soldiers have come to Peking where you
> live to study in the universities. We owe this great
> happiness to you. We are determined to win honor for
> you and for our great socialist motherland! We pledge
> that though our work posts have changed, our conscious-
> ness of continuing the revolution will not change. . . .
> Whatever changes may take place, our loyalty to you
> will never change!

A selected group of workers and soldiers known as the Mao Tse-tung Thought Propaganda Team is a new body of authority representing the proletarian leadership and control of education in the university. Members of the team, like the students, are trusted revolutionaries, but they have had little schooling. They are vested with authority to supervise the curriculum and work of the faculty as well as the students. They are charged with the responsibility of wresting the control of education from the "bourgeois scholars." Faculty scholars now take a back seat. They are not the only teachers; their ranks are augmented by workers and technicians whose political and production experience is rated higher than the theories of the intellectuals. Moreover, the "bourgeois intellectuals" must undergo ideological remolding under the supervision of the Propaganda Team. (The management of schools by Mao Tse-tung Thought Propaganda Teams is more fully discussed in Chapter 5.)

Revolutionary changes have taken place in the lower schools, too. The programs are designed to directly meet the immediate needs of production work. The study of Mao's writings occupies a central place in the curriculum. A large part of the time of students and teachers is devoted to labor and production and active participation in revolutionary (political) movements. Preparation for further study in higher schools is definitely not one of the objectives of any school or its students.

There are also new-type schools in which production and politics play an even more dominant role. Ideological remolding through labor and political education is the central objective. Teachers are recruited from among workers, peasants, and cadres. The curriculum is determined by practical needs perceived by workers, peasants, soldiers, and cadres. There are also planned programs of education not directly related to the schools in which students and "intellectuals" are "re-educated" by workers and peasants by living and working with them: They learn in the process of working and living as active revolutionaries and supporters of the proletarian cause. Whether in schools or outside, they are being trained—educated—to become successors to the proletarian revolution.

Successors to the revolutionary cause, says Mao Tse-tung, are produced "in mass struggles and are tempered in the great storms of revolution."[5] Active participation in the "mass struggles" and "the great storms of revolution" educates just as truly as study in school. Indeed, it is often considered a more vital form of educative experience than book knowledge or classroom instruction.

These are not isolated innovations. They are characteristics of a program that can only be described as revolutionary. It is revolutionary because it is radically different from the conventional education of other countries, especially those of the West. It is revolutionary because its central aim is to continue and to advance the revolution.

Prelude to Educational Revolution

Mao's educational revolution was preceded by years of educational experimentation before the establishment of the new regime in

1949 and by more than a decade of educational reform after 1949. Educational experimentation began at the Kiangsi-Fukien base of the Chinese Soviet Republic before 1934. It was interrupted by the Long March of 1934-35, but resumed at the Yenan base in the northwestern part of China. While Mao Tse-tung had always recognized the importance of education as a cornerstone of the revolution, in earlier years he had spoken of education and culture only in general terms, and his discussions of education and culture were interspersed in discourses on political and economic problems. At Yenan, he turned his attention more specifically to the problems of education and schooling.

Mao has written no treatise on education comparable to his philosophical essays on "Practice," "Contradiction," "Chinese Revolution and the Chinese Communist Party," "New Democracy," "People's Democratic Dictatorship," and other expositions of what is now called Mao Tse-tung Thought. In 1958, probably as harbinger of a drive for revolutionary changes in education, the People's Education Publishing House in Peking published a volume that put together Mao's scattered statements on education, culled from his speeches and writings from 1927 to 1958.6 It is worth noting that of the 42 titles under which the quotations were grouped, only three were for the period before the Long March, and most of the quotations that were labeled as dealing with education were concerned with problems of culture in its broad aspects. A large portion of the compilation consisted of Mao's statements during the period of the rectification campaign of 1942-44.7 Aside from ideological questions, most of the statements dealt with the method of hsüeh-hsi (learning, or study, meaning ideological study rather than school study) and the problem of intellectuals (a major document of this period spelling out the Communist policy toward intellectuals was composed of Mao's lectures on "Problems of Art and Literature" in 1942).

Educational Experimentation in Yenan

After the establishment of the Communist base in Yenan, in the northwestern part of China,* the Communists were in some measure relieved of the pressure of military campaigns and they began to dig in and think about a long-range program. The United Front they agreed upon in 1937 called for a suspension of radical economic measures of land reform and collectivization in favor of moderate reforms such

---

*The area is known as the Shensi-Kansu-Ninghsia Border Region. For convenience, the word "Yenan" is here used to refer to the entire area in northwestern China under Communist control from 1936 to the end of World War II.

as the reduction of rent and interest. Meanwhile, they were looking beyond the temporary expediency to the future. To consolidate their position, they set out to strengthen their internal organization and to pay more attention to work among the masses in pursuance of their "mass line." Educating the masses to win their support and training cadres to work among the masses now engaged the leaders' attention.

At the same time, the arrival of intellectuals and young students who were attracted to Yenan by the proposed program of "going to the people" to work for their welfare brought in its wake the problem of assimilating the unproletarian elements, remolding their outlook, and inculcating the Marxist-Leninist ideology without which there could be no sure guide for thought and action. The infusion of new elements also accentuated the need for intensified ideological indoctrination among the cadres and Party members, who were now exposed to harmful bourgeois ideology. Moreover, the suspension of radical reform produced a tendency for the revolutionary spirit to weaken.[8] These circumstances led to the ideological remolding campaign of 1942. Since ideological remolding has always been a central objective of Maoist education, much of what Mao said about ideological remolding has been considered applicable to education in general.

The Kang Ta

Education in Yenan was concerned with mass education[9] as well as the training of cadres and the remolding of intellectuals. Communist literature seems to have accorded a greater importance, or at least more publicity, to Kang Ta, and Mao Tse-tung himself often speaks of the "spirit of Kang Ta" as the symbol of Yenan education. "Kang Ta" is an abbreviated name for the Chinese People's Anti-Japanese Military and Political College.* The educational practice of Kang Ta is now upheld as a model for all to follow—not only institutions of higher learning but lower schools as well.

The mother institution of Kang Ta was the Anti-Japanese Red Army College established in June 1936 in the town of Wayapao in northern Shensi. A few months later it was moved to Yenan, where it assumed the name Chinese People's Anti-Japanese Military and Political College. As the name indicates, it was established to train military and political cadres during the period of resisting Japanese aggression. Lin Piao was the president but Mao Tse-tung, as chairman of the

---

*The Chinese K'ang means "to resist," or "anti"; it serves as an abbreviation for "K'ang Jih" (Anti-Japanese or Resist Japanese). Ta is an abbreviation of Ta Hsüeh (university or college). The aspirate sign is usually dropped in the current usage of Kang Ta.

Education Committee, determined the institution's direction and operational procedures.

When the training of revolutionary successors was stressed as an educational task of first importance in the late 1950s, the "Kang Ta type" of school was proposed as the most suitable form. According to Yeh Chien-ying,* ten characteristics of Kang Ta are worth perpetuating today:

1. Correct objectives: politics in command, Mao's Thought as guide for all activities; study and production go together.
2. Firm leadership: direct supervision by Mao Tsetung; strict adherence to his principles.
3. Good school spirit, characterized by unity of spirit, intense absorption in work, strict discipline, and vivaciousness. Political and military atmosphere dominant.
4. Political education as curriculum core. Mao's writings as basic teaching materials.
5. Integration of theory and practice.
6. Simplified content. Fewer but more concentrated courses; elimination of non-essentials.
7. Shortened period of schooling; 6 to 8 months for completion of course.
8. Attractive and lively methods of learning; collective study, mutual assistance among students; group discussion as a method of learning; open book examination.
9. Teachers imbued with revolutionary spirit.
10. Self-reliance; thrift and economy in running the school.[10]

These ideas were already in evidence in the education of the Chinese Soviet Republic in the early 1930s. We begin our story with Yenan education, rather than the earlier period, partly to avoid repetition and partly because current Chinese literature on the educational revolution seems to attach more importance to Yenan education.[11]

---

*Yeh became well known to the world when, as vice premier and the Number 2 man in the cabinet, he played a conspicuous role during President Nixon's visit to China in 1972. He has always been a prominent military figure, and his political fortunes rose rapidly during the Cultural Revolution and became even more firmly established afterward.

To publicize the Kang Ta in the early stage of the Cultural Revolution, a special exhibit of Kang Ta memorabilia was held in Peking in August 1966. Commenting on the exhibit, the Peking Review called Kang Ta "a college of the newest type, that is most revolutionary and progressive."[12] Kang Ta, said the Peking Review article, was "run entirely in accordance with Chairman Mao's thinking on education"; it was "the most thorough and lively embodiment of Chairman Mao's great thinking on education, a prototype of proletarian education." The students engaged in production to support themselves, they dug caves to build dormitories, and they wasted no time in theoretical studies not directly related to practical needs. Concentrating on essentials made it easier to shorten the period of training and enabled the institution to train more than 100,000 cadres and army officers from 1936 to 1945.[13] Speaking in favor of shortened training, Yeh Chien-ying said, "The longer the period, the greater the tendency toward impractical learning."[14] These features of Kang Ta also characterize the new schools after the Cultural Revolution.

Mass Education

The Kang Ta was not the only institution of higher learning in the Yenan period. Others were the Lu Hsun Academy of Literature and Arts, the Chinese Women's University, the Institute of Natural Sciences, and other separate units that became part of Yenan University. The Bethume Medical School was well known, and in Manchuria were the Harbin University, the Workers' University, the New School for Young Intelligentsia Cadres, and teacher-training colleges. These were closer to the normal pattern of four-year colleges, but they were influenced by Kang Ta and adopted such methods as discussion in small groups and the investigation of practical problems; teachers and students were to engage in production.[15]

On the lower levels there were elementary and secondary schools, but they were not systematically planned and there was no clear pattern of development. It is therefore difficult to talk about an educational system under the government of the Border Region. Significant innovations were introduced in mass education, but elementary education did not get as much actual attention as the verbal commitments would lead us to expect. The training of cadres and the reduction of adult illiteracy were more pressing needs, and the consequent neglect of elementary education may be attributable to the Communist principle that education must serve immediate needs. Adult education was given a higher priority than the education of children, because adults could be taught to take up the duties of armed struggle and production immediately while the education of children would have only "limited utility."[16]

The training of cadres was recognized as a more pressing need than mass education, one that deserved the "greatest attention" of the government.[17] This meant the development of education on what may be considered the secondary level. Adult literacy was another need that could not wait. Along with literacy, adult education emphasized political and ideological training that would enable the masses to understand the nature of the revolutionary struggle and take an active part in the class struggle. Adult education seemed more free to depart from the conventional pattern than secondary schools. The relative maturity in the age of students encouraged the use of the discussion method. The most popular institutional form seemed to be the winter school, which followed a flexible schedule adjustable to the seasons and the production demands of the rural areas. Reading groups and the use of school children to teach adults in their families were other methods designed to meet the needs of rural life.

In elementary education, the formula of min-pan kung-chu (people management, government assistance)* meant that the schools were to be established by the local people with the government standing by to render assistance when needed. Government assistance did not mean financial support; it meant government supervision over the broad plans and outlines of education. From the favorable viewpoint, this decentralization not only made the local community conscious of its responsibility for the schools but also put the schools in the direct service of the local community and, ideally, would make the schools more responsive to local needs and conditions. At the same time, government supervision would make sure that the general spirit and objectives of education were followed by local communities. At its best, this form of decentralization could encourage local initiative and participation without relinquishing government control over fundamentals.

From a more critical viewpoint, the decision to decentralize schools might have been a way to resolve the contradiction between the government policy of putting secondary and higher education ahead of elementary education and the mass line calling for a greater commitment to mass education. Even in the Communist area in the northeast, where education was more developed than in the northwest, as late as September 1946 an official resolution stated that "education at the middle-school level should be considered more important than primary-school education."[18] Since the government was not ready to play a big role in primary education, decentralization seemed a neat

---

*The term may also be translated as "establishment by the people, with assistance from the government"; "people-run" would also be an acceptable translation for min-pan.

way out. It not only relieved the government of financial responsibility but also fit in well with the theory of the mass line by making the schools directly answerable to the masses. Furthermore the provision for "government assistance" enabled the government to lay down guidelines of education to make sure that nothing would conflict with government policy. According to a directive issued in 1944:

> ' People-managed' primary schools follow the line of the
> masses. . . . The form of the school and the educational
> content are decided by the people themselves. The admin-
> istration and organization of the school are managed by
> the people themselves; the teachers are chosen by the peo-
> ple themselves, and so on. In this way, primary school
> education can then be best suited to the wants of the people,
> can best serve the people and can most easily be spread.
> . . . But ' people-managed' cannot be separated from
> ' public [government] help.' People's management needs
> strong leadership, not laissez-faire.[19]

The directive went on to specify that government help was needed for "leadership in administration, system, and methods of instruction" and for the "introduction, cultivation, and training of teachers." It is evident that the government kept a firm hand on the direction of educational development.

Unfulfilled Promise

Yenan education left a legacy of ideas and innovations that later served as powerful stimulants to the educational revolution during and after the Cultural Revolution. Among those ideas and innovative practices are the integration of theory and practice, the close link between education and politics, the shortening of the period of schooling, education to meet immediate needs, the use of the discussion methods, the min-pan schools, and new forms such as the winter schools, the half-day schools, and other unconventional schooling facilities. During the Yenan period, however, these remained fragmentary experiments and did not lead to fundamental changes in the educational system.

There was no educational revolution yet, partly because Communist educational thinking was in an early stage of development and partly because during most of the period the overall plan was to build a "regular" system of schools along conventional lines (the slogan was that the schools should be "cheng-kwei-hua," meaning "regularized" or "standardized"). Another reason is that educational administration was in the hands of either intellectuals who came from outside the Communist areas or those who had been influenced by the influx of "bourgeois intellectuals." Mao's rectification campaign of 1942-44 was in part directed against the infusion of bourgeois ideology and against the intellectuals who only knew the conventional form of education. It was at this time that he inveighed against book knowledge and the impractical theories of the scholars. But Mao Tse-tung himself was not ready for a full-scale educational revolution. He was in favor of retaining the conventional schools, to exist side by side with the innovative schools; thus he actually was advocating two parallel kinds of schools, for which the Liu Shao-ch'i revisionists and bourgeois scholars were severely condemned during the Cultural Revolution. Mao said in 1944:

> Hence, in our education we must have not only regular primary and secondary schools but also scattered, irregular village schools, newspaper-reading groups and literacy classes. Not only must we have schools of the modern type but we must also utilize and transform the old-style village schools.[20]

This position was also clearly stated in an article in the Chiehfeng Jih-pao (Liberation Daily) of May 27, 1944, which was supposed to reflect the view of the Central Committee of the Chinese Communist Party:

> Education at the middle-school level should follow multiple or double lines. . . .
> For a long-period plan, a long-period regular school may be run. To meet immediate urgent needs short-term training courses may be arranged. In general, for the time being, the ordinary middle school should still use the 3-3 system; that is, lower-middle school 3 years, and higher middle school 3 years. Teachers' training schools should be divided into two kinds. One is the normal school on the 3-3 system; that is, a lower stage of 3 years, which will receive graduates from higher primary school, and a higher stage of 3 years, which will receive graduates from lower-middle school. The other kind is the short-period training course which will last from one half to one year and which will receive lower-middle school graduates or students of similar standard. These will give political and vocational training.[21]

The system here advocated was essentially the system under the Kuomintang and what was in effect under the Communist regime until the educational revolution. The retention of the conventional schools, however, was not accepted without reservation. New ideas of a revolutionary nature were already in the making, and the planners for proletarian education were groping for something different from the conventional or the "regular," despite the call for cheng-kwei-hua (regularization). The same Liberation Daily made a searching criticism of conventional education:

> First, it is the product of countries at a high stage of capitalist development and not suited to the Chinese demands; secondly, it is the product of a capitalist ruling class and not suited to Chinese democratic bases; thirdly, it is the product of peaceful conditions and not suited to the demands of the war of resistance; fourthly, it is the product of the big cities and not suited to the demands of agricultural villages. . . .
> Present education trains people for the next stage of education. Because of this, to graduate even from primary school does not pay; to graduate from middle school pays even less. Those who return home are dissatisfied and cannot become model workers; they are actually worse off than if they had not gone to school.[22]

There was educational ferment and dissatisfaction with urban and capitalist education, which was considered unsuitable for rural and proletarian society. But there was no proposal to scrap the old schools and replace them with a new system of proletarian schools. Consequently, Yenan did not go beyond the stage of educational experimentation. The germs of revolutionary change were sown, but a full-blown educational revolution was delayed for nearly two decades.

Educational Reform After 1949

Early Changes

When the Communists established their rule in 1949, their first and most urgent task was of course the consolidation of political power. But they did not neglect education. They began early to introduce important changes in education. One of the early reports on education and culture was made by Kuo Mo-jo, then chairman of the Committee of Cultural and Educational Affairs of the Central Government. He wrote:

> A large-scale study movement was set in motion throughout the country after the Central People's Government was

14

established. It is a movement of liberated people to educate and re-educate themselves by democratic methods of learning.23

This was a nationwide movement not restricted to the schools. "Workers, peasants, and urban citizens have been organized for education and study," Kuo said. The trade unions were involved. Newspapers and radios joined in a common effort to impart knowledge about the new regime and its characteristics. Classes were held inside and outside the schools, for adults as well as children, to study the basic documents spelling out the organization of the new government and to learn how the new China was different from the old. Government offices, factories, business enterprises, urban neighborhoods, and villages organized "study" sessions for their personnel, and the entire nation was involved in an information program of unprecedented scale. Besides the "study" of official documents, the movement brought together millions of people in small groups to listen to news reports, to read and hear discussed the works and ideological concepts of Marxism-Leninism. Some of these "study" sessions were used for "criticism and self-criticism," the effective vehicle for ideological remolding that has been extensively used down to the present day. The "study movement" is a clear example of the Communist concept of education extending far beyond the schools.

In the schools, the first year of the regime saw the introduction of significant changes. Political education was made a core subject of the curriculum. Starting with the elimination of the Kuomintang-sponsored civics study and instruction in San Min Chu I (Three People's Principles), the new program in political education provided for the study of the works of Marx, Lenin, Stalin, and Mao Tse-tung (the "Thought of Mao Tse-tung" had not yet been proposed as a specific subject for study). The new textbooks were to emphasize the importance of labor and science and their contributions to production as well as ideological outlook, and students were to be led to make critical examinations of imperialism and capitalism in contrast with socialism. Besides classroom study, political education required students and teachers to engage in "revolutionary work" such as anti-imperialism parades and demonstrations, campaigning for the Stockholm Peace Appeal and for closer ties with the USSR, the Resist America/Aid Korea campaign, and other approved political activities.

New methods included different forms of "collective learning"24 and "collective living" and wider use of seminars and group discussions. In administration, the committee system was tried for a brief period. Later it became general practice to have a Communist Party member as vice-principal of a school.

Besides the regular schools, new institutional forms were introduced. A number of special institutes and short-term courses appeared on the scene in higher education. Among new institutions specifically guided by the Marxist-Leninist ideology were the North China People's Revolutionary University (also in other cities) and the Chinese People's University.[25] On lower levels, worker-peasant schools were a concrete expression of the Communist commitment to increase the educational opportunity of workers and peasants. The government early issued an order for schools and universities to open their doors to young men and women of the worker-peasant class, and even to give priority to worker-peasant applicants for admission. In addition, special schools were established to enable promising worker-peasant youths to encompass the essence of the six-year secondary school curriculum in three years, after which they were considered qualified for admission into colleges and universities.[26] These are among the shortcuts devised to turn out a "proletarian intelligentsia."

A new facility beneficial to adult learners and applicable to worker-peasant education is spare-time education. Tried with success during the Yenan period, spare-time education proved a very effective way of extending educational opportunity to those who would otherwise be deprived. It was now vigorously promoted and extensively provided. Spare-time classes were organized for the benefit of workers, peasants, and other adults during seasons or hours that would not interfere with their work. They are held in government offices, in factories, in village temples, in homes, on boats for the crew in after-work hours, and in any other convenient place. The basic condition is that there be no interruption of production or work. There are classes for the illiterate as well as the barely literate. Winter schools in rural areas are a form of spare-time education. In all cases, political training is an essential part of the program.

Achievement and Dissatisfaction

Later developments follow more or less the same direction indicated in the early changes. Education under the Communists is subject to sudden shifts and reversals. Institutional forms, content, and methods are constantly being modified to meet observed needs. Whatever fails to meet the needs is quickly discarded, and there is no hesitation to try new methods. The Worker-Peasant Short-Term Middle School, for example, was discontinued after five years. The Revolutionary University was dropped after the Chinese People's University took over enlarged functions.[27] Some colleges were closed, others were merged or consolidated, and new ones were established.

A new development was the implementation of the concept of unifying theory and practice by the combination of education with productive labor. Students alternated between production and study; schools established factories and production enterprises in which students and faculty sought to integrate theory into practice, and factories and production enterprises established schools to attain the same end. The schools thus evolved into three main types: the full-time school, the work-study school (with time divided between work and study), and the spare-time school. The literacy campaign was vigorously pushed ahead. Language reform, especially in the unification of the spoken tongue and the use of abbreviated written characters, aided learning among adults and children alike.

The educational record of the regime's first decade was impressive. Statistics presented a bright picture of rapid growth and expansion. According to official reports published in 1958, student enrollment in higher institutions soared from 155,000 to 660,000; in technical middle schools from 383,000 to 1,470,000; in middle schools from 1,496,000 to 8,520,000; in primary schools from 23,683,000 to 86,400,000; and in kindergartens from 130,000 to 29,501,000. Reports for 1958 also showed 150,000 people attending spare-time middle schools and 26,000,000 in spare-time primary schools.[28]

This record of growth is as impressive as the economic progress and political strength of the first decade, yet there was something wanting in the eyes of Mao Tse-tung and his fellow revolutionaries. Significant as some of the reforms were, they did not challenge the educational system already in existence in 1949. The old system remained basically unchanged. The spare-time and work-study schools were harbingers of a new era, but the old "regular" schools continued to command respect and prestige, even to the disparagement of the new-type schools. Worst of all, the old spirit of education had not changed. Young people were still motivated by ambitions of personal success and advancement through education. They considered advanced education and the professions a higher calling than labor and production. With all the changes and expansion, education was not producing the new man needed for the building of a socialist society. From the standpoint of the proletarian revolutionaries, the educational changes of this period were not much more than efforts to remedy the shortcomings of an outmoded system by patchwork. At best, this was a period of educational reform, not educational revolution. A thorough revolution would scrap the old and start anew with the actual needs of proletarian society.

Notes

1. Mao Tse-tung, "Khrushchev's Phony Communism and Its Historical Lessons for the World" (July 14, 1964) in Quotations from Chairman Mao Tse-tung (Peking: Foreign Languages Press, 1966), pp. 276-77.

2. For an elaboration of this point of view, the reader is referred to the author's article, "A Nation in Agony" in Problems of Communism, November-December 1966, pp. 14-20.

3. Some colleges and universities reopened in 1970, and more in 1971 and 1972. Even by 1973 not all the institutions of higher learning closed in 1966 had resumed work. For a brief report on the reopening of colleges and universities, see China News Analysis (Hong Kong), no. 906 (January 12, 1973).

4. Quotations from Chairman Mao Tse-tung, op. cit.

5. Peking Review, July 17, 1964, p. 27.

6. Mao Tse-tung T'ung-Chih Lun Chiao Yu Kung-Tao (Peking: Jen Min Chiao Yu Ch'u Pan She, 1958). English translation in successive issues of Chinese Education, beginning with Vol. 2, nos. 1-2 (spring-summer 1969).

7. Other documents of the 1942-44 rectification campaign appear in Cheng Feng Wen Hsien (Hong Kong: Hsin Min Chu Ch'u Pan She, 1949). English translation by Boyd Compton in Mao's China: Party Reform Documents, 1942-1944 (Seattle: University of Washington Press, 1952).

8. Mark Selden, The Yenan Way in Revolutionary China (Cambridge, Mass.: Harvard University Press, 1971), p. 208.

9. See Peter J. Reybolt, "The Yenan Revolution in Mass Education," China Quarterly, no. 48 (October-December, 1971).

10. See Yeh Chien-ying's article in Kuang-ming Jih-pao, August 2, 1966, p. 2.

11. For education in the Chinese Soviet Republic, see Wang Hsueh-wen, "A Study of Chinese Communist Education During the Kiangsi Period," Issues and Studies (Taiwan), April 1973 and subsequent issues.

12. Peking Review, August 5, 1966, pp. 12-14.

13. Ibid.

14. Ibid.

15. Michael Lindsay, Notes on Educational Problems in Communist China (New York: Institute of Pacific Relations, 1950), p. 41.

16. See article in Chieh-fang Jih-pao, May 27, 1944, translated in ibid., p. 59.

17. Ibid.

18. Ibid., p. 63.

19. Ibid., p. 103.

20. "The United Front in Cultural Work," in Selected Works of Mao Tse-tung (Peking: Foreign Languages Press, 1965), Vol. III, p. 235.

21. Lindsay, op. cit., pp. 64-65.

22. Ibid., pp. 55-56.

23. Kuo Mo-jo, "China: A Cultural Survey," People's China, August 16, 1950, p. 16.

24. Theodore H. E. Chen, "Collective Learning in Communist China's Universities," Far Eastern Survey 26 (January 1957), pp. 8-11.

25. See Yueh Fung, "Ke-Ta—'A Furnace of Revolution,'" People's China, April 16, 1950, p. 18; Hu Hsi-kwei, "Chung Kuo Jen-Min Ta-Hsüeh Ti Chien Lüeh Chieh-Shao" (A brief introduction to the Chinese People's University), Hsin Hua Yüeh Pao, January 1951, p. 663.

26. Regulations for these Worker-Peasant Abbreviated Middle Schools were published in the Jen-min Jih-pao, February 17, 1951.

27. Kuang-ming Jih-pao, January 1, 1953.

28. State Statistical Bureau, Ten Great Years—Statistics on Economic and Cultural Construction Achievements of the People's Republic of China (Peking: Foreign Languages Press, 1960), pp. 192, 198.

THE EDUCATIONAL REVOLUTION

The educational scene in China at the time the Communists proclaimed the birth of a new regime in 1949 reflected a composite of influences from a variety of sources. It consisted of a modern system of schools that was originally adopted in the beginning of the century to take the place of the traditional classical education and examination system, but that then underwent marked changes when the republican form of government replaced the monarchy. Later, the Nationalist government under the Kuomintang revamped the program to suit its ideology and its political and economic policies. An additional strand was woven into the pattern during the first decade of the regime with the wholesale importation of Soviet ideas and practices. This complex pattern of schools and educational practices formed the background for the educational revolution.

Modern Chinese Education

The first modern Chinese school system was patterned after Japanese education, which in turn had followed the German model. Japan was at that time a shining example of successful modernization and much of her success was attributable to the modern education she had developed. Chinese students went in large numbers to Japan for study. With the establishment of the Republic of China in 1912, the model of monarchical Japan became less attractive and China adopted a new school system that greatly resembled the American. (However, Chinese scholars educated in Japan continued to exert influence on Chinese educational thought and practice, even after the abandonment of the Japanese model.) In the ensuing years, American ideas and educational theories played a major role in shaping the intellectual outlook and educational development of the infant Republic of China.

John Dewey became a household word among Chinese educators, and Chinese scholars who had studied at the feet of Dewey, Paul Monroe, E. L. Thorndike, L. M. Terman, William H. Kilpatrick, E. P. Cubberley, and other noted American educators became molders of the Chinese mind in Chinese university centers. Missionary effort loomed large on the educational scene, and most of the missionary schools and colleges were established and run by Americans. When the junior high school movement in America culminated in a revision of the school system to form the 6-3-3 sequence, China followed suit and divided secondary education into two levels, with junior middle schools and senior middle schools. The 6-3-3 pattern, with a four-year college, continued with only minor changes until the Cultural Revolution.

During and after World War I, Wilsonian ideals of democracy and self-determination stirred the imagination and hopes of Chinese intellectuals, and Dewey's visit to China in 1919 further stimulated student activism and educational liberalism. The May Fourth Movement drew the attention of the world as an aggressive reaction of Chinese youth against the political and social status quo, and a new spirit of rebelliousness and self-expression that the new education had helped to foster. This brief reference to the background of the contemporary educational situation does not allow a discussion of the May Fourth Movement. Suffice it to say that this very significant movement was one of the concrete expressions of the intellectual and educational ferment that characterized this era of intellectual freedom and self-expression when China opened her windows and doors to new currents of thought from all over the world, especially the Western world. Some observers use the word renaissance to describe the intellectual vitality of this period, but the Chinese term Hsin Ssu-ch'ao (New Thought Movement; a literal translation would be "New Tides of Thought") is perhaps more descriptive of the intellectual and educational mood of the time.[1]

Unfortunately, the political climate was not favorable to the growth of education or the realization of the hopes and dreams stimulated by the New Thought Movement. Warlordism left little room for long-range constructive plans. Liberal ideas and ideals were emerging and significant educational experiments appeared here and there (notably in mass education and rural education), but growth was impossible amid political turmoil and instability. Government inaction and indifference left education sadly neglected. Absence of leadership and positive planning resulted in educational stagnation and chaos.

The Kuomintang Program

The Nationalists who came to power in 1927 had a positive educational policy and a definite plan to use education as a means of attaining the projected goals of the Nationalist revolution. The Kuomintang ideology of San Min Chu I (Three People's Principles: people's nationalism, people's rights, and people's livelihood) was made the guide for all educational effort. Education was considered an instrument of national regeneration. The structure of the school system remained unchanged, but much was done to regularize, standardize, and upgrade the schools. The schools were now assured of financial support, and state schools and national universities rose in prestige and began to attract capable students who had previously preferred the private colleges and universities. A new emphasis was given to adult education, to the reduction of illiteracy, and to what was known as "social education," which includes museums, libraries, and other educational media outside the schools. To help forge national unity, a campaign was launched to unify the spoken tongue, to teach it in the lower schools, and to use it as the medium of instruction in all schools and universities.

Education was now strictly controlled by the state. Private education was allowed but required to conform to the same rigid prescriptions as the public schools, and enjoyed little more freedom. (Private education has now been abolished in China.) Laws and regulations spelled out in detail the curriculums, teaching materials and methods, as well as equipment and building standards for all levels of schools. Determined to bring order out of chaos, the Nationalist government adopted a policy of centralized control and administration to replace the laissez-faire policy of the warlord regime. A premium was put on uniformity rather than variety, discipline rather than freedom.

The American model of decentralized administration and its concept of educational freedom were found unsuitable to attain this purpose. Nationalist China turned to Europe and saw attractive models in French and German education. The French tradition of centralized control, enforced to the point of regimentation, appeared to Nationalist leaders to be what China needed, and the exacting nature of German scholarship seemed a much better way to raise the quality of education than the American approach. Chinese scholars who had studied in French and German universities gradually took over positions of educational leadership, and European educators were invited to come to China to advise on educational reform.

A group of European educators whose advice exerted great influence on the educational policy of the 1930s was the League of Nations' Mission of Educational Experts invited to make a survey of Chinese education in 1931 and to propose reform measures to the Chinese government.[2] The mission made concrete recommendations regarding a more equitable geographical distribution of schools, the administration of education, the teaching of science, more systematic planning for an organized system of public and private education, financial support, and other problems of educational reform. Most of the recommendations were accepted by the Chinese government and translated into official policy. In making their recommendations, members of the mission doubtless drew from their experience in their homelands and reflected their belief that there were distinctive features of European education worthy of careful study by Chinese educators. They deplored "the remarkable, not to say alarming, consequences of the excessive influence of the American model in Chinese education."[3] While stressing the need for a system of national education to meet Chinese needs and cautioning against blind imitation of foreign practices, the mission "came to the conclusion that the cultural conditions of Europe are more suitable than American conditions for adaptation to Chinese requirements."[4] The mission's criticisms and recommendations were accorded high respect and close attention by the leaders of the Nationalist government.

The shift from the American to the European model seemed at that time an important change in Chinese education. From the standpoint of the Maoist revolutionaries, however, there was no change in the essential nature of an educational program borrowed from capitalist Western countries or Japan. They would argue that the differences between American and European education are minor variations of a common model that reflects the exploitative nature of capitalist society and designs a program for the elitist few and out of the reach of the masses. Furthermore, American and European education alike exalt knowledge and theory divorced from practice and exclude labor and production from the pursuit of academic learning. Therefore the revolutionaries would maintain that the introduction of European influence did not basically change the direction and social purposes of the Western-oriented education of modern China.

Even within the framework of Westernized education, the progress made in the decade prior to the outbreak of the Sino-Japanese War in 1937 was cut short by the devastations of war. Many stories have been told of the heroic efforts made by the Chinese to save education from destruction and keep schools going under the most difficult conditions during World War II. Schools and universities were uprooted and students and teachers trekked to their temporary wartime quarters hundreds of miles (or over a thousand) away from the original campus. The spirit was indomitable and admirable, but the effort to raise standards had to be temporarily abandoned. There were significant developments during the long war,[5] but the prewar system of schools was maintained without great change. After the war, educational rehabilitation was severely hindered by the very precarious political and economic situation. By 1949 the prewar system of a coordinated sequence of schools and universities had been restored and most of the schools and universities had been reestablished on their original campuses. But numerous postwar problems of educational instability and frequent interruptions of work were unsolved.

The Soviet Model

A part of the initial educational task of the new regime in 1949 was to continue postwar rehabilitation and encourage the uninterrupted operation of the schools. Teachers, who had been apprehensive of losing their jobs, were asked to remain in their posts. Private schools were for the time being permitted to function. Even the missionary schools, soon to be attacked as bastions of cultural imperialism, were not threatened with immediate closure and many missionary educators were hopeful that the Christian schools and colleges would continue to operate for an indefinite period of time as long as the constitutional provision of freedom of religion was observed (this provision was contained in the Common Program, which partially served the purpose of a constitution from 1949 to 1954).

Besides the changes mentioned in Chapter 1, one of the most important phases of educational reform after 1949 was the adoption of the Soviet model. For several years, "Learn from the Soviet Union" was a slogan officially sponsored for nationwide observation and a guide for major reforms in curriculum, teaching methods, and school organization. The short-term worker-peasant schools were not unlike the Soviet rabfacs (workers' faculties) of early years. The Soviet five-point system of grading was adopted. Russian replaced English as the most important foreign language, and many a teacher of English had to learn Russian in a hurry in order to continue as foreign language teacher. Teams of Soviet educators toured China and gave lectures publicizing Soviet educational ideas and practices. Chinese delegations went to Russia to study Russian education.

The "Learn from the Soviet Union" campaign was carried into schools of all levels. It also reached out to include the adult population. The officially sponsored Sino-Soviet Friendship Association, which in its first year had more than 3 million members, mostly from the school population,[6] organized spare-time evening schools to teach Russian to adults. Radio stations broadcast Russian language lessons. In 1956 the Guozi Shudian (International Bookstore) in Peking was reported to have imported 777,551 Russian books from the USSR.[7]

Soviet influence was especially pronounced in higher education. Higher education was reorganized according to plans drawn up by Soviet advisers. The American-style higher education was abandoned in favor of "comprehensive universities" and technical universities. Departments and colleges were reorganized and regrouped according

24

to the Soviet plan. The college course was extended to five years. The new Chinese People's University was set up "as a model of Soviet higher education and exemplar for learning from the Soviet experience." Curriculum organization and areas of specialization followed Soviet examples, and the "seminar" approach was hailed as a new method of teaching developed in Soviet universities. Soviet scholars occupied key positions in the university faculties.

As late as 1957, the minister of higher education called for redoubled efforts to learn from the Soviet Union. "To learn from the Soviet Union" he said, "is a firm and unshakable policy of our nation's socialist construction."[8] He reported that the Soviet government had sent 700 experts to work in Chinese institutions of higher learning, and they trained 8,285 graduate students and teachers, inaugurated 889 new courses, and provided guidance for 443 courses taught by Chinese teachers.[9] They wrote 629 kinds of teaching materials and helped build 496 laboratories, 192 research libraries, and 34 factories for students to gain practical experience. Soviet experts also lectured in teacher training classes, thus extending their influence to many lower schools through the teachers they trained.

Soviet scholarship was highly exalted in all fields of study. Soviet textbooks were translated for adoption in classes. Soviet theories were accepted in science, economics, pedagogy, psychology, and other fields of study. Michurin and Lysenko dominated the study of biology. The translation of Russian books reached astounding proportions. In 1957 it was reported that 12,400 Russian textbooks had been translated into Chinese and more than 12 million copies printed for wide distribution.[10] The use of Russian-language textbooks was also encouraged. As late as 1971 a foreign visitor found that the "greater part" of textbooks sold in a second-hand bookstore in Peking were Russian books.[11]

"Bourgeois" Intellectuals

The Maoist revolutionaries declare that education must be purged of the pernicious influence of Western capitalism, Kuomintang reactionarism, Soviet revisionism, and the bourgeois intellectuals who are the carriers of nonproletarian ideology and revisionist thought. In their view, the educational revolution was delayed for more than a decade because the schools and universities were dominated by "bourgeois scholars" after 1949. Therefore, a specific demand of the educational revolution is to terminate "the phenomenon of our schools being dominated by bourgeois intellectuals" (see section 10 of the 16-Point Decision, Appendix 10).

Who are the bourgeois intellectuals? They are the products of old education who could not break away from their past. They are the scholars who commanded respect in the old society. They are the educators who served as the presidents of the colleges and universities. They are the admirers of the Western capitalistic educational tradition. They are the teachers in schools and universities who influence the thought and action of youth. They are the purveyors of knowledge for its own sake, of book study divorced from practice. They are the artists and literary writers whose works spread revisionist ideas and abound in veiled criticisms of socialism. They are the professional educators who have controlled educational development. They mouth the new slogans but continue their old ways. They declare allegiance to Chairman Mao but, after paying lip service, they proceed to violate the spirit of his teachings. Hiding behind the shield of acceptable slogans and a revolutionary vocabulary, they worked to sabotage proletarian education. They are the people who dominated the educational scene after 1949 and concerned themselves with quality education and scholarship standards, actually protecting the Western-oriented bourgeois-revisionist educational system from radical change. They appeared as educational reformers, but they confined themselves to minor reforms that would not disturb the system in which they had deep vested interests. Under their influence, young people became unfit for the role of revolutionary successors.

It is significant that among the first targets of the Cultural Revolution were literary writers whose works were denounced as revisionist and antiproletarian. Other specific targets were intellectuals in leading positions of culture and education, some of whom had been trusted members of the Communist Party. Take, for example, Lu Ting-i, for almost two decades the chief of the Propaganda Department of the Chinese Communist Party, who was appointed minister of culture in 1965. On many occasions he had been the official spokesman for important policy decisions. He was the man who elaborated on Mao Tse-tung's "contending-blooming" policy,[12] and he made public the conclusions of a 1958 educational conference that declared that the primary purpose of education was to serve politics and production needs.[13]

Early in the Cultural Revolution Lu Ting-i was identified as one of the chief protagonists of copying the Soviet revisionist educational system. Later, after Liu Shao-ch'i was publicly named China's Khrushchev and the Number 1 man "taking the capitalist road," Lu was accused of working hand-in-hand with Liu Shao-ch'i to preserve and strengthen revisionist education. He was also charged with being in league with bourgeois intellectuals intent upon "regularizing" and "standardizing" the schools. According to his accusers during the Cultural Revolution, Lu criticized the educational revolution for lowering educational quality. At the same time, he and other "capitalist-roaders" advocated elitist education and proposed the establishment of a system of elite schools known as "little treasure pagoda."[14] The pagoda was meant to be a system of quality schools maintaining high standards of scholarship unattainable by schools whose students had to engage in labor and production and consequently were unable to devote their full effort to study. This plan not only would result in two parallel systems of schools but, by putting physical labor in a bad light, would widen the gap between mental and physical labor.

One of the most important documents of the educational revolution was a chronology of educational events in the May 6, 1967 issue of Chiao-yü Ke-ming (Educational Revolution), a publication of the Education Revolution Committee of the Peking municipality.[15] Titled "Chronology of 17 Years of the Two-Line Struggle on the Educational Front," it told the story of a long struggle between the Maoist revolutionaries and the revisionists allied with the bourgeois intellectuals. It accused Lu Ting-i of opposing the educational revolution at every turn: In 1961 and 1962 he reportedly criticized the chaos and confusion of the new schools and said they were even inferior in quality to the schools of the warlord regime and the Kuomintang period. He was held responsible for the abolition of the short-term worker-peasant middle schools, and he was reported to have opposed the work-study schools, preferring to concentrate on the development of "regular" full-time schools in which no time would be wasted on labor and politics.

Among the bourgeois intellectuals singled out for severe attack in the Cultural Revolution was Lu P'ing, the president of the prestigious Peking University, which became famous not only as the oldest state-supported university in modern China but also as the home of liberal thought that played a stellar role in the New Thought Reform and the May Fourth Movement in the second decade of this century. Beginning with his membership in leftist youth organizations in the 1930s, Lu gained prominence as a youth leader and rose rapidly until he was made president of China's foremost university. He became a major target of attack, largely because of his position in an exemplary comprehensive university and liberal arts college. The charges against him were not very different from those against Lu Ting-i. Instead of bringing up students to be successors to the revolutionary cause, he reportedly tried to bring up successors to the bourgeois cause. Pretending to be supporting the educational revolution, he adopted a policy of "learning from the Soviet Union and using the American and British education as reference material."[16] Under his leadership, Peking University neglected the Thought of Mao Tse-tung; amid the plethora of courses on ancient and foreign culture, the study of Mao Thought was conspicuous by its absence. Bourgeois scholars occupied leading positions and bourgeois scholarship dominated the entire University, so that it was no different from the Peking University of the Kuomintang period. Lu P'ing was reported to have held the view that any competent scholar deserved recognition and promotion as long as he did not oppose the Chinese Communist Party and socialism. Student participation in productive labor and the class struggle was only grudgingly allowed and actually discouraged. Pressed to admit students from worker and peasant families, Peking University treated the worker-peasant students badly and subjected them to difficulties in their studies, with the result that they finally had to withdraw. In the name of quality education, Peking University pursued the bourgeois line instead of the Maoist line.

The "Chronology" mentioned above named other bourgeois scholars most influential in upholding the revisionist-capitalist-Kuomintang system of education. Among them are Mao Hsü-lun, minister of higher education in 1952-54; Chien Chün-jui, vice minister of education in 1949-50; Yang Hsiu-feng, minister of higher education in 1964-65; Chiang Nan-hsiang, president of Tsinghua University and an active leader in education and culture who at different times held such high posts as vice minister of education, minister of higher education, and president of the Party Higher School. According to "Chronology," these men dominated the Ministry of Education and adopted policies contradictory to Mao's educational line; from 1949 to the high tide of the educational revolution, the Ministry of Education, under the direct administration of bourgeois scholars, was concerned mainly with the "intellect first" type of education and preoccupied with raising educational quality to measure up to bourgeois standards of scholarship. It issued regulations and policy statements reflecting the elitist concept of education. Examples are:

- The length of schooling was increased; higher education was extended to five years, Soviet style.
- Courses of study were multiplied to fulfill the specialization plans recommended by Soviet advisers.
- Instead of compiling new teaching materials, Kuomintang textbooks and outdated Chinese classics were used.
- Academic study and the acquisition of knowledge were stressed; labor and political study were slighted. Labor was reduced to a minimum; politics was confined to specific courses and not allowed to interfere with intellectual study. Participation in social and political activities was frowned upon. Class struggle was deemed unnecessary.
- It was proposed that the schools should be run by experts, namely, the bourgeois scholars. Intellectuals who were identified as Rightists in the rectification campaign of 1957-58 held key positions in the schools and universities. Bourgeois intellectuals were commended for their "teaching experience."
- Technical education, or the study of technique, was considered more valuable than physical labor.

● Academic degrees and titles (borrowed from Soviet universities) encouraged the selfish motive of studying to achieve personal fame. Students aimed to become famous specialists removed from the masses.

Whether the accused educators actually committed the alleged offenses is not so important for understanding the background of the educational revolution. What is important is that Mao Tse-tung became increasingly aware of the urgent need to produce a new type of man to fulfill his dream of socialist society and he was convinced that the existing educational system could not do the job. The period of reform was now seen as an interruption of what had been started in the Yenan experiment, and the culprits were identified as those who carried on the Kuomintang tradition, those who went all out to copy the Soviet model, and the bourgeois scholars who would not give up the Westernized capitalistic system of education. These educational culprits were linked with the revisionists, whose influence was seen to have extended beyond the political and economic areas into the fields of education and culture. The bourgeois intellectuals and their ideology became inseparable from the revisionists and "capitalist-roaders." To remove them and destroy their influence was the negative phase of the educational revolution that was needed to clear the way for the new changes.*

The Maoist Educational Line

Mao Tse-tung's thinking on education may be said to have developed by degrees. He tried out some of his ideas in the Yenan period, but he does not seem to have then visualized a revolutionary system that would take the place of the old. He was therefore willing to have the old schools exist alongside the new and experimental (see Chapter 1, "Unfulfilled Promise"). After 1949 he himself was one of the most eloquent protagonists of the "Learn from the Soviet Union" campaign. In December 1949 he spoke in favor of a program based on the Yenan experiments, the "useful experience of the old education," and "the

*The list of bourgeois scholars subjected to severe condemnation is too long to be included here. To those already mentioned may be added Li Ta, president of Wuhan University; Kuang Ya-ming, president of Nanking University; the president of Chiaot'ung University in Sian; the vice president of Peking University; the vice president of Nankai University; the president of Chekiang University; the vice president of Shanghai First Medical College; the vice president of Shanghai College of Drama; and many others.

experiences of the Soviet Union."[17] It may be said that the educational revolution marks the maturation of Mao Tse-tung's educational thinking, or at least its translation into schools and educational practices to constitute a new system to replace the old. It is not easy to fix the date for the start of the educational revolution. According to the "Chronology," it began in 1958-60, met with obstruction in 1961-63, flared out in open confrontation with the obstructionists in 1964-65, and finally reached the stage of positive and aggressive action in 1966.

Mao Tse-tung's educational moves in 1958-60 were a part of his aggressive push toward the socialist society he conceived. The anti-Rightist campaign was launched to still the criticisms that burst out during the "Hundred Flowers" interlude. The "Red versus Expert" issue came to the fore, with the official view identifying "Redness" with the position of "politics in command" (see Appendix 2). The anti-Rightist struggle, said "Chronology," prepared the way for the educational revolution. The decisions to speed up the organization of communes and to launch the Great Leap Forward were also made at this time, finally precipitating the cleavage within the Communist hierarchy beginning with the ousting of P'eng Teh-huai, the defense minister, and culminating in the attack upon Liu Shao-ch'i and other revisionists and capitalist-roaders. The fact that some veteran leaders of the Communist Party were openly critical may have led Mao to take more drastic measures to combat policies and ideas opposed to his own.

In 1958 an educational conference convened by the Central Committee of the Chinese Communist Party set forth three basic guidelines for education: (1) education must serve proletarian politics; (2) it must be combined with productive labor; and (3) it must be under the direction of the Communist Party.[18] In the same year, Mao called upon the schools to establish factories or farms in order to link study with production, and to adopt schedules providing for half work and half study. The agricultural schools were new work-study schools of this type. The work-study plan was to be adopted in the universities, too, as Mao clearly stated after his visit to Tientsin University and Wuhan University (see Appendix 29). It was probably on the basis of these changes that "Chronology" claimed that the educational revolution started in 1958.[19]

A combination of circumstances caused the failure of the Great Leap Forward and the socialist drive. The failure gave the dissidents an opportunity to raise their voices. Pragmatic elements in the Communist leadership adopted ameliorative measures that seemed to turn the tide of popular dissatisfaction, although they were later labeled as revisionist. There came a period of slackened control when intellectuals were emboldened to assert their views, and during this period such writers as Wu Han and Teng T'o disguised their criticism in allegorical writings, historical anecdotes, and satire.

The Ministry of Education, as noted above, espoused regular schools that would pursue quality education and engage students in full-time study. Lu Ting-i proposed a ten-year system of schools that would not release youth for labor manpower until age 16 or 17.[20] In the same vein, Ch'en Yi, foreign minister holding concurrent positions in education and culture, declared that experts with good professional education could still be useful even though they had not spent much time on political study, and that students in the professional schools should be allowed to concentrate on their specialized studies without politics.[21] The "old" intellectuals were being reinstated in positions of respect, and young intellectuals were told they had much to learn from the experienced.[22] Peking University restored courses in ancient philosophy and capitalistic thought.[23] In a wave of bourgeois educational ideas, students signed up in large numbers for foreign language classes and old-style academic study.[24] The library became a popular place for students. Labor, production, and politics were being neglected. From the standpoint of the Maoists, the educational revolution was being undermined.[25]

At that time the educational revolution was not officially stressed. The new developments seemed to herald a new era of liberalism, and there was no indication that Mao Tse-tung was opposed to them. It is possible that Mao was already making plans for a full assault upon educational revisionism, but it is also possible that the storms of the Cultural Revolution were just beginning to brew and that the escalation of political and economic conflicts later pushed Mao to a more extreme position in regard to the educational revolution.* A full-scale educational revolution was not in evidence until Mao Tse-tung called for the termination of the domination of education by bourgeois scholars in 1966, although the ideas that later became the major guidelines of the educational revolution were expressed in the preceding years (see Appendixes 5-7). In 1964 he frankly told a visiting Nepalese delegation that "many people" were opposed to the educational reforms he proposed.

The Socialist Education Movement

Among the direct antecedents of the educational revolution, Mao's call for the training of millions of successors to the proletarian

---

*Something like this happened in 1955 when, in reaction against the tendency to slow down the drive for higher cooperatives, Mao ordered redoubled efforts to speed up collectivization in an "upsurge" of the "high tide of socialism."

revolution (1964) and the socialist education movement (1962-66) deserve mention. The former clearly set forth the aim of education, namely, to produce revolutionary successors with the attributes he stipulated;[26] the latter was the first organized effort to combat the ascending liberalism of the period. The call for revolutionary successors came after Mao Tse-tung was disenchanted with Chinese intellectuals and with the Soviet Union. As he himself explained, he had once hoped to select worthy successors from among the intellectuals and the products of education, but the intellectuals were steeped in bourgeois ideology and it was necessary to produce a new generation of successors. To design an educational program to achieve this end, where could he turn to find a model? Certainly not the Kuomintang system, nor the American or European type of capitalist education, nor the education of the revisionist USSR. There was only one way out: to devise a new revolutionary program.

The socialist education movement was a rectification movement not unlike that of 1942-44. It was an effort to arrest the relaxation of social and political controls, to turn the tide away from capitalism, and to rectify the mistakes of cadres indulging in corrupt practices.[27] It was another ideological remolding campaign, and the remedy it prescribed for the prevailing evils was a new emphasis on the all-important concept of class struggle. It was also known as the Four Clean-Ups (Ssu-Ch'ing) movement, which ordered the clean-up of undesirable practices in politics, ideology, organization, and the economy.[28] The movement was not directly concerned with the schools, and its literature made virtually no reference to schools. But in Chinese Communist terminology it was rightly called an educational movement because: (1) ideological remolding is recognized not only as an important function of education but as its central purpose and (2) changing the behavior, thought, and attitudes of adults outside the schools is an educational task of even greater immediate importance than the education of children in schools.

"In all its works," said Mao Tse-tung, "all schools should aim at transforming the ideology of the students." Speaking of the "revolutionary and historical significance" of the socialist education movement, Chou En-lai said that it involved "hundreds of millions of people."[29] "Socialist culture," he said, "must serve the politics of the proletariat . . . and serve the economic basis of socialism." This is a reiteration of the principle that education is inseparable from politics and economics. Chou continued:

> In this movement it is necessary to carry out a cleaning up and "capital construction" in the political, economic, ideological and organizational fields in accordance with the socialist principle of thorough-going revolution and

to conduct a profound class education and socialist education among the masses of the people so as to promote proletarian ideology and eradicate bourgeois ideology.

Production was said to have lagged because the masses and the cadres were under the pernicious influence of bourgeois ideology: The former demanded material rewards and were not putting forth their best efforts; the latter engaged in theft and corruption and failed to provide leadership for the masses. Since all action issues from thought, according to Communist theory, and problems of behavior and attitudes are traceable to ideological shortcomings, what the masses and the cadres needed was an intensified program of ideological remolding. This program was to center on the concept of class struggle, and the process of teaching its importance was known as class education.

The principal method of class education was to recall the evils of past society and contrast them with the progress since "Liberation" (1949). The content consisted of the "three histories" or "four histories." There were variations of the histories. In the early stage, the three histories were personal history, family history, and village history. Other histories making up a variety of combinations were commune history, factory history, street history, neighborhood history, and so on. In all instances the approach was the same: to relate the evils of the past in detail and to hail the achievements of the present. The slogan was "I K'u Ssu T'ien" (to recall past bitterness and reflect on present sweetness). Recollection of the dismal past was made by the individual or in group discussion or by listening to the personal experiences of the poor and the exploited.

No details were spared in describing the evils of the past. Peasants and workers were encouraged to tell how they had been abused by exploiting landlords, oppressive gentry, and merciless factory owners who treated workers as slaves and chattel. Women related their experience with lustful landlords; poor peasants told how usurious money-lenders cheated them out of all their earnings and the fruits of hard labor; all stories concluded with high praise of the new life that had been made possible by Chairman Mao and the Communist Party.

This form of class education is a part of the legacy of the socialist education movement and has become a salient feature of the educational revolution. As will be seen in later chapters, the recalling of past miseries and contrasting them with the bright present is a method still widely used in political education. The most moving narratives by peasants, workers, and activist students have been written and compiled into teaching materials for use in the classroom. It is considered important to teach about class enemies and class exploitation in past society because young people who grow up in the new society did not personally experience the bitter struggle of the past and consequently tend to minimize the importance of continued class struggle. The purpose of class education is to arouse and keep alive class consciousness so that the people do not forget the indispensable class struggle, stay on the alert to detect and fight against class enemies, guard against relaxation of the class struggle, and constantly strive to serve as valiant warriors of the proletarian class revolution.

The Opposing Lines

To sharpen the contrast between "two opposing educational lines," educational thinkers other than the maligned bourgeois scholars and revisionists have also been chosen as targets of mass criticism in education. One of them is Confucius. "Down with the Confucius Shop" is a slogan that has been heard every now and then in the past twenty years. It was reactivated during the Cultural Revolution and given new emphasis in the educational revolution. Confucius is attacked as an "idealist" in the service of the slave-owning class whose ideas were promulgated by such purveyors of reactionary thought as K'ang Yu-wei and Hu Shih. He is called the idol of Chiang Kai-shek and Liu Shao-ch'i.[30] The Four Books, "the epitome of the doctrine of Confucius and Mencius," are condemned as "the trash of the Confucius Shop."

Educationally, it is said, Confucius aimed to train bureaucrats for the reactionary slave-owners.[31] He taught his disciples "to seek fame and personal gain" and considered officialdom the acme of a scholarly career. He thus exploited the selfish motive of studying in order to climb up. He looked down on manual labor and the laboring people, who were denied the opportunity of education. His theory of human nature, summarized in the dictum "by nature men are nearly alike," runs counter to Chairman Mao's teaching that human nature has a class character and that "there is no human nature above classes."[32] His statement that in teaching there shall be no distinction of classes is considered typical of the "supra-class mentality" of feudal and bourgeois intellectuals. On the occasion of the ninetieth anniversary of the birth of the leftist writer Lu Hsün, the People's Daily prominently displayed a full-page article supporting and elaborating on his repudiation of Confucius and Confucian influence on Chinese culture. It pointed out that Confucius' concepts of "benevolence" and "love" represented the thought of the exploiting class and were designed to consolidate the power of the reactionary rulers.[33] Obviously, Confucius is still a live issue in the educational revolution.

Among the foreign educational theorists attacked as opponents of the Maoist educational line is Iran Andreevick Kairov. Since Kairov's

Pedagogy was used in teachers' colleges during the period when Soviet influence dominated Chinese education, this Soviet educator has been singled out for mass criticism during the educational revolution. Kairov's definition of education as "purely a human phenomenon" is condemned because it "completely denies a most fundamental fact: In class society, education is a phenomenon of class struggle."34 "Education," the critics argue, "develops out of the need of class struggle, not of an abstract 'human' need." A quotation from Kairov's Pedagogy to the effect that schools have two tasks to perform, namely, "to prepare students for advanced study and to train students in labor and production" is criticized as the advocacy of "two kinds of education," a viewpoint prevalent in the years of revisionist dominance.

Mass criticism of Confucius and Kairov underscores the ideological overtones of the educational revolution. The two men are put in the same category as the bourgeois scholars in order to present a clear contrast between the Maoist educational line and the non-Maoist line, and to make it easier for the masses to understand the meaning of the "two-line" struggle.

What, then, is the Maoist educational line? The answer will be clearer after the following chapters on concrete changes in the school system. The following summary of basic concepts may help point up the significance of the revolutionary changes:

- The educational revolution is opposed to elitist education; its program is mass-oriented.
- The Maoist line is opposed to knowledge for its own sake, education for its own sake, art and literature for their own sake; all must be guided by politics and economics (see Appendix 1 for Mao's theory of knowledge).
- Mao taught the unity of theory and practice. In education, the study of theory must be linked with its application to the political and the economic (production) struggle.
- The period of schooling should be shortened, and courses of study should be fewer.
- Examinations and marks should be dethroned.
- Full-time study alienated students from labor and production; study should go hand-in-hand with production and participation in the political (class) struggle.
- Intellectuals must be reformed by labor and learn to identify themselves with the laboring class. They must be aware of the class nature of all educational and cultural work.
- Workers and peasants must be educated to become a new force of proletarian intelligentsia.

Notes

1. See Chow Tse-tsung, The May Fourth Movement (Cambridge, Mass.: Harvard University Press, 1960).

2. The experts were Professor C. H. Becker of the University of Berlin, formerly Prussian minister of education; Professor M. Falski, director of the primary education department at the Polish Ministry of Education in Warsaw; Professor P. Langevin of the Collège de France in Paris; and Professor R. H. Tawney of the University of London. Their report and recommendations were published by the League of Nations' Institute of Intellectual Cooperation under the title The Reorganization of Education in China (Paris, 1932).

3. Ibid., p. 25.

4. Ibid., p. 28.

5. See Hubert Freys, Chinese Education During the War (Shanghai: Kelly and Walsh, 1940).

6. Kuang-ming Jih-pao, June 18, 1951.

7. See article on the high tide of learning Russian language in Kuang-ming Jih-pao, April 16, 1957.

8. Yang Hsiu-feng in Kuang-ming Jih-pao, November 6, 1957.

9. Another report stated that 3,000 to 4,000 course outlines used in the USSR were adopted by Chinese higher institutes. See Chinese Education, spring 1968, p. 15.

10. Article by Ch'ien Chün-jui, then vice minister of culture, in Jen-min Jih-pao, January 12, 1957; also April 18, 1957.

11. Klaus Mehnert, China Returns (New York: E. P. Dutton, 1972), p. 26.

12. Lu Ting-i, Let Flowers of Many Kinds Blossom, Diverse Schools of Thought Contend! (Peking: Foreign Languages Press, 1957).

13. Lu Ting-i, "Education Must Be Combined with Productive Labor," Peking Review, September 9, 1958.

14. See article on the "pagoda" in Jen-min Jih-pao, December 17, 1967.

15. "Chronology of 17 Years of the Two-Line Struggle on the Educational Front," English translation in Chinese Education, spring 1968.

16. Article attacking Lu P'ing's revisionist education in Jen-min Jih-pao, July 19, 1966.

17. See "Chronology," op. cit.

18. Lu Ting-i, "Education Must Be Combined with Productive Labor.

19. "Chronology," op. cit.

20. Lu Ting-i, "Reform in Educational Work," Peking Review, May 10, 1960.

21. Kuang-ming Jih-pao, September 3, 1961.

22. See article on relationship between young and old intellectuals in Jen-min Jih-pao, August 26, 1961.

23. Kuang-ming Jih-pao, April 4, 1961.

24. China News Analysis, no. 407 (February 9, 1962), p. 3.

25. See section 4 of "Chronology," op. cit., dealing with the 1961-63 period.

26. Peking Review, July 17, 1964, pp. 26-27.

27. Richard Baum and Frederick C. Teiwes, Ssu-Ch'ing: The Socialist Education Movement of 1962-66 (Berkeley: University of California Press, 1968), p. 12.

28. Peking Review, September 16, 1966, p. 11.

29. Peking Review, January 1, 1965, p. 13.

30. Chi Fan-hsui, "Ghost of Confucius' Shop and Actual Class Struggle," Peking Review, December 12, 1969.

31. The Writing Group of the Shantung Provincial Committee of the Chinese Communist Party, "A Criticism of Confucius' Thinking on Education," Peking Review, September 17, 1971; Chinese text in Jen-min Jih-pao, September 19, 1972.

32. Ibid.

33. Article by Lo Ssu-ting in Jen-min Jih-pao, September 25, 1971.

34. "Who Transforms Whom?—A Comment on Kairov's 'Pedagogy,'" Peking Review, March 6, 1970, p. 7.

The School System

A new school system was promulgated on October 1, 1951, two years after the birth of the regime. After the acceleration of the educational revolution, this system was considered unacceptable because it was planned and administered by bourgeois scholars guided by Soviet advisers.

At that time, the system seemed to reflect the new ideology. It provided for a sequence of schools on different levels: an elementary school (6 years), a junior middle school (3 years), a senior middle school (3 years), and various institutions of higher learning. There were some new features, including a variety of technical schools and short-term worker-peasant schools. The latter offered abbreviated courses that enabled workers and peasants with little or no schooling to encompass the essence of five years of elementary education in two or three years, or six years of secondary education in three or four years. By attending such schools in the evening, they could qualify for higher education within a few years. This reflected the proletarian ideology of giving priority to worker-peasant education and followed Mao Tse-tung's educational thinking in regard to shortened schooling and simplified content. Various forms of spare-time education were also recognized as parts of the school system. The ideological basis of the system was underlined by the People's Daily in an editorial greeting the promulgation of the new school system:

A school system is the reflection of the development of production and science in a given society. . . . The school system of capitalist states is a reflection of capitalist production and serves the purpose of the monopolistic economy of the capitalist class. The school system of the socialist states is, on the other hand, a reflection of the advanced methods of socialist production and meets the needs of the ever-expanding socialist and Communist construction. The school system of old China was an imitation of the system of capitalist states and reflected the reactionary ideology of landlords, bureaucrats, and the comprador class of semi-colonial semi-feudal society. It is opposed to the actual needs of the Chinese people.[1]

After the educational revolution gained momentum and the reforms of the first decade were discredited, it was pointed out that the system introduced in 1951 actually preserved the Kuomintang-capitalist-Soviet system of "regular" schools governed by the philosophy of elite and "quality" education. The People's Daily was then controlled by the revisionist bourgeois scholars, it was said, and the ideological allegations were only a show and a shield concealing the plot to forestall a thoroughgoing educational revolution. The worker-peasant schools and spare-time education did not represent a wholehearted effort to extend educational opportunity to the laboring masses; instead, they were makeshift arrangements designed to supplement the regular full-time schools, which remained the mainstay of the system.

In support of these charges, the critics cited the decision of the Ministry of Education to discontinue the short-term worker-peasant schools in 1955. In announcing this decision, the ministry expressed dissatisfaction with accelerated programs "which did not follow the method of gradual, orderly progress" and suggested that a way of producing a worker-peasant intelligentsia was to absorb many workers and peasants into the regular schools for systematic, orderly study.[2] This, the critics say, clearly shows that the Ministry of Education, controlled by the bourgeois intellectuals, thought and planned in terms of the bourgeois-revisionist type of schools.

Dissatisfaction with the school system of the reform period culminated in the decision to close all schools in 1966 (see Appendix 7). As noted in Chapter 1, the reopening of schools took place very slowly. The reopened schools are certainly very different from those of the past. A definite pattern is emerging in higher education, and radical programs are being launched on the elementary level and in adult education. The form of secondary education is less definite. If a system is viewed as a sequence of schools articulated for advance from one level to another, a system is yet to be developed. The dividing lines between elementary and secondary education and between the lower schools and higher education are so indefinite that there are really no clear-cut levels and the traditional terms of "elementary," "secondary," and "higher" have little meaning in the new situation.

On the other hand, if one accepts the Maoist contention that the purpose of study is not to advance to higher levels and that it is unnecessary and unwise to encourage students to climb the well-graduated rungs of the educational ladder, then the question of articulation of schools fades into unimportance. It may be contended that a revolutionary "system" rejecting the continuum of traditional schools is emerging today.

The Reopening of Schools

The reopening of the schools after their closure in 1966 was delayed for several reasons. The students had enjoyed a gala holiday when as Red Guards they could travel from one big city to another without paying travel expenses, and were accorded welcome and hospitality and provided with free board and lodging wherever they went. They had been hailed as true revolutionaries and they enjoyed the temporary power and authority of chastising all those they identified as reactionaries. They had taken upon themselves the right to enter households and public buildings to investigate evidences of the Four Old (old habits, customs, ideas, and culture). They had had the excitement of mammoth rallies and the privilege of seeing Chairman Mao in person. After such an exhilarating experience, what inducement was there to return to the dull quietude of the classroom?

Nor was it easy to get the teachers to return to their work. They had been denounced as bourgeois scholars and upholders of the old educational system. They had been subjected to personal inquisition, to abuses and insults, even physical assaults in some cases. They had sat or stood quietly to listen to the charges hurled against them by the Red Guards, among them their own students. The thought of facing these recent accusers and the possibility of further humiliation chilled them and dampened their enthusiasm for teaching.

The government order to return to school and continue "to wage revolution" (see Appendix 11) offered no reassurance to the skeptical and the hesitant. Young people who were urged to wage revolution in schools wondered what advantage the new way would have over the much freer way of waging revolution in the city streets. Teachers wondered what the order to continue to wage revolution would mean to their personal safety and peace of mind.

Supporting the order to resume classes, newspaper editorials pointed out that a small handful of "capitalist-roaders" were plotting against the revolution and inciting the students to stay out of school. To resume classes, said Wen-hui Pao, an influential Shanghai daily newspaper faithfully reflecting the official view, is to continue the class struggle, to overthrow the capitalist-roaders, and to ferret out the bad elements among the teachers and staff members.[3] If the school was to be the new battleground for continued "revolution," what would it be like in terms of curriculum, teaching schedule, relations between teachers and students, and other prosaic details of running a school?

After the students and teachers returned to the schools, other problems vexed those in charge. The buildings, many of which were used to house the roving Red Guards, were in disrepair. Equipment was gone or badly damaged. The revolutionaries knew what to condemn, but they were not sure what to advocate. The old curriculum had been abolished, but a new curriculum was yet to be developed. The old textbooks were banned, but new ones had not appeared. Old administrative organs had ceased to function, but new ones had not been devised. According to one observer, a few months after the order to reopen schools, "it appears that perhaps an average of one-half or two-thirds of the children at primary and secondary schools attend classes for one or two hours every morning, during which they read or sing quotations from Mao Tse-tung and undergo military training. That is all."[4] For some time, there was only a partial opening of the schools.

Disciplinary problems further complicated the situation. They arose not only from the difficulty of getting the rampaging Red Guards to settle down in the relatively restrained life of the school but also from internecine strife among competing youth factions. Interfactional strife flared up at times in physical combat and bloodshed. To quiet things down and curb disruptions, it was necessary to bring in the military to enforce order.

It seems that an important motive for ordering the youngsters to return to their schools was to take them off the streets and put a stop to the excessively disruptive activities of the Red Guards. Orders to cease their travels and rallies in the cities were also designed to rectify the chaotic conditions. Since the central emphasis was on returning to school to wage revolution, revolutionary activities dominated the school scene in the first few months after reopening. Political activities of youth were still encouraged, but they were now put under supervision and control. As far as the school program was concerned, people were waiting for instructions from the authorities. In the meantime, it seemed safe to stick to an approved political program and avoid venturing into what might be condemned as academic or bourgeois. Singing such songs as "East Is Red" and "The Great Helmsman" was certainly safe, and the study of the Chairman's quotations and the glorified "Three Great Articles"* constituted the core

---

*The "Three Great Articles" (sometimes translated as "Three Constantly Read Articles) are short and simple articles written by

of the new curriculum. After the initial uncertainty and confusion, the broad outlines of a school program slowly began to take shape.

The Draft Program

The "16-Point Decision" of the Central Committee of the Chinese Communist Party in 1966 stated, among other things, that the period of schooling should be shortened and courses should be fewer and better (see Appendix 10). The schools reopened after 1967 were guided by these instructions. Theoretically, the primary school is now reduced from six to five years, and the secondary school from six to four years, divided into two levels of junior middle school and senior middle school, each offering a two-year course. However, there are no clear-cut lines of demarcation between levels of education and no standardized criteria for judging qualifications for advance. Moreover, many primary schools offer a course shorter than five years. Where there are well-established five-year primary schools, some of them add junior middle school classes that come under the primary school administration. Bearing in mind the absence of clear-cut lines of division, we may think of an emerging system as indicated in the chart on page 43.

The Communist Party's call for the reopening of schools in 1967 gave preliminary instructions on the school program (see Appendix 14). It proposed that primary schools focus on political education, the study of Chairman Mao's quotations, the singing of revolutionary songs, the organization of Red Little Soldiers, and the teaching of "some general arithmetics and scientific knowledge." For the secondary schools, political education was to be continued, the Red Guard organizations were to be promoted, and the students should "attend their lessons on the one hand and make revolution on the other." The students should "devote some time to reviewing mathematics, physics, chemistry, foreign languages and other essential courses of study." Later, with Mao's "March 7 Directive" putting the army in charge of political and military training in schools and universities, military training was added to the regular school program (see Appendix 15).

Mao Tse-tung at different times. They are: "In Memory of Norman Bethune" (1939, 917 words in Chinese); "Serve the People" (1944, 697 words in Chinese); and "The Foolish Man Who Moved the Mountains" (1945, 928 words in Chinese). The third is an old Chinese story that used to appear in primary school textbooks, but was modified to suit the new purpose. The Three Great Articles have become required reading for political education inside and outside the schools for the entire population.

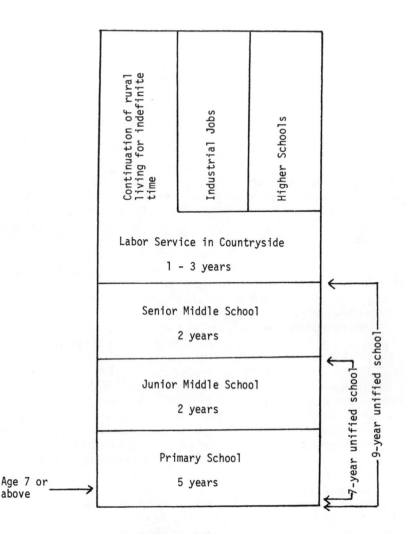

By 1969 the educational revolution had progressed to a stage where more detailed prescription of school work was possible. The "Draft Program for Primary and Middle Schools in the Countryside" went beyond the earlier proposals and spelled out more clearly what was expected of the schools (see Appendix 16). This program was not an official directive. It was proposed by the revolutionary committee of a county in Kirin province, but its publication in the People's Daily gave it an official stamp of approval. In the absence of a formal program proclaimed by the government, this Draft Program is the most specific and detailed prescription of the way the new schools should be run.

It declares that the reopened schools "are a new type of socialist school directly managed by the poor and lower-middle peasants under the leadership of the Chinese Communist Party." The principle of peasant management under Party leadership is thus clearly affirmed. Education must serve politics and production and lead the young to "temper themselves in the three great revolutionary movements of class struggle, the struggle for production, and scientific experiments in order to become "reliable successors to the revolutionary cause loyal to the great leader Chairman Mao." Peasants manage the school as part of the 'three-in-one revolutionary committee" and it is their responsibility to make sure of the "ideological revolutionization" of teachers and students by the process of struggle-criticism-transform tion.‡ The revolutionary committee is now the administrative body of the schools.

The Draft Program underlines the principle that "politics is the commander, the soul in everything." Mao Tse-tung's Thought must "take firm root in all positions of education . . . and [be] put in first place in all the work of the schools," including extracurricular activities. Teachers and students should "raise their consciousness of class struggle and the struggle between the two lines." The Communist Youth League and the Red Guards are to assist the Party and the school revolutionary committee to provide leadership in ideologica and political education.

Management by peasants goes with the local establishment and financial support of schools. The Draft Program stipulates that the primary school should be run by the production team and the middle school by the commune "or branches of it set up in several villages or run jointly by brigades." The addition of the junior middle school to the primary school, mentioned above, is in accordance with this provision. Theoretically the complete system will have "an uninterrupted nine-year school" (5-2-2), but at this moment it is only a goal for future development. The old system of promotion by examination is abolished and replaced by the method of "recommendation and selection, giving priority to the children of workers, poor and lower-middle peasants, revolutionary martyrs and armymen."

---

*Scientific experiment refers mainly to the use of scientific techniques to devise new methods and tools for the improvement of production.

†The three-in-one combination consists of representatives of "revolutionary mass organizations, army units, and revolutionary cadres."

‡Struggle against selfishness, criticism of revisionists, and transformation of ideology. Struggle is also directed against class enemies.

Students who complete primary and middle school education are expected to return to the production front and remain in the countryside. This means that young people join the ranks of full-time labor at the age of 16; even before age 16 their attendance at work-study schools means they are already a part of the production force. No mention is made of further study in higher institutions; there is no definite articulation between secondary education and higher education to make a continuous school system.

The intent of the government is to move as fast as possible toward universal education, at least on the primary school level. The most serious problem is financial. A convenient solution to the financial problem seems to have been found in the principle of local management of schools. The min-pan (people-managed) schools, which gained prominence in the Yenan period (see Chapter 1, "Mass Education") and were revived in the 1950s, now became the standard form of primary and secondary education, and the Draft Program's advocacy of peasant management of schools is an application of the same idea. Local management makes possible the adaptation of the schools to local conditions and local needs and the compilation of teaching materials derived from the local environment. At the same time, inasmuch as the peasants and other members of the "three-in-one" revolutionary committee* function under the leadership and guidance of the resident Party committee in the schools, the control of the educational program still rests in the Party-state.

It is evident that local management does not mean the relinquishing of centralized control of the fundamentals: the aims of education, the ideological and political commitment of teachers and students, the cultivation of revolutionary successors and worker-peasant (proletarian) intelligentsia, and a close link with production and political movements. In education as in economic development, Mao's instruction is to "let the localities undertake more work under unified central planning."[5] What is involved is more than a simple issue of educational decentralization or centralization. The financial consideration seems to be basic to the plan: The local community relieves the state of financial responsibility for the establishment of schools. Local responsibility is bolstered by the psychological motivation engendered by the doctrine of self-reliance, which calls for a determined effort to carry on with as little state aid as possible. The constant exhortation to practice thrift and economy and the repeated warnings against

---

*The three elements that constitute the revolutionary committee in charge of school administration are the poor and lower-middle peasants, the cadres, and the revolutionary teachers and students. The peasants are supposed to be the mainstay.

extravagance and waste further focus attention on the financial advantages that will accrue from the local management of schools (see, for example, article 29 of the Draft Program, Appendix 16). "Unified central planning" is not sacrificed.[6]

There is no private education, no school not controlled by the Party and the state. As nonstate schools established by the local people and such nongovernment agencies as factories, farm collectives, and business concerns, the min-pan schools at first seemed to be a relaxation of the ban on private education. However, since the factories, farms, and business enterprises are all controlled by the Party-state, the schools they establish are not private schools at all, as normally understood in Western countries. The communes and factories certainly cannot be considered private enterprises. All of them accept the leadership of the Party-state, and all their schools exist to serve politics and production according to the guidelines of the Party-state. No one has any doubt that the Party representatives in the schools represent the "leadership" that must be respected and obeyed.

Although the Draft Program was adopted for the rural schools, the general principles apply to the city schools as well. Responsibility for the management of schools in the cities also belongs to the local community. Urban schools are run by the factories and neighborhood organizations. The "three-in-one" organization of administrative personnel is also in effect, and workers are recognized as the mainstay just as the peasants are in the countryside. The Party leadership is the invariable principle, and close linkage is maintained between schools and factories.

Much is said about the "open-door" policy of running the schools. "Open-door" means the removal of barriers between the school and society. Students learn not only in school but also outside. The school should cooperate closely with outside agencies—the factories, the communes and brigades, the revolutionary committees of various units, and the families—and coordinate all activities so they may become parts of a planned program working for common objectives. The "open-door" also means that students and teachers should learn from the workers and peasants and in turn help to solve the problems of the masses. They should also join the masses in pushing ahead the three great revolutionary movements.[7]

In accordance with Mao Tse-tung's "May 7 Directive" of 1966 (see Appendix 9) that students should "learn other things, that is, industrial work, farming and military affairs," urban middle schools have set up branch schools in rural areas where students and teachers may learn farming and relate learning to farming practice. Teachers and students go to these rural bases in rotation, and they work on reclaimed land and put up school buildings, using local materials. A report on these rural branch schools stated that "many of these schools harvested rice, peanuts and other products . . . some have also developed side-line production."[8] An additional convenience for the rural branches of city schools is that poor and lower-middle peasants are asked to help in class and "line" education by relating their family and village history to the students.

The Draft Program was intended to be tentative. Comments and suggestions were solicited. Some schools launched programs according to the guidelines of the Draft Program, and they stimulated other schools to emulate or follow suit. The local management of schools leaves the way open for variations in light of local situations, but there is no departure from the principles set forth in the Draft Program. Progress has been slow and uneven in the adoption of what may be considered a stable program. Few statistical reports are available, and reports on schooling conditions in some localities and provinces do not give a national picture. The well-organized schools that foreign visitors see in China are not representative of the whole country, but they do indicate what the educational revolution is trying to achieve.[9]

Preschool Education

Attention has been directed to the education of young children before they are ready for elementary school. The People's Daily (June 2, 1969) raised the rhetorical question whether small children should be positively taught and nurtured in the Thought of Mao Tsetung or whether they should be left alone to live and learn in a nonproletarian environment until they reach school age. The answer was that education in class consciousness and the proletarian outlook should begin from the early years. A program of "infant education" for children between ages 3 and 6 is considered crucial for the molding of correct thought and action. This program is carried on in nurseries, kindergartens, and prekindergarten classes; also in homes, in factories and communes, and in various programs outside the schools.

Nursery rooms where working mothers come to feed their children and nurseries where children may be left for the entire day or even overnight are considered strategic places for starting the molding process. Habits of physical labor can be formed; thrift and the endurance of hardship can be cultivated. Within the home, it is suggested that parents seize every opportunity to impart class education. Children who object to old and worn-out clothes can be taught to be more appreciative when they are told how much worse life was in the old society and how conditions are constantly improving in the new society. There are also opportunities for education in "struggle-criticism," that is, struggle against selfishness and criticism of revisionism. It is suggested that the names of revisionists be made known to small children. In the old days, the Chinese used to say that parents reared children so that they might have the young to rely on when they reached old age. Now, it is suggested, in lieu of rearing children as protection for old age, parents should learn a new concept, namely, to rear children in such a way as to protect against revisionism ("yang-erh fang-hsiu" instead of "yang-erh fang-lao"). In the 1950s Communist leaders used to say that society could do a better job than the home in the training of children, but in recent years the family is recognized as a valuable agency in children's education.

A production brigade in a commune in Anhwei province organized "Red children's classes" for children of age 3 or above for education in Mao Tse-tung Thought by means of "daily study of Chairman Mao's quotations."[10] The children are taught to overcome self-interest by making a clear distinction between public interest and self-interest. In other communities, the school, the family, and the commune or factory cooperate to hold exhibits designed to develop class consciousness by the identification of class enemies and by contrasting the old and the new society. Children are led to watch the poor and lower-middle peasants work in the field and to observe their spirit of working hard and not fearing hardship. The Red Little Soldiers play a role by sending propaganda teams into villages or city neighborhoods to help educate the small children and mold their emotional attitudes and ideological ideas.

The Goal of Universal Education

In elementary education, the aim is to popularize the five-year primary school. Theoretically, the hope is expressed that five-year primary schools will be established in the area of the production teams; junior middle schools (or seven-year schools) in the production brigades; and senior middle schools (or nine-year schools) in the communes. This goal is approached in only a few areas. Many areas are unable to provide five years of primary education and have to improvise such makeshifts as irregular courses of one or two years in length, or literacy or newspaper-reading classes of even shorter duration. Besides the financial problem, obstacles to universal schooling lie in the attitudes of children and parents. In stressing the importance of practice, Mao Tse-tung has used strong language to condemn book study and knowledge divorced from practice. The more books a person reads, Mao once said, the more stupid he becomes: Even in the study of Marxism, reading too many books may be harmful (see Appendix 5). Evidently, some people have misunderstood the Chairman's intentions and jumped to the conclusion that "it is useless to study." One ideological problem of the educational revolution is to combat the notion that study is useless. For example, a primary school girl student was found to have no interest in study. She was usually late to class and often absent. Investigation revealed that she was influenced by the idea that study was useless. The cure, of course, was ideological education, which taught her the importance of study in order to serve the revolution. An article on the teaching of "socialist culture" in schools reported that a stumbling block was the students' attitude: "some students had the idea that the less they studied, the more revolutionary they would become."[11]

The fallacious thinking in regard to study is reinforced in the minds of many young people and their parents by the great emphasis on labor and production. If one's primary duty is to serve the cause by active participation in the "production struggle," wouldn't it be better to take it up as soon as possible? Since children start to perform labor early anyway, wouldn't it be better for them to continue on the production front instead of interrupting it to go to school? There is an obvious advantage in starting early to accumulate more work points. Furthermore, it is often said that education has been dominated by the bourgeois ideology and schooling tends to remove the students from the masses. If so, wouldn't it be safer to stick to labor and not bother about schooling?

The officially approved rejoinder to such questions is that the old educational system removed the students and teachers from the masses and study was motivated by the desire to achieve personal fame and success or, according to the Confucian tradition, to become an official, whereas the aim of the new education is to serve the people and the school now teaches students to become successors of the proletarian revolution. Consequently, there is no inconsistency between the previous strictures against book knowledge and the current effort to popularize primary education. This sounds logical enough, but ideological niceties are often too abstruse for the masses, and some doubts still remain. Dropouts today constitute a serious problem in primary education and authorities are enjoined to strive to reduce the number of dropouts. But didn't Chairman Mao point out that some of the greatest names in history were dropouts? (See Appendix 5.) Evidently much remains to be done to clear up ideological confusion before primary education can be made universal. There is so much emphasis in current literature on attacking the notion that "study is useless" that it must be fairly prevalent, and it is being attacked as one of the poisonous ideas disseminated by the revisionists and the "black gang of swindlers."

A report in the People's Daily (May 17, 1972) states that the dropout rate increases with the advance in primary school grades

49

and is higher among girls. Pupils who are sent out to take part in labor are tempted to stay out of school permanently. Parental cooperation is recognized to be important in the attempt to solve this problem, and various methods have been proposed to carry out ideological education among parents so that wrong ideas may be corrected and more favorable attitudes engendered.[12] An investigation carried out by a district in Honan province also revealed that the percentage of dropouts was higher among girls than boys, that the rate increased with the advance in grades, and that economic needs had a good deal to do with the decision of parents to withdraw their children from school.[13] No report has made any reference to withdrawals resulting from the loss of interest on the part of the pupils, but the sabotage of class enemies spreading revisionist ideas is often mentioned as a major cause of the high dropout rate. To combat such ideas, the district in Honan sent teams of old peasants to visit the homes to remind parents of the bitter past so that they might be more appreciative of the opportunities now available to them.

Even with primary courses reduced to one or two years, full-day sessions are not always popular because they interfere with the need for labor. Half-day classes are common; in other cases, evening classes better meet local needs. Holding classes every other day of the week has been tried. Sometimes the school organizes out-of-school literacy classes for pupils of the higher grades who cannot attend school during the day because of their work. In the cities, the neighborhood primary school offers instruction in the first two grades. Practicing thrift and economy, and trying to get along with a minimum of equipment and physical needs, these schools claim that they are following the spirit of Kang Ta (see Chapter 1).

One observes much ingenuity in the variety of forms in which primary education is carried on. There are no fixed standards, but much diversity in the light of local conditions. In Inner Mongolia, where settlements are scattered and travel is difficult, mobile classes are held in the homes of the herdsmen and a small corps of traveling teachers can take care of a large number of such classes.[14] In other cases, more advanced pupils serve as "little teachers" to help conduct classes between the visits of the traveling teachers. School children also have been sent into homes to teach young and old the quotations from Chairman Mao and his "Three Great Articles."[15] Flexibility and adaptation to local needs characterize the effort to popularize primary education. At the same time, it is obvious that the goal of universal five-year primary education is not anywhere near attainment for most areas of the country. Here and there a report appears that school attendance has increased 200 percent or more, but no absolute statistics are available. Other reports say that universal education has been "basically" attained in selected areas, but the meaning of "basic" is not made clear.

Secondary Education

It has been noted that there exists no distinct dividing line
between elementary and secondary education. Since preparation for
further study is not an important function of education, it does not
much matter whether a particular school is classed as elementary
or secondary or higher. Indeed, there are secondary schools in technical fields that are elementary in nature and "colleges" that actually
are secondary schools. The term "middle school" was used in the
old days to refer to the academic middle school considered a prerequisite to institutions of higher learning. Today it is used for a variety
of secondary schools "including intermediate technical schools and
schools run on part-work and part-study or part-farming and part-
study basis." As a matter of fact, the technical schools now dominate
the secondary field, and the work-study type is more common than
the full-day school.

The guidelines for secondary schools also stress the importance
of politics. The schools "must resolutely execute the proletarian
revolutionary line represented by Chairman Mao and thoroughly criticize and repudiate the bourgeois reactionary line." This is the meaning of the "two-line" struggle or "line education." Schools must "carry
out struggle, criticism, and transformation"; they must "practice
economy while making revolution." Political and military training is
prescribed for teachers as well as students, and "the ranks of teachers
must be reorganized and purified seriously." Besides the all-important
political education, "it is also necessary" to study mathematics, physics, chemistry, foreign languages," and other essential courses of
study." In the study of academic subjects, political and ideological
themes must be interwoven with the subject matter (examples are
given in Appendix 22).

There are many kinds of technical schools. It is hard to identify
their role or position within an organized system because many seem
independent of other schools on lower or higher levels. They offer
courses of varying length and are designed to produce personnel to
meet the immediate needs in such areas as agriculture, industry,
communication, transportation, medicine and pharmacy, trade, accounting and bookkeeping. The technical schools suffered a setback during
the Cultural Revolution on account of the ideological assault on the
revisionist policy of "technique first" and the trend to put "expertness"
above "Redness." However, the need for trained personnel became
urgent with the inauguration of a rehabilitation program following the
disruption of the Cultural Revolution. When Chairman Mao put his
stamp of approval on the Shanghai machine tools plant, the status of
technical education rose again (see Appendix 33). To avoid lapsing
into the "technique first" error of revisionist education, the technical

schools of today put a premium on loyalty to the Maoist line and unceasing criticism of the revisionist concept of "technique first." The technical schools exist to produce personnel for the proletarian revolution, but the quality of their product is judged in terms of ideological correctness and political dependability. Politics, in other words, must be put in command.

Some technical schools are on the junior middle school level, others on the senior middle school level. Courses vary in length. However, some general characteristics are common to all. They follow the min-pan principle of local establishment and support; they are part-study and part-work schools; in all cases, political education occupies a central place. Local needs and conditions guide the program: the school calendar, the schedule, the curriculum, and teaching materials. The agricultural schools that appeared before the Cultural Revolution are today modified to conform to the new pattern.[16] Other types of technical schools have been established in answer to local needs. They are designed to meet immediate needs and to train persons who are able to put theories into immediate practice and make direct contributions to the "three great revolutionary movements." If, for example, there is a need for electrical repair work, a special course in electrical repairs is in order; if there are not enough bookkeepers, a course or school is set up to teach bookkeeping. When the need is specific and urgent, a short-term course of a few months to a year or two is likely to appear.

Much publicity has been given to "four kinds of new-type schools" established in Kwangtung province.[17] In response to the recognized needs of agriculture and locally managed industries, such as the shortage of teachers and mechanics able to repair farming implements and machinery, a plan was adopted to establish industrial schools, agricultural schools, health schools, and normal schools. The industrial schools were established in advanced factories, agricultural schools in advanced communes, schools for health and hygiene workers in hospitals and advanced clinical centers, and normal schools in "advanced units of educational revolution." They are short-term courses, three to six months in length. From the first day of classes, students study the "Three Great Articles" and engage in "mass criticism" of the ideological fallacies of "study to become officials," "technique first," and "occupational competence in priority." They study Mao's teaching on practice and integration with poor and lower-middle peasants. They take active part in the "three great revolutionary movements." They listen to the oral narrative of peasants on the "three histories."

Students for these schools are selected from among experienced workers, poor and lower-middle peasants, and "educated youth" sent to the countryside for reeducation or settlement; admission is subject

52

to the approval of the Party leadership. The curriculum consists of industrial knowledge, agricultural knowledge, the use and repair of the most important agricultural implements and machines, herb medicine, acupuncture, and the treatment of common animal diseases. Reports on these schools underline the political and ideological training but do not give many details about instructional content and methods or other academic matters. They make frequent mention of the Kang Ta spirit of education and stress self-reliance and the ability of students and teachers to build their own classrooms, construct roads, irrigate rice fields, plant fruit trees and vegetables, and raise hogs, sheep, chickens, and ducks.

The Curriculum

The previously mentioned Draft Program provides for five subjects to be taught in the primary school, and five in the middle school. The primary school subjects are politics and language, arithmetic, "revolutionary literature and art," military training and physical culture, and productive labor. The primary aims of serving politics and production are evident. "Revolutionary literature and art" means that the subject matter must be linked with the "three great revolutionary movements." Music, sometimes an additional subject of the curriculum, teaches the singing of "revolutionary songs." (Two songs that are much publicized are the "Internationale" and "The Three Great Rules and the Eight Points"; the former expresses the spirit of worldwide Communism, and the latter is Mao's formula for army discipline.)

In the middle school, the curriculum consists of Mao Thought and politics (including history), agriculture ("including mathematics, physics, chemistry, and economic geography"), military training and physical culture, and productive labor. The academic subjects are thus closely integrated with politics and production (as often as not, such academic subjects as mathematics and chemistry are not taught separately but as parts of "agricultural knowledge" or "industrial knowledge"). Even military training is supposed to include "the study of Chairman Mao's concepts on people's war." Industrial instruction takes the place of agricultural instruction in the city schools, but the pattern remains the same. In the initial period after reopening, political study completely dominated the curriculum, but later programs make greater provision for "cultural courses," which is the term commonly used for subjects other than what is definitely labeled as political. It includes physical training. The Draft Program proposed that 70 percent of scheduled teaching in middle schools and 60 percent in primary schools be concerned with courses "in general knowledge and culture." "Cultural study" often means no more than basic reading and writing to overcome illiteracy.*

However, "cultural study" does not exclude political education because politics permeates the entire curriculum and all activities in school and outside. The "revisionist" idea that cultural courses are concerned mainly with intellectual education is unacceptable: "There is no such thing as 'pure' cultural courses divorced from politics" (see Appendix 17). The chemistry or mathematics teacher has as much responsibility as the teacher of the political course to teach the Thought of Mao Tse-tung and to remold the students' ideology. Moreover, any difficulties in teaching and learning are traced to ideological problems. The People's Daily (July 6, 1972) reports the experience of a primary school in which one-third of a fifth-grade class was falling behind in language and mathematics. Finding that the backward students had been influenced by the notion that study is useless, the teacher adopted a program of ideological education to raise the pupils' revolutionary consciousness. To give the class a vivid lesson in revolutionary struggle, the pupils were led to visit a site of Mao Tse-tung's early revolutionary activities. It is thus evident that while the assignment of 60 to 70 percent of time to cultural study does provide for more academic work,† it does not in any way dilute the political and ideological character of the curriculum or of school life.

The study of foreign languages suffered a setback during the Cultural Revolution but has regained its place in the school curriculum. Foreign language study begins with the fourth grade in some primary schools.[18] The Foreign Language Institute has been reopened,[19] but it is now contended that it is not enough to train specialists in the Foreign Language Institute, and that knowledge of foreign languages is important and useful for the cultured socialist worker. Foreign languages, it is pointed out, are a useful tool for such tasks as publicizing Marxism-Leninism and the Thought of Mao Tse-tung, and supporting the worldwide struggles against imperialists, revisionists, and reactionaries.[20] Thus the two cardinal principles of political purpose and practical use enter into the teaching of foreign languages.

The teaching of foreign languages before the Cultural Revolution is criticized today because it paid exclusive attention to listening, speaking, reading, and writing to the neglect of politics. Instead of

---

*Sometimes the study of politics is also included in the category of cultural courses (see Appendix 17). Labor, production, and political activities would then belong to the other category.

†The word "academic" is used here in the ordinary meaning commonly accepted in the West, not in any derogatory sense.

politics in command, it put languages in command, and that is now considered wrong. In the first decade of the regime, the Russian language was given first priority and English, previously the first foreign language for schools and universities, was relegated to a secondary position. Now English has risen to push out Russian, no doubt as a result of the government's new international policy. Radio lessons in English reach many people outside the schools, in all walks of life. A Canadian reporter in Shanghai spoke of "a craze to learn English."[21] The radio lessons, he said, "are most popular among middle school students, but the program has also caught on among hotel employees, factory workers, and even pedicab drivers." The first of the radio lessons in Shanghai sets the tone for the program: "We study English for the revolution." Also: "Chairman Mao is our great leader. We must listen to Chairman Mao and follow the Party." Lesson 2 contains the following: "This is a badge. This is a book. Is this a badge? Yes, it is. It is a Chairman Mao badge. Is that a badge, too? No, it is not. It is a book. It is a copy of Quotations from Chairman Mao Tse-tung. We love our great leader Chairman Mao." Other foreign languages taught are Japanese, French, German, Arabic, and Spanish,[22] but they are not as popular as English.

Teaching Materials

Inasmuch as old textbooks are found to be replete with bourgeois ideas, they are no longer usable. It is therefore necessary to compile new teaching materials and write new textbooks. Since the entire school program is in flux, no standardized teaching materials have yet appeared. Materials supplied by the state are supplemented by those based on local conditions. The local character of the teaching materials is enhanced by the manner in which they are compiled. The cooperation of workers, peasants, and soldiers, as well as "revolutionary teachers and students," is enlisted in the selection of curriculum materials. Writing them up for class use is a collective effort of "writing teams" or "compiling teams" rather than the work of educators or professionals. The teams are constituted according to the three-in-one principle: workers-peasants-soldiers, revolutionary teachers, and students. Selected cadres also serve on the teams.

Practical use and political steadfastness are the guides. Materials drawn from the actual problems of farming and industry and the common diseases of the locality ensure that knowledge gained in study is applied to practice, while the study of Mao's speeches and writings ensures the correct political orientation and ideological vigilance. History texts center on the Chinese Communist Party, world Communism, and the worldwide revolutionary struggle for the liberation of the oppressed. Locally compiled materials include local "histories" of class exploitation and the testimony of workers and peasants. The Party revolutionary committee of a hsien (county) in Kiangsu province reported a textbook based on lectures given by old peasants. It contains vivid descriptions of how the landlords of yesteryear forcibly occupied the land of the people and oppressed the peasants until the latter rose in indignation to resist paying rent and to beat up the landlords. It told how, under the Red Flag and Chairman Mao's guidance, the people learned to organize cooperatives and communes and acquired a determination to carry on the struggle against class enemies.[23]

Old textbooks are not merely discarded; they are critically analyzed and severely condemned for their feudal and revisionist ideas in order to sharpen the distinction between the old and the new—the two opposing "lines." Stories used in elementary textbooks for decades and centuries are put under scrutiny to examine their ideological background. For example, the old story of four-year-old K'ung Yung who chose for himself the smallest pear and left the bigger ones for his elder brother is criticized because the little boy in the story later became an official to serve the ruling class.

The story of little Ssu-ma Kuang who alertly picked up a rock to smash a water jar into which a playmate had fallen, and that of Tsao Ch'ung who devised a way of weighing an elephant by putting it on a boat, marking the water line on the side of the boat, and later loading it with rocks to reach the same line and then weighing the rocks, are familiar stories known to many generations of Chinese children, but they are now rejected as reflections of feudal society glorifying the ruling class and the selfish motive of personal fame. In the past the story of a black goat and a white goat coming from opposite directions to a narrow bridge, each unwilling to yield and fighting until both fell into the water, was told to teach the lesson that it was better to defer than to fight, but it is now repudiated because it teaches "conciliationism" which is detrimental to the will to "struggle."

It is also felt that the old textbooks—teaching such "stupid things" as "a cat jumps; a dog barks" and irrelevant matters such as birds and flowers—completely ignored the social and political struggle and were meant to lull the people into complacency with the status quo. In line with Mao's teaching that destruction must precede construction, intensive criticism of old teaching materials is deemed a necessary prelude to the preparation of new ones. A frequent criticism is that the old primary school textbooks devote too much space to describing emperors, kings, generals, prime ministers, and beautiful women; they fail to cultivate the revolutionary spirit.

There is much oral instruction without the use of textbooks: listening to old workers and poor peasants tell their experience with exploiting landlords and local gentry, singing revolutionary songs, and so forth. When compiling teams produce written materials, they always indicate that the materials are of tentative nature and issued for temporary use. Most are mimeographed materials. While these temporary materials vary in content, they follow the same basic pattern.

Take, for example, two sets of primary school textbooks, compiled by writing teams in Yunnan province and Shanghai, which happen to be available to the author. Book One on language study in each series begins with "Long Live Chairman Mao," followed by other "Long Live" slogans (Mao Tse-tung Thought, the Chinese Communist Party, and so forth). In each series Book One has 32 lessons, and not one of them fails to mention Chairman Mao or his "quotations."

Chairman Mao and Mao Thought are also integrated into middle school texts on farming, science, and mathematics, as well as language. For example, an exercise in subtraction may ask how much grain was left for the poor peasant who toiled all year to harvest ten piculs of grain but had to pay nine piculs for rent to an oppressive landlord.

Notes

1. Jen-min Jih-pao, October 3, 1951.
2. Chung Hua Jen Min Kung Ho Kuo Fa Kwei Hui Pien (Laws and regulations of the People's Republic of China) (Peking: Fa Lu Ch'u Pan She, 1956), Vol. II, pp. 775-78.
3. Reprinted in Kuang-ming Jih-pao, February 18, 1967.
4. Harold Munthe-Kaus, "School Holidays," Far Eastern Economic Review (Hong Kong), June 15, 1967.
5. Peking Review, September 24, 1971, p. 9.
6. Even the "revisionist" Ministry of Education encouraged the establishment of min-pan schools in the 1950s. The ministry directives candidly admitted that establishment of schools by the people was meant to relieve the state of financial responsibility, but "political education and rural activities" must be under the direct supervision of the Communist Party. For another interpretation of the decentralization policy, see Donald J. Munro, "Egalitarian Ideal and Educational Facts in Communist China," in John M. H. Luidbeck, China: Management of a Revolutionary Society (Seattle: University of Washington Press, 1971), pp. 256ff.
7. Kuang-ming Jih-pao, April 2, 1973.
8. Peking Review, December 25, 1970, p. 26.
9. The New York Times, May 14, 1972, published a report from Hong Kong saying that "a more temporary type of classroom operated on a part-time basis" and "scattered irregular village

schools" are more common than what foreign visitors see in the large cities and more advanced communes.

10. Foreign Broadcast Information Service, Daily Report, Communist China, June 2, 1970, p. C7, (Hereafter cited as FBIS.)

11. FBIS, June 30, 1969, p. C3.

12. Kuang-ming Jih-pao, August 14, 1972; report on a primary school in Kirin province.

13. Kuang-ming Jih-pao, April 25, 1973.

14. In one county, nine teachers in one commune took care of 40 mobile classes meeting in herdsmen's homes. FBIS, January 7, 1971, p. F.

15. Hung-ch'i (Red flag), July 21, 1970; report on rural education in Kansu province.

16. See Robert D. Barendsen, Half-Work Half-Study Schools in Communist China (Washington, D.C.: U.S. Office of Education, 1964).

17. Tsu Kuo (China monthly; Hong Kong), January 1, 1972, pp. 39-41; also Hung-ch'i (Red flag), July 21, 1970.

18. According to Donald Bremner, Los Angeles Times, May 7, 1972, English is taught in the first grade of a primary school in Shanghai.

19. "Renewed Attention to Foreign Language Training," Current Scene 10, no. 2 (February 7, 1972).

20. Jen-min Jih-pao, March 7, 1969.

21. John Burns, New York Times, August 22, 1972.

22. Ibid.; "Renewed Attention," op. cit. The New York Times on April 1, 1973 reported an escalating interest in the study of Japanese and the inauguration of radio broadcasting of Japanese-language lessons in Shanghai.

23. Jen-min Jih-pao, January 11, 1970.

4

POLITICS AND IDEOLOGY

"Put politics in command" is one of the most frequently repeated slogans in the Chinese Communist movement. Politics is the "soul" of all economic work, social reform, and education. Since politics is inseparable from ideology and the two words are often used interchangeably, it would be just as appropriate to use the slogan "Put ideology in command." All problems are reducible to ideological terms. Whenever there is difficulty of any kind, be it a lag in production or too many dropouts from school or young people dissatisfied with life in rural areas, the source of trouble is invariably believed to be ideological. Conversely, all successful policies and all forms of good behavior are attributed to correct ideological stand. The success of the revolution, therefore, hinges on correct ideological guidance.

It is not easy for an individual to attain ideological competence. Mao Tse-tung has said many times that ideological remolding cannot be achieved once and for all, and that there are no short cuts. People are constantly subject to the corroding influence of bourgeois ideology, which abounds in present-day society and in a world dominated by the bourgeoisie and bourgeois ideology. The danger of revisionism arises from the tendency to relax and consequently become vulnerable to the infiltration of unproletarian ideas, which come from various forms of "idealism," "transcendentalism," "apriorism," or any "ism" other than the correctly interpreted brand of Marxism-Leninism or the Thought of Mao Tse-tung. Even without the threat of external influences, a person is likely to hold within himself unwholesome ideas that are hangovers from his past, and there is always the danger that these may reassert themselves. Ideological remolding must be a long, continuous process. It cannot be accomplished by the use of stark force; it can be brought about only by the slow and continuous process of persuasion, and according to Communist thinking, the process of persuasion is that of education. It follows that while education is concerned with the acquisition of knowledge, skills, and habits, its major function is ideological remolding.

It is not possible to explain the Chinese Communist ideology in a few words, but a few concepts stand out prominently and loom large in political and ideological education. A major concept is class. The Communists call their revolution a class revolution, and their party a class organization. They are the vanguard of the working class and their mission is, in the words of the Party Constitution revised in 1969, "the complete overthrow of the bourgeoisie and all other exploiting classes" in order to establish the dictatorship of the proletariat.

Society is divided into classes and every person is a member of a class, molded by it and reflecting its thinking and outlook. It is extremely difficult for a person born into a nonproletarian class to have the proletarian point of view; only by determined and sustained effort can he learn to identify himself with the proletarian class. Mao Tse-tung's famous analysis of Chinese society listed the landlord class, the bourgeoisie, the petty bourgeoisie, the peasantry, and the proletariat.[1] With official encouragement, Chinese scholars have rewritten the history of various periods centering on the concept of classes in Chinese society. Awareness of classes and their special interests is regarded as essential to political and ideological awakening. It is thus understandable why there is so much emphasis on class education, and why the major effort of education is devoted to raising the class consciousness of students and the population at large.

Much is heard and said of "class origin," and every person is made aware of his class origin. In education, privileges and advantages are accorded to youths of worker-peasant class origin. Intellectuals are constantly reminded of their bourgeois class origin, and their children are made to realize that they have handicaps to overcome by virtue of their bourgeois background. A specific task of political and ideological education is to teach how to differentiate between "friend and foe," to recognize "class enemies" and learn how to combat them.

Class consciousness is inseparable from class struggle, and "struggle" is another key concept in the Communist ideology. Life is one struggle after another, and history is in effect the story of class struggle. Progress comes from struggle and is quickly nullified by hostile forces as soon as struggle is relaxed. According to Mao Tse-tung, there are two major forms of struggle: class struggle and the struggle for production. All human knowledge comes from these two forms of struggle (see Appendix 1). Continuous revolution means continuous class struggle, which is the only guarantee of the success of the proletarian revolution. Since the Cultural Revolution, class struggle has been stressed more strongly than ever before, and it is the dominant theme of ideological indoctrination today. "Politics," said Mao Tse-tung, "whether revolutionary or counterrevolutionary, is the struggle of class against class."[2] Contrary to the revisionist theory that class struggle will die out, Mao teaches that even after the establishment of the dictatorship of the proletariat, class struggle will still be necessary in order to combat the class enemies who will appear in different forms.[3]

"Never forget classes and class struggle," warned Mao Tse-tung on the eve of the Cultural Revolution.[4] The continued emphasis on class struggle in the post-Cultural Revolution era is illustrated in the rectification campaign launched to upgrade the ideological consciousness of youth. An article in the People's Daily (December 25, 1972) on the ideological rectification campaign in the Communist Youth League of a production brigade in Honan province stated that most of the young workers, even members of the Youth League, failed to appreciate the acute nature of the class struggle and the struggle between the two lines. It cited the instance of a young couple who had a newborn baby. Their former landlady came to offer felicitations with a gift of ten eggs. When the husband expressed displeasure with a gift from a person of the landlord class, his wife showed appreciation for the gift by saying that the landlady "meant well." Then followed an argument, which came to the attention of the Youth League. Alert to the ideological implications, the Youth League organized a study session to examine the incident. How could a landlady have good intentions? Careful analysis showed that she probably came with the intention of bribing the young couple because both were Youth League members— the wife was a member of the revolutionary committee of the production brigade, and the husband was a leader of a militia platoon. Viewed in this light, the eggs were "sugar-coated bullets" fired by a class enemy. This revelation led to a penetrating criticism of such insidious ideas as "the gradual dying out of the class struggle" and the "theory of human nature," which could blind the unwary to the real intentions of the landlady. The conclusion was that it is necessary to be vigilant and combat the intrigue and deception of the enemy by never forgetting for a moment the importance of the class struggle.

Forms of Political Education

Political education takes place in a variety of ways. The content of classroom study consists of the works of Marx and Lenin and the Thought of Mao Tse-tung as revealed in his writings, speeches, and numerous statements and directives. Government and Party documents dealing with major policies and ongoing mass campaigns are included. Outside the classroom there are "study sessions" and "group discussions" to clarify ideological issues. But knowledge is not enough; it must be applied to and reinforced by "revolutionary action," which ranges from extracurricular activities in the school to direct participation in mass campaigns and "revolutionary movements" beyond the school walls. The youth organizations have a planned program of ideological remolding for their membership and other young people. Finally, since the Cultural Revolution, the politically active workers, peasants, and soldiers have been brought into the picture to share the responsibility of teaching young people—and older intellectuals, too— the practical significance of the class struggle and ongoing revolutionary movements.

On the elementary level, ideological study is concerned with simple quotations from Chairman Mao and current events as transmitted by official news and propaganda agencies. Ongoing mass campaigns and rectification campaigns are given much attention. Official documents such as the speeches and resolutions of the latest Party Congress and National People's Congress and statements of government policy constitute a regular part of the study content. The joint editorials of the People's Daily, People's Liberation Army Daily, and Red Flag on important occasions always reflect government views and are studied carefully. On more advanced levels, the study moves on to more theoretical questions of ideology. From the "Three Great Articles," students advance to such expositions of Mao Thought as "On Practice," "On Contradiction," "On Liberalism," and "Talks at the Yenan Forum on Literature and Art." The familiar slogan popularized during the Cultural Revolution chants: "Sailing the seas depends on the helmsmen; making revolution depends on Mao Tse-tung Thought." Not so many Russian writings are now required for study as in the heyday of Sino-Soviet friendship, but selected works of Marx, Engels, and Lenin are still considered the storehouse of proletarian wisdom. Among these are the Communist Manifesto, Marx's Critique of the Gotha Program, Engels' Anti-Dühring, and Lenin's Imperialism: The Highest Stage of Capitalism, Materialism and Empirio-Criticism, and State and Revolution.

The most important materials for ideological education are found in the Thought of Mao Tse-tung. "In putting politics first," declared a Peking Daily editorial (April 22, 1966), "it is essential to put the Thought of Mao Tse-tung in command." Another editorial of the same paper on May Day in 1966 said that Mao Thought is the summit of Marxism-Leninism in the present era and "the most powerful weapon in our struggle to defeat bourgeois and revisionist ideology." Mao's writings are to be studied intensively and repeatedly. His quotations are recited again and again in order to etch a permanent impression on the mind. The "Three Great Articles," short as they are, are read and reread in schools at all levels and in adult classes outside the schools. His terse statements on educational reform, on learning from workers and peasants, on the class struggle, and so forth are read and heard over and over again in study and in group discussions.

In 1970 a campaign began to study Marxist-Leninist philosophy, with the contention that philosophical writings can be well understood by the masses and serve as a guide to their thinking and behavior.[5] The Central Committee of the Chinese Communist Party issued a call for the whole Party to study Mao's philosophical works conscientiously. Five "philosophical essays" by Mao Tse-tung were selected for nation-wide study: "On Practice" (1937), "On Contradiction" (1937), "On the Correct Handling of Contradictions Among People" (1957), "Speech at the Chinese-Communist Party's National Conference on Propaganda Work" (1957), and "Where Do Correct Ideas Come from ?" (1963). At the same time, Mao's concepts—such as "one divides into two" and "unity of opposites"—are hailed as sure guides to the solution of ideological and practical problems, from controversial questions of Redness versus expertness in education to the planting of agricultural crops or the building of an irrigation canal.[6] (The concept "one divides into two" is contrasted with what Maoists call the "revisionist" concept "two combines into one." The latter was attacked by the Maoists as a negation of the importance of struggle because it opened the way to reconciliation.)

The "living study" of Mao Thought is expressed in the faithful execution of his "line" and the struggle against the revisionist line opposed to the Maoist line. The basic line that Mao formulated for the revolution is as follows:

> Socialist society covers a considerably long historical period. In the historical period of socialism, there are still classes, class contradictions and class struggle, there is the struggle between the socialist road and the capitalist road, and there is the danger of capitalist restoration. We must recognize the protracted and complex nature of this struggle. We must heighten our vigilance. We must conduct socialist education. We must correctly understand and handle class contradictions and class struggle, distinguish the contradictions between ourselves and the enemy from those among the people and handle them correctly.[7]

Line Education

A method of "line education" now being stressed is "revolutionary mass criticism." It consists in continuous and "penetrating" criticism of ideas other than the strict Maoist line. It constantly draws distinctions between the Maoist proletarian ideology and all forms of non-proletarian ideology. It carries out Mao's "March 7 Directive" to practice struggle-criticism-transformation and the "16-Point Decision" directing that students in the reopened schools engage in the criticism of the bourgeoisie and "bourgeois and feudal ideology" (see Appendixes 10 and 15). Such ideas as "the dying out of class struggle," "profession above politics," "education for the gifted," "study comes first," and "two combine into one" are repeatedly condemned in order to reaffirm the Maoist line in education and in all areas of "socialist construction." For example, the revisionist "theory of human nature," which exalts personal feelings, clan and family solidarity, and friendship for all, is found to be the root of apathy to the class struggle. It is said that politics is often neglected in schools because teachers and administrators are too much occupied with academic matters or because students feel that they are too busy with study. Such a situation is also indicative of the presence of class enemy intrigue attempting to win over the young people to the anti-Maoist line of thinking. It calls for more intensive "line education."

Line education was given an impetus in 1970 when the Central Committee of the Chinese Communist Party called upon the entire nation to resolutely carry out the proletarian revolutionary line of Mao Tse-tung by means of ceaseless struggle-criticism-transformation and a determined "struggle between the two classes, the two roads, and the two lines." In January 1971 a joint editorial by the People's Daily, the Liberation Army Daily, and the Red Flag launched a national campaign on a more intensive scale. While a large part of line education concerns the population outside the schools, it is also emphasized as a central theme of political education in the schools. The most effective materials for line education are often found in sources beyond classrooms and textbooks. Oral instruction by poor peasants and old workers is used to tell the "three histories" or "four histories" to present a sharp contrast between the old society and the present.

The method of recalling past miseries developed during the socialist education movement is used extensively (see Chapter 2; examples are given in Appendix 8). There are four major forms of comparing the "bitter past" with the "sweet present" (I K'u Ssu T'ien): (1) inviting workers and peasants to give lectures in schools, (2) going into the factories and communes to interview workers and peasants, (3) visiting places of historical interest to unearth more facts about pre-1949 society, and (4) exhibits. The method of sending students into factories and communes is known as "social investigation." On-the-spot investigation of this kind helps break down barriers between the school and society at large. Moreover, it brings workers and peasants into the center of the educational process. Social investigation also provides information for the "histories" of the factories, communes, families, etc., to be compiled into new teaching materials.

In the cities, students interview old men and women in the neighborhood to learn about their misery and bitter experience in the exploitive society of the past. After such "social investigation," they become fired with "determination to master Mao Tse-tung Thought, remember class bitterness and blood debt, do a good job as successors to the revolution, and insure that the socialist motherland will not change color."[8] A middle school in Shanghai hailed as an "advanced model on the educational front" reported how the Party branch of the school led the teachers to provide effective lessons in class and line education.[9] To prevent the contamination of poisonous ideas from outside, the Party leadership declared that it was necessary to take the initiative in attacking the bourgeoisie instead of waiting until they won over wavering youth. To do this, teachers took classes to visit the nearby former British police station and learn about the methods of oppression and torture employed by the imperialists.

Exhibits are another means to keep fresh the memories of past struggles. A village exhibit displayed tattered clothes passed on from one generation to another in a family of poor peasants and tools used to dig up wild roots for food in the old society.[10] Urban exhibits contain reminders of imperialist exploitation, relics from old prisons, and samples of extravagant living by those who grew wealthy at the expense of the masses. Ugly images of landlords, whips used in Kuomintang prisons, and blood-stained clothes of victims of brutal beating are among materials considered fit for class education exhibits. The practice of recalling the bitter past is described by an American school teacher who visited China in 1971:

> A new tradition is evolving in the People's Republic today—the tradition of "the bitter remembrances." The bitter remembrances are one of China's methods for dealing with the problem of a generation of young people growing up without the knowledge of widespread famine and twenty years of war. . . .
> One example of this new tradition are meals of bitter remembrance. On New Year's many families cook leaves, bark, and the bitter herbs that once were common fare during famines in pre-revolutionary China. This frugal meal is then served amid stories of the bitter past. . . .
> Old people play a special role in bringing the bitter remembrances alive today. Schools and residential areas invite them to become teachers and tell of their experiences before the revolution. They come carrying old

tattered pants and blouses, their only set of clothing in pre-Liberation days. They tell of lost brothers and sisters, sold to keep families from starvation. They also relate their own personal stories.

In Shanghai a few of our group listened to one old woman tell such a tale. As she sat upon her bed, neatly dressed in a white blouse and blue pants, tears running down her face, she told us of her experiences as a child when she had been sold. "I was beaten at whim, and illness was no excuse for rest. Even the household dogs ate before I did."

Art and culture, too, often use themes from China's bitter heritage. Many of the national revolutionary ballets draw on the miserable plight of the peasant for dramatic material.

In the Ming Tombs Museum, the life of the peasant is displayed alongside the magnificent gold artifacts of the Ming emperors. In paintings, peasants are portrayed being conscripted for work on the tombs while their heartbroken families watch. A set of clay statues show how peasants were taxed to pay for the tombs.

In village performances we saw songs and dances that used the bitter remembrances as themes. In Sian we watched a puppet performance about the Japanese occupation and observed acrobats leap upon each other's shoulders to scale imaginary watchtowers and engage in mock battle with the Japanese.

Photographic displays of scenes of children working in textile factories and British civil servants living in luxury are also used to recall bitter memories.[11]

"Line education" is in some respects only a variant of class education. It may be considered an expansion of the concept of class education to include the struggle between the Maoist line and the anti-Maoist line that became prominent during the Cultural Revolution. This way of modifying and reinterpreting basic concepts is characteristic of the Communist method of ideological education. In the process, new terms and new slogans are coined to make a fresh appeal, but the basic purpose of political conformity and ideological uniformity remains unchanged. At one time, mass criticism and struggle were directed against the Kuomintang reactionaries, at another time the capitalist-imperialists, later the social-imperialists and Soviet revisionists. On the home front, rectification campaigns have been waged against the Rightists and bourgeois intellectuals, against capitalist-roaders in league with the revisionists, against Leftist as well as

Rightist deviations. Whenever the "line" shifts, a new need for political education arises. Today the "three great revolutionary movements" and the "strike-one oppose-three campaign"* are all merged into the defense of the Maoist line, and teachers and students are expected not only to study and understand their purposes but to take an active part in them.

Ideology in Curriculum and Extracurricular Activities

Courses in political education have appeared under different titles: current events, general political knowledge, knowledge of the revolution, basic knowledge in social science, Marxist-Leninist Thought, Mao Tse-tung Thought, socialist construction, cultivation of youth, and so on. Since the Cultural Revolution, there has been greater stress on the ideological and political permeation of the entire school life and the teaching of ideology through regular school subjects. Geography is taught with the "international class struggle" in view and in connection with Lenin's and Mao's analyses of the world situation.[12] Agricultural lessons teach students to raise more pigs and accumulate manure and fertilizers "for the revolution." In a chemistry class studying fire extinguishers, students are asked to consider what to do in the event of fires caused in a war started by the imperialists.[13] When students working in a factory expressed fear of electricity, an alert teacher taught them that electricity is, in the words of Chairman Mao, both a real tiger and a paper tiger; it is to be strategically despised but tactically taken seriously.[14]

A noteworthy feature of contemporary Chinese education is the breakdown of the isolation of the classroom and the recognition that much education goes on outside the classroom and that it is often even more effective than classroom instruction. Education beyond the classroom is especially important for ideological remolding. A well-planned program of education beyond the classroom makes sure that young people are under the molding influence of an all-embracing ideology during all their waking hours and that classroom instruction, extracurricular activities in school, and life beyond the school all work together toward the same end of producing a generation of successors to the proletarian revolution.

---

*"I-ta san-fan" stands for striking the counterrevolutionaries, opposing corruption and theft, opposing speculation, and opposing waste and extravagance.

Students take part in the activities of youth organizations, which play a leading role in all phases of school life. Extracurricular activities, as well as classroom instruction, are under the supervision of the school's Party Committee. One of these activities is the criticism of "bad books" (on criticism of bad textbooks, see Chapter 3). "Bad books" are leisure reading materials that do not cultivate the revolutionary ideological viewpoint. They are novels, cartoons, and books containing bourgeois ideas. The notion that leisure reading is a harmless hobby is condemned as a revisionist trick to poison the mind of youths, who should realize that all works of literature and art are tools of class struggle and serve a political purpose. To this end, the third grade of a primary school initiated a project of building a collection of more than 50 books of revolutionary literature, revolutionary novels and dramas, and Mao's philosophical writings for after-school leisure reading. Students form groups to read books from the collection; some borrow books to take home to read.[15]

The Maoist concept of extracurricular activities is much broader than school activities. It embraces the entire social life: family, farm, factory, afterschool hours during the schooling period, vacations between school terms. The Communists speak of "a network of extra-curricular activities." Under the leadership of the Party branch, the revolutionary committees of schools and those of the county or town join to enlist the cooperation of peasants, workers, cadres, demobilized soldiers, and responsible personnel of communes or factories or urban neighborhoods to map out a program that will keep youngsters profitably occupied when they are not in school. The program provides for a variety of activities. The study of Mao Thought is never neglected; in addition, youngsters are organized for labor, military training, supplementary school work, and propaganda teams to publicize any new instruction or directive from Chairman Mao or any call issued by the Party's Central Committee to launch a new campaign of some kind, whether the collection of manure fertilizers or the killing of pests or a stepped-up struggle against class enemies. Literary, recreational, and athletic activities are planned, but line education is of crucial importance. Plays and music are among the approved "cultural activities" outside the classroom, but recreation or entertainment without political significance is rejected. The ideologies condemn "recreation for its own sake" just as they reject literature and art for their own sake. All activities must serve a political purpose; extracurricular activities are designed to continue what is done in the schools, where politics rules supreme.

School teachers are supposed to keep in close touch with those in charge of out-of-school activities, and vice versa, so that they may share information and experiences in regard to the students. Parents, teachers, representatives of propaganda teams, youth organizations,

Party committees, and revolutionary committees of various units meet to plan a coordinated program of extracurricular activities. This kind of concerted effort was illustrated in the instance of a girl student who reportedly neglected her study, did not attend classes regularly, and was generally guilty of "bad behavior." The "leadership" planned a program of class education to rectify her ideological confusion. She and her fellow students were asked to attend meetings at which they listened to the story of hardships suffered by the girl's own father in the bad old days. The teachers and cadres of the neighborhood organization joined the school authorities to make more than 40 visits to the girl's home and talk with the family more than 120 times. Finally, she underwent an ideological change and got rid of such revisionist ideas as "study is useless." According to the report, she then joined the Red Guards and became an active revolutionary.[16] A good deal of the work of changing this girl was done outside the classroom, by the cooperative effort of out-of-school agencies.

Party organizations play a leading role in such programs. The slogan is to put Mao Tse-tung Thought in command of the students' out-of-school life. A municipality in Hupeh reported that 93 percent of the students in primary and middle schools took part in the Mao Tse-tung groups organized by the Party and revolutionary committees.[17] Within the municipality a force of 5,500 workers, peasants, and soldiers was organized to guide the out-of-school activities of youth. Coordinated effort to guide young people assumes even greater importance during vacations. At the approach of the summer or winter vacations, the cooperating agencies begin to plan a program of exhibits, visits, social investigations, lectures by workers and peasants comparing the present with the past, and classes for the intensive study of Mao's works. "Big" and "small" criticism meetings are held to carry on the struggle-criticism-transformation activities.[18] Close attention is given to the behavior of youth and disciplinary problems. There is no relaxation of the remolding process, whether schools are in session or not. Vacation plans also provide for the ideological study of teachers and engaging them in revolutionary mass criticism.[19]

Anticipating the need to guide youth in the use of leisure time during the winter vacation, the Peking municipality organized study and activity groups under the auspices of the Municipal Youth Palace. Students joined these groups for political and ideological study, for the study of science and technique, and for music, games, and so on. For class education, the method of recalling past miseries was again used, and old workers and poor and lower-middle peasants related to the students their bitter memories of past sufferings and their deep hatred for the class enemies.[20]

Youth Organizations

Youth organizations under the direction of the Communist Party have always been a major vehicle for the training and control of youth. Before the Cultural Revolution, the Youth Pioneers, the Communist Youth League, the All-China Youth Federation, and the All-China Student Federation were officially recognized. The first two were well-organized youth groups, while the latter two were catchall "federations" designed to bring together a variety of youth activities not related to the Pioneers and the Youth League.[21] The Young Pioneers (for ages 7-15) and the Communist Youth League (ages 16-25) were linked with the Chinese Communist Party by a direct line. The Pioneers were "founded by the Communist Party" and "under the direct guidance of the Chinese Communist Youth League" and dedicated "to become builders and protectors of Communism." The Youth League, according to its constitution, was "a school for the study of Communism and an assistant to the Chinese Communist Party." The Youth League also served as the training ground for membership in the Communist Party; its most active and trusted members were selected for Party membership.

During the Cultural Revolution, Communist Party leaders responsible for the youth organizations were accused of ideological deviation and the Youth League and Pioneers were displaced by the Red Guards as the true followers of Mao Tse-tung. The two organizations lapsed into inactivity, but they were not disbanded. For a while the Red Guards became the symbol of militant youth with fiery loyalty for Chairman Mao, but factional strife as well as indulgence in indiscriminately destructive activities spelled their decline and finally led to official action to restrain and even suppress their activities. The call to return to the schools to wage revolution was in part an effort to put the Red Guards under supervision, and the introduction of military discipline over school youth marked the end of the unrestrained militancy of the Red Guards. The Red Guards continue to exist as an organization, but they are a more disciplined and subdued group.

The Pioneers, with a membership of one million on the eve of the Red Guards' outburst, have evidently been dropped. Their function has been taken over by the Red Little Soldiers, who are active in the primary schools and in out-of-school activities for the 7-12 age group. The Red Little Soldiers organize study classes after school to heighten political consciousness and seek deeper understanding of the "Three Great Articles" and other constantly read writings by Mao. Outside the schools, they organize children to turn from play to revolutionary activities, and form propaganda teams to go into the villages to spread the Thought of Mao and information about government policies. They lead in teaching revolutionary songs and criticizing bourgeois literature and art. According to one report, the Red Little Soldiers of an elementary school in Liaoning province, "nurtured by Mao Tse-tung Thought . . . made profound changes in their spiritual outlook through tempering in the Great Proletarian Cultural Revolution."[22] From another distant area, the People's Daily (June 2, 1972) reported that primary school children in Lhasa organized Red Little Soldier propaganda teams to give performances on festivals and holidays, with songs and acts to eulogize Chairman Mao and his teachings, and to promote such campaigns as "Support the Army" and "Learn from Tachai."

The Red Guards serve an older age group than the Red Little Soldiers. They have ceased factional strife and carry on well-regulated activities "to help the Party organizations and the school revolutionary committees to do a good job in ideological and political work" (article 9 of Draft Program, Appendix 16). Many Red Guards have been sent to the countryside for productive labor and reeducation. After ideological rectification, to rectify past mistakes, they are recognized as a useful force in the education of youth inside and outside the schools. Their most active and trustworthy members are recommended for membership in the Communist Youth League. They hold regular meetings to plan their activities, and discipline is stressed.

The Communist Youth League had a membership of approximately 30 million on the eve of the Cultural Revolution purge. Always organizationally and ideologically linked with the Party, the Youth League virtually passed out of existence when the Party structure was attacked as the tool of the anti-Mao revisionists. Now that the Party structure is being rebuilt and the local Party branches have begun to function, the Youth League is being reconstituted as an appendage to the new Party organs. The Youth League is more selective in membership than the Red Guards and the Red Little Soldiers; only Red Guards of outstanding record are admitted. The total number of Youth League members may be well below the 1966 level, but no statistics have been published. Youth League organizations are not limited to the schools. They carry on important work in factories, brigades, communes, business enterprises, administrative bureaus and offices, and other units that employ young workers. They not only stimulate greater effort in work but carry on an active program of ideological and political education. For example, a Youth League organization in a commune was called to task because it was concerned only with work efficiency with the result that enthusiasm for work did not last on account of the lack of proper ideological motivation. More attention to ideological and political education was the remedy.[23]

The New Year's message issued jointly by the People's Daily, the People's Liberation Army Daily, and the Red Flag on January 1, 1973, called for "centralized Party leadership" over all organizations.

71

It said: "The Trade Unions, the Communist Youth League, the Red Guards, the Red Little Soldiers, the poor and lower-middle peasant organizations, and the women organizations should be rectified and strengthened step by step." Party branches are now instructed to pay more attention to exercising positive leadership over the Communist Youth League, in order to cultivate and strengthen the "new seedlings" for successors to the revolution.[24] Youth League members have been found to be weak in ideological conviction and revolutionary dedication, and consequently in need of education to strengthen their class consciousness: Like youth in general, they do not have the experience of the old workers and peasants in the struggles of the past and they are subject to the temptations and enticements of class enemies who are constantly plotting to take advantage of their ideological instability. Youth League members are thought to need firm leadership and constant ideological remolding.

The Communist Youth League has been revived as the most important and influential of the youth organizations. The revival is accompanied by a vigorous program of rebuilding and rectification. A part of this program has been to convene provincial or regional youth conferences centering on the problems of the Youth League. One of the well-organized conferences was the "Sixth Shanghai Municipal Congress of the Chinese Communist Youth League," held in Shanghai on February 12-19, 1973. It was attended by 1,500 delegates, representing "League members who are industrial workers, peasants, People's Liberation Armymen, office workers, national minority people and returned overseas Chinese."[25] The failure to mention Youth League members from schools may indicate that the conference was designed for leaders of Youth League work rather than for direct participation by students. The delegates attended sessions to study Chairman Mao's instructions and to repudiate the revisionist line in youth work. Nevertheless, the People's Daily (February 22, 1973), hailed the "great significance" of the conference in "uniting and educating young people" and bringing up a revolutionary younger generation under the guidance of Mao's revolutionary line. The Communist Youth League, said the paper's editorial, "is the assistant of the Communist Party of China and a mass organization of advanced young people." "The most important task at present for the entire Party," it continued, "is the criticism of revisionism and rectification of the style of work. League organizations at all levels should mobilize and organize League members and other young people to take an active part in this militant task."

A municipal congress of the Communist Youth League held in Peking from March 28 to April 3, 1973, was slightly different in the nature of representation. It was attended by 2,201 delegates, consisting of workers, peasants, urban youths who had settled in the countryside, college students of worker-peasant origin, members of minority groups, and returned overseas Chinese. The congress passed a resolution calling on the Youth League to turn itself into "a school for young people to study Marxism-Leninism-Mao Tse-tung Thought, and strive to train the young generation to become successors to the cause of the proletarian revolution."[26] Similar congresses have been convened in other parts of China in a nationwide program of rebuilding the Youth League.[27]

League members are expected to engage in criticism-rectification and to get other young people to do so (the term criticism-rectification refers to the criticism of revisionism and rectification of the style of work). They are to be diligent in ideological and political study and to lead other young people in such study. A positive campaign has been launched to recruit new members. A report on a Youth League congress in Liaoning province stated that 1.7 million out of 6 million young people in the province had become Youth League members.[28] In comparison with the pre-1966 days, there is a greater emphasis on discipline and more definite provision for the participation of the military in the leadership and overall planning. Youth League committees have been established in all the provinces and autonomous regions. Many of the secretaries of these regional committees are also members of the revolutionary committees or the Communist Party organs. The Youth League has become a positive force in political affairs.

The New Man

Mao Tse-tung once named five requirements for worthy successors to the revolutionary cause: In his words, revolutionaries must wholeheartedly serve the majority of the people of China and the whole world; they must be proletarian statesmen capable of uniting and working together with the overwhelming majority; they must be models in applying the Party's democratic centralism and leadership based on the mass line; and they must be modest and prudent and have the courage to correct mistakes.[29] People with such qualifications are the new type of man that education must produce. The task is not an easy one, but the Communists believe it can be done. The Peking Review (February 18, 1966) optimistically editorialized: "As the pace of socialist revolution and social construction in China grows swifter, a new type of man is emerging in growing numbers. They are highly political-minded, dedicated heart and soul to the revolution, and they perform remarkable feats despite great odds."

What are the specific characteristics that education must strive to cultivate in the new man? Besides such general concepts as "good pupils of the age of Mao Tse-tung" or "good daughters of the Communist Party," several formulations of specific characteristics have been publicized at different times. Before the Cultural Revolution, much was said about "five-good youth": one who was obedient to the Party, a diligent worker, able to overcome difficulties, alert in protection of public property, and mindful of the unity of the Youth League. During the Cultural Revolution, the "four-good" became the goal of education: youth was to be trained to be good in ideological work, good in military training, good in arranging everyday life, and good in working style. This formula was originally adopted for the army, but after the campaign to mobilize the whole country to "learn from the People's Liberation Army," "four-good" became a goal for the education of youth all over the country. (The term has not been used so generally after the purge of Lin Piao, but the general concept is still valid.) The People's Daily (December 26, 1969) pointed out that the four attributes are interrelated, but ideological work is of primary importance. To be good in political and ideological work, commented the Peking Review (August 6, 1969), is to put Mao Tse-tung Thought in command.

The supreme virtue of the new man is wholehearted dedication to the revolution led by Chairman Mao and the Chinese Communist Party. This dedication means absolute loyalty and obedience to the Chairman and the Party. From Liu Shao-ch'i to Lin Piao and down to the present time, a good revolutionary is always expected to put away all personal plans and ambitions and to put the interests of the revolution and the Party above all. The Cultural Revolution called for the criticism of revisionism and the struggle against selfishness (p'i-hsiu tou-ssu). The new man must be selfless. He is undaunted by difficulties, undeterred by hardship or personal danger. Indeed, death for the sake of the revolution must be considered a great honor. Most of the heroes and models selected for public emulation were honored posthumously for their readiness to make the supreme sacrifice.

The new man seeks no personal fame or glory. In the words of an industrial hero, "I'm willing to be an 'ox' serving the people all my life." He was described as an indefatigable worker "nurtured by Mao Tse-tung Thought," one who displayed "the revolutionary spirit of fearing neither hardship nor death" and gave his life for the revolutionary cause.[31] Another hero was quoted as saying that he would be content with being a screw in a big machine. The new man does not seek physical comfort, nor does he expect material reward for his labor. He has only one thought in mind: to serve the revolution.

To serve the revolution is to accept the leadership of the Communist Party and to be guided by the Thought of Mao Tse-tung. Labor and production are essential, beyond any doubt, but it is not enough just to excel in labor and production. The new man must be properly motivated, ideologically sound, and "highly political minded." He must be a "Red expert," and he must be correct in thought as well as in action.

Ideological remolding is concerned not only with thought and action but also with emotions. The new man must have the emotions of a proletarian revolutionary. He must learn to hate class enemies "passionately" just as he loves Chairman Mao and the Chinese Communist Party. He must hate feudalism and imperialism as he loves socialism and Communism.[32] He has acquired proletarian tastes, hating luxury and comfort but loving labor and thrift. He hears sweet music in the strong and loud call that summons people to labor;[33] he delights in the smell of the natural fertilizers that he carries to the fields. In a word, the new man is distinguished not only by his Marxist-Leninist-Maoist ideology and his devotion to labor and production and political activities but also by his proletarian tastes and emotions. He stands ready at all times to heed the call of the Party-State and Chairman Mao.

In recent years, journalists and other visitors to the Chinese mainland have reported that whenever they ask students what they plan or hope to do after graduation, the ready answer always is, "I shall serve the revolution according to Chairman Mao's instructions," or the same idea in slightly different words (to "serve the people" and to "serve the revolution" have practically the same meaning). Even marriage must be subordinated to the needs of the revolution; the good revolutionary consults the Party leadership before he makes any decision in regard to employment or study or love and marriage.

Adult Education

The education of adults is of major importance in the Communist program; in the Yenan period, for instance, adult education was given even greater prominence than the education of children (see Chapter 2). The Communist "mass line" calls for mass support of all policies and this support is obtainable only when the masses can be reached by propaganda and indoctrination, and by information transmitted by mass media. Literacy is therefore a basic necessity. But literacy is only a means; the real goal is political intelligence. Teaching to read and write is inseparable from political and ideological education. From the first day of a literacy class, politics and ideology furnish the content of the lessons. Everything that has been said about the supremacy of politics in school education applies to adult education with equal or even greater force. There are three phrases of adult education: the liquidation of illiteracy, the acquisition of occupational knowledge and skills, and ideological-political education. The third gives meaning and direction to the other two. Without the proper ideological orientation and the support of right attitudes and habits, it is believed that occupational skills would not go very far.

Adult education is effective because it is a continuous day-to-day program that overcomes the limitation of sporadic efforts and because it actively uses a wide variety of methods and channels from schools to "study sessions" and classes in factories, in communes, on trains and boats. Museums, cinema, radio, plays and exhibits are all planned with their educational functions in view. Much has been done to reduce illiteracy and much success has been achieved, but the new regime did not start from scratch in this undertaking. Both in the use of new and unconventional agencies of adult education and in the unification of the spoken tongue, a good foundation had been laid in China before 1949. Even in the use of a phonetic script, significant progress had been made under the Nationalist government before the outbreak of World War II. Nevertheless, the new regime has successfully built on past foundations and advanced beyond earlier achievements. While meaningful statistics are not available, there is reason to believe that illiteracy has been greatly reduced in the past two decades. Posters, leaflets, and propaganda materials using a simple vocabulary help to popularize the written word.

Language reform has given further impetus to the literacy campaign. The reform continues the effort to unify the spoken tongue and make learning easier by the adoption of simplified written characters. The new simplified characters have fewer component strokes and so are easier for the learner to recognize and write. The simplified characters are now used in all writing and all publications, and a new generation of children and adult learners knows only the simplified writing. Theoretically, the simplification of written characters is only an intermediate step of the language reform, which aims to eventually abolish the written characters and adopt a "Latinized" written language. But the Latinization proposal has met with resistance from educated Chinese as well as other practical difficulties that necessitated postponement of this radical change. At this time, the simplified written characters remain the most revolutionary and successful change produced by the language reform.

It is not easy to judge the extent to which illiteracy has been reduced in the country at large. Reports of successful literacy campaigns in selected areas do not give information for the whole country. Moreover, the reports usually state that in a certain area the majority or almost the entire adult population has attained "basic literacy," but there is no recognized standard of literacy and the meaning of "basic literacy" is far from clear. Moreover, the percentage of literates in a selected area right after the completion of an intensive campaign may not remain a stable figure because there is a tendency for new literates to slide back into illiteracy if they do not actively use what they have learned. Therefore we can only state in general terms that noteworthy progress has been made in the literacy campaign, and that probably more people than ever can read and write and understand the written messages transmitted through posters, leaflets, newspapers, and a wide variety of propaganda publications.

The political education of the adult population is more extensive and reaches more people than the literacy campaign. All mass media are used for this purpose. If one takes into account the radio, the "study" groups, the mass meetings, the exhibits and demonstrations, one may say that the population is subject to political education during all waking hours. As a result, no matter whether they read or write, it is safe to say that the "masses" are well aware of what happens in the country, beyond their local community or immediate environment. To be sure, they are told only what the Party-state wants them to know, and they have access to only the official point of view and the officially approved sources of information, but they do have a higher degree of social awareness and interest in public affairs than the masses of previous generations.

In addition to the informal and vicarious means of imparting political intelligence, there are organized forms of political education similar to those for young people. Cadres and administrative personnel, militiamen and demobilized soldiers, as well as workers, peasants, and the population in general, have been enlisted to join classes for the study of the Thought of Mao Tse-tung and the philosophical works of Marxism-Leninism. A "mass movement of philosophical study" has familiarized the masses with such ideological vocabulary as dialectical materialism, "one divides into two," empiricism, idealism, metaphysics, revisionism, continuous revolution, class struggle, and line struggle. On the anniversaries of major speeches by Mao, such as his Talks at Yenan Forum and his treatises on practice, contradiction, and so on, special study sessions and symposiums are held to reread and discuss the "brilliant works" and try to apply them to current problems. After the Ninth National Congress of the Chinese Communist Party in 1969, the new Party constitution and other documents of the congress were studied and discussed by groups all over the country.

Mention should be made of the use of literature and art for political education. The famous Chinese opera has been completely reconstructed to portray the class struggle and foster revolutionary sentiments among the masses, and the cinema is judged according to its success in developing proletarian attitudes and emotions. Even the street storyteller, who in pre-1949 days used to set up platforms on streets and attract crowds with entertaining stories drawn from classical themes or contemporary fiction, have been commandeered for service in political education. Study classes have been organized to instill in storytellers a firm ideological outlook and to teach them how to use their skills for the benefit of the revolution. In one such class, the storytellers carefully studied Mao's Yenan Talks and learned to examine their own ideological position from the viewpoint of "one divides into two."[34] Study sessions aboard trains lend themselves well to learning about such current affairs as the Chairman's "latest directive" or important "decisions" of the Communist Party or the government.[35] Official policies are thus quickly publicized in order to enlist the understanding and support of the masses.

Just as storytellers and artists must undergo continuous ideological study to know what message to bring to the people, so cadres and administrative personnel (such as members of revolutionary committees) must keep their ideological status in top shape in order to provide effective leadership. They must be conversant with the Thought of Mao and his writings. Even in local areas the Party leadership must engage in ideological study, under the guidance of the higher authorities. Unceasing "study" keeps the leaders on their ideological toes, and the practice of criticism and self-criticism helps avoid the pitfalls of arrogant bureaucracy in violation of the "mass line."[36]

With coordinated planning under centralized direction, communes and factories have established "political schools" for programs sustained over longer periods of time. One reads about efforts to build a "network for the popularization of socialist education." One county in Fukien province reported that more than 90 percent of the production teams run political night schools, attended by 80 percent of the adult commune members.[37] Another commune in Hupeh province reported political night schools where "commune members and masses" meet daily for "hour long" periods of concentrated study of Mao Thought.[38] Other reports indicate that the political night school is a fairly common form of political education.

Spare-Time Education

The political night school is a form of spare-time education, which is one of the most creative aspects of Chinese Communist education. It is a major vehicle of adult education for literacy, for production skills, and for ideological remolding. It has achieved outstanding results. In earlier years, it admirably served the purpose of teaching more people to read and write. During and after the Cultural Revolution, political education became the dominant aim.

It was noted in Chapter 3 that a salient feature of the new school system adopted in 1951 was the recognition of spare-time schools as an integral part of the system. The short-term worker-peasant schools of earlier years and the winter schools in rural areas were examples of spare-time education that brought education within the reach of millions of people who would otherwise have been deprived of any educational opportunity. Government statistics in 1958 reported 26 million spare-time primary schools, 5 million spare-time middle schools, approximately 600,000 spare-time technical middle schools, and 150,000 spare-time "institutes of higher learning."[39] In addition to the "schools" there were a large variety of "classes" serving such diverse groups as ship crews and housewives. Some were organized to teach the illiterate to read and write, others stressed production efficiency; political education was the essential element in all programs.[40] The minister of education reported in 1960 that 37,560,000 workers and 130,000,000 peasants were attending spare-time schools or classes.[41]

The spare-time schools were established by factories, industrial and business enterprises, and the full-time schools and universities. Before the Cultural Revolution, the Ministry of Education attempted to introduce general standards for spare-time schools of primary, secondary, and higher levels, in the hope of establishing a complete system enabling adults to advance from illiteracy to some form of advanced study. This imaginative approach to adult education also suffered a setback during the disruptive period of the Cultural Revolution, but it is being revived now, with even greater emphasis on ideology. The People's Daily (October 15, 1972) reported that 80 percent of factories and stores in Shanghai had organized spare-time schools enrolling 700,000 workers taught by 30,000 spare-time teachers. In Liaoning province, general and technical spare-time courses were established for peasants by production teams, brigades, and communes; one county reported an enrollment of 36,000 persons.[42] For the benefit of workers who had advanced beyond elementary literacy and made outstanding contributions in production, the Shanghai Municipal Spare-Time Industrial University offered courses in technology—machine building, electronics, metro-chemistry—as well as the study of Maoism and education in the struggle between the two lines.[43]

Some spare-time programs concentrate on political education. For example, the Party Committee of the Peking locomotive and carriage works organized study classes that workers attended for one hour each day after work and a half-day each week for concentrated study of the philosophical essays of Chairman Mao and the Marxist-Leninist texts Anti-Dühring and State and Revolution.[44] Under the impetus of the Communist Youth League, a semiconductor parts plant in the same city launched a program of "line education" for its 1,200 workers, over half of whom were graduates of middle schools.

"Political and theoretical studies," wrote the Peking Review, "have helped the workers deepen their understanding of Marxism-

Leninism-Mao Tse-tung Thought and enhance their political consciousness." In the rural communes, spare-time agrotechnical schools
train agrotechnicians who "consciously carry out Chairman Mao's
revolutionary line and lead the masses in scientific farming."[45] "Red
and expert" evening schools teach technical skills as well as political
subjects.[46]

In a county approximately 120 miles from Peking, it is reported
that about 90 percent of the adult peasant population has attended spare-
time classes of some kind. The illiterate learn to read and write,
while the literate attend night schools to study "political theory or
farming techniques." The peasants study the works of Marx, Engels,
Lenin, Stalin, and Mao, and "the Party's policies and principles."
The teachers are drawn from "cadres, commune members, demobilized
armymen and young peasants who have graduated from middle schools."[4]

The importance of political education for workers and peasants
arises from the Communist theory that a person must be both "Red"
and expert and that occupational ability is not enough unless it is guided
and motivated by a correct ideological stand. Moreover, workers
and peasants, like young people, are considered subject to the intrigue
and propaganda enticements of class enemies who try to lure them
away from the proletarian class. Bourgeois ideas can sneak into their
thinking and dampen their ideological fervor. When workers think of
material comfort instead of production goals, or when peasants lose
enthusiasm for collective farming, they are considered clearly under
the influence of bourgeois ideas and consequently in need of firm ideological guidance. As often as not, spare-time political education in
factories and communes is launched by the Communist Youth League
under Party direction.

Labor and Production

Labor and production occupy a prominent place in the Communist
ideology and in the practical program of building a new society. "Labor
creates man" is a concept taught in the primary school textbooks.
To become one with the laboring masses is to identify with the proletarian class. To acquire "the viewpoint of the laboring class," it is
necessary for intellectuals and others of nonproletarian class origin
to spend much time in labor. Labor is also supposed to have an ideologically therapeutic value; the Common Program adopted in 1949
provided that landlords, bureaucratic capitalists, and other reactionaries "shall be compelled to reform themselves through labor so as to
become new men" (article 7). Intellectuals are still being sent to
communes, factories, and mines for long-term labor to temper and

reform themselves so that they may be fit for service to proletarian society.

According to Mao Tse-tung, there are two forms of human struggle: class struggle and the struggle for production (see Appendix 1). Therefore, education must serve politics and economics. The Communist Manifesto of 1848 advocated the "combination of education with industrial production." In 1958 the Central Committee of the Communist Party ordered that education must be combined with productive labor, and Mao Tse-tung declared that "schools should run factories and factories should run schools" (see Appendixes 4 and 29). Thus began a drive to establish schools in factories and factories in schools. Factories, communes, and business enterprises established schools of all grades from nurseries to "colleges" and institutions of higher learning. At the same time, schools and universities set up factories, farms, engineering firms, and business enterprises that were more than laboratories for student experience—they were actual production units that fulfilled orders and carried on business as regularly as their counterparts outside the schools.

According to the Communist claim, the farms and factories became centers of learning as well as centers of production, while the schools and universities were to be centers of production as well as centers of learning. As centers of production, colleges and universities manufactured scientific equipment, machinery, building materials, chemicals, and so on. They designed bridges and contracted construction projects. Even elementary schools joined the campaign to serve as centers of production. Within a few months the elementary schools in Kirin province were reported to have established 18,048 "factories" producing steel, metal, tools, chemical fertilizers, tiles, cement, textiles, and stationery, in addition to orchards, apiaries, and poultry farms.[48] According to another report, elementary schools in the whole country in 1959 operated 490,000 small factories and worked on 400,000 small farms.[49]

Linking education with production was given further impetus during the educational revolution by Mao Tse-tung's "May 7 Directive," in which he ordered that in addition to study, students should "learn other things, that is, industrial work, farming, and military affairs; they should also criticize the bourgeoisie" (see Appendix 9). The combination of education with production is also in line with Mao's teaching that theory must be closely linked with practice. Alternating between study and production, students learn to apply their study to practical problems of production and refer production problems to the classroom for study. The trend is to restrict the growth of the full-time schools and to accelerate the development of work-study schools. The latter will thus become the major type of school for youth, with spare-time education the major type for adults.

The part-work part-study school adopts a variable schedule; work and study may be scheduled on alternate days or alternate weeks or there may be several weeks of study alternating with several weeks of work. In some schools, students spend half a day in study and the other half in work. In the rural areas, the schedule is adjusted according to the needs of the farming seasons. Ideological and practical advantages are claimed for the work-study schools. They are said to help keep teachers and students close to reality and avoid the pitfalls of theory divorced from practice; to bridge the gap between mental and physical labor and help break down the barriers between the intelligentsia and the laboring masses; and to help produce the versatile man capable of both mental and physical work. And one may add that the school factories have markedly enhanced the production manpower and output of the nation.

The Peking Review reported that primary and middle schools in Peking had established factories "turning out machine parts, metal products, electronic products, and optical instruments," as well as "printing, wood work, and processing factories or handicraft shops."[50] With the help of their teachers, a group of students "successfully solved through study the problem of replacing organic glass with ordinary glass in producing an element with digital readings for automatic meters." In another case, middle schools in Nanking were reported to have established more than 100 factories in the fields of machinery, electronics, foundry, chemical industry and pharmaceutical manufacture producing medical equipment, diodes, triodes, broadcasting supplies, cement products, chemical fertilizers, and industrial chemicals. Factories reportedly cooperated by sending some of their experienced workers to help the schools run their factories.[51] Similar claims have been made for other parts of the country.

The Role of the Military

The military played a prominent role in the Cultural Revolution and has remained a potent force in shaping the development of education. Even before the Cultural Revolution, the entire nation was called upon to "learn from the People's Liberation Army." Model PLA soldiers were hailed as national heroes for all to emulate (as in the "Learn from Lei Feng" campaign). The PLA was instrumental in launching the cult of Marxism. On its thirty-ninth anniversary on August 1, 1966, it issued a call to "turn our Army into a great school in Mao Tse-tung Thought." The Worker's Daily (August 3, 1966) promptly responded with an appeal to workers to turn their factories into great revolutionary schools for the study of the Thought of Mao Tse-tung. The direct participation of the military in school affairs and the education of youth came about when the PLA was asked to help curb the undisciplined activities of the Red Guards, to end their factional strife, and to bring young people back to the classroom after prolonged suspension of school sessions.

Since early years, Mao Tse-tung has spoken of the triumvirate of workers-peasants-soldiers as the major elements that constitute the masses; in his Yenan Talks, for example, Mao ordered that "writers and artists must weld their ideas and emotions with those of the workers, peasants, and soldiers." Today, more than ever, the soldiers are recognized as an active partner in the triumvirate and an integral part of the proletarian leadership that education must accept. Their representatives are stationed in schools and universities, some serving as members of the revolutionary committees, others as members of the Mao Tse-tung Thought Propaganda Teams, still others as teachers for political education. Outside the schools, the demobilized soldiers are active in the planning and management of extracurricular programs for youth, and of ideological and political education in general. The soldiers are praised as ideologically reliable elements, because most of them came from the poorer classes and also by virtue of the ideological and political education they receive in the army.

The reopening of schools after 1966 would have been delayed for an even longer period of time if the army had not been called in to enforce the order to resume classes. After the Red Guards returned to the schools, factional strife among them created not only disorder and chaos but violence and bloodshed. It was necessary for the army to use its authority to establish order and discipline. In his "March 7 Directive" Mao not only directed the army to "help in reopening school classes, strengthening organization" but also to take responsibility for "political and military training" in schools and universities (see Appendix 15).[52] In the year following Mao's directive, it was reported that "more than a million teachers and students" in Peking were given such military and political training "under the unified leadership and organization of the Peking Garrison's general headquarters for military and political training."[53] Furthermore, the army assumed administration functions and became a part of the "leading bodies" of the educational institutions. According to the New York Times (March 14, 1968), military representatives occupied a dominant position in the revolutionary committees that functioned as the new administrative bodies of the schools and universities.

Recent visitors to China have been impressed by the discipline and orderliness of the schools. No doubt much of this condition is due to the presence of the army. A journalist observed that the PLA "plays a significant, perhaps decisive role in the administration of China today, in Communist Party politics, in industry, agriculture, education, propaganda and in the fundamental ordering of Chinese society. . . . Mao and his leadership consider the army to be the most reliable force in the country at present."[54] In the same vein, a visiting American scholar wrote of the "ubiquitousness of the rank-and-file military men" and the "enormous number of ordinary soldiers, sailors, and airmen scattered through China's cities. Rarely were we out of their sight. Most of them were not armed; remarkably few were engaged in military activity of any kind. They were simply there, walking the streets or traveling from one place to another."[55] In educational literature, one reads about military cadres in schools, PLA soldiers in charge of the ideological remolding of teachers and students, demobilized soldiers in the countryside engaged in a wide variety of activities from lecturing in schools to the organization of spare-time educational programs.

Notes

1. Theodore H. E. Chen, The Chinese Communist Regime (New York: Frederick A. Praeger, 1967), pp. 52-53.
2. Peking Review, April 22, 1966, p. 15.
3. Peking Review, May 10, 1968.
4. Peking Review, October 6, 1972, p. 11.
5. See Current Background, no. 932 (May 21, 1971), for articles on the "upsurge of the study of philosophy by the masses."
6. See "A Philosophical Discussion," Peking Review, September 24, 1971, pp. 14-16, 22.
7. Peking Review, March 23, 1973, p. 5.
8. Peking Review, September 22, 1970; report on a primary school in Peking.
9. Report on P'ei Kuang Middle School in Jen-min Jih-pao, January 4, 1973.
10. Kuang-ming Jih-pao, June 28, 1963, p. 2.
11. Ann Kruze, "The Bitter Remembrances," Understanding China (New York: American Friends Service Committee, November 1971).
12. Peking Review, December 1, 1972, pp. 5-8.
13. For further information on this subject, see "Put Mao Tsetung Thought in Command of Cultural Courses," Peking Review, September 25, 1970; "Revolution in Education Brings About New Outlook," Peking Review, March 7, 1969.
14. Quotations from Chairman Mao Tse-tung, (Peking: Foreign Language Press, 1966) pp. 72, 79.
15. Article on training the students to criticize the bourgeoisie and bourgeois concepts of universal human nature, of putting intellectual development first, and so on, in Jen-min Jih-pao, July 7, 1971.

16. Report by the revolutionary committee of a district in Anshan municipality, in Jen-min Jih-pao, July 29, 1972.

17. Foreign Broadcast Information Service, Daily Report, Communist China, September 2, 1971, p. D1. (Hereafter cited as FBIS.)

18. Jen-min Jih-pao, July 29, 1972.

19. Kuang-ming Jih-pao, January 21, 1973.

20. Jen-min Jih-pao, February 4, 1973. For a story on the Shanghai Children's Palace (for ages 7-16), see Peking Review, June 8, 1973.

21. See Chen, op. cit., pp. 124-26, 166-80, 265-66.

22. FBIS, June 3, 1970, pp. G1-2.

23. Kuang-ming Jih-pao, January 27, 1973.

24. Jen-min Jih-pao, September 20, 1972.

25. Peking Review, March 2, 1973, p. 3.

26. Peking Review, April 13, 1973, pp. 3, 22.

27. See, for example, a report on Youth League congresses in Tientsin, Anhwei province, and Shansi province, in Jen-min Jih-pao, April 27, 1973.

28. Peking Review, May 11, 1973, p. 7.

29. Peking Review, July 17, 1964, pp. 26-27.

30. Jen-min Jih-pao, March 6, 1961.

31. Kung Yeh, "Wang Chin-hsi—Outstanding Representative of the Chinese Working Class," Peking Review, November 19, 1971.

32. Theodore H. E. Chen, "The New Socialist Man," Comparative Education Review, February 1969.

33. Words of hero Lei Feng, reported in Ta-kung Pao (Tientsin), September 12, 1964.

34. FBIS report from Shanghai, October 28, 1971, p. C4.

35. FBIS report from Peking, March 10, 1969, p. F11.

36. See Kuang-ming Jih-pao, March 1, 1973, for report on ideological study for cadres, secretaries, and deputies of Party branches.

37. FBIS, June 21, 1971, p. B1.

38. FBIS, December 15, 1969, p. C7.

39. State Statistical Bureau, Ten Great Years (Peking: Foreign Languages Press, 1960), p. 198.

40. Paul Harper, writing in 1964, called political education the keystone of spare-time education for workers and said that "intensive political education in industry preceded the implementation of systematic workers' education in all fields and has remained the central facet of industry-centered spare-time education." Spare-time Education for Workers in Communist China (Washington, D.C.: U.S. Office of Education, OE 14102, 1964), p. 3.

41. Report of Yang Hsiu-feng in Kuang-ming Jih-pao, February 9, 1960.

42. Survey of China Mainland Press, no 5171 (July 11, 1972), p. 58.

85

43. Kuang-ming Jih-pao, December 29, 1972.
44. Jen-min Jih-pao, January 24, 1973.
45. Peking Review, October 27, 1972, pp. 22-23.
46. Kuang-ming Jih-pao, December 29, 1972.
47. "Night Schools for Peasants," Peking Review, June 8, 1973.
48. Hung-ch'i (Red flag), November 1, 1958.
49. China News Analysis, no. 332 (July 15, 1960), p. 5.
50. Peking Review, January 8, 1971.
51. FBIS, September 23, 1970, p. C4.
52. See also Circular of Communist Party Central Committee and State Council, December 31, 1966, and other related documents in Current Background, no. 852 (May 6, 1968).
53. Peking Review, March 15, 1968, p. 10.
54. Richard Reston, "Army Woven Fabric of China Society," Los Angeles Times, February 17, 1972.
55. A. Doak Barnett, "There Are Warts There, Too," New York Times Magazine, April 8, 1973.

PROLETARIAN LEADERSHIP VERSUS DOMINATION BY INTELLECTUALS

Dethroning the Intellectuals

Perhaps the most revolutionary development of the educational revolution is the institution of "proletarian leadership" to put an end to the dominant position of intellectuals in education. No other Communist country has gone so far in rejecting the bourgeois educational tradition and the role of intellectuals in educational development.

The Maoist policy of putting workers, peasants, and soldiers in a "leading role" is the result of several trends that have now merged into one. A deep distrust of "bourgeois intellectuals" has been a characteristic of Mao Tse-tung's thinking for many years. This attitude led to the double-barreled policy of "absorbing" and "reforming" the intellectuals, which was enunciated by the Chinese Communist Party at its Yenan base in 1939.[1] The intellectuals could be useful in many phases of revolutionary work, but before they could be of service they had to undergo thorough remolding and be cleansed of bourgeois ideas and attitudes.

The "problem of the intellectuals" has been a thorn in the Communist side for many years. Official policy has vacillated between severe criticism and ameliorative measures to win over the intellectuals.[2] A policy of moderation toward intellectuals reached a climax in the decision to "let a hundred flowers blossom, let a hundred schools contend." Even during that "blossoming-contending" period, the demand that intellectuals should be reformed and remolded was never slackened. In his famous speech in 1957 on the "Correct Handling of Contradictions among the People," Mao Tse-tung devoted a section to "the question of the intellectuals." He said:

The mass of intellectuals have made progress, but they should not be complacent. They must continue to remold

themselves, gradually shed their bourgeois world outlook
and acquire the proletarian, Communist world outlook so
that they can fully fit in with the workers and peasants.
This change in outlook is something fundamental, and up
till now most of our intellectuals cannot be said to have
accomplished it.[3]

Ideologically, Mao Tse-tung accepts Lenin's dictum that education apart from politics has no meaning. He has repeatedly declared
that the first duty of education is to serve proletarian politics. Until
the Cultural Revolution, he seemed to be asking no more than that the
intellectuals who held leadership in education should identify themselves with the proletariat and see that education served the workers,
peasants, and soldiers who make up the majority of the laboring masses.
To put the laboring masses in direct charge of education is therefore
a step far beyond Mao's previous thinking and explicit directives. He
must have come to the conclusion that no amount of remolding could fit
the intellectuals for leadership in proletarian education, or have felt
that the workers-peasants-soldiers have sufficiently advanced in
ideological conviction and political intelligence to be able to take over
the leadership.

Education for the benefit of workers and peasants was stressed
in the educational reform of the first decade. It was expressed in the
special schools for workers and peasants and the policy of ordering
all schools and universities to increase the percentage of students
from worker-peasant families. At the end of the first decade, official
statistics reported that worker-peasant students had reached 90 percent of the total in primary schools, 75.2 percent in middle schools,
77 percent in technical middle schools, and 48 percent in institutions
of higher learning.[4] Among new students admitted into higher institutions in 1958, 62 percent were reported to be of worker-peasant class
origin.

This transformation of the class composition of the school population has been consummated by the educational revolution. Elitist education has been replaced by education of the masses from the lowest
to the highest levels. At all levels, young people from worker-
peasant-soldier families are given priority of opportunity, and those
of other family background often find the doors of higher institutions
closed to them. The next step beyond extending educational opportunity
to workers, peasants, and soldiers is to put them in the position of
leadership. If we were to use a cliché to describe the change, we
might say that the educational revolution wants not only education for
the masses but also education by the masses.

Proletarian leadership in education is expressed in a variety
of ways. First, workers, peasants, and soldiers are sent into schools

and universities to "manage" them and lead them toward set goals.
Second, workers, peasants, and soldiers "mount the rostrum" and
become classroom teachers. It is claimed that their ideological
fervor makes them effective teachers in political education and that
their practical experience in production and revolutionary work enables
them to relate knowledge to practical problems. Third, workers, peasants, and soldiers take an active role in the compilation of teaching
materials. Fourth, they are put in charge of the "reeducation" of
students, teachers, and other intellectuals who are sent in large groups
to the countryside and mountain areas to be remolded under the tutor-
ship of workers, peasants, and soldiers. In all cases, the changes
mean a diminution of the role of intellectuals in education. (Reference
to the role of worker-peasant teachers was made in earlier chapters;
the first and fourth types of activity are the main topics of this chapter.)

Mao Tse-tung Propaganda Teams

Mao Tse-tung had earlier sent army units into the schools and
universities to give political and military training to teachers and
students. In 1968, to implement proletarian leadership, he sent
workers and peasants to join hands with the army in the enforcement
of the educational revolution (see Mao's directive, Appendix 19). Now
that Mao Thought is recognized as the heart of the new program, its
propagation becomes the central task of the proletarian leadership.
Hence the organization of the Mao Tse-tung Thought Propaganda
Teams. The teams in the cities are spearheaded by select workers
while those in the rural areas consist of poor and lower-middle peasants. Both serve on the same teams with the PLA soldiers already
stationed in the schools. Besides the schools and universities, Mao
Thought Propaganda Teams are sent into factories, communes,
hospitals, research institutes, government offices, and so on. They
organize classes for political study in such locales as professional
schools, technical institutes, banks, radio stations, newspapers, and
shipyards.
The workers' teams are manned by activists who distinguished
themselves during the Cultural Revolution, older workers who are
adept in depicting the evils and sufferings of pre-1949 society, retired
workers who are ideologically adequate and who would not be missed
on the production front, PLA soldiers, and cadres trained in special
schools.[5]
Among the workers and peasants who serve on the Mao Tse-tung
Propaganda Teams, some are actually illiterate and few, if any, have
had as much schooling as the students and teachers whom they are
commissioned to lead in ideological study. Literate or illiterate, all

89

are distinguished by their ideological steadfastness and their unswerving loyalty to Chairman Mao and the Chinese Communist Party. Asked how an illiterate person could help run a university, a woman team member replied, "With the backing of Mao Tse-tung, anything can be attained."[6] Another illiterate team member sent into Hangchow University had never spent a day in school. He had not even dreamed that he would be a student at a university much less a member of the governing body.[7]

Mao's directive stipulated that the Propaganda Teams "should stay permanently in the schools and colleges . . . and will always lead these institutions." The march of the first team into Tsinghua University, for many decades one of the most highly respected institutions of higher learning in China, on July 27, 1968, was hailed as a turning point in the educational revolution. The workers and soldiers marched into the university "holding aloft portraits of Chairman Mao and with red-covered copies of Quotations From Chairman Mao Tse-tung in their hands." Their arrival "put an end to domination by intellectuals in Tsinghua University."[8]

A Propaganda Team entering a university is manned by hundreds of workers and soldiers. Futan University in Shanghai had a team of more than a thousand members for a student body of 6,000 to 8,000 persons.[9] "In a matter of weeks after Mao's order," according to another report, ". . . 10,000 workers, strengthened by military personnel, had arrived and set about their jobs in the city's 26 institutions of higher learning."[10] Even larger contingents went to universities in Peking. Estimates of the total number of Propaganda Team members for the whole country reached a figure as high as 10 million.[11] A major team is divided into subteams, and there may be more than 100 subteams in a university. The impact of so many workers and soldiers "permanently" stationed in the universities to exercise control and leadership can only be imagined. At the same time, the transfer of so many workers to the educational institutions must necessitate new adjustments on the production front. According to one estimate, 10 to 20 percent of workers in factories were sent to schools and universities to serve on the educational front in response to Mao's call for proletarian leadership in education.[12]

How the Teams Function

The work of the Propaganda Team in the schools and universities falls under four major categories: the enforcement of discipline, general administration, political and ideological education, and teaching. The workers joined the military in the enforcement of political and military training; at the same time, they enhanced the strength of the forces charged with the quelling of continued disorder.

A part of the disorder arose from the difficulty of getting rambunctious youths to settle down to school life, but no small part was due to continued strife between factions of Red Guards and other revolutionary groups that arose during the Cultural Revolution. Violence and bloodshed were common occurrences for a while. In Tsinghua University, factional strife continued for 100 days and resulted in the death of ten students. The militant students even opposed the arrival of the Propaganda Team and opened fire to resist its entry into the university. The gunfire resulted in the death of five workers and the wounding of more than 700 workers and soldiers.[13]

After the restoration of order and discipline, the teams took up regular duties of general administration and teaching. In administrative work they assist the revolutionary committee—now the "leading body" or administrative organ of a school or university—in the management of daily affairs. Their role in political education is extensive and commanding. They preside over the ideological remolding of teachers and students. They pass on the adequacy of teachers and have a voice in their hiring, rating, promotion, and dismissal. They organize classes for ideological study and see that directives and instructions are carried out simply and unequivocally. They send teachers and other intellectuals to the countryside for labor and re-education. They lead the students and teachers to take part in the "three great revolutionary movements" outside the schools.

Mao's directive charges the teams with the duty of "fulfilling all the tasks of struggle-criticism-transformation in the schools." Consequently, a major activity is to organize classes and discussion groups to criticize revisionism and bourgeois ideology, to repudiate educational ideas not compatible with the Maoist line, and to expatiate on the failings of intellectuals and their educational influences. Armed with Mao's directives and Party guidelines, the teams visit classes and check on the performance and attitudes of teachers and students. Many a college teacher has been called to task for expressing ideas in the classroom that do not adhere strictly to what the team members understand to be the correct ideological line. Some have been relieved of teaching and permitted to resume their work only after satisfactory evidence of ideological change.[14]

A popular slogan used by the Propaganda Teams is: "Working class leadership means leadership by Mao Tse-tung Thought." Inasmuch as the implementation of Mao Thought requires curbing the ideology of bourgeois intellectuals, the teams take seriously their task of guiding the reform and remolding of the intellectuals. They lead the intellectuals in an unceasing attack on such bourgeois and revisionist ideas as "intellectual development comes first," "technical ability is all-important," and "mastery of knowledge and theory before practice." Teams attached to the research institutes and to industrial enterprises—such as the famous Taching oilfield—consider it their specific duty and authority to help remold the technical personnel in order to correct the "pure vocationalism" attitude of apolitical intellectuals.

Activities of a similar nature are carried out by Propaganda Teams in primary and middle schools. Teams made up of more than 300,000 workers, peasants, and soldiers carry on their work in 10,000 primary and middle schools in Kwangtung province.[15] Their instructional role in the lower schools is, for obvious reasons, even more pronounced than in the higher institutions. In teaching, team members use a variety of methods to drive home basic ideological concepts. To supplement their lectures on the superiority of socialist society over the old society, they supervise the preparation of scanty "bitterness meals" in schools and universities to show how people suffered in the past with little food available to them. In one case a Futan University student who came from a poor peasant family was given a sickle to bring to the university to remind him of his laboring background. But after a period of study he developed bourgeois attitudes and cast aside the sickle. A team member found the rusty sickle and lectured him on his "rusty" thinking as illustrated by the rusty sickle. The young man was reportedly put to shame for his unworthy ambition to become a nonlaboring intellectual, and he thus was saved for the revolution.[16] (Other examples of the work of the Propaganda Teams may be found in Appendixes 20-23).

Problems

The exercise of proletarian leadership by the Mao Tse-tung Thought Propaganda Teams has not been easily accomplished. Many problems have arisen, some of which admit of no simple solution. It has been noted that the arrival of the teams met with opposition in schools and universities. Backed by high authority, the teams were able to overcome overt opposition. But inner resentment, accentuated by contempt for unschooled workers and peasants occupying positions of authority in halls of learning, was not always easy to suppress. For their part, team members have at times been debilitated by a sense of inadequacy in dealing with people they recognize as better educated and more knowledgeable. The simplistic ideological training they have received often sounds hollow in the classroom. Whenever any problem arises, the only source of guidance they can turn to consists of quotations from Chairman Mao and the officially approved political texts. They repeat such clichés as "one divides into two," "unity of opposites," and "struggle between two lines," but how many of them really understand what the words mean?

The ambivalent Maoist policy in regard to intellectuals tends to compound the difficulties of the proletarian representatives. While it condemns the ideological shortcomings of the intellectuals and demands their abdication of the traditional position of leadership, it at the same time calls for the "wise use" of the remolded intellectuals in revolutionary work. The workers-peasants-soldiers do not find it easy to distinguish between the task of remolding and that of "wise use." They are sometimes told that they should not be timid in the exercise of proletarian leadership, but at other times they are warned not to lose sight of the Party policy of absorbing and utilizing the remolded intellectuals. How can they tell whether in a given case there should be more attention to remolding than active use, or vice versa? They are asked to be careful in making a clear distinction between those who do not understand Marxism-Leninism-Maoism and those who are recalcitrant and antagonistic, between insufficient remolding and stubborn reactionism. This is not easy for them.

The need to make such distinctions has been the subject of repeated instructions to the Propaganda Teams. Evidently the authorities have been a little concerned over the performance of the teams. It is now emphasized that team members need ideological and political study in order to sharpen their understanding of their mission. To avoid slipping into mistakes, they must practice self-criticism and submit to the supervision of the "masses." An article in the authoritative Red Flag (September 1, 1971) warns against conceit, arrogance, and inadequate ideological understanding on the part of team members. Some team members, it is said, do not know how to make use of old cadres and intellectuals and fail to lead in a democratic way, with the unfortunate result that old teachers and old cadres tend to stand back and wait for the team to lead. Team members are told it behooves them to engage in more study, to be more cautious and humble, and to remold their own world outlook.

Team members find themselves in a quandary. If they do not push hard for remolding, they are in danger of neglecting their ideological mission. But if they push too hard, they are guilty of misunderstanding the Party policy of making wise use of the intellectuals. In the midst of uncertainty and puzzlement, no wonder some workers and peasants have requested return to their production units.

A part of the confusion may be due to the changing status of the Propaganda Teams. The teams were sent to the schools and universities at a time when the Party organizations were in disarray and the revolutionary committees as administrative organs of schools (as well as governments at different levels) had not been established. They were vested with administrative authority as well as the authority to restrain the Red Guards and other rebellious youth groups. After the establishment of the revolutionary committees and the Party organizations, the teams were divested of a part of their power and authority. They still have work to do in the propagation of Mao Thought and the area of political and ideological education, but now they must learn to adjust to multiple relationships: a relationship with the Revolutionary Committee of the school in which they operate, a relationship with the Party branch of the school and the Party organizations in the area in which the school is located, and a relationship with the Revolutionary Committee of the Commune or factory.[17]

Major problems that come to the teams are now referred to the Party branch for guidance and approval. When the Team and the revolutionary committee do not see eye to eye in regard to methods of class education and struggle-criticism-transformation, it is necessary to hold meetings for discussion and for "criticism and self-criticism." In the event of an impasse, the Party organization may step in to resolve the difficulty.

Theoretically, the Revolutionary Committee is the administrative body of the school and the Propaganda Team works under the Revolutionary Committee. As the symbol of proletarian leadership, the team still plays a big role in the ideological realm. At the same time, the Revolutionary Committee and the Propaganda Team both accept the leadership of the Party organization. Actually, the Party organization is the most important of the three interlocking control agencies. Propaganda Teams explicitly declare their acceptance of the authority of the Party branch in the schools as an expression of their allegiance to the Chinese Communist Party. Proletarian leadership, they declare, can be achieved only through the Chinese Communist Party, the vanguard of the working class.[18]

In a way, a system of multiple mutual checks is being developed. The Revolutionary Committee as the "leading body" of the school organizes study classes for the Propaganda Teams to keep them on their ideological toes, the Propaganda Teams take upon themselves the responsibility of reeducating members of the revolutionary committee whenever they show signs of bourgeois and revisionist thinking or behavior, and both are subject to the criticism and supervision of the "masses." The core of the "masses," it may be added, is the proletariat, and the "vanguard organization" of the proletariat is the Chinese Communist Party. In the last analysis, proletarian leadership means a more positive control of education by the Party, with the workers, peasants, and soldiers serving as the conduit through which Party leadership is channeled.

Reeducation of Intellectuals

Another formula conceived by Mao Tse-tung to assert proletarian leadership and reduce the influence and status of intellectuals is to send large numbers of intellectuals, including students or "educated youth," to the countryside and mountain areas to be reeducated by workers, peasants, and soldiers (see Mao's directives in Appendixes 24 and 25). The idea of "sending them down" to the countryside for long or short periods of labor is not new. As early as 1945 Mao Tse-tung said that intellectuals "should gladly go to the countryside, put on coarse clothes, and willingly take up any work, however trivial."[19] At different times in the first decade of the regime, students as well as more mature intellectuals were urged to go to the rural areas to take part in agricultural production. In 1957 the hsia-fang (downward transfer) movement was launched to send bureaucrats and intellectuals to the countryside for labor. After 1960, the campaign to send "educated youth" to the rural and mountain areas gained momentum. At the beginning of 1954 it was estimated that 40 million young people had been "sent down."[20] In addition, over a million government and Party workers as well as teachers and other intellectuals were "transferred downwards" to "re-educate themselves by working directly among the peasants."[21]

The "up-to-the-mountains down-to-the-villages movement" (shang-shan hsia-hsiang yun-tung) was given a fresh impetus in 1968. The target of this movement is described as "intellectuals" or "intellectual youth" (chih-shih ch'ing-nien). The latter actually refers to students; "educated youth" is used here as a possibly more appropriate term. The purpose of the movement is to bring about the reform and remolding of the intelligentsia, or the educated class in general. The current campaign to send the intelligentsia to the countryside surpasses all previous efforts in proportion and scope. There is now a broader meaning in reeducation: not only do the intellectuals who are the products of bourgeois education need to be reeducated by the laboring class but the young people who attend schools dominated by intellectuals and their revisionist educational ideas must be purged of the ill effects of the wrong kind of education; only by identification and integration with the workers-peasants-soldiers can such products of bourgeois and revisionist education become useful to the proletarian revolution.

There are no accurate statistics for the total number of people sent to the countryside since the stepped-up campaign of 1968. Estimates vary from 25 to 30 million to 40 to 60 million. Nearly one million young people went from Shanghai from 1968 to 1972.[22] An officially released report to the effect that 400,000 middle school graduates left for the countryside and frontier regions in the first eight months of 1972[23] seemed to indicate a slowdown in the rate of exodus, but the same report reaffirmed the policy of reeducation of intellectuals in the countryside.* As a rule, the intellectuals and students are sent to distant areas or areas where living conditions are harsh and work is strenuous so that they may learn to be tough and unafraid of hardship. Those from the big cities are sent to the border areas of Kirin province in the northeast, the rural areas of Hainan island, the less developed areas in faraway Yunnan, Szechuan, Sinkiang, the northwest, and other areas offering opportunities for the reclamation of wasteland or the development of the frontier. One student related his experience as follows:

> When we arrived at Chingtushan, after traveling over 50 li of mountainous road, we became quite disheartened. This was not like the ordinary mountain village we had imagined. The 20-odd households were scattered over the 20-li-long ravine. A walk of 3 to 4 li is needed to reach a neighbor. [A li is about a third of a mile.] When we saw this, each of us was busy with his own thoughts, and some even sounded the drum of retreat.[24]

In the countryside, the intellectuals live among the peasants and engage in labor and production. Some are there for a specific period of time while others are assigned for indefinite terms; many are sent to join the production teams and brigades to settle down permanently in the rural areas. Documents and writings reflecting the official view stress the importance of physical and ideological "tempering" and the need of all intellectuals to integrate themselves with the laboring masses. Very little is said or written about the reformative or punitive aspects of the "reeducation program," but there is evidence that the present program has incorporated some form of reformative labor that was prescribed for recalcitrant intellectuals (including landlords and uncooperative capitalists) in earlier years.

Besides the intellectuals and the graduates of schools and universities, cadres and functionaries of government offices and Party organizations are included in the program. Many of them are sent on a rotation basis for a definite period of reeducation, after which they are supposed to return to their original posts with fresh dedication and ideological enthusiasm. They usually attend training classes

---

*If there is any slowdown in the exodus, it may be due in part to the need for more manpower in the cities arising from the program of industrial recovery and rehabilitation, and perhaps to the less pressing manpower need in the rural areas. Additionally, a new policy may be emerging to permit more talented students to pursue advanced study.

along with labor and production; some are assigned to the "May 7 Cadre Schools" (these schools are discussed more fully in Chapter 6). Some are members of the Communist Party or the Communist Youth League who have shown signs of ideological vacillation or the influence of bourgeois and revisionist ideas. There is some evidence that a small number of trusted cadres and Party members have joined the urban exodus in order to serve as activists working within the ranks of urban youth and leading them in ideological reform. The reeducation program has also been a means of dispersing and rectifying the Red Guards, whose factional strife was a serious obstacle to the restoration of order and discipline in the schools after reopening. At the same time, Red Guards with a good record of service and loyalty have led the way in responding to the Chairman's call for the reeducation of intellectuals.

The Medical News-Tribune in London reported that many doctors had been sent to the countryside: "Few older doctors are seen in the country's hospitals now. They are all in the countryside undergoing reeducation . . . [or] doing manual work in factories."[25] Radio technicians from Shanghai went in groups to stay a month at a time to learn "how to make manure compost piles, harvest cotton, and reap rice crops."[26] Teachers, bureaucrats, and other urban inhabitants further swell the ranks of new arrivals in the countryside.

Life in the Countryside

Besides the experience of working and living with peasants to learn their hard-working and frugal way of life, the intellectuals are "steeled" or tempered physically and ideologically by strenuous labor and intensive political education. Labor is performed under the most challenging circumstances. The daily schedule is rigidly adhered to: out of bed at 6:30 a.m., labor during the day, study periods after breakfast and in the evening. A report from an "old revolutionary base" in Fukien province tells how the "young intellectuals" transformed a mountainous area into farmland. Under the guidance of experienced peasants, they went up the mountain to reclaim the land and lived in an old abandoned temple. Life was strenuous and conditions were rough, but the students were reminded that even greater difficulties were overcome by Chairman Mao and the Red Army when they established a base there in the late 1920s.[27]

In the villages, urban youths learn how to take care of crops and perform such chores as wading into the pigsty to dig out the mud, to be used as fertilizer. In the mountain villages, where the carrying pole is a daily necessity, the young people from the cities learn to use it to carry heavy loads on their shoulders. They cross hills and dales to go to the farms; they brave biting cold winds to climb up the mountains "to chop firewood or reclaim wasteland and terrace the slopes." In this way, they gain a respect for labor, at the same time tempering themselves to endure hardships and acquire "revolutionary fortitude."[28] One 1972 report stated the young people earned from 200 to 275 yuan a year; the exchange rate at that time was 2.25 yuan to a U.S. dollar.[29]

Urban youth is expected to learn the simple virtues of the peasants who work hard and indulge in no luxuries, who are satisfied with plain food and simple lodging. There are no paved roads, no concrete buildings. Young urbanites who easily feel tired are put to shame when they watch the peasants toil without rest, braving wind and snow. They learn to discard their bourgeois aversion to filth and stench. They see the value of practice, without which theory is useless. They learn to build and to repair tools on the basis of the practical experience of the peasants, rather than on theory. They watch the inventiveness of the peasants in devising makeshifts with simple materials, using discarded pieces of wood and scraps for the construction of windows and bamboo broomsticks for door frames. They thus practice economy and "scientific experimentation" at the same time.

Most important of all is the ideological remolding that is to be achieved while living among the workers-peasants-soldiers. The peasants and other people in charge of the program, as well as the young people undergoing reeducation, are constantly reminded that it is a mistake to think of reeducation in terms of labor and production only. Just as the school must consider ideological remolding its primary and most important task, so the experience in the countryside will have failed in its most fundamental objective if it does not bring about a transformation of ideology with the attendant changes in attitudes, outlook, and loyalties. The toughening process of labor and the specific contributions in rural construction and production, significant as they are, can have meaning only when they are guided and motivated by a vigorous political consciousness and by firm ideological conviction.

To focus attention on the need for a fundamental change on the part of the intellectuals, Mao's statement in regard to cleanliness and dirtiness is frequently quoted and repeated. In his highly revered Yenan Talks on literature and art, Mao said:

Whenever I compare unreformed intellectuals with workers, peasants, and soldiers, I realize that not only were the minds of those intellectuals unclean but that their bodies were also unclean. The cleanest people in the world are the workers and peasants. Even though their hands may be soiled and their feet smeared with

cow dung, nevertheless they are cleaner than the bourgeoisie and the petty bourgeoisie. That is what I mean by
a transformation of sentiments—a changing over from one
class to another.[30]

The use of this piece of Maoism is illustrated in the case of a
girl student from medical school who tried to learn to transplant rice
seedlings but felt repelled by the dung around the roots. She overcame
her aversion when she was reminded of Mao's statement about the
cleanliness of peasants with dirty hands and dung-smeared feet.[31]
Another girl reportedly used to wash her hands thoroughly with soap
after handling manure fertilizers, but also changed her attitude after
studying Mao's writings under the light of a kerosene lamp.[32] Still
another girl from Peking University had blisters on her palms after
tying up bundles of hay. After studying Mao's instruction to fight
self-interest, she realized that her tender hands were the product of
revisionist education and her blisters a severe indictment of revisionist
education. She vowed: "I must make the blisters rupture, I must rub
my hands with hay and cover them with unfeeling calluses. These
tender hands must be transformed into the hands of laboring people."[33]
The aim of reeducation is to transform the ideological outlook
of the intellectuals. Its content consists of labor, production, and the
proletarian ideology as taught by Mao Tse-tung; its method is to
serve the workers-peasants-soldiers and integrate with them. Politics
is paramount. The ideological significance of every action and attitude
is scrutinized. A music student who feared that pulling weeds would
hurt her fingers and make them unfit for playing the p'i-p'a (Chinese
guitar) was found to be obsessed with the bourgeois ambition of seeking
personal advancement, and was finally led in the reeducation process
to denounce the bourgeois ideology which had dominated her thinking.
The young people must learn the story of the class struggle in the
villages and the "boundless love" of the villagers for Chairman Mao.
They are told: "Chairman Mao sent you here to be changed politically,
ideologically, and emotionally.[34] It is easy to change clothes and don
overalls, they are told, but the more crucial test is the transformation
of thought and ideology.[35]
Integration with workers-peasants-soldiers entails integration
in outlook and feelings. It calls for the shedding of the "ideological
baggage" of bourgeois ideas that fills the minds of unreformed intellectuals: the scorn of manual labor, the fear of hardship, the hanker-
ing for physical comfort, the ambition of personal advancement through
study. Study classes, symposiums, and discussion groups are the
media for threshing out the ideological issues and sharpening the focus
on the struggle between the "two lines." Another method is to organize
"Red Pairs" in which an urban student teams up with a peasant of high

political consciousness who stirs his imagination and emotions by relating from personal experience how the village has been transformed under the Red flag.

The role of soldiers as agents of reeducation is underscored in the army camps to which some of the young people are assigned. Managed by PLA units, these camps are run like army companies. Physical work and political study are the two main types of activities. Labor is performed in the open fields: building houses, growing vegetables, cleaning pigsties and latrines. Classes are conducted to study the Chairman's directives on the educational revolution and the class struggle. Students are led to appreciate the contributions of the PLA to the revolution and the high political consciousness and firm loyalty of the soldiers. They sing songs praising the valiant fighters of the PLA. Army concepts of discipline and good conduct hold sway. Girls in the army camps learn to drive horse carts, to tend animals, even to wear military uniforms as female mounted soldiers.[36] There is some indication that graduates of colleges and universities are more likely to be sent to army camps than to production teams or brigades.

In one instance a graduate of a veterinary institute related his experience in a PLA production base. Under the evil influence of revisionist thinking, he had been unhappy over admission into the veterinary institute, for he did not like the dirty work and wanted to become an engineer. At the army base he learned to appreciate manual labor and to integrate with the masses. He lived in a shabby shed with a pigsty and a manure pool in front. He slept on a mat on the bare ground, although on rainy days leakage from the roof turned the ground to mud. Pigs came into the shed and messed up his bedding. Earnest study of Mao's writings finally purged him of revisionist ideas, and disgust gave way to a determination to serve the revolution. When his wife came to see him she was shocked by the miserable conditions, but he asked her to join him in the study of Mao's directives and she too became convinced that he was doing the right thing to stick to his reeducation.[37]

There is a third phase of the rural program for intellectuals: in addition to physical labor and ideological reform, they are to make contributions to the rural community. They contribute not only by participating in production but in various forms of service that the peasants of lesser education cannot adequately perform. They teach in night schools, sometimes technical subjects applicable to agriculture but always Mao Thought and ideology. They serve as medical workers and "barefoot doctors," as bookkeepers and accountants in the communes, and as writers of news-sheets and materials for adult education. They make new insecticides and fertilizers, they increase the yield of farmland, and they help develop industries in rural China. Furthermore, there may be an indirect contribution that is not readily visible: the presence of so many intellectuals in the rural community may start a leavening process whose effects may not be immediately seen or felt.

Planning

All phases of the program are carefully planned with the central objectives in view. Immediately after Mao's "latest instruction" on reeducation, a nationwide campaign was under way to persuade young people to obey the Chairman's call and parents to send their children to the countryside. In the schools, the Propaganda Teams and the Communist Youth League launched a drive to urge students to volunteer for rural service. They organized study classes to dwell on the value of labor and production and the significance of Mao's call to the pro-letarian revolution. Outside the schools, all government offices, factories, business enterprises, and mass organizations joined to promote citywide campaigns for the mass exodus of youth to the countryside. Pressure was brought to bear on families so that parents would agree to "sending down" their sons and daughters. Parents were invited to meetings at which Mao's directives were read and explained and exhortations were made to respond to the call. For example, in the Tientsin cigaret factory, a campaign among the workers reportedly resulted in 97 percent of their children signing up to go.[38] When a member of the Party committee of the factory led the way by sending his eldest son, it was difficult for workers not to follow.

Family conferences, often used as the medium for struggle-criticism-transformation, are utilized for discussions leading to a decision to accept integration with workers-peasants-soldiers. The Red Flag (August 11, 1972) reported the story of a cadre who sent his daughter to the countryside in 1968. The grandparents were at first unwilling to see their eldest granddaughter leave home, and the cadre father wavered for a while until he carefully studied Chairman Mao's instructions and decided to obey his call. The grandparents objected because the girl was the first child in several generations to complete middle school education and they felt that it would be a waste of talent to send her to the countryside. Whereupon the father convened a family conference at which they recalled their unhappy past and finally decided to accept the call for integration with workers-peasants-soldiers. The next question was, "Where to go?" The girl said she would go "where the Party wants me to go," but the grandparents preferred some place near the city. Another family conference brought the realization that the desire to be near home would not be an expres-sion of true revolutionary love, and the family agreed that the girl should accept the distant mountain area to which the authorities had assigned her.

After some time in the mountain area, the girl became dissatisfied and complained of hardship. Realizing the significance of the two-line struggle, the father sent 90 books of Marxism-Leninism-Maoism to strengthen her will and ideological stand. In 1969 the authorities were about to send some young people back into the city and the girl wanted to take advantage of the opportunity. Again, according to the officially approved story, the father went into an ideological struggle and decided to ask his daughter to remain in the countryside for lifetime settlement, and not to be tempted by the lures of city life.

The importance of parental attitude is recognized in Mao's "Instructions" on reeducation, in which he urged "cadres and other people in the cities" to encourage their children to answer the call to go to the countryside (see Appendix 25). To ensure parental cooperation, the authorities continue to enlist parents in ideological study throughout the whole period of their children's stay in the countryside. The Party branch of a neighborhood in Shanghai organized weekly study sessions that parents have attended for more than two years. The sessions try to show the peasants that their worries about their children's exposure to inclement cold weather, wild beasts, and poisonous snakes in remote Heilungkiang areas are incompatible with Chairmen Mao's instructions to fear neither hardship nor death. The parents are taught to live and act as revolutionary parents teaching their children the revolutionary spirit.[39]

In the countryside, revolutionary committees and the Party organizations mobilize the workers-peasants-soldiers to prepare for the arrival of the intellectuals. Workers, peasants, and soldiers are taught how to make use of their ideological conviction and proletarian outlook in the reeducation of the urban arrivals. Special organs are set up to supervise the program, and every effort is made to ensure success and prevent preoccupation with labor and production to the neglect of politics. In many communes, brigades, and production teams, select activists among poor and lower-middle peasants, cadres, and educated youth are chosen to constitute "reeducation leadership groups" to look after the entire program.

It has been found that workers-peasants-soldiers are quite ready to teach the urbanites to perform labor, but they are hesitant when it come to teaching them ideology and politics, partly because they are not sure that they know how and partly because some still retain the traditional respect for educated people. It is thus necessary for the authorities to organize classes and symposiums for the workers-peasants-soldiers to inform them of their new duties and responsibilities and show them how to discharge them, how to relate all work to ideology and use the Chairman's teachings as their supreme weapon, and how to use their personal knowledge of the unhappy past in their

102

families and villages for the ideological remolding of the intellectuals. Those who have suffered oppression in the past and those who have shown high political consciousness are selected to live, work, and study with the urban arrivals.

The intellectuals are not left to the workers-peasants-soldiers after their arrival. The workers-peasants-soldiers discharge their duties under the supervision of the Revolutionary Committee of the brigade or the commune. The Revolutionary Committee, the special organs set up for reeducation, and all government offices and production units share the responsibility of reeducation work under the "unified leadership" of the Party. The Communist Youth League also has a role to play. Youth League members visit homes to talk with parents and children. They are active in the countryside and organize classes, symposiums, exhibits, and plays for education in the two-line struggle.

Exercising "unified leadership," the Party organization coordinates the work of all participating agencies and sees that no agency neglects its responsibility because it is too engrossed in its ordinary, routine work. Whenever any participating agency becomes lax in its work, the Party organization sets up special study classes to recall the Chairman's instructions and to stress the crucial importance of reeducating the intellectuals. In one county in Kiangsu province, over 300,000 poor and lower-middle peasants attended classes and forums to exchange experiences in reeducating urban youth.[40]

Occasionally, young people in the countryside are allowed to return to the city on home leave, especially at the time of the lunar New Year (now called the Spring Festival). Not everyone is granted this privilege. As a matter of fact, officially sponsored propaganda takes the position that the cold winter provides a good opportunity for youths to test their ability to endure hardship in the countryside and that progressive youths should not think too much of going to their city homes, even for short visits.[41] Nevertheless, many are granted home leave during the Spring Festival, and the cooperating agencies in the countryside and the cities again engage in careful planning to utilize the brief stay in the cities for continued reeducation. City authorities organize welcome meetings at which integration with workers-peasants-soldiers is hailed as the best way of turning intellectuals into worthy successors of the revolution.

The welcome meetings are followed by symposiums and report meetings at which the activists among those on home leave speak with enthusiasm of their experiences in the countryside and express their determination to return to their countryside posts after the home leave. These meetings are held throughout the period of home leave. They serve multiple purposes—not only to bolster the morale of the youths on leave but also to keep them away from activities tainted with bourgeois and feudal ideology (especially during the lunar New Year season, which traditionally is given over to fun and amusement). Parents and young people who have not been "sent down" are invited to such meetings. To further ensure that the ideological remolding in the countryside is not diluted through neglect or the unproletarian influences of city life, classes are organized for young people to continue to study Mao's directives and other writings to keep up their ideological vigilance while on leave.

For example, a young girl on home leave in Shanghai tells how she joined the class and line struggle during her Spring Festival visit. She also served as a "voluntary propagandist" to persuade other young people to take the road of integration with workers-peasants-soldiers. She was kept so busy that she did not spend much time at home, but she had a rich and meaningful experience in the continuing struggle between the bourgeoisie and the proletariat for the loyalty and devotion of the young generation.[42]

The cooperation of government offices, production units, propaganda agencies, the home, and the school, and the coordination of their activities under the "unified leadership of the Party" furnish further evidence of the broad and bold concept of education. The school is considered only one of the many agencies of education, with the process of education something that goes on everywhere and all the time, 24 hours a day and every day of the year, with no interruption for vacations or any other periods of idleness.

Results

The rustication program has produced some good results that must be gratifying to the planners. Wasteland has been reclaimed and turned to productive use. Frontier areas have been developed. The area of farmland has been expanded, and the augmentation of labor manpower has boosted production and construction work.

The original idea of sending urbanites into the countryside was part of the rectification campaign of 1957 and an effort to reduce the evils of bureaucratism. Although the reduction of an oversized bureaucracy was not a major consideration in the current program, it must be considered one of the incidental benefits. Chou En-lai is reported to have said in 1971 that the bureaucracy in the Central Government had been reduced from 60,000 people to 10,000.[43]

The need to thin out the urban population may have been another factor in the planning. About 15 percent of the urban population has gone to the countryside; millions are there for permanent settlement. The cities were troubled by unemployment and listless youths creating problems of delinquency. Rural settlement under strict supervision helped clear the cities of troublesome elements. Certainly the Red

Guards needed to be curbed and dispersed, and sending them into the countryside offered a convenient way out in the name of an ideological principle, namely, integration with the masses. Some of the Red Guards were rural youths who had left the countryside to join the roving bands at the height of the Cultural Revolution. They did not choose to return home after the Cultural Revolution, and they exacerbated the congestion of the cities and the turmoil in the schools. When urban youths were sent to the countryside in large numbers, it seemed easier to persuade rural youths to return to their villages.

The intellectuals, young and old, have made positive contributions to rural life. The ideological study at the heart of the reeducation program serves to raise the political consciousness of workers, peasants, and soldiers as well as intellectuals. The permanent settlement of so many educated people makes for a higher level of knowledge and intelligence and a change of outlook on the part of the rural community; even the few who are selected to enter institutions of higher education after two or three years of rustication are supposed to return to the countryside after graduation. Furthermore, obvious benefits are brought by the night schools in which the urbanites serve as teachers. Together with the acceleration in production and construction work, these changes add up to a significant advance in the development of rural China.

The aim of reeducation is to produce millions of worthy successors to the revolutionary cause. From the Communist point of view, progress has been made in this direction. Of the 300,000 young people who left the city of Peking for the countryside and mountain areas in the past few years, 16,000 joined the Communist Youth League, 3,200 were admitted into the Communist Party, and 10,000 were judged ready to take up leading posts in the production brigades and various levels of the provincial government; others have become accountants, storekeepers, agrotechnicians, teachers, and barefoot doctors.[44] Among the 20,000 Peking students who went to Yunnan, 600 have joined the Communist Youth League, 100 have become Communist Party members, and 7,000 are recognized as activists.[45] Out of 100,000 "educated youth" sent to remote Sinkiang from big cities near the coast, 2,000 have joined the Communist Party and 20,000 the Communist Youth League.[46] In many places, reeducated urbanites have been elected leading members of Party organizations as well as revolutionary committees at various levels. Besides labor and study, the intellectuals take part in the "three great revolutionary movements" in the countryside, thus helping to fulfill the plans to engage the entire population in these movements.

To the ideology-minded Communists, the ideological gains are certainly no less important, if not more so. They have taken another big step in making the entire nation aware of the importance of ideological remolding. With the reeducation program goes a major nationwide propaganda campaign, and every propaganda campaign of this scope arouses the entire population and helps to muster popular support for the program of the Party-state. In other words, the campaign is another educational movement destined to change the thought and feelings of intellectuals, parents, workers-peasants-soldiers, and all who take part directly or indirectly in the reeducation program.

Another giant step is taken in bringing the intellectuals down from the favored position they traditionally occupied in Chinese society. Many intellectuals have been remolded and shorn of their bourgeois and revisionist ideas and attitudes. They have gained a new respect for labor and the working masses. The Communists may well feel proud of their progress in eliminating the gap between mental and physical labor, in the "combination of agriculture with manufacturing industries [and] the gradual abolition of the distinction between town and gown" (provision of the Communist Manifesto). The program also serves to reinforce the Maoist theory of agriculture as the "foundation" of the national economy. Incidentally, the Communists could hardly be unaware of the fact that uprooting young people from their city homes and sending them into remote areas would also contribute to the loosening of family ties and thus pave the way for the development of loyalty to the revolutionary cause and the Party-state.

Problems

The reeducation program is not without problems and difficulties. That current literature and official statements constantly attack ideological deviations that hamper successful execution may be taken as an indication that such deviations do exist and are not merely isolated instances. It is emphasized that ideological remolding is a long process and not easily achieved. Young people transferred to the countryside do not quickly shake off their bourgeois and revisionist thinking; while some hold onto the ideology of "intellect first" and "study for personal advancement," others take the defeatist view that study is now useless. Even those who seem to accept integration with workers-peasants-soldiers may harbor the erroneous notion of "rustication as a process of gilding"—the feeling that it is necessary to perform labor to acquire a proletarian veneer but the whole experience will be a thing of the past after returning to the cities. Much is said and written these days in condemnation of this "gilding theory."

Another ideological deviation frequently attacked in the current propaganda campaign and study sessions is the notion that rustication is a form of punishment. The correct view is that intellectuals should consider it an opportunity and an honor to identify themselves with the masses and to become qualified for service to the revolution. But whether they think in terms of gilding or punishment, there is evidently no small number of intellectuals who secretly long for early release from rustication in order to resume their work and life prior to the "downward transfer." Commenting on reeducation in an army farm, an article in the People's Daily (October 24, 1968) observed that many young people were still under the influence of feudal and bourgeois ideology and had a long way to go to establish the new philosophy of studying to serve the revolution.

Official reports on reeducation abound in stories of successful remolding and enthusiastic response to Mao's call. Little information is available in regard to negative responses among young people. Nevertheless, there is little doubt that discontent does exist. There are reports about students who worry that after a few years of rural service they will have forgotten what they studied in school and will not be able to continue from where they left off. Others are depressed because they see no chance to make use of the schooling to which they gave precious years. Those troubled by such dissident ideas are not likely to perform well in labor and production.

There are rumors of discontent flaring up in overt rebellion, but no factual confirmation is obtainable. However, the fact that official statements and newspaper writings so often warn of the presence of class enemies who plot to create trouble and sabotage the reeducation program leads one to suspect that some resentment has emerged on the surface. Whenever there are observable signs of vacillation in thinking on the part of the young people or decline in their enthusiasm for labor or ideological study, the authorities always attribute them to the insidious influence of class enemies who try to turn youth away from the proletarian cause. Reports on "hooligans and Teddy boys" who damage farm crops and attack peasants provide further evidence that some young people have not accepted reeducation without protest (see Appendixes 27 and 28).

The New York Times (January 14, 1973) reported that among 20,000 refugees who fled from China to Hong Kong in 1972, "most were discontented young people who had been sent from urban areas to rural communes, where they were expected to spend the rest of their lives." Another report by the same paper (August 14, 1972) stated: "Discontent among young people in China's Kwangtung province, arising out of their objection to rural work assignments, has reportedly led to an upsurge of crime in Canton, the provincial capital, and has brought the number of refugees reaching Hong Kong to its highest level in 10 years." The problem seemed serious enough to be discussed in a symposium sponsored by the Kiangsu Provincial Revolutionary Committee. At the symposium it was declared: "We must deal a telling blow to the handful of class enemies who undermine the work of young intellectuals settling in the countryside."[47]

107

Articles also have appeared in Mainland Chinese journals and newspapers urging special attention to the problems of girl students from urban areas. Little information is available in regard to the specific problems of girl students, but it is possible that girls find it even harder than boys to perform heavy labor and adjust to the harsh conditions in the undeveloped areas. They are more likely to miss their homes and families.[48] It is also possible that the campaign to delay marriage has caused uneasiness among girls who see their best years go by without any prospect of marriage.

The attitude of the peasants also poses a problem. Mao's directives stated that workers, peasants, and soldiers should welcome the intellectuals from the cities (see Appendixes 24 and 25). But the workers-peasants-soldiers have their own worries. Some feel that the foodgrain produced by urban youth is not enough to balance what they consume, since young people unaccustomed to labor do not produce as much as the seasoned workers-peasants-soldiers. Others complain that the young people from the cities are more of a burden than a help. The influx of so many intellectuals puts a strain on the food supply, and the local population watches the process with apprehension. Moreover, many workers-peasants-soldiers feel that they are too busy with their own work to teach the urbanites how to work on the farm and construction projects. They are even more hesitant in taking up the role of political mentors to guide the ideological remolding of the intellectuals, who have far more schooling and better knowledge of the writings of Chairman Mao and Marx and Lenin. They are taught to lecture on past miseries and the history of their families and villages, and to use such quotations as "one divides into two" and "serve the people," but after much repetition the limited repertoire begins to sound monotonous.

Those who are supposed to join in the undertaking have been called to task for insufficient awareness of their responsibility. It is emphasized that the proletariat is engaged in a life-and-death struggle with the bourgeoisie and the revisionists to win over the young generation, and that the masses and their organizations—farms, communes, factories, government offices, families—must rearrange their work so as to regularly set aside time for discharging their duties in the reeducation program. The alibi of being "too busy" is not acceptable. Constant prodding by the Party leadership seems to be required to get all participating agencies to do their share. Normally the revolutionary committees furnish the guidance and organize the classes and symposiums. But revolutionary committees are known to have become lax in leadership. In such cases, study sessions are organized for the benefit of members of the revolutionary committees, presumably at the prompting of the Party organizations.

Sometimes even "comrades in the Party branch became complacent, saying that the work of reeducating the educated youths was 'about done.' This led to a slackening in the work of reeducating the young intellectuals."[49] Who, then, keeps the local Party organization on its toes? Presumably, in the system of multiple mutual checks that we observed in connection with the Mao Tse-tung Thought Propaganda Teams, the revolutionary committee may also check on the Party branch or, in the spirit of the mass line, the "masses" may criticize the Party branch or the revolutionary committee. Some system of mutual check may be signified by the fact that workers-peasants-soldiers preside over the ideological remolding of the intellectuals but also attend political study classes in the evening at which intellectuals serve as political instructors. Most likely, however, the Party branch is subject to the authority of higher-level Party organizations, and in the last analysis it is the top Party leadership of the "Party Center"—the Central Committee, the Politburo, and Chairman Mao—that lays down the line and calls the tune.

Notes

1. Theodore H. E. Chen, Thought Reform of the Chinese Intellectuals (Hong Kong: University of Hong Kong Press, 1960), Chapter I.
2. Cf. Chou En-lai, Report on the Question of Intellectuals (Peking: Foreign Languages Press, 1956).
3. Mao's speech was made on February 27, 1957. The official English translation appears in Peking Review, June 23, 1967.
4. State Statistical Bureau, Ten Great Years—Statistics on Economic and Cultural Construction Achievements of the People's Republic of China (Peking: Foreign Languages Press, 1960), p. 200.
5. See Peking Review, May 22, 1970, for a report on the Liuho "May 7 Cadre School."
6. Robert S. Elegant, in Los Angeles Times, December 19, 1968.
7. Chinese News Analysis, no. 713 (November 1, 1968), p. 5.
8. "Anniversary of Entry of Working Class into Realm of Superstructure," Peking Review, August 1, 1969.
9. Wen-hui Pao, August 27, 1968.
10. Peggy Durdin, "The Bitter Tea of Mao's Red Guards," New York Times Magazine, January 19, 1969.
11. "Worker Teams Spread in China," New York Times, December 9, 1968.
12. China News Analysis, October 18, 1968.
13. Wang Ch'un-sheng and Wang Cheng-fang, Tsai Chung Kuo Ta Lu Ti Chien Wen (What we saw and heard in Mainland China) (Hong Kong-Wen Chiao Ch'u Pan She, 1972), p. 93. For a fuller story on

violent strife in Tsinghua University, see William Hinton, Hundred Day War: The Cultural Revolution in Tsinghua University (New York: Monthly Review Press, 1972).

14. Foreign Broadcast Information Services, Daily Report, Communist China, February 25, 1969, p. C3. (Hereafter cited as FBIS.)

15. FBIS, April 21, 1969, p. D1.

16. FBIS, April 30, 1969, p. C3.

17. For example, the revolutionary committee of the factory that sends workers to serve on a team tries to keep in touch with their work and ideological progress. See Jen-min Jih-pao, August 19, 1971.

18. See report on the educational revolution in a middle school in Tientsin, in Kuang-ming Jih-pao, March 20, 1970. See also an article by Propaganda Teams in Heilungkiang province, FBIS, August 3, 1970, p. G3.

19. Li Fang, "Why Intellectuals Go to the Countryside," Peking Review, March 25, 1958.

20. Reported in a speech given at a conference of representatives of youth activists engaged in rural construction, in Chung-kuo Ch'ing-nien Pao (Chinese youth journal), January 25, 1964.

21. Li Fang, op. cit.

22. Jen-min Jih-pao, February 16, 1972.

23. Peking Review, September 22, 1972, p. 5.

24. FBIS, May 13, 1970, p. C11.

25. Los Angeles Times, May 3, 1971.

26. FBIS, January 20, 1970, p. C1.

27. Survey of China Mainland Press, no. 5136 (May 18, 1972), p. 169.

28. "Marching Forward along the Road of Integration with the Workers, Peasants, and Soldiers," Peking Review, July 24, 1970.

29. China Monthly (Hong Kong), January 1, 1972, p. 39.

30. Mao Tse-tung, Problems of Art and Literature (New York: International Publishers, 1950) p. 13.

31. "Marching Forward with Big Strides under the Leadership of the Working Class," Peking Review, August 1, 1969.

32. Hung-ch'i (Red flag), September 21, 1970, p. 64.

33. Kuang-ming Jih-pao, January 17, 1969.

34. Jen-min Jih-pao, February 2, 1969.

35. FBIS, November 10, 1969, p. H9.

36. China News Analysis, March 19, 1971, p. 5.

37. Jen-min Jih-pao, May 4, 1969.

38. Jen-min Jih-pao, January 18, 1973.

39. Jen-min Jih-pao, April 2, 1973.

40. FBIS, July 3, 1969, p. C3.

41. FBIS, December 28, 1970, p. B9.

42. Kuang-ming Jih-pao, January 19, 1973.
43. China Quarterly, April-June 1971, p. 392.
44. Kuang-ming Jih-pao, January 30, 1973.
45. China News Analysis, no. 835 (March 19, 1971), p. 4.
46. Peking Review, July 6, 1973, p. 22.
47. FBIS, August 4, 1970, p. C8.
48. Report of the revolutionary committee of a brigade in Kiangsu province, Jen-min Jih-pao, October 16, 1972.
49. FBIS, September 10, 1970, p. C12.

REMOLDING OF CADRES
AND INTELLECTUALS

The ideas and practices contained in the reeducation program are not altogether new. For many years, Maoist thinking has insisted that ideological remolding must be the central aim of education, that labor is essential to the process, that education must be combined with production and politics, that intellectuals must be reformed and remade and integrated with the laboring masses, that workers-peasants-soldiers constitute the core of the masses, and that rugged life in the countryside helps remold the outlook and ideology of urban intellectuals.

On the practical side, reformative labor has been prescribed for intellectuals since the beginning of the new regime, labor was made a major theme of the curriculum shortly after 1949, close links between the schools and the factories and farms were forged before the Cultural Revolution, the "downward transfer" of intellectuals to the countryside had already assumed huge proportions in the mid 1960s, and workers-peasants-soldiers were used as political instructors to relate personal experiences of abuse and oppression in the old society. But putting together all these ideas and practices into one program is a new development born of the educational revolution.

The May 7 Cadre Schools

Another important product of the educational revolution is the "May 7 Cadre School." Schools for the training of cadres have occupied the attention of Communist leaders for many years. Mao Tsetung declared in the early years of the Communist movement that cadres are a decisive factor in the revolution, that "everything depends on the cadres." Through the years, the cadres have consisted largely of proletarian elements with little or no schooling. They obviously need training, and various forms of cadre schools have been tried. The training of cadres has now merged with the reeducation of intellectuals, and the result is a new form of cadre training that embodies the main concepts and practices of the rustication program described in Chapter 5.

The new form of cadre education also puts a premium on integration with workers-peasants-soldiers by living among them and working in rural surroundings. Cadre education of the past, it is now charged, followed the revisionist line. Although it provided for ideological and political study, it did so by studying behind closed doors without actual participation in the class struggle and working among the masses. It was divorced from the masses, from labor, and from the revolutionary movements outside the schools. The May 7 Cadre School is supposed to be inspired by Mao's "May 7 Directive," really a short letter he wrote to Lin Piao, then his confidant and "close comrade-in-arms," on May 7, 1966 (see Appendix 9). This directive is now hailed as a major document spelling out Mao's educational philosophy.

The letter to Lin Piao was concerned with the army and instructed that the PLA "should be a great school" in which "the armymen should learn politics, military affairs, and agriculture," and "take part in the socialist education movement in the factories and villages." The army should engage in three major tasks: "agriculture, industry, and mass work." After these specific instructions for the army, Mao's letter went on to apply his ideas to education in general, stressing the importance of "learning other things." Workers and peasants should study "military affairs, politics, and culture" and engage in criticizing the bourgeoisie. Students should "learn other things, that is, industrial work, farming, and military affairs. They should also criticize the bourgeoisie." The same principle holds for government and Party personnel and for people in trade and commerce. The section on students includes Mao's often repeated statements on the need to shorten the school term and terminate the domination of the schools by bourgeois intellectuals.

The May 7 Directive produced no immediate impact, as far as actual implementation was concerned. Perhaps the country was too much embroiled in the Cultural Revolution. Two years later, Mao followed up the original directive with another "Instruction" that specifically linked cadre training with the new emphasis on labor in the countryside. "Sending the masses of cadres to do manual work," said Mao, "gives them an excellent opportunity to study once again; this should be done by all cadres except those who are too old, weak, ill or disabled. Cadres at work should also go group by group to do manual work."[1] The May 7 Cadre School is the product of both the

113

May 7 Directive and the later instruction on cadre training (now called his "Latest Instruction" on cadre training). In all official statements, however, credit is given principally to the May 7 Directive; hence the name of the new schools.

The first May 7 Cadre School was established in a farm at Liuho in Heilungkiang province in May 1968, a few months before Mao issued his "Latest Instruction" on cadres. It became the prototype of the May 7 Cadre Schools. A major nationwide drive to establish such schools was inspired by Mao's "Latest Instruction" on October 4, 1968; according to the Peking Review, "In the single month of October [1968] alone, new ones appeared almost every day."[2] Within a short time, hundreds of these schools appeared in different parts of the country, with millions of cadres receiving new training in labor and ideological rejuvenation. In Kwangtung province some 300 schools were established and took care of more than 100,000 cadres; in Honan province, 20,000 cadres from former provincial Party offices were sent to the new schools; in Kweichow province, 20,000 were dispatched;[3] the municipality of Tientsin established twenty-one May 7 Cadre Schools accommodating more than 11,000 cadres.[4] That the May 7 Cadre School has become a major educational institution of the post-Cultural Revolution era is evidenced by the fact that the itinerary of most visitors to China in recent years includes a visit to one of these schools.

Civil servants, technicians, teachers, trade and commerce personnel, office workers, artists and writers, doctors, nurses, university graduates, and other "intellectuals" are included in the training program. An American visitor reported that "all faculty and administration members, without exception," of the prestigious Tsinghua University underwent training in the May 7 schools. "Most of them spent two years living a peasant life, digging in the fields, planting rice, driving the night-soil carts, studying Marxism-Leninism and The Thought of Chairman Mao."[5] Among the cadres are those in active service sent for training in rotation, "old cadres" who were criticized or lost their jobs during the Cultural Revolution, and others waiting to be rehabilitated or reemployed.

Ministries of the central government, the provincial revolutionary committees, and individual counties as well as cities and autonomous regions have their own May 7 schools for their personnel. More than a hundred have been established by the Central Committee of the Chinese Communist Party and the State Council (see Appendix 18). In line with the philosophy of the reeducation of intellectuals, people working in the cities are believed to have been contaminated by bourgeois and revisionist ideas; it therefore behooves them to be reeducated by poor and lower-middle peasants so that they may be cleansed of their nonproletarian ideology and learn to serve the masses of workers, peasants, and soldiers.

Teachers have been sent for lack of enthusiasm for the educational revolution. Scholars who rely excessively on foreign knowledge, foreign books, and foreign equipment are sent to learn self-reliance and the use of indigenous materials. Writers are said to need the training because their writings do not reflect the needs and interests of the proletarian revolution. Spendthrift officials must learn the frugality of the poor peasants. At the same time, there are cadres and bureaucrats in good standing who accept the rotational training simply because they want to keep close to the masses or to lead other cadres to integrate with workers-peasants-soldiers. Members of revolutionary committees have volunteered or have been urged to enroll. It is reported that Huang Hua, vice-chairman of the first United Nations delegation from the People's Republic of China, and his wife asked to attend a May 7 Cadre School between his diplomatic assignments abroad.[6] As in the reeducation of young intellectuals, it seems to be regular policy to send trustworthy cadres and personnel of unquestionable ideology to live with the others in order to set good examples.

The long-range plan is to give all cadres a turn at a May 7 school; moreover, they should return for retraining every few years. The revolutionary committees of counties (hsien), municipalities, and lower units make sure that personnel of all levels take their turn. Some cadres are assigned to posts after six months; most stay a year or two, while others stay even longer.[7] The May 7 Cadre School is hailed as a "revolutionary furnace" turning out active fighters of the proletarian revolution, and the "May 7 Road" is described as the essential road for all intellectuals and revolutionaries who want to make themselves worthy of service to the proletarian cause. May 7 of each year, the anniversary of Mao's Directive, has been made an occasion for kindling greater enthusiasm for the schools by means of rallies and symposiums dealing with their aims and methods.

As in other forms of reeducation, the central aim is ideological remolding to change the students' outlook and way of thinking.[8] In all the work of the school, whether labor or study or participation in mass work and revolutionary movements, this central aim must be kept in mind. Labor and production are essential but they must not be allowed to interfere with political study, and political study is fruitless unless it transforms thinking and strengthens ideological commitment. Labor must be integrated with study; when there is a conflict in the time allotment for labor and study, the solution must be found in the overriding aim of transforming the students' ideology. "Politics in command" means that labor must be a means of ideological transformation. To say that a good record in labor and production is enough is just as wrong as to neglect labor in order to have more time for study.

It is claimed that the schools of the educational revolution have torn down the walls separating them from the society outside. Actually, many May 7 Cadre Schools are located in areas of poverty and under-development where there are no buildings, much less walls. Necessary buildings are constructed by the students with their own hands and with materials they find locally. Frugality and self-reliance are the watchword; no external assistance is sought, no state subsidy is expected. An American journalist describes a May 7 Cadre School as follows:

> Most women live in simple brick dormitories built with their own hands. . . . Four years ago . . . nothing was here but a sandy swamp, flooded frequently by a nearby river. Now there are rice paddies, acres of tomatoes, and all sorts of other vegetables. All the land was reclaimed by hard labor and with no machines. . . . There are a carpenter shop and a small dye factory . . . with the exception of a small electrical switchboard in the dye factory, all machinery was rebuilt from discarded factory models, they say . . . The youngest in the camp was 19, the oldest 60.[9]

Much of what was said in the preceding chapters about the toughening process of plain living and hard labor is applicable here. The first test of physical endurance is often a long walk on dirt roads to the site of the school, sometimes as far as thirty miles or more.[10] Upon arrival, the trainees are likely to be struck by the sight of barren land devoid of crops and buildings. They set about to clear the wasteland for farming. In mountain areas they dig caves for sleeping quarters and classrooms; where needed, they dig canals for irrigation. Many an urban intellectual learns for the first time to cook, to take care of his own laundry, and not only to use but also to clean the most primitive type of latrines.[11] Labor, study, and "mass work" keep the trainees occupied from dawn to dusk and in the evening, allowing no time to be alone. Thinking and reflecting, if at all, are supposed to be done collectively, in discussion groups and study classes. Life is Spartan. Military training and discipline lead some observers to describe the schools as training camps.[12]

Many of the women are teachers, but there are also women leaders of the Communist Youth League and from industry. They, too, perform hard manual labor. Men and women have separate quarters. They live in tents or huts. There are no single rooms and each "room" has half a dozen or more bunks, built by the trainees; the rooms are usually without doors. The trainees continue to receive their regular monthly salaries, but they get no income from what they produce. They have few belongings with them; there is actually no need beyond the simplest clothes, towels, and a bunk to sleep on. After a day's hard work, a full schedule of study, and participation in "revolutionary criticism" and revolutionary movements, there is little energy left for anything but sleep.

Agriculture and the development of frontier territory are the major pursuits of the labor program. Study is chiefly concerned with ideology and politics but also includes agricultural knowledge and technique. In line with Mao's May 7 Directive, agricultural pursuits include forestry, animal husbandry, side occupations, and fish breeding; the trainees also run small industries to repair machines, manufacture chemical fertilizers and insecticides, make paper and bricks, refine sugar, and so forth. They create a diversified economy, and all work is done on the principles of frugality and self-help. Going to the site of labor often requires a daily walk of many miles over rugged territory, and that is a part of the toughening process and the essential experience of sharing the life of the workers-peasants-soldiers.

The study curriculum consists of the works of Marx, Engels, Lenin, Stalin, and Chairman Mao. The Communist Manifesto, Critique of the Gotha Program, The State and Revolution, "On Practice," "On Contradiction," and Mao's "philosophical essays" are among the works that constitute the treasure house of ideological wisdom. They are to be read and reread, studied and discussed until they become a part of daily thinking. But book knowledge is not enough. The "living study and creative application" of Mao Thought means that the concepts must be applied to present-day problems and issues. On the negative side, the trainees must engage in "criticism-rectification." They must criticize the bourgeoisie and the revisionists. They must attack "swindlers of the Liu Shao-ch'i type" and pinpoint the fallacy of such concepts as "the dying out of the class struggle," "the universal character of human nature," and "manual labor as a form of punishment."* On the positive side, ideological study must be reinforced by revolutionary action, by active participation in the "three great revolutionary movements" in the countryside.

---

*After 1971 criticism was directed against the specific target of the purged Lin Piao. In his report to the Tenth National Congress of the Chinese Communist Party on August 24, 1973, Chou En-lai said: "First of all, we should continue to do a good job of criticizing Lin Piao and rectifying style of work."

Integrating theoretical study with production practice and community service for the benefit of the masses furnishes opportunities for the application of Chairman Mao's teachings. In all thinking and action, the utmost effort must be made to uphold the Mao Tse-tung line in opposition to the bourgeois and revisionist line. An important test of ideological remolding is a growing awareness of the struggle between the two lines and its implications for the trainees in their respective fields of work. The trainees are expected to link ideological study with reality, and to learn to detect ideological issues in the problems of daily work and living.

An article in the People's Daily (January 13, 1973) on the crucial importance of the "line struggle" tells the story of the secretary of a production brigade who took the mistaken view that the Cultural Revolution had solved the issue of the class struggle and so it was now time to concentrate on production. As a result of his ideological slackening, his leadership role was weakened and production in the brigade suffered. Thanks to his retraining in the May 7 Cadre School, he learned to energetically pursue the class struggle and line struggle. The result was said to be a more positive leadership and a consequent boost in production. In other instances, cadres of communes reportedly had neglected diversified subsidiary production and concentrated only on the production of food grain, with the result that there was an unfortunate drop in the production of tobacco and raw silk. Again, their mistakes were reportedly corrected after ideological study in the May 7 Cadre School.

To facilitate integration with workers-peasants-soldiers and to get rid of their bureaucratic work-style and bourgeois life-style, trainees are asked to live with the peasants as well as working and studying with them. Two methods are used: "inviting in" and "sending out." On the one hand, teams of poor and lower-middle peasants are invited to come and live in the school to relate their personal knowledge of the miserable past. On the other hand, trainees are sent out in groups to live among the peasants to become one with the masses. Recently, the method of "sending out" has been expanded as an expression of the policy of running schools on an "open-door" basis. Trainees of the cadre schools are sent by rotation to production teams to live among the peasants for ten-day periods.[13] During these periods they engage in ideological study and learn to love Chairman Mao and his teachings as the peasants do. They also join the peasants in the denunciation of Liu Shao-ch'i and his revisionist gang.

Results

According to official claims, the May 7 Cadre Schools have proved an effective means of remolding intellectuals and ensuring the dedication of cadres. Many are said to have gotten rid of their revisionist ideas and bourgeois habits. They are reported to gain a new respect for labor and for workers-peasants-soldiers; to acquire a clearer understanding of the line struggle and a greater determination to combat such ideas as "technique first"; and to appreciate more than ever the vital importance of correct ideology—Mao Thought—as a guide to all action and policy-making.

After its first year, the Liuho May 7 Cadre School in Heilungkiang, the first in the country, graduated 330 cadres, who took up leading positions in the revolutionary committees of various levels and in the Mao Tse-tung Thought Propaganda Teams.[14] Within a period of eight months another cadre school trained some 3,000 barefoot doctors who "acquired the basic technique of the new acupuncture therapy and are able to use it in the treatment of many common and recurrent diseases" among the peasants.[15] Many intellectuals have joined the Communist Party or the Communist Youth League after training in the May 7 Cadre Schools.

Statistics on economic gains are impressive. For example, 48 schools on the outskirts of Shanghai reportedly produced within a two-year period "7.14 million catties* of grain, 0.23 million catties of oil-bearing crops, more than 9.1 million catties of unginned cotton, and 8.13 million catties of vegetables." They had become "basically self-sufficient in grain, edible oil, and meat" and vegetables.[15] A school in Kiangsi province reported that it reclaimed 1,200 mou of land for farming and reaped 178,000 catties of grain and 7,700 catties of edible oil, as well as building 138 dormitory rooms, kitchens, warehouses, 65 pigsties and cattlepens, and a "15-li-long highway."[16] Many other similar examples have been reported.

The official view attributes such outstanding results to the intensive ideological and political education that motivates the cadres to maintain a firm grasp on the class struggle and the line struggle and to take part in the struggle-criticism-transformation movement in the villages and factories. But encouraging as the production gains are, the most important work of the May 7 Cadre Schools is to turn out men and women with a transformed outlook and ideological rejuvenation (see Appendix 18 for examples of ideological transformation in the cadre schools). Some who returned to the cities and were found not firm enough in ideological commitment have been sent either to the May 7 Cadre Schools for another period of training or to the rural communes for long-term settlement and reeducation.

---

*A cattie is equal to 1.1 lbs. or 500 grams.

Problems

Current Communist literature on the May 7 Cadre Schools has mentioned other problems besides persons found to have been insufficiently remolded. Some are said to have resisted enlisting and needed persuasion to accept the high road of integration with workers-peasants-soldiers designated by Chairman Mao. There are indications of some discontent among trainees in the schools, but there is no way of determining its extent. Some are dissatisfied with living conditions; others are unable to keep up the strenuous labor and have become sick; still others are unhappy for fear of forgetting the technical knowledge they acquired before coming to the May 7 schools. The existence of discontent is evidenced by frequent references in official reports to "class enemies" who stir up trouble in the May 7 Cadre Schools. The enemies, it is alleged, sabotage production and "viciously attack the schools."[17]

Class enemies are also blamed for spreading many concepts that interfere with the successful operations of the schools. Among concepts that have been made specific targets of "revolutionary mass criticism" in the schools, the following may be mentioned:

● Attending the cadre schools is a necessary stepping-stone to a better and more secure position.

● To attend the May 7 schools is to acquire a "veneer of gold" or a gilding that does not change the intrinsic substance.

● To be sent to a May 7 school is a form of punishment.

● To relate theory to practice, students can go to the factories attached to city schools; it is unnecessary to go to the countryside.

● There are workers in city factories from whom urban intellectuals can learn; learning agriculture has no value for cadres working in the cities.

● It is enough to excel in labor and production; ideological study is not essential.

● Those who have had labor experience and undergone ideological remolding do not need any further tempering.

The fact that so much effort has been made to prove the fallacy of these concepts makes one think that they do frequently appear in the thinking and attitudes of the trainees.[18]

Other "May 7" Approaches

Besides the May 7 Cadre School, a variety of other institutions and practices owe their inspiration to the May 7 Directive. There are May 7 experimental classes, May 7 farms, May 7 communes, May 7 production teams, May 7 factories, May 7 middle schools, May 7 universities, and so on.

Agricultural middle schools and other middle schools have modified their programs to incorporate the ideas contained in the May 7 Directive. Some call themselves May 7 Middle Schools, offering one-year courses (sometimes shorter or longer) in agriculture, trade, medical service, veterinary problems, and so on.[19] The All-China Federation of Trade Unions has established a May 7 School for the study of agriculture and Mao Thought. A middle school in Kirin was converted into a May 7 Middle School by adopting a program requiring students to "learn other things" (that is, agriculture, industrial work, and culture) and combining classroom education with "on-the-job training in the three great revolutionary movements."[20] The school also "set up small farms and small iron works" to facilitate the integration of theory and practice.

A May 7 Agricultural Middle School in Honan province was established to train indigenous experts in agriculture. Applicants for admission are selected by the poor and lower-middle peasants; 82 percent of those selected were sons and daughters of poor and lower-middle peasants of good political, ideological, and work record.[21]

"May 7 universities" have also appeared on the scene. In Anhwei province, 40 May 7 universities were born in 1970-71.[22] They reportedly were the scene of "a fierce struggle between the two classes, two roads, and two lines." Other universities have set up May 7 agricultural courses, May 7 animal husbandry courses, May 7 experimental classes, and so forth. There are also "May 7 political night schools" to popularize Mao Thought and push forward the revolutionary movements. Many of them do not have any special characteristics; they have adopted the new name "May 7" in order to join the nationwide campaign to respond to the Chairman's call.

Reform of Intellectuals

The situation within China and the respective roles of the Communists and the intellectuals have undergone modification since the early years, but the essential nature of Communist policy toward intellectuals has not changed. The ambivalent attitude of welcoming the intellectuals but at the same time distrusting them still remains. The current policy of "uniting with, educating, and remolding" the intellectuals is little different from the earlier policy to "absorb and reform," although the vocabulary has been modified and new methods of reform have been adopted.

Pressure on the intellectuals on a nationwide scale began with the Communist assumption of power in 1949. A nationwide "study" program (hsüeh-hsi) involved the entire population, and intellectuals in particular were enlisted in the study of the new ideology and politics.

With the acceleration of the agrarian reform, intellectuals were sent to the rural areas to observe and participate in the class struggle against landlords and village gentry who had oppressed and exploited the peasants. Well-known scholars were asked to testify how their experience in the agrarian reform had aroused their class consciousness and exposed the error of their former "supra-class mentality."23 More pressing demands on intellectuals to remold their thinking came with the "resist-America aid-Korea" movement of 1950-51, which set out to eliminate American influence on Chinese education and the mentality of U.S.-educated Chinese scholars. Individual intellectuals were subjected to criticism and to self-criticism in which they confessed their failings due either to their bourgeois class origin or the "bourgeois idealism" they had assimilated in their education: individualism, liberalism, neglect of politics, lack of class consciousness, aloofness from the class struggle, preoccupation with personal success and fame, infatuation with the bourgeois concept of freedom.

A shift in the policy seemed to be in the offing by the mid-1950s. The intellectuals had made confessions and seemed to have accepted the need for ideological conversion. But many of them assumed a negative attitude of silence and passivity. Most of them, said Chou En-lai in 1956, belonged to an "intermediate section who support the Communist Party and the People's Government and generally complete the tasks assigned to them, but are not sufficiently active politically."24 In other words, they were "generally" passive, willing to do what they were asked to do, in order to stay out of trouble, but no more. This was not good for "the upsurge of the socialist tide," which brought with it an urgent need for more intellectuals to take up actively and energetically the many tasks of "socialist construction." A new look at the "question of intellectuals" was in order.

A period of relatively liberal and moderate treatment of the intellectuals was thus ushered in. Ameliorative measures were adopted to ease their physical and psychological stress in an attempt to win them over. Among these measures were an improvement in living and working conditions, better housing, higher salaries, access to professional literature from foreign countries, and improved library and research facilities. A number of well-known intellectuals were even admitted into the Chinese Communist Party. This policy of relaxation culminated in the "100 Flowers" episode of 1956-57.

The "wilting of the Flowers" is now a well-known story. The anti-Rightist campaign and the rectification campaign that ensued signified a pendulum swing from "absorption" to "reform" and certainly did not enhance the confidence of the intellectuals. Then followed new forms of pressure: more self-criticism and self-denunciation in "heart surrender" meetings and forums at which the intellectuals pledged to surrender their "whole heart" to the Communist

Party and the socialist revolution. University professors were censured for seeking extra remuneration and spending too much time on research and writing with the purpose of achieving personal fame. Scholars who immersed themselves in the study of antiquity in order to avoid the delicate task of dealing with contemporary issues were denounced for having removed themselves from reality. "Academic criticism" was another medium through which intellectuals were brought to see the harmful effects of divorce from labor, aloofness from the working class, pursuit of knowledge unrelated to the practical problems of the present, and uncritical acceptance of the ideology of the reactionary class from which they came.

The "question of the intellectuals" came to the fore again with the advent of the Cultural Revolution. The first phase of the Cultural Revolution was an assault on literary writers, artists, and intellectuals engaged in education and propaganda work who had continued to serve as purveyors of bourgeois and revisionist thought and who, under the guise of following Mao Tse-tung, were actually perpetuating an anti-Mao and antiproletarian ideology. University presidents and professors, editors, novelists, and philosophers were singled out one by one for attack by official newspaper organs as well as by the Red Guards. Many were divested of their positions and relegated to obscurity.

The Chinese term for intellectuals, chih-shih fen-tzu, literally means "knowledgeable elements" or "people of knowledge." Chou En-lai made a distinction between "higher intellectuals" and "ordinary intellectuals" and said the former are "engaged in scientific research, education, engineering and technology, public health, cultural work, the arts and other occupations."[25] He estimated in 1956 that there were "roughly 100,000 higher intellectuals," with the number still growing. One-third of them, according to Chou, were "recruited since the liberation." The term "intellectuals" also applies to young graduates of colleges and universities. All together the two groups of intellectuals made a total of 3,840,000. Mao Tse-tung may have included the students in the general category of intellectuals (or intelligentsia) when he spoke of a total of 5 million.[26] Additionally, persons holding leading positions in industry and commerce are included in the general category of intellectuals.

The intellectuals not only constitute a reservoir of talents greatly needed in "socialist construction" but, by virtue of their traditional prestige in Chinese society and the respect that the masses usually accord to them, they hold vast potential for effective leadership. As Chou En-lai said in 1956, "To mobilize our intellectuals to the fullest possible extent and bring into full play their existing strength is imperative for China's rapid construction at present."[27] But even in that period of goodwill toward intellectuals, in the same speech, he lamented the fact that many intellectuals "are dissatisfied with the policies and measures of the Party and the People's Government and hanker after capitalism or even feudalism. . . . They have enormous conceit, thinking themselves Number One in the world, and refusing to accept anyone's leadership and criticism." In his speech on "Contradictions Among the People," Mao made a similar assessment when he said that remolding is fundamental but "most of our intellectuals can not be said to have accomplished it."[28]

Those remarks were made after half a dozen years of intensive effort to reform and remold the intellectuals. Since that time, the intellectuals have lived through successive remolding campaigns all the way down to the Cultural Revolution. Mao's call in 1966 to put an end to the dominant influence of the intellectuals was reinforced by his decision to institute proletarian leadership in the schools and universities and to send intellectuals to the countryside for integration with workers-peasants-soldiers. These developments indicate that in his judgment the intellectuals have not yet been sufficiently reformed and so, while remolding must continue, their influence must be curtailed. This view governs the policy of the educational revolution toward intellectuals. It is important to make "wise use" of the talents of the intellectuals, but it is necessary to be aware of their limitations. A report about Yunnan University stated that most of the teachers, even the younger ones, are indifferent to politics and the majority "still retain a bourgeois class outlook."[29] Essentially the same view was expressed by an editorial of the New Anhwei Daily:

> Except for a few who hold a relatively firm proletarian view and a very small number of counterrevolutionary elements, the overwhelming majority of the present intellectuals are in an intermediate status. They often tend to be impractical in their thinking and irresolute in action. Unless we strengthen the work of educating them, they are likely to be victims of revisionism. . . . At the same time, we shall also understand that the class enemies are always competing with us in capturing the intellectuals. Taking advantage of the intellectuals, they desperately try to poison them.[30]

The alleged shortcomings that remain as targets of necessary reform may be briefly summarized: The intellectuals are not enthusiastic about the class struggle and believe that it will fade in importance. They prefer to mind their professional business and stay out of politics. In teaching, they value knowledge for its own sake and theory not directly related to practice. They scorn labor and the laboring masses. They are addicted to the bourgeois way of life. They love physical comfort and shun hardships. They are the products of elitist education and subscribe to the philosophy of elitist education. Their major shortcomings are a "three-fold alienation" from politics, from the masses, and from reality.

The intellectuals are believed to be motivated by selfish individualism, to spurn collective effort and the collective good. They are said to hold ambitions of personal success and fame, and to impart such ambitions to their students and thus reinforce the old feudal motive of studying to become high officials, or to win recognition as an expert. They reportedly shut themselves in the library or laboratory to pursue knowledge that makes no direct contribution to either the political struggle or economic construction. They may study Marxism, but they have no firm convictions and vacillate between the proletarian and the bourgeois ideology. It is recognized that not all intellectuals are guilty of such failings, but the "majority" cannot yet be trusted to serve as leaders in the proletarian revolution; some have even served as agents of the bourgeoisie and the revisionists and secretly plotted to sabotage the revolution.

Self-criticism and confession of mistakes are still used as methods of remolding. A new facet of the remolding program is the role of workers-peasants-soldiers as agents of reforms to lead the intellectuals (under the leadership of the Party) in ideological study and to teach them the virtues of labor, hard work, unequivocal acceptance of the proletarian ideology, and single-minded devotion to Chairman Mao and the Communist Party. For example, a geological surveyor testified that he once "shut himself in a small room to pore over books and study data" in the hope of making innovations in drafting that would bring him fame and advancement, but he achieved nothing until he went to work among the workers and learned from their practical experience. With the help of the workers, he said he developed a new technique of making drawings on polyester film that could withstand acid, soda, and weather changes.[31] A professor devoted himself to research on an uncommon lung disease in the hope of achieving fame until ideological remolding turned him to research on schistosomiasis in order to serve the people more directly.

In another case, a well-known writer whose novels revolved around the theme of motherhood, depicting its beauty and lasting value, underwent reeducation in a cadre school. After more than a year of labor experience she affirmed that her outlook had been transformed and she was brought to realize that class love is greater than mother love.[32] A professor of history had written a treatise on the Opium War. He, too, came to see his errors after reeducation by workers-peasants-soldiers. Under the leadership of the Party organizations, the poor and lower-middle peasants held meetings for "mass criticism" of his writing. His idealistic viewpoint was exposed and found to have permeated his entire treatise. Writing about the anti-British struggle in the area which was now the scene of his reeducation, he had mistakenly given credit to heroes rather than the masses. He exaggerated the role of Lin Tse-hsu and put too much emphasis on a rainstorm that helped to defeat the British. His failure to give due credit to the valiant struggle of the peasants was found to have originated in an ideological viewpoint which refused to recognize that ordinary peasants could be a positive force in the struggle against imperialism. Only after reeducation and the ideological remolding that went with it did he wake up to the fact that the masses were the main force in the anti-British struggle.

An interview with a 66-year-old professor of engineering at Tsinghua University recalls the confessions of an earlier period. He said:

> I studied in the United States and Germany from 1926 to
> 1931 before I came to teach in this university. I studied
> only to become famous and I became a bourgeois spiritual
> aristocrat. I regarded knowledge as my personal wealth.
> When I later taught, I inculcated my students with the
> same ideas.

He also said that as a result of his ideological transformation he came to appreciate the wisdom of Chairman Mao's stand that the domination of schools and universities by bourgeois intellectuals should not be tolerated any longer. He reported that labor experience and learning from the workers in a petrochemical factory enabled him to comprehend the full meaning of the Chairman's statement that "the lowly are the most intelligent, the elite the most ignorant."[33] Many other similar cases have been reported.

So goes another round of the "absorb and reform" or "unite, educate, and remold" campaign. How does it differ from the preceding rounds? Basically, the same issues are involved. "The question of intellectuals," Mao once said, "is above all one of ideology." Needless to say, the transformation of ideology is far more difficult for the intellectuals than for workers-peasants-soldiers. They have a more cumbersome "ideological baggage" to get rid of, and they have too many questions and doubts in their mind. It is not easy for them to read and reread the "Three Great Treatises" and find fresh inspiration in them every time. It is not so simple for them to accept the leadership and ideological tutelage of workers-peasants-soldiers whose understanding of Marxism-Leninism-Maoism is so simple and uncomplicated. It is easier for them to conform in action than in ideology, to change habits of living rather than to transform their mode of thinking. But it is precisely the transformation of outlook and ideology that they are expected to achieve. From the Communist point of view, the only sure guarantee of loyalty is a firm ideological commitment and wholehearted acceptance of the Marxist-Leninist-Maoist ideology. Moreover, the most dangerous threat to the revolution comes from the antiproletarian ideology of the bourgeoisie and the revisionists, and more than any other sector of the population the intellectuals are likely to be the carriers and breeders of bourgeois and revisionist ideology, unless they are thoroughly remolded.

Will this latest round in the reform of intellectuals be more successful than previous efforts, in terms of their acceptability to the authorities as well as their firmness of conviction? This is not the first time that the intellectuals have acknowledged their inadequacies and pledged to remedy them. No doubt many of them are sincere in their pledges and will honestly endeavor to "serve the people" and the revolution. However, there may still be some who belong to the lukewarm "intermediate section" and will in time slide back to passivity or political indifference until the pressure mounts again. For them, more ideological remolding is in store.

For all intellectuals, constant vigilance is necessary. Mao has said on many occasions that ideological remolding is not to be accomplished once and for all. The ideological struggle, like the class struggle, never ends; new situations develop, new contradictions arise, and the conflict between the "two lines" assumes different forms. Loyalty is constantly put to the test in new manifestations of ideological struggle. Take, for example, the dichotomy of "Red and expert" or "politics and vocational competency." Theoretically both are needed and one should not exclude the other. But the practical question of relative emphasis is not a simple one. The official line veers from one to the other and it takes acumen and dexterity to always be on the correct line.

It has been pointed out that to overestimate or underestimate the importance of technique in relation to politics are both manifestations of anti-Maoist thinking.[34] According to a "writing group" in the Soochow area, the revisionists and "swindlers of Liu Shao-ch'i type" often swing from the rightist to the leftist position, from neglect of politics to neglect of vocational work, all the time trying insidiously to sabotage the educational revolution. When compiling teaching materials for language classes, they pay attention only to political content and disregard the style of writing, thus defeating the purpose of language study. In mathematics, even the most practical problems are loaded with an excess of unsuitable political terms. This is obviously wrong, but in the same article one reads: "In the selection of teaching materials, we must put the political criterion first."[35] What, then, is the correct line?

For more than two decades, the position and status of China's intellectuals has been under assault. They have been subject to pressure, denunciation, and humiliation. They have also been per-suaded, cajoled, and given a chance to transform themselves into new men. From "heart surrender" to reeducation by workers-peasants-soldiers, each campaign is a further step in downgrading the tradi-tionally exalted intellectuals. Although they also occupied leading positions in such areas as government, industry, commerce, scientific research, and technical advance, their stronghold lay in the schools and universities. Now they have been pushed off the academic pedestal; even in the classroom they must defer to the representatives of prole-tarian leadership. Some must feel discouraged, but the more intrepid and resourceful are challenged to discover new opportunities for serv-ice and new ways of giving expression to their talents and their basic loyalty to the nation and its people.

There must be many intellectuals who have undergone genuine transformation or ideological conversion. In their student days and subsequent life, most intellectuals have been stirred by idealistic dreams of serving the common people. If they can lay aside their doubts and skepticism in regard to Marxist dogmas they did not readily accept at first, they can still build a new life in response to the chal-lenge of serving the people under the leadership of the Communist Party. Some may even find it possible to accept the new ideology with-out serious reservations, making personal interpretations to satisfy their inner selves. Regardless of the degree of acceptance, those who succeed in making peace with the new order probably can find happiness in hard work in the service of a rising nation. At the same time, there probably exists no small number of intellectuals who feel disheartened and frustrated.

What the future holds for the intellectuals will depend (1) on the degree to which they genuinely support the new order and have trans-formed themselves sufficiently to satisfy the ideological remolders and (2) on the stability of official policy or the pendulum swings and vacillations inherent in the policy. The two are interrelated.

There are currently some indications of greater emphasis on the "bold use" of intellectuals, that is, on "absorb" and "unite." But politics is still in command and official statements warn that a proper balance must be maintained. At what precise point the balance should be kept varies with the changing needs of the situation and the official assessment of the threat posed by dissent or deviation. Greater em-phasis on "use" and expertness or vocational competence entails a more lenient and tolerant policy toward the intellectuals, but it is dif-ficult to predict whether or when the pendulum will again swing to more emphasis on remolding.

Transformation of Teachers

Mao Tse-tung has said repeatedly that the educational revolution cannot succeed without a transformation of the teaching personnel. The Draft Program for Schools devotes a section to the problem of teachers (see Appendix 16). It begins with the statement that "in the problem of transforming education it is the teachers who are the main problem." It points out that the problem of teachers is actually a part of the problem of intellectuals and its solution lies in "Chairman Mao's policy of uniting with, educating, and remolding intellectuals." New teachers must be fully in accord with the spirit and objectives of the educational revolution. In the meantime, it is necessary to make "bold and wise use" of the "old" teachers, at the same time educating and remolding them. In the selection of teachers, the guiding criteria are ideology-politics and the ability to relate teaching to the practical problems of production.

The use of workers, peasants, and soldiers in classroom teaching is a part of the proletarian leadership they are supposed to exercise. They may be weak in the knowledge of school subjects, but they are ideological-political stalwarts who have had experience in the class struggle and in production. They are especially effective in class education and line education and in lectures on the history of villages, families, and so forth. They serve as part-time teachers and in teams moving from one school to another to give lectures. For example, in one county in Honan province, 2,209 poor and lower-middle peasants form 328 teaching teams, each consisting of five to ten persons. Besides lecturing in classrooms, they help compile teaching materials. Their weapon is the "invincible thought of Chairman Mao." An old peasant lecturing in an arithmetic class used the title "A Debt of Blood and Tears" and taught the students to calculate the amount of interest paid to a landlord over a period of years at a usurious rate of interest. He succeeded in stirring up class hatred and the room resounded with shouts of denunciation and "class bitterness." He thus turned an arithmetic lesson into a vivid lesson in class education.[36]

From the standpoint of the everyday job of teaching the various subjects of the curriculum, the role of the original teachers is still indispensable. The program of the Communist Party for the reopened middle schools stipulated that "the ranks of teachers must be reorganized and purified seriously," and the Draft Program also states that while it is important for the schools "to build up their ranks of proletarian teachers," they must also "conscientiously purify and strengthen the ranks of teachers." So while those who are politically unacceptable are eliminated, the majority of the "old" teachers must be remolded or reeducated to be of service. The methods of remolding are essentially those described in previous chapters: ideological-political study, active participation in revolutionary movements, labor and production, integration with workers-peasants-soldiers, recalling the "bitter past." Special attention is given to ideological fallacies common to teachers: teaching without application to practice or reference to ideology and politics; believing that teaching offers no future and only results in frustration and humiliation; sharing the false pride of intellectuals who deem themselves superior to the laboring classes; arousing in students the revisionist ambition of attaining personal fame and success; putting intellectual development first; emphasizing examinations and grades; regarding teaching as an independent or autonomous profession. The "teacher as center" concept is singled out for criticism. In a word, the old teachers must be led to discard all vestiges of bourgeois and revisionist ideology and to identify themselves with the proletarian cause under the leadership of Chairman Mao and the Chinese Communist Party.

Few worker-peasant-soldier teachers have had enough schooling to teach the regular subjects. Most are part-time teachers who teach lessons in class education and lead the "old" teachers in ideological study and in constantly heeding the directives and instructions of Chairman Mao. New "proletarian teachers" are being produced but training takes time, especially since many of them must start with rudimentary basic education. In the meantime, the bulk of teaching must be done by the "old" teachers. In fact, after implementing the policy of "purifying the ranks of teachers" cadres are now told that they must try to bring the old teachers into an active role and make use of their professional skills.

The People's Daily (July 9, 1972) published an interesting article calling for a return of teachers who had been assigned to other posts or to participation in the struggle-criticism-transformation campaign "on various fronts." It indirectly sheds light on the practice of taking teachers out of the schools in the process of "purification of ranks" and assigning them to other posts that help them in remolding themselves and also utilize their knowledge and skills. It also reflects the shortage of teachers in schools and the realization that the workers-peasants-soldiers and the new proletarian teachers are not yet able to carry on the educational program.

The Party Committee of a middle school in Liaoning province reported that an old teacher who had acquired a good ideology and understanding of the Thought of Mao Tse-tung was put in charge of a mathematics teaching demonstration class in the district, but some young teachers were skeptical and raised the specter of "walking the old road" (that is, restoration of the old order). So the authorities organized all teachers to study and apply the "one-dividing-into-two" method in order to understand the importance of utilizing the successful experience of the old teachers. The old teachers, it is said, can even help raise the level of teacher training.[37]

While the current emphasis on a positive role for old teachers indicates a more favorable attitude toward intellectuals, the ambivalent policy of "absorb and reform" remains in force. It is wrong not to provide for the active use of the old teachers, wrong to refuse to listen to their voice of experience. At the same time, it is necessary to bear in mind that they are the products of bourgeois society and bourgeois education, and their remolding requires close supervision and guidance. They are not proletarian teachers. To fail to make this distinction is to lose sight of the demarcation between classes and to neglect the grim struggle between the two lines. Therefore, the need to use the old teachers must not be allowed to divert attention from the equally important task of reform and remolding.[38]

Teacher Training

Teachers are trained in normal colleges or while they are in service. In all cases, ideological-political training is of paramount importance. Even when those being trained are deficient in the knowledge of subject matter on account of insufficient schooling, the major portion of training still consists of ideological-political study and activities. It is argued that in "culture study," which means academic subjects, ideological-political motivation is of supreme importance so that the students will always be aware of why they are studying and what they are preparing to do. They must be taught to view teaching as a means of serving the revolutionary cause. They must vigorously attack such revisionist concepts as knowledge for its own sake and professional knowledge divorced from politics.

The Hopei Normal University graduated its first class of worker-peasant-soldier students in 1973, after the completion of a two-year course preparing them for teaching in middle school.[39] The majority of the 1,044 students were from poor and lower-middle peasant families, and 92 percent were members of the Communist Party or the Youth League. The university offers courses in mathematics, Chinese language, political education, history and geography, foreign languages, physics, chemistry, fundamentals of agriculture, military-physical culture, and literature and art. The study of these subjects is closely integrated with political study. It is claimed that training in the normal university has effectively enhanced awareness of the class struggle and the line struggle.

In view of the shortage of teachers, in-service training plays a major role. Spare-time classes and short-term institutes and symposiums are widely used. All training is under the supervision and leadership of the Party authorities. Members of the local Party branch regularly inspect the schools and visit classes, paying special attention to ideological-political study for teachers. A report by the Party branch of a middle school in Anhwei province mentions the following methods of teacher training: study of the educational thought of Mao Tse-tung; tempering by manual labor; listening to old workers and poor peasants who "recall the bitter past and dwell on the present happiness"; deep involvement in the three great revolutionary struggles; and advancement of professional knowledge for the purpose of serving the revolution.

Another form of in-service training is provided by "mobile groups" moving from one school to another. Some mobile groups are organized by the normal colleges; others may consist of old teachers of high political consciousness and ideological conviction. The mobile groups pay special attention to the ideological-political upgrading of the teachers; they organize classes for ideological-political study and promote the integration of teaching with the three great revolutionary movements in the countryside. In other words, they "put Mao Tse-tung Thought in command of teaching."[40]

The preponderant emphasis on ideological-political training is understandable because many of the problems of teaching, in the Communist view, are ideological-political in nature. For example, experienced teachers who look down upon worker-peasant-soldier teachers are really unwilling to accept proletarian leadership in education; moreover, putting a premium on scholarship and academic knowledge, they fail to appreciate the commanding role of ideology and politics. Those who are discouraged and hesitate to take initiative may be holding the mistaken view that since intellectuals are not allowed to play a dominant role, there is no future for the "old" teachers and the simplest way to stay out of trouble is to sit back and wait to be told what to do. Even new teachers are influenced by this view, and there is a spate of articles in journals and newspapers refuting the notion that there is no future for teachers.[41] The refutation is always made in ideological terms, basing all arguments on quotations from Chairman Mao.

Problems

Teachers are confronted with vexing problems. Textbooks and other teaching materials are not easy to get. Guidelines are not specific and it is easy to commit the error of misinterpreting them. The new teachers who have had only a minimum of schooling lack confidence because they are unsure of the subject matter they teach. Old teachers, on the other hand, are uneasy because their ideological-political stand is under critical scrutiny. They fear not only the reprimand of authorities but also the censure of students and workers-peasants-soldiers. In the criticism-rectification campaign in schools, students have taken their teachers to task for neglecting politics, for adhering to the outmoded practice of placing teachers in the central position, for failing to consult students in teaching content and methods, and other offenses that may easily lead to official censure by the authorities.

Teaching morale is low. The traditional respect and prestige accorded to Chinese teachers are now absent. Salaries are unattractive.[42] It is not easy to teach students who are inadequately prepared and vary widely in academic knowledge and ability. Teachers are afraid to assert their authority for fear of being accused of the revisionist practice of teacher domination. They hesitate to demand too much from students in the learning of subject matter because they do not want to expose themselves to the charge of stressing useless book knowledge. Discipline is virtually impossible when students have the right to attack teachers for anti-proletarian ideas and practices.

These are not imaginary difficulties. The Party branch of a middle school in Liaoning province stressed the need for positive leadership to help teachers solve their problems.[43] According to a report, some of the old teachers "did not dare hold classes" for fear of being considered old-fashioned, while some of the young teachers also avoided too much emphasis on knowledge for fear of committing the error of "professionalism" divorced from politics. The dilemma that confronts some teachers is described in an article by the Party branch of a middle school in Inner Mongolia. A language teacher selected two essays written by students for class discussion and evaluation. One had good content and was written in a clear style. The other had no clear central theme but contained many political slogans, only vaguely discussed. Comparing the two, the teacher was inclined to favor the first, but when some students said that the second essay had a "clear political viewpoint" the teacher quickly changed his evaluation. Fearful of being accused of neglecting politics, he concluded that each essay had its merits.[44]

To rectify the thinking of teachers and to boost their low morale, teacher training has stressed the proper understanding of the two lines and Chairman Mao's policy of uniting with the intellectuals, while at the same time educating and remolding them. It behooves teachers to maintain the current balance between Redness and expertness, between theoretical knowledge and its practical use, between professional competence and ideological-political activism. Politics must be in command, of course, and Mao Thought must guide all effort. But this should not exclude vocational study. As a matter of fact, vocational study is important and necessary, as long as it is guided by Mao Thought. For example, the Party branch of a middle school sent an Educational Revolution Investigation Team to factories and countryside to find out how its graduates were getting along in the rustication program. The team received reports from workers and peasants to the effect that the students were high in political consciousness and good in labor but weak in scientific knowledge.[45] This is the result of an educational program that relegates academic study to a secondary position, the outgrowth of a situation in which teachers are afraid to commit the error of "putting intellectual achievement first" and students are plagued by the idea that "study is useless." Both teachers and students have expressed a preference to go to the farms and factories, because after all labor and production are what really counts. Teachers may feel there are fewer ideological hazards and more security in labor and production than in teaching.

Teacher training and remolding now stress that technique and knowledge are needed. What is important is that they must be taught and acquired with Mao Thought as guide; the relationship between politics and vocational work is that of the commander and the commanded.* It would be wrong, of course, to put vocational work in command, as was done in bourgeois and revisionist education. Study and vocational preparation have their rightful place, but ideological transformation still remains the ultimate aim of all school work.[46] Is the distinction difficult to make? Is the ambivalence confusing? Does it present an unsolvable dilemma? The solution, according to the official line, lies in the Maoist doctrine of the unity of opposites.

Notes

1. Peking Review, October 11, 1968, p. 2.
2. The " 'May 7' Cadre School," Peking Review, May 12, 1972.
3. China News Analysis, March 21, 1969, p. 3.
4. Current Background, no. 899 (January 19, 1970), p. 4. This issue contains ten articles from the People's Daily on the operation of May 7 Cadre Schools.
5. Harrison E. Salisbury, To Peking—And Beyond (New York: Quadrangle, 1973), p. 36.
6. Seymour Topping, Journey Between Two Chinas (New York: Harper and Row, 1972), p. 407.
7. Salisbury, op. cit., p. 66.
8. "All for the Transformation of the Students' Thinking," Jen-min Jih-pao, April 30, 1972.

---

*Vocational work and cultural study are terms used to refer to school subjects other than ideological-political study and military-physical training; in other words, academic study.

9. Report by Wes Gallagher, president of the Associated Press, in Los Angeles Times, August 14, 1972.

10. Report on a Kirin school, Foreign Broadcast Information Service, Daily Report, Communist China, May 14, 1971, p. G1. (Hereafter cited as FBIS.)

11. Klaus Mehnert, China Returns (New York: E. P. Dutton, 1972), p. 68.

12. Gallagher, op. cit.

13. Jen-min Jih-pao, March 2, 1973.

14. Jen-min Jih-pao, August 18, 1969.

15. FBIS, July 7, 1971, p. B9.

16. FBIS, May 17, 1971, p. C7.

17. FBIS, October 14, 1969, p. H4.

18. See Current Background, no. 899 (January 19, 1970), esp. pp. 3, 6, 31-32.

19. FBIS, September 4, 1970, pp. D2-4.

20. FBIS, December 3, 1970, pp. G2-3.

21. FBIS, May 10, 1971, pp. C1-2; Kuang-ming Jih-pao, November 18, 1971.

22. Jen-min Jih-pao, April 21, 1969.

23. Theodore H. E. Chen, Thought Reform of the Chinese Intellectuals, (Hong Kong: University of Hong Kong Press, 1960), Chapter IV.

24. Chou En-lai, Report on the Question of Intellectuals (Peking: Foreign Language Press, 1956), p. 10.

25. Ibid., p. 11.

26. "Chronology of 17 Years of the Two-Line Struggle on the Educational Front," Chinese Education, Spring 1968, p. 24.

27. Chou, op. cit., p. 16.

28. Mao's speech was made on February 27, 1957. The official English translation appears in Peking Review, June 23, 1967.

29. China News Analysis, no. 906 (January 12, 1973), p. 6.

30. FBIS, March 14, 1969, p. C2.

31. FBIS, July 1, 1970, p. F1.

32. Kuang-ming Jih-pao, December 1, 1972.

33. FBIS, September 27, 1971, p. B2.

34. Jen-min Jih-pao, April 8, 1972.

35. Jen-min Jih-pao, April 29, 1972.

36. Kuang-ming Jih-pao, January 11, 1969.

37. Jen-min Jih-pao, November 13, 1972.

38. See article on the use of old teachers, in Jen-min-Jih-pao August 16, 1972.

39. Report in Kuang-ming Jih-pao, January 29, 1973.

40. Report on mobile teaching groups in Kwangtung province, FBIS, July 2, 1971, pp. D2-4.

41. See, for example, article in Hung-ch'i (Red flag), April 1, 1970.

42. A. Doak Barnett reported after visiting China in 1973 that a primary school teacher was paid 40 yuan a month, a middle school teacher 50 yuan, a college professor 75 to 300 yuan, while industrial workers were getting 30 to 100 yuan a month. A. Doak Barnett, "There Are Warts There, Too," New York Times Magazine, April 8, 1973.

43. Kuang-ming Jih-pao, November 8, 1972.

44. Jen-min Jih-pao, October 15, 1972.

45. Report on Sha Ch'eng Middle School, Jen-min Jih-pao, October 29, 1972.

46. Jen-min Jih-pao, October 27, 1972.

The radical changes brought about by the Maoist educational revolution are especially striking in higher education. They go far beyond the organization and reorganization of institutions, courses of study, and methods of teaching. The new enrollment policy, the content of advanced study, and the personnel of the teaching staff reflect a concept of higher education vastly different from what the term means in other countries.

Reform Under the Revisionists

Educational reform after 1949 gave much attention to higher education. Institutions of higher learning were merged or consolidated, and the immediate result was a reduction in number. The Soviet model guided the reorganization of departments and areas of specialization; Soviet scholarship and theories were embraced; the "pedagogical seminar" and the "five-point grading system" were among the new methods; and the curtailment of liberal arts courses and colleges was accompanied by the expansion in science and technology. The "comprehensive university" that replaced the nonscience colleges and universities was another product imported from the USSR.

In 1958 an effort was made to bring higher education into the service of the Great Leap Forward and the commune movement. Mao Tse-tung ordered that "Schools should run factories and factories should run schools" (see Appendix 29).[1] An ambitious proposal was made to popularize higher education and make it available to the masses. The revolt against elitist education had begun. Higher education was to be made universal in 15 years. Needless to say, this was not the form of higher education accepted as the norm in capitalist countries. The new forms included the "spare-time universities" and the "Red-and-expert universities," which sprang up within weeks and months and opened their doors to workers and peasants.[2] Thousands of these "universities" hurriedly opened their doors and reportedly enrolled millions of students. There was no time to plan for equipment or libraries. Students attended either in their "spare time" or on a work-study basis. In view of the rapid quantitative expansion of education and the emergence of a program radically different from the conventional patterns, some Communist writers have marked 1958 as the year when the educational revolution was born.

The sudden appearance of ill-equipped "colleges" and "universities" and the influx of students ill-prepared for higher learning must have greatly disturbed the scholars and professional educators on the university faculties. In the midst of the general readjustment of policies after the failure of the Great Leap Forward, the educators launched a program of consolidation designed to restrain the excesses of hasty expansion. According to the Maoists, the revisionists now took control of the country and the educational revolution was foiled by bourgeois scholars who set out to restore the bourgeois type of elitist education. Difficult examinations that put a premium on theoretical knowledge unrelated to practice forced the worker-peasants to drop out, leaving the universities to remain as citadels of academic learning far removed from politics, from reality, and from the masses. Old professors who had been denounced as Rightists in the rectification campaign of 1957-58 were reinstated and put in key positions. Qualitative growth was advocated to the disparagement of quantitative expansion and the cultivation of an intellectual elite at the expense of workers and peasants (see Chapter 2 on charges against bourgeois scholars). Politics and labor were relegated to a secondary position; students were encouraged to devote more time to study.

The Program After Reopening

The institutions of higher learning were specific targets of attack during the educational revolution. The order to close schools in 1966 was primarily directed against institutions of higher learning, and it was synchronized with student demands for fundamental reforms in higher education (see Appendixes 6 and 7). The shortcomings of colleges and universities were detailed: They exalted book knowledge; they inspired the selfish ambition to attain fame and become an expert; they put intellectual achievement above all else and neglected the "ideological revolution of Youth"; they ran counter to Mao's theory of knowledge; they discriminated against workers and peasants, and widened the gaps between town and countryside and between physical and mental labor; they ignored politics and productive labor; in a word, they failed to produce worthy successors to the revolutionary cause. As has been noted, the order to close for six months actually led to a suspension of higher education in the entire country for four years.

After the order to reopen schools and universities, the Central Committee of the Chinese Communist Party promulgated a Draft Program for institutions of higher learning.[3] As in the case of the lower schools, teachers and students of higher institutions were ordered to return to their campuses to "take part in the great cultural revolution there." They were to engage in military and political training to "carry out struggle, criticism, and transformation" and struggle against the handful of Party persons in authority taking the capitalist road and the bourgeois academic 'authorities' politically, ideologically, and academically. They must study ways to reform the old educational system, policy of teaching, and methods of teaching." In other words, just as students of primary and secondary schools were to resume classes and continue to wage revolution, so the teachers and students of colleges and universities were to carry on the Cultural Revolution and the educational revolution. The new spirit was expressed by the first contingent of workers-peasants-soldiers who entered Tsinghua University in 1970: "our consciousness of continuing the revolution will not change. . .our style of hard struggle will not change" (see Appendix 34).

The guidelines for the reopened colleges and universities were fairly simple and definite. Four-year and five-year courses were shortened to two or three years. There are fewer departments and fewer courses of study, with simplified and condensed content. The entrance examinations have been abolished to make it easier for workers-peasants-soldiers to enter. To break the monopoly of bourgeois intellectuals, the teaching staff consists of a "triple alliance" of worker-peasant-soldier teachers, cadres (or "revolutionary technicians," that is, those with production experience and good ideological motivation), and the original faculty. Such revisionist practices as knowledge for its own sake, teaching and study unrelated to practical needs, and the neglect of the class struggle and line struggle are banished from the educational scene. The purpose of higher education is not to produce elite scholars and intellectuals but "Red experts" equipped with the knowledge and skills actually needed in production and "socialist construction" and, motivated by the proletarian ideology as enunciated by Chairman Mao and the Communist Party.

Institutions of higher learning have thrown their doors wide open to admit workers, peasants, and soldiers in large numbers. The ratio of students from the proletarian classes to those from previously privileged classes is reversed; the former now constitutes the bulk of the students. They take no entrance examinations and are not required to present academic credentials. Some of the worker-peasant-soldier students have had no previous schooling. Applicants for admission are theoretically supposed to have the "equivalent" of middle school education, but the term "equivalent" is interpreted loosely and flexibly. There are four steps to the application for admission: (1) application by the worker, peasant, or soldier concerned, (2) recommendation by the "masses," which means essentially the workers-peasants-soldiers of the production unit, (3) approval of the "leadership," which means the revolutionary committee and the Party branch, and (4) final acceptance by the school. Of those who apply, a small number are selected for recommendation on the basis of production and ideological-political record. Physical fitness is also an important criterion.

No student advances directly from secondary education to higher education. A graduate of the middle school must go to the production front and will not be eligible for application to a college or university until after two or three years of good record in production and ideological-political performance. Even then, he must win the selection and recommendation of the "masses" and the authorities. In any case, only a small number of eligible applicants are selected for recommendation and endorsement. Until 1972, worker-peasant-soldier class origin was a primary factor of eligibility, but this criterion seems to have been relaxed to some extent. Statements have appeared in newspapers and journals to the effect that it is wrong to consider class origin alone in the screening of applicants for higher study, and that applicants of nonproletarian class origin also merit consideration if their production and ideological-political record warrants it. But the procedure of application and selection remains unchanged; the ideological-political criterion is still of primary importance.

The first class of entrants into the reopened universities consisted of workers, peasants, and soldiers recommended by factories, mines, communes, and army units. Between 70 and 90 percent are members of the Communist Party or Communist Youth League. A small number were selected from among outstanding urban youths who had been successfully reeducated in the countryside. Upon final acceptance for admission, the "new-type university students" were invited to farewell meetings and rallies in their production units marked by spirited ideological-political appeals. They were reminded of their responsibility to the masses who had selected them. They attended special sessions to study Chairman Mao's directives and writings (with which they were already familiar) in order to assure a firm determination to carry on the class struggle and the line struggle. For farewell gifts, they were presented with the writings of Chairman Mao and such symbols of the laboring masses as a shoulder carrying pole, a hoe, or a sickle. Upon arrival at the universities, they vowed to make the best of their opportunity, to overcome all difficulties, and to transform higher education with the Thought of Mao Tse-tung. In compliance with Mao's directive (see Appendix 33), they pledged to return to the production front at the completion of their study.

Many advantages are claimed for the new enrollment policy. Admission is no longer limited to middle school graduates. The selection of new students no longer is made by bourgeois scholars. Examinations and marks have been thrown out, and the practical ability and ideological-political record of new students assure their devotion to the revolutionary cause. The mass line is followed and the class revolution is accented. Instead of self-centered youths who become successors for the bourgeoisie, the universities now exist for the cultivation of a proletarian intelligentsia pledged to "serve the people."

Science and Engineering

There is much more emphasis on the polytechnical universities and institutes than on what are called liberal arts colleges in the West or general universities with offerings in arts and sciences. For each type, the programs of a few leading institutions have been given wide publicity as models for others to follow. Symposiums have been held in different parts of the country to study the examples of Tsinghua University, T'ung-chi (Tongji) University, Peking University, and others. In his directive on universities (July 21, 1968), Mao stated frankly that he was thinking "mainly" in terms of colleges of science and engineering (see Appendix 34). Inasmuch as he specifically mentioned the Shanghai machine tools plant, the training of technicians at this plant has become a center of interest in the revolutionization of higher education.

The Shanghai machine tools plant is not a university; it is not primarily an educational institution. It is a factory for making precision grinding machines. The work of designing the machines is done by a staff of engineers and technicians. Not satisfied with the technicians turned out by the colleges and universities, the plant set up a program of on-the-job training to enable select workers to learn to become technicians. This program must have appealed to Mao Tse-tung not only because it implemented his proposal of having "factory-run schools" but also because the workers who were trained to be technicians were reported to be superior, in practical ability and in ideological-political devotion, to the graduates of institutes of higher learning. In his directive of July 21, 1968, he ordered that colleges of science and engineering should "take the road of the Shanghai Machine Tools Plant in training technicians from among the workers."

The "road" is contrasted with the bourgeois method of education. It replaces "the reactionary bourgeois technical authorities" with "revolutionary youth technicians and revolutionary cadres . . . [who]

141

are proletarian revolutionary fighters with deep class feelings for Chairman Mao and the Communist Party." An investigation report on the plant was given wide publicity as a major document in the educational revolution (see Appendix 32). Of the 600 engineers and technicians, 45 percent have risen from the ranks of the workers, 50 percent are college graduates since 1949, and the remaining few are old technicians trained before the Liberation. Having passed from bourgeois leadership to proletarian leadership, the plant faithfully carries out Mao's "proletarian revolutionary line" and sharply attacks the revisionist line of "China's Khrushchev" and the reactionary bourgeois world outlook. These "revolutionary technicians" of worker origin are described as "more advanced ideologically and more competent in practical work" than the products of colleges and universities. Reportedly they work closely with the worker, have overcome the gap between those engaged in mental work and those who work with their hands, and do not indulge in useless theories. Free from the evils of bourgeois and revisionist ideology, they reportedly do not seek personal gain or fame and are impelled by "profound proletarian feelings for Chairman Mao and the Party."

Two months after Mao's directive of July 21, 1968, the Shanghai machine tools plant set up a "July 21 workers' college" with a class chosen from among the workers of different workshops, on the basis of advanced political consciousness and production experience. The college is permeated with "proletarian politics" and Maoist Thought. Study of Mao's writings goes hand-in-hand with unceasing criticism of the revisionist line in education. With "proletarian politics in command," the students and teachers condemn the 'revisionist' line of relying on specialists to run factories." The "line struggle" is reflected in the conflict between two different views of the role of workers and worker-technicians. Instead of a plethora of courses of specialization, only seven are offered. In compliance with Mao's May 7 Directive, students learn military affairs in army units and farming in the communes. They participate in struggle-criticism-transformation and the three great revolutionary movements. They learn on the job in order to integrate study with practice. The first class graduated after 34 months of work-study.

The most famous university of science and engineering is Tsinghua University in Peking. Tsinghua was a major battleground of rival factions and conflicting viewpoints during the Cultural Revolution, and it was the first university entered by a Mao Tse-tung Propaganda Team to inaugurate proletarian leadership. In forums in different parts of the country to study the exemplary experience of Tsinghua University, it is hailed as "a typical case in the educational revolution personally nurtured by Chairman Mao" and a 'reflection of Chairman Mao's brilliant thinking on proletarian education."[4] The university was a pacemaker for the rest of the country when it admitted the first class of students in September 1970. Among the 2,800 students in the entering class, 45 percent came from worker families, 40 percent from peasant families, and 15 percent from PLA units.[5] The governing body of the university is a Revolutionary Committee of 31 members, comprising eleven soldiers, three workers from the Thought Propaganda Team, seven professors, seven students, and three cadres. Its chairman is a military man who is also the first secretary of the Party Committee of the university.

The new students are supposed to have the "equivalent" of junior middle school education, that is, about eight years of schooling, but this is not a rigid requirement. The length of study has been reduced to two or three years, and short-term courses vary from a few months to a year. The program is production-oriented and designed to produce technicians rather than scholars. A high-precision machine tool production unit that used to be only an experimental unit is now a real production unit. The study of books receives less emphasis; a journalist reported that during his visit he did not see a single person in the library reading rooms. But, he added, "the new breed of intellectuals will have callused hands."[6]

Students are taught to "use the Marxist method to observe, pose, analyze, and solve problems."[7] In the classroom, lectures play a lesser role, and self-study by students is encouraged. Students are helped to solve problems by study, and teachers "teach students both scholastically and politically [and] do ideological work in the course of teaching." The old type of examinations has been abolished in favor of giving questions and topics for students to answer and study, using whatever books they need; "the main object of giving marks is to induce students to follow Chairman Mao's ideas on education in regard to the attitude and method of study."

It would be unrealistic to expect that the changeover from an academic university to an action-oriented and production-centered "socialist university of science and engineering" could be effected without difficult problems. Some of the professors miss the academic atmosphere and do not easily discard their old attitudes; they worry about standards and systematic knowledge. Teaching subjects without specific prerequisites taxes patience and ingenuity. Students with insufficient schooling do not easily benefit from the study of basic theories, and even those who have had some form of secondary education tend to have forgotten what they studied after three, four, or five years of full-time labor in production. Faculty members who plan makeup work for students of weak academic background are sometimes opposed because they seem to be reverting to the revisionist method of academic cramming and book knowledge. Realizing the need, however, the more enlightened authorities now take the position that some makeup work for worker-peasant-soldier students is desirable and that this form of makeup study to enable the proletarian intelligentsia to understand the basic theories essential to the solution of practical problems is different from the old reprehensible approach of knowledge-centered cramming.[8]

Another university of science and engineering praised for adherence to the Maoist educational line is the T'ung-Chi (Tongji) University in Shanghai (Appendix 30 explains the T'ung-Chi plan, and Appendix 31 reports its actual operation). Before 1949 T'ung-Chi was one of the national universities known for its work in medicine, engineering, and science. After the May 7 Directive (1966), it was reorganized into a "May 7 Commune" consisting of a teaching unit, a designing unit, and a building unit. These units have replaced the original departments and faculties. Close links are established with factories and construction sites, and the teaching personnel and students and workers are "organized under military lines." The five-year course has been reduced to three years, prominence is given to political work and the study of Mao Thought, teachers and students engage in productive labor, and the study of specialized courses is closely linked with actual construction projects.

Mao's Thought guides all three phases of the program: teaching, designing, and building. Domination by bourgeois intellectuals is brought to an end (1) by placing power in the hands of "commune" leaders elected by the "members" of the commune by virtue of "high proletarian consciousness and political levels," and (2) by having "workers and designers as well as students" share with the original teachers the role of classroom lectures. Teachers and students work and live with the workers; they go to PLA companies to work as soldiers. The military organization of the "commune" is evident in terms used for its activities: the engineering instruction given in preparation for the beginning of a construction project is called "precombat training," construction work in the course of carrying out the project is "learning while fighting."

Study, designing, and construction work have become phases of construction projects. Before designing a factory building, for example, study is concerned with the Party's general line in building socialism and Mao's teaching on the class struggle, integration with laboring masses, and other related subjects. Designing is done collectively by the students, the designers, the worker-teachers, and the original professors. After the completion of designing, students join the workers in construction. Theory, practice, and politics are thus integrated. It is claimed that after eight months of study, worker-students with no more previous schooling than the equivalent of junior middle school education were able to design a factory building.[9]

The ideological-political struggle in higher education is also stressed in a report published by the Red Flag in 1968.[10] What

144

happened at the Shanghai Institute of Mechanical Engineering is taken
as an example of the two-line struggle that is basic to the educational
revolution. Originally founded by the Central Government in 1952 under
the name of the Shanghai Technical School for Machine Building, it
followed the revisionist line. Workers and peasants were admitted,
but the bourgeois intellectuals who were in charge blindly worshipped
foreign models and prepared difficult examinations that more than half
of the worker-peasant students failed. The study of theoretical knowledge was divorced from practice. Departments and teaching personnel
multiplied and expensive equipment accumulated. This was the
revisionist line, the capitalist road. The other line, the proletarian
line, is shown by the road taken by the Shanghai machine tools plant.
The current reform is said to hinge on the outcome of the "sharp
struggle between the two classes, the two roads, and the two lines."
The report adds, "the central question in the struggle [is] one of
power."

The Liberal Arts Colleges

The Chinese term for "liberal arts" institutions is the "college
of arts" or the "arts faculty" in a university. It actually refers to
departments and schools other than science, engineering, medicine,
agriculture, and teacher training. In this category belong the social
sciences, the humanities, the fine arts, law, philosophy, and so on.
It has been noted that Mao's directive on higher education definitely
favors science and engineering and implies a more restrictive policy
toward the "arts" colleges and universities. The reasons are obvious.
The latter are further removed from the cardinal principles of putting
education in the service of politics and production. It is easier to
link the teaching of science and engineering with production and
practice; the way to apply teaching in the "arts" to practice is not so
clear. As for politics, the old science and engineering colleges were
guilty of neglecting the teaching of ideology, but the arts colleges and
universities often committed serious errors of teaching ideas and
thought systems contrary to Marxism-Leninism-Maoism. In other
words, the arts institutions have a more unsavory past to overcome
before they can be made into "socialist universities." As early as
1964, Mao expressed his view as follows:

Broadly speaking, the intellectuals of the industrial
field are better because they are in contact with reality.
Those in the scientific field, that is in the field of pure
science, are poorer, but they are somewhat better than
those dealing with arts. Those who are most divorced

from reality are the ones in the departments of arts, be they students of history, philosophy, or economics. They are so divorced from reality that they know nothing about world affairs. . . . Comparatively speaking, China's faculty of arts is most backward. [See Appendix 5.]

Since it is not feasible to set up workshops in a college of arts as in a college of science or engineering, Mao's formula for the arts colleges is that they "should take the whole society as its own workshop" (see Appendixes 5 and 36). Philosophy, he said, could not be learned from textbooks; it is necessary to "go to society or among the masses of people or to a Mother Nature to learn philosophy." Arts students must also "go to the lower levels to work in industry, agriculture, and commerce." Ideological study is of utmost importance, of course. The Mao Thought Propaganda Team in Hongchow University wrote as follows:

The basic task of the arts faculty of a socialist university is to study, publicize Marxism-Leninism-Mao Tse-tung Thought, criticize and repudiate the bourgeoisie and train revolutionary public-opinion fighters fighting for the consolidation of the proletarian dictatorship. The arts faculty must take Chairman Mao's works as basic teaching materials.[11]

A major form of ideological-political activity is the organization of "revolutionary mass criticism writing groups." As a matter of fact, a popular cliché is that arts colleges must turn themselves into writing groups to practice mass criticism. The groups apply their mass criticism to writing essays, stories, and plays repudiating revisionist ideas and bourgeois ideology. The writings kindle enthusiasm for the two-line struggle and attack concrete targets such as alienation from labor and politics, studying for personal gain and ambition, and the belief in "art for its own sake." Students go to the masses and write to propagandize the Thought of Mao Tse-tung. In doing so, they are following Mao's dictum that intellectuals must learn to write for the masses. Students in the literature classes center their attack on the major literary targets of the Cultural Revolution, now known as the "four villains": Chou Yang, Hsia Yen, T'ien Han, and Yang Han-sheng. These revisionists stressed style and technique of writing, rather than its revolutionary content and appeal. To relate their study to practice, students write to make literature a weapon of the ideological-political struggle and a positive force for the implementation of Mao's ideas and instructions. Propaganda work in connection with various revolutionary movements and mass campaigns is among the regular activities of the writing groups. Besides producing "revolutionary literature," they help other worker-peasants to form writing groups, sometimes in connection with their spare-time education.

Just as Tsinghua is hailed as a model socialist university of science and engineering, Peking University is held up as a good example of a reformed arts college. The "liberal arts" in this university, usually abbreviated as Peita in Chinese, include Chinese language and literature, history, philosophy, political economy, international politics, law, and library science. All of them are guided by Mao's directive to take all society as the workshop of the arts. Students and faculty go "deep into the factories, communes, and PLA units to take part in production and in the class struggle." Instead of confining themselves to classroom study, they go out to make "social investigations" and get their ideas from the investigations.

In discussing "Where Do Correct Ideas Come From?", Mao had said that ideas came from "three kinds of social practice: the struggle for production, the class struggle, and scientific experiment." Accordingly, students and faculty base their study and teaching on what they actually find in the production units and the scenes of political struggle. They spend four months a year out in society to find live materials for study and also to apply what they study to social practice (see Appendix 35).

Philosophy students discover "the law of class struggle" by social investigation of conditions in factories, shops, industrial enterprises, and schools. They carry out "mass criticism together with the workers." Students of political economy find a rich source of study materials in the brigades and the cooperative system that led to the establishment of the brigades. In international politics, the study of Lenin's Imperialism, the Highest Stage of Capitalism is linked to reality by social investigations in an adjacent coal mine, an iron-smelting mill, and a power plant formerly owned and controlled by imperialists.

Literature students went to a locomotive rolling-stock plant and discovered "corruption, theft, straggling, waste and speculation—as well as the activities of counter-revolutionaries" and produced posters and articles to oppose these evils. They also wrote plays and dramas to portray the revolutionary spirit. The study of Mao's Yenan Talks is directly applied to and reinforced by the social investigations, and this reportedly enabled the writing groups to produce a revolutionary literature with the single purpose of advancing the socialist revolution under Communist leadership.

Unity of theory and practice, one of Mao's central ideas in education, is achieved by combining classroom study with production on the one hand and politics on the other. Classroom study of the class struggle is made real by listening to workers who recall how they were oppressed and exploited by the bourgeoisie. Mao's Thought permeates all studies. There are courses on Mao Thought and the history of the Chinese (Communist) revolution. Mao's writings are used in the grammar class as well as the physical education class, in literature as well as international politics, in the English class and in the class for training interpreters. All students acquire a rich ideological-political vocabulary and presumably a corresponding mental outlook. As in the lower schools, Mao's works are read and reread, studied and discussed in every course and on all occasions.[12] How else could Mao Thought be put in command?

The numerous courses once offered by Peking University have been reduced and organized under three major categories: (1) Marxism and Mao Thought, (2) history (including philosophy), with emphasis on the Communist movement in China and abroad, and (3) revolutionary criticism. The educational thought of Confucius and John Dewey is subject to severe criticism. Students and teachers are called upon to engage in "three repudiations" and "three acquisitions": They repudiate the ideas of "natural Redness" (which means that those who are already "Red" by family origin or by training do not need further remolding), of "intellectual development above all," and of the "backwardness of the masses"; instead, they must acquire a new world outlook, a determination to put politics in command of vocational work, and a willingness to learn from the masses.[13] The governing body of the university, as in all other schools and universities, is the revolutionary committee. It consists of 39 members, with an army representative as chairman, as at Tsinghua University. The Party committee of the university is also headed by a PLA representative.[14]

Peking University has been chosen to be the model for the "arts" colleges and universities by virtue of its high reputation and the respect it has commanded through the years. Its history spans three-quarters of a century and mirrors the turbulent as well as invigorating intellectual currents of modern China. It was the birthplace of the May Fourth Student Movement and its faculty and students led the nation in the New Thought Movement (see Chapter 2). It was noted for intellectual freedom and it was no accident that it was at Peking University that Mao Tse-tung himself came into contact with socialism, Communism, and other schools of thought, all of which were welcomed in those days in the spirit of free inquiry. In recent years, however, Peking University has been under fire as a center of intellectual recalcitrance, and its successive presidents have been denounced for their bourgeois ideology and their revisionist educational theories and practices. The fundamental reform of Peking University has therefore become a major task of the educational revolution in higher education.

Nationwide Reform

Reforms undertaken by institutions of higher learning in different parts of the country have more or less followed the patterns set by Tsinghua University and Peking University. Futan University in Shanghai has organized its liberal arts studies into a "May 7 experimental class," admitting worker-peasant students, using Mao's writings as "basic teaching materials," and putting Marxist-Leninist-Maoist ideology in command of all studies.[15] Nankai University, once a private university catering to the upper classes and stressing high standards of scholarship, is a different institution today with worker-peasant-soldier students and worker-peasant-soldier teachers. Besides setting up ten "small and medium-sized" factories, Wuhan University has established close ties with 40 other factories to insure integration with practice and with the masses.[16] After the Second Plenary Session of the Ninth Central Committee of the Chinese Communist Party in August-September 1970, Wuhan University launched "a campaign to study, propagate, and implement the communiqué" of the Session.[17] Chiaotung University in Shanghai compiled new teaching materials on the basis of Mao's teachings and the social investigations, to meet the needs of the three revolutionary movements.[18]

Elsewhere, students in Foochow University direct their revolutionary criticism against waste and extravagance, and against the desire for "bigness" and "modern equipment." Biology students in Chungshan University help the peasants in "scientific experimentation" (one of the three revolutionary movements) in the control of insect pests. The classrooms of the July 21 Water Conservancy College of Tientsin University are scattered among water conservancy construction sites throughout various mountain valleys, and the "open-door" policy applies to admitting worker-peasant-soldier students and carrying on study programs outside the school.[19] From Heilungkiang and Kirin provinces in the northeast to Yunan and Kansu provinces, colleges and universities seek to carry out the educational revolution.

Medical Education

Radical changes have been made in the medical schools. The basic guideline is provided by Mao's instruction: "in medical and health work, put the stress on the rural areas." The long-term, costly medical course has given way to short-term courses that send students and faculty to get their practical training among the poor and lower-middle peasants. Teaching bases are established in the countryside to facilitate the study and treatment of common diseases of the rural population. Ideological-political indoctrination is an essential

149

part of medical and health education so that students may be aware of the significance of their work to the revolution and inspired by a determination to serve the masses rather than to seek personal gain or professional advancement. The study of traditional Chinese medicine, including the use of herbs and acupuncture, is in line with the current trend to deemphasize reliance on foreign theories and practices.

Workers and peasants of higher political consciousness are admitted for study in the medical schools. Here, too, academic requirements for admission are of little importance. Courses of study have been shortened to two or three years at most. Shorter courses and training classes produce health workers and "barefoot doctors" in a few months. Workers are sent to hospitals to learn specific techniques for meeting immediate needs, and it is claimed that after two months of training they are able to diagnose diseases, detect cardiac murmurs, and perform appendectomies.[20] A number of half-farming half-study medical schools have appeared. One such school in Shensi province has produced hundreds of barefoot doctors, with ideological-political education interwoven with technical training; Mao's Three Great Articles and his instructions on health work are among the required readings. Workers and peasants are admitted with 'ho admission restrictions on age or previous educational background."[21] The Chungshan Medical College shortened the length of training and reduced courses of study from 36 to 15, to be taught in three years. It has trained thousands of barefoot doctors able to treat common and recurrent diseases in the rural areas and industrial plants and mines, using both Western and traditional Chinese medicine. Instead of the old schedule of proceeding from basic cures to clinical theories and finally to clinical practice, the new program starts with a brief orientation and then sends students to communes to learn about the common diseases and to gain some preliminary clinical experience by offering medical services and lectures. They also engage in the three great revolutionary movements and in revolutionary criticism of revisionist ideas and practices in medical and health work. After such practical experience and social investigation, the students undertake their classroom study in a more systematic way. Finally, they return to the communes for further clinical practice. Theory and practice are thus integrated and the students are constantly reminded of their central purpose—to serve the masses and to improve health conditions in the countryside.[22] Throughout the entire period of schooling, the students spend two-thirds of their time in actual practice.

Other professional schools such as agricultural and industrial colleges have been reorganized along similar lines of integrating theory with practice and putting ideology and politics in command of vocational study. Courses of specialization are simplified and reduced in number, and teaching materials are selected with the three great revolutionary movements in view. An agricultural college that has attracted much attention is the Kiangsi Communist Labor University. Established in 1958 as a part-work, part-study school, it was accorded high praise by Mao Tse-tung. Writing in celebration of its third anniversary in 1961, Mao endorsed its program as follows:

> I fully approve your endeavors of half-work half-study, and of hard work and study with frugality, without spending a single cent of the state. . . . Other provinces should send capable and intelligent responsible comrades to Kiangsi to observe school operation and absorb experience so that they may initiate such schools after returning to their own respective provinces.[23]

The students of the Kiangsi Communist Labor University are workers and peasants of high political consciousness and rich labor experience, regardless of age and previous schooling. Worker-peasant-soldier teachers give the staff a proletarian character. The students work in agriculture, forestry, and animal husbandry, and their studies are coordinated with their work. Current events and ideological study are, of course, a regular part of the curriculum. Financial support comes from the income accruing from the labor of teachers and students. The university maintains 132 branch campuses scattered in the mountain areas of the province. Altogether they enroll more than 50,000 students and have produced 120,000 graduates, many of whom "have become basic level cadres of bookkeepers, weather forecasters, stockholders, technicians, agro-mechanics, and barefoot doctors in their communes and production brigades and teams."[24] They operate "more than 390 cultivated farms, tree nurseries, and animal husbandry farms and about 250 factories throughout Kiangsi."[25] In a conference of the various branches of the university in 1970, the delegates studied the reports of Tsinghua University and the Shanghai machine tools plant, and discussed ways and means of doing a better job of making the Labor University "a new-type socialist university which has grown in strength in the struggle between the two classes, two roads, and two lines."[26]

Ideological Remolding

In a way, the need for ideological-political remolding is even more pressing in higher education than in the lower schools. Institutions of higher education are a repository of intellectual traditions that are more tenacious and more resistant to change than those in the primary and secondary schools. The doctrine that the ultimate aim

151

of all educational work is to remold the thought, attitudes, and ideological-political commitment of students and teachers applies with an even greater force here. When Mao warned that ideological remolding is an acute and drawn-out struggle that must be continued for a very long time, he probably was thinking of the intellectuals rather than the masses, and more of those in higher education than those at the lower levels.

Ideological-political remolding is imperative not only for those whose earlier education took place under bourgeois and revisionist auspices but also for the workers-peasants-soldiers, even for members of the Communist Party and Communist Youth League. Such fallacious notions as "priority on intellectual development" and "vocational competence apart from politics" are believed to have a firm root in colleges and universities. Besides, worker-peasant-soldier students and members of the Party and Youth League have an additional problem to contend with. Under the misleading assumption that they are "already Red" by training or "born Red" by virtue of class origin, many of them let down their ideological vigilance and fall prey to bourgeois and revisionist enticements.

Take, for example, the story of a peasant student selected by poor and middle-lower peasants for study in Amoy University. As a send-off gift, the peasants presented him with a pair of straw sandals and asked him to wear them at the university as a symbol of his peasant origin and revolutionary thinking. But at the university he fell under the influence of Liu Shao-ch'i and his followers and was attracted by the "theory of dying out of the class struggle." He discarded the straw sandals. Fortunately, his transgression was caught in time and ideological remolding made him realize his error. He became an even more ardent revolutionary than before and was finally admitted into the Communist Party. This incident was cited to show the acute need for continuous remolding, even for the workers-peasants-soldiers.[27]

Some worker-peasant-soldier students are so awed by the scholars that they unconsciously and gradually fall prey to their revisionist ideology. Others, at the other extreme, are so arrogant that they feel they have nothing to learn and have come only to exercise proletarian leadership. Still others labor under the mistaken idea that they have come to the university primarily to study and are disappointed that they still have to engage in labor and production. For all such deviations, ideological remolding is the only sure remedy.

Ideological remolding is more than a negative process of rectification. It is the implanting of the correct ideology and the shaping of a proletarian revolutionary outlook. "In all its work and lessons, if a school is not educating students with proletarian ideology, it is poisoning them with bourgeois ideology." In other words, it is possible to lose the ideological struggle by default, and this can be prevented only by a positive program of intensive ideological-political education. And this process does not merely involve the teachers as the educating agents and the students as the learners. The teachers themselves need remolding and the workers-peasants-soldiers, as students and as members of the Mao Tse-tung Propaganda Teams, play an active role in pressing for the ideological-political reform of the teachers. Moreover, the students can do much in helping one another to keep up their ideological-political vigilance. For example, women students from worker-peasant-soldier families living in the same dormitory in Futan University formed a group for ideological-political study. Every day, they studied the works of Marx, Engels, Lenin, Stalin, and Mao, and gathered to discuss them.[28]

A worker-student in Tsinghua University wrote about the three-fold tasks of "study, management, and transformation."[29] Besides their own study, he and his fellow students help to "manage the university" (in cooperation with the Mao Thought Propaganda Team) and to "transform" it by means of "mass revolutionary criticism" of revisionist tendencies. They criticize the bourgeois teachers for teaching theory apart from practice and for the use of expensive foreign equipment characteristic of the revisionist line. In other universities, too, students actively oppose any expression of revisionist ideology or bourgeois theories of education on the part of the faculty. At the same time, the Revolutionary Committee and the Mao Thought Propaganda Team always look out for ideological-political deviations and see to it that the ideological-political remolding of teachers and students is never relaxed.

Inasmuch as more intellectuals are found in the colleges and universities than elsewhere, much of the reform of intellectuals concerns the activities of college faculties. The various methods used to reform the teachers may be briefly summarized. First, the role of the bourgeois intellectuals has been greatly curtailed, by the inauguration of proletarian leadership and the introduction of worker-peasant-soldier teachers. Second, the intellectuals are held responsible for any remaining vestiges of bourgeois and revisionist education. Third, they are required to regularly engage in ideological-political study and in critical examination of their own teaching methods and materials. Fourth, they are expected to join the students in labor, in production, and in "social investigation." Fifth, they are sent to the countryside or May 7 Cadre Schools for reeducation and integration with workers-peasants-soldiers. The scholar-teachers take turns in reeducation; a visitor found that of the 2,133 persons originally on the faculty of Peking University, "over a thousand are currently engaged in productive labor" and are to continue for one to three years.[30]

The favorite "three-in-one" formula applies to the teaching staff, which consists of workers-peasants-soldiers, "revolutionary technical personnel," and the original teachers. The worker-peasant-soldier teachers are rated "the most vigorous and revolutionary" of the teaching staff. For example, workers serve as full-time or part-time teachers in Tsinghua University. Their class lectures are very different from those of the intellectuals. They stress "class education and education in the struggle between the two lines." They tell the history of their families or their factories and the sufferings of the past.[31]

Nevertheless, the old teachers still outnumber the new ones. In T'ung-Chi University, after three and a half years of the "May 7 Commune," there were still 117 old teachers among the three-in-one teaching staff of 143 persons.[32] Reports on colleges and universities have given examples of bourgeois intellectuals who stand in the way of educational reform and others who have been successfully remolded. In Futan University, a proposal to establish a factory for the production of transistor parts as a step in the reform of the physics department met with opposition from "a handful of class enemies . . . seriously influenced by the poison of revisionism."[33] After the establishment of the factory, "a sharp struggle arose on the question of leadership." Some "academic authorities" who at first balked at the new program were remolded by working on the production line and "underwent a profound change after half a year's tempering." In another case, a mathematics professor at Amoy University designed a culvert on the basis of his bookish theory, which required each piece of rock to be cut to an exact angle. But experienced workers simply used uncut pieces of rock and successfully put them in place to build the culvert. The workers' success was hailed as a triumph of Mao Thought over bourgeois scholarship. The teacher was led to study Mao's teachings and finally learned to integrate with workers and peasants.[34]

The New Higher Education

To summarize, revolutionary change has overtaken Chinese institutions of higher learning. They are fundamentally different from what they used to be and from what higher education is in the West. The "academic" atmosphere has disappeared or been altered beyond recognition. Academic requirements have been waived or minimized. Academic degrees have been abolished. The university exists for service and for the revolution; its mission is to produce a proletarian intelligentsia, not an intellectual elite. It is no place for academic research on topics of no immediate practical use. The dominance of the triad of "teachers, classrooms, textbooks" has been shattered.

The influence of the scholarly intellectuals has been sharply curtailed. The governing body of the university is the Revolutionary Committee in which workers-peasants-soldiers have a big voice, but most policy decisions are made by the Party committee or the Party branch at the university, which in turn is answerable to the higher Party hierarchy. The Mao Tse-tung Thought Propaganda Team and the Communist Youth League share administrative functions under the leadership of the Revolutionary Committee and the Party committee. The new campus atmosphere is described as follows:

> Revolutionary teachers and students, who have just eaten their recall-bitterness meal, are recalling past bitterness and thinking of the present sweetness and chatting intimately with old workers and peasants who have suffered much and hate the old society. Together they sing the praise of the great leader Chairman Mao and denounce big renegade Liu Shao-ch'i.

> In their spare time and on Sundays, the revolutionary teachers and students, their trouser legs rolled up and with hoes in their hands, reclaim the several hundred mou of wasteland in the campus, in which they will grow crops.

> Unafraid of becoming dirty and defying fatigue, some of the teachers and students, who in the past would cover their noses when they passed a manure cart, are now cleaning lavatories and digging up mud from rivers in an effort to accumulate manure.[35]

Gone are the Christian colleges and universities established and supported by American mission boards which played a prominent role in Chinese higher education for three decades until 1949. Their buildings have become the property of state universities. The campus of Yenching University is now a part of Peking University, Lingnan University has been merged into Chungshan University, Fukien Christian University is a unit of Foochow University, and so on. The original identity is completely lost.

There are fewer institutions of higher learning with fewer students. All studies must directly serve the needs of production and the ideological-political struggle. The humanities, if they exist at all, must meet these criteria as much as science and technology. Knowledge for its own sake is unacceptable; the development of the mind and its use in "free inquiry" would be unthinkable. "Revolutionary literature and art" are used as instruments of propaganda on behalf of the revolutionary movements and the ideological-political struggle. The content of philosophy and the social sciences consists essentially of the ideology of Marxism-Leninism-Maoism, reinforced by a denunciation of all other thought systems. The humanities and the social studies must be purged of all reactionary ideology, and it is safe to say that at present and in the near future few students will major in the humanities or social sciences. In compliance with the May 7 Directive, all students must learn agriculture, industry, military affairs, and politics and "should take part in the socialist education and in the criticism of the bourgeoisie."

Problems and difficulties are to be expected. Reports frequently mention the fierce struggle on the various campuses between the two opposing lines. Not all scholars can be happy with their dwindling role in an area in which they have excelled. No doubt some of them hanker after the old system, and the charge that revisionists among them are engaged in sabotage against the new system may not be entirely without foundation.

The frustrations of intellectuals described in the preceding chapters are certainly present on college campuses, and even those ready to cooperate are not always sure which way to turn. Opening the doors of colleges and universities to workers-peasants-soldiers is a noble intention, but there are practical problems. Factories and communes have sometimes hesitated to recommend their best talents because they are reluctant to release them from production work. Those selected to go do not always jump at the opportunity: some are afraid that the studies may prove too difficult and they feel more secure in the production jobs they already know well; a small number may also feel that "study is useless" because one ends up in production and labor anyway. After entering the colleges and universities, some worker-peasant-soldier students have objected to scholarly lectures that they neither understand nor find useful, while others have been disappointed that they are not given more opportunity to study and acquire the technical knowledge they lack; still others decide to quit because they feel unequal to the problems and difficulties of combining study with proletarian leadership. The old teaching materials have been discarded, but there is a scarcity of new teaching materials that can be safely used.

Theoretically, with the dethronement of the bourgeois intellectuals, a proletarian intelligentsia should rise to take their place. Now the bourgeois scholars have been shoved aside, but a proletarian intelligentsia is yet to be born. At best, higher education is in a stage of transition, grouping for new patterns and new methods, and awaiting concrete guidelines on how to implement the directives and instructions of Chairman Mao. There is much confusion and puzzlement on all sides, but perhaps these are the unavoidable difficulties of a transitional period.

Notes

1. See Lu Ting-i, "Education Must Be Combined with Productive Labor," Peking Review, September 9, 1958.
2. Theodore H. E. Chen, The Popularization of Higher Education in Communist China (Washington, D.C.: U.S. Office of Education, OE-14002, August 1959).
3. Text translated in Current Background, no. 852 (May 6, 1968).
4. Foreign Broadcast Information Service, Daily Report, Communist China, August 27, 1970, p. G7; also August 25, 1970, p. F1. (Hereafter cited as FBIS.)
5. Current Scene (Hong Kong) 9, no. 9 (September 7, 1971), p. 22.
6. Mark Gayn in the Washington, D.C. Evening Star, May 19, 1971.
7. Article by the Tsinghua University Revolutionary Committee, in Peking Review, February 23, 1973; also article on new-type students of Tsinghua, in Peking Review, March 2, 1973.
8. See article by the Tsinghua Propaganda Team in Hung-Ch'i (Red flag), September 1, 1971.
9. FBIS, August 11, 1970, p. C8.
10. Translation in Peking Review, September 13, 1968.
11. Jen-min Jih-pao, July 30, 1971.
12. Report on Peking University by Michael Frolic, in New York Times Magazine, October 24, 1971.
13. Article by the Propaganda Team in Peking University, in Jen-min Jih-pao, June 19, 1971.
14. Frolic, op. cit.
15. Hung-ch'i (Red flag), June 1, 1971, reprinted in Jen-min Jih-pao, June 29, 1971.
16. Kuang-ming Jih-pao, July 12, 1972.
17. FBIS, September 15, 1970, p. D7. The communiqué called on the entire nation to "hold high the great red banner of Mao Tse-tung Thought . . . to carry out the tasks of struggle-criticism-transformation consciously . . . to grasp revolution, promote production and other work and preparedness against war," etc. Text of communiqué in Peking Review, September 11, 1970.
18. FBIS, December 9, 1969, pp. C3-5.
19. Kuang-ming Jih-pao, October 2, 1970.
20. New York Times, March 2, 1969.
21. FBIS, September 23, 1971, p. H1.
22. Kuang-ming Jih-pao, June 22, 1971.
23. For a translation of Mao's letter, see Issues and Studies (Taipei), January 1970, p. 80.
24. FBIS, September 24, 1971, pp. C7-8.
25. Richard M. Peffer, "Serving the People and Continuing the

Revolution," China Quarterly, no. 52 (October-December 1972), p. 644.

26. FBIS, August 4, 1970, pp. C14-15. This dispatch mentions 177 branches of the Kiangsi Communist Labor University.

27. Kuang-ming Jih-pao, August 12, 1972.

28. Peking Review, March 9, 1973, p. 22.

29. Kwei Yu-peng, "Revolution in Education: Our Experience," Peking Review, August 20, 1971, p. 12.

30. Frolic, op. cit.

31. "Worker-Teachers in Tsinghua University," Peking Review, January 15, 1971.

32. Hung-ch'i (Red flag), June 1, 1971, p. 74.

33. FBIS, July 30, 1970, p. C2.

34. Kuang-ming Jih-pao, March 22, 1972.

35. A report on Tsinghua University, in Jen-min Jih-pao, May 9, 1969. Translation in Survey of China Mainland Press, No. 4423, May 26, 1969.

The Ninth National Congress of the Chinese Communist Party in 1969 supposedly terminated the stormy Cultural Revolution and marked the beginning of a period of recovery and rehabilitation. Education is one of the most sensitive areas of national life both in terms of the convulsive effects of the Cultural Revolution and from the standpoint of the urgent need for a positive program of rebuilding. Two years of suspension of all school work was a costly price to pay for a new revolution under a regime that had just begun to achieve stability and progress, politically and economically. Moreover, the indulgence of youth in unrestrained disruptive activities entailed a breakdown of discipline whose effects could not be quickly obliterated. In higher education, the closing of colleges and universities for four years or more deprived the nation of hundreds of thousands of trained personnel who could have been produced. [1] The nation could not well afford such a heavy loss. Educationally, one of the direct results is a severe shortage of teachers that constitutes a major problem in the post-Cultural Revolution era.

The task of educational rehabilitation is complicated by the decision to scrap the system that existed before the Cultural Revolution and to start out in a new direction. Mao Tse-tung has always recognized education as the cornerstone of the new society that the proletarian revolution aims to establish. In the early years he was more concerned with the broad aspects of education as the process of changing people than with the specific problems of schooling. He identified education with propaganda and indoctrination and frequently made light of book study and the acquisition of useless knowledge. [2] Teachers, he said, are propagandists; so are journalists, literary writers, artists, even the army comrades. [3]

In regard to actual school practice, some of Mao's basic ideas were already in evidence in the educational practices of the Chinese Soviet base in Kiangsi province in the early 1930s. At Yenan, Mao enlarged on his ideas concerning knowledge and practice, thought and action, and applied them to the problems of learning and ideological remolding. The opportunity for large-scale educational reform came with the establishment of the new regime in 1949. But as the regime consolidated its position, it tended to become relatively conservative, more concerned with stability and strength than with radical change. The initial policy of moderation, originally intended to be a transitional phase, created an atmosphere in which "revisionism" grew rapidly and found expression in education as well as in economics and politics.

Mao Tse-tung must have been alarmed by what he saw as an alliance between the revisionists and the bourgeoisie to thwart his revolutionary dream and "plot for the restoration of capitalism." In education, bourgeois scholars, who despite remolding efforts were waiting for a chance to reassert their old ideology, appeared to have joined hands with the revisionists to turn the educational reform into a moderate program of piecemeal innovations within the framework of bourgeois education. Soviet influence pushed Chinese education farther away from the Yenan model. The educational revolution was aborted. To turn the tide it was necessary, in Mao's view, not only to launch a fierce attack on bourgeois and revisionist ideology but also to depose those who were responsible for its preservation, namely, the bourgeois intellectuals. A major effort had to be made to shatter the dominant influence of bourgeois intellectuals in education.

The bourgeois intellectuals were in control of education during the period of weak educational reform in the first decade. They held positions of authority in the Ministry of Education of the Central Government and the organs of educational administration in the provinces. They controlled the universities. Today, the Ministry of Education, the Ministry of Higher Education, and the Departments and Bureau of Education on lower levels have been abolished, and revolutionary committees and "education groups" have taken over educational administration. Chapter 2 outlined the policies of the bourgeois scholars in contrast with the Maoist educational line. Some major features of the Maoist program may be summarized as follows:

- The primary aim of education is to produce an educated proletariat, not an intellectual elite.
- Revolutionary education is action-oriented, not knowledge-centered; practice-centered, not study-centered.
- It is geared to present needs, not future needs.
- It avoids dependence on foreign models and foreign materials.
- It substitutes proletarian leadership for the dominating role of bourgeois intellectuals.

- It puts ideology and politics in command of all school work.
- It serves politics and economics and accepts the direction of the Communist Party.
- It helps bridge the gap between mental and physical labor, between the city and the countryside.
- It does not recognize intellectual development as its primary aim.
- It places little value on academic quality and scholarship standards, which are the central concern of bourgeois scholars.
- It repudiates the bourgeois tradition of selfish individualism which makes the attainment of personal advancement and success the prime motive of study.
- It plays down the importance of formal schooling and puts a premium on practical experience and self-study.
- It deemphasizes systematic knowledge, well-defined levels of learning, and academic prerequisites for advanced study. It consequently challenges the traditional concept of higher education.

The new changes tend to blur the distinction between the full-time schools, the part-work, part-study schools, and the spare-time schools. Since all students are required to engage in labor and production and to participate in educational programs after school hours and during vacations, the three types of schools are gradually losing their distinct characteristics. Actually, there are few or no full-time schools where students devote all their time to study. The worker-peasant school used to be a distinct type of school, but it is no longer needed since all schools now exist for workers, peasants and soldiers. Prior to the Cultural Revolution, educational statistics used to point out the increasing percentage of worker-peasant youths in the schools from year to year. Now that all schools and universities put priority on the admission of students from worker-peasant-soldier families, the question of percentages has disappeared.

Accomplishments

Educational opportunity for the masses has been greatly expanded. The campaign to obliterate illiteracy is making headway. Although development throughout the country is uneven and some areas fall way behind the more progressive areas, there is no doubt that the wide variety of adult education, spare-time education, and social education have greatly increased educational opportunity for the entire population. The many forms of village schools, part-time schools, short-term schools, and locally improvised classes together make schooling more accessible to children in the rural areas. The poor and the heretofore underprivileged are now given opportunities that used to be beyond their reach.

Higher education is much more restricted. Even worker-peasant-soldier youths must undergo a rigorous process of "selection and recommendation" before admission into institutions of higher learning. The academic requirements for admission have been waived, but the net result of the new criteria of high ideological-political conscious-ness and a good production record is that higher education is even more selective than before. Enrollment in the big universities has declined in comparison with the pre-educational revolution years, and many of the smaller institutions that existed before the Cultural Revolution either have been merged or failed to reopen for one reason or another.

Any discussion of educational opportunity must take into account the broad concept of education in Communist China, which recognizes the importance of numerous forms of education that take place outside the schools. The statement that the whole society educates is more than a theoretical concept. Those in charge of museums, recreation centers, and production units are constantly reminded of their educa-tional responsibility and ordered to make specific provisions to dis-charge their duties, either in helping school programs or in organizing out-of-school activities of educational value. The Draft Program for schools provides that "education by the school, society, and the family should be combined." The Party organizations and revolutionary com-mittees see to it that the school and out-of-school agencies coordinate their efforts to make sure that they reinforce one another and are directed toward the same objectives.

The wide range of educational activities and their close coordina-tion make it possible to use the school as an agency of social change. Students who are taught the importance of the three great revolutionary movements in political education in school go out to arouse popular enthusiasm and to lead the masses in the class struggle, in production, and in scientific experiment. After they are taught in school that the high cost of weddings, funerals, birthday celebrations, and seasonal festivities is wasteful and harmful to the socialist cause, they spread these ideas in their families and communities and help to change deeply entrenched customs and habits. Young people are taught to rebel against early marriage and to see the wisdom of having small families, and they are consciously directed to influence the thinking of their elders in such matters. Thus, the school becomes a driving force for social reform.

There is close cooperation between the school and out-of-school agencies in the education of youth and adults. Teachers and those in charge of production, the mass media, and various agencies of social education meet in conferences to make coordinated plans and discuss problems under the unified leadership of the revolutionary committee and the Party organs. As noted in the discussion of extracurricular activities in Chapter 4, education extends far beyond the classroom and the schoolground, and beyond the school hours; it consists of the total impact on young and old during all their waking hours. By an unceasing barrage of information, instruction, and exhortation, all designed to produce the same impact, the mind is saturated with messages from the planners of the socialist-proletarian revolution and remolded with the Thought of Mao Tse-tung. Portraits of Mao, his quotations, and the constantly repeated slogans confront the individual no matter where he goes, and there is no escape from the conditioning process.

Many of the new changes help to close the gap between school and society. Teachers and students engage in production and the revolutionary movements. Parents take part in school affairs; workers-peasants-soldiers manage the schools; and "social investigation" puts students and teachers in the stream of social life to produce teaching materials that reflect the conditions and needs of the local community. Worker-peasant teachers may not be very effective in academic teaching, but they help to bring schools and society more closely together. There also are institutional links between the schools and the factories and production teams and brigades. And there is a constant emphasis on the integration of study with practice. These provisions, plus the "network" of educational programs in and out of school, result in an "open door" policy for running the schools.

Local establishment and management of schools also helps to bring the school close to the community. The compilation of local teaching materials may be the characteristic of a transitional period when experimentation is encouraged and the state must depend on local support for schools rather than state aid. The time may come when experimentation gives way to more standardized curriculums and teaching materials, and when the state will have the resources for increased support of schools, incidentally bringing more state control and less local authority. Even then, the "open-door" way of running schools will probably remain a salient feature of Maoist education.

Problems

Problems encountered in the work of the Mao Tse-tung Propaganda Teams, in the education of youth, and in the reeducation of intellectuals have been discussed in previous chapters. It has been noted that a major objective of the educational revolution is to push the bourgeois intellectuals and the children of the bourgeoisie off the center of the stage and to put workers-peasants-soldiers in their place. The idea seems logical enough, but the implementation is not an easy matter. The admission of large numbers of worker-peasant-soldier youth to schools and colleges is an obvious gain to the proletarian revolution, but to shut out young people simply because they are from bourgeois families may not turn out to be such a wise policy. Many bourgeois children are youths of high ability whose exclusion from education means a loss of talent for the country, and for the revolution. These youths are psychologically eager for higher education, and indefinite postponement of further study in order to devote year after year to labor at a farm or factory has resulted in frustration and unhappiness for many.

On the other hand, the worker-peasant-soldier students have their adjustment problems, especially in the higher schools. Catapulted, so to speak, into advanced study without the foundation of basic academic education, they find it difficult to digest what they are taught. Some lose interest quickly, while others put the blame on bourgeois teachers who fail to relate teaching to practical situations within the experience of the laboring masses. They can participate vigorously in the criticism of bourgeois education and its aloofness from labor, production, and politics, but beyond that they too can feel frustrated. Some are baffled by questions that are not easy to answer. Since they have been chosen for advanced study by virtue of their political and production record, why should they as students be required to devote so much time to politics and labor? As a matter of fact, a specific target of ideological remolding is the alleged complacency that comes from the feeling that one is "already Red." To use the vocabulary of ideological remolding, the "doctrine of original Redness" is an error that workers-peasants-soldiers are apt to commit and must consciously "struggle against." Still, there are worker-peasant-soldier students who feel that they have come to school or college to learn the "technique" and "knowledge" that they cannot get in their production practice, and they, unlike those who complain of difficult studies, are disappointed when labor and production do not leave much time for the study they want.

The exercise of proletarian leadership has not proved an easy task for the workers-peasants-soldiers dispatched into the schools and universities. The initial task of criticizing the bourgeoisie and the dominant influence of bourgeois scholars is relatively simple, but the task of "leadership" in education is much more difficult and complicated. How can they, with their limited schooling, provide positive leadership in educational matters for the scholars at the universities? Their only sure weapon is the Thought of Mao Tse-tung, but the big question is how to apply Mao Thought to concrete problems of school management. An article on proletarian leadership laments that "poor and lower-middle peasants unconsciously slipped into the mire of routinism where the teachers are giving the lessons and the poor and lower-middle peasants have nothing to do."[4]

Mao is firm in his precept that intellectuals should learn from the workers-peasants-soldiers. Certainly, they have much to learn from the worker-peasant-soldier way of life: hard work, frugality, simple living, acceptance of hardship. They can learn the unswerving adoration of Mao and unquestioning acceptance of his teachings. But what about the study of the works of Marxism-Leninism-Maoism and the discussion of ideological-political problems? How can the workers-peasants-soldiers lead in such study? How can the intellectuals be expected to sit at the feet of the workers-peasants-soldiers in learning to grasp the full meaning of Mao Thought? Some of the workers, peasants, and soldiers may be very eloquent in recounting their past woes and venting their hatred for class enemies. But after much repetition, the oral "histories" lose their appeal and effectiveness.

Among other problems, the shortage of adequate teaching materials is a major difficulty. Theoretically, locally compiled teaching materials can be adapted to local needs and conditions and practice, but they consist mostly of materials with political significance: the "histories" of families, villages, production teams or brigades, and factories, of individual workers, peasants, and soldiers. "Social investigation" also has been concerned mostly with ideological-political materials. Oral instruction is extensively used for the principal reason that written materials are not available for the use of teachers and students. The new materials have been slow in appearing, even in tentative mimeographed editions. Old materials are to be expunged or purged of objectionable content, but it is not so easy to determine what part of the old is retainable and what part is a clear reflection of feudal or bourgeois ideology. In the university, curriculum content is judged according to its practical value; some study of theory is needed, but how much? The three-in-one teams are not able to answer such questions. Beyond quoting Chairman Mao and repeating ideological-political clichés, they really do not have many ideas about the organization of teaching content. The "old" teachers who know more about the practical problems in school work than the new teachers and worker-peasant-soldier teachers are so afraid of the charge of restoring bourgeois practices that they tend to sit back and wait.

Maoism and Formalism

In 1942 Mao issued a stern warning against "Party formalism." He assailed the "eight-legged" type of stereotyped writing (and thinking) in which the old classical scholars punctiliously observed a standardized form of writing. A large part of learning under the old system of education was devoted to learning the accepted formalistic style of writing. In time, thought became the prisoner of form, style became more important than content, and an essay was judged by its conformity to stereotyped form rather than by the ideas expressed. This formalism stunted the development of thinking and killed the creative spirit that marked early classical thought in China. Mao was worried that the indoctrination of Party dogmas might degenerate in the same way and result in beautiful words without much meaning. There was a tendency, he said, to "mouth empty phrases and words without substance." A great danger lay in using formalistic words as a means of "flaunting authority and terrifying people into submission." Listeners and readers of such formalistic speeches and literature were left in a fog. Mao described the process as follows:

> If a person writes in the style of Party formalism the
> consequence may not be too serious, but if he shows
> it to another person, he doubles the harm done. If
> he goes further and posts his writing on the wall or
> mimeographs it or publishes it in a newspaper or
> prints it as a book, then the problem becomes even
> more serious and many people are affected. But those
> who write in the "eight-legged" style always want
> many people to read what he has written.[5]

Was Mao prophetic ? Unfortunately, the above quotation could well be a description of what is happening today. The danger today lies not only in a new "eight-legged" form of writing, but in an "eight-legged" type of thinking. Granted that education must serve proletarian politics and, to do so, must put Mao Thought in supreme command, the question may still be raised whether the methods used in ideological-political indoctrination are likely to produce intelligent persons who may become worthy successors to the revolutionary cause. The current method is to saturate the mind with ideology and to accept Mao Thought as the sure guarantee of success, happiness, health, and prosperity, and the panacea for all troubles and problems, individual and social. One can understand how devotion to Chairman Mao and repeated study of his "Three Great Articles" can motivate a spirit of sacrificial service and steel the will to achieve despite obstacles, and how Mao's instruction to "fear neither hardship nor death" can inspire a determination to forge ahead in the face of difficulties and even danger. But when it comes to using Mao Thought as a source of wisdom for the solution of technical problems of agriculture and industry and all problems of personal life and social relations, one begins to wonder whether formalism in the use of big words has begun to develop.

For example, a poor peasant with a "low level of education" was honored for his ability to apply Chairman Mao's philosophical

essays to growing trees on a mountain. Here is what he was reported
to have testified at a Congress of Activists in the Living Study and
Application of Mao Tse-tung Thought:

[Chairman Mao's] On Contradiction has this statement:
"It (materialist dialectics) holds that external causes
are the condition of change and internal causes are the
basis of change, and that external causes become
operative through internal causes." With this in mind,
I thought about our grafting jujube on wild sour jujube
shrubs. It seemed to me that the sour jujube itself
had the condition for being made into a jujube. That
is the internal cause. Grafting is the external cause.
The grafting is an operative factor when done to the
sour grape. The sour grape cannot become a jujube
without grafting, which means that "external causes
are the condition of change." After all, a rock cannot
be made into a jujube tree no matter how skillfully you
graft, which means that "internal causes are the basis
of change" and "external causes become operative
through internal causes." Well, when I can figure out
what internal and external causes mean and their
dialectical relationship, I am sure philosophy is
no mystery.[6]

One must give credit to the peasant for his ability to expound
materialist dialectics, but one wonders if his practical experience in
grafting came before his study of Chairman Mao's philosophical
essay and then he wrote an "eight-legged" essay on Mao Thought, or
whether it was the study of Mao Thought that enabled him to graft a
jujube shrub successfully.

Another worker testified that he applied the two-line struggle
to production problems. According to "foreign technical data,"
spindles must not revolve more than 200 times a minute, but he and
his fellow workers wanted to increase the speed in order to step up
production. Ideological study made them realize that the question of
whether the speed of the spindles could be increased was "a mani-
festation of the clash of two kinds of philosophy . . . . The clash between materialistic dialectics and metaphysics"; the solution of the
production problem must come from the "remolding of my world
outlook."[7]

Mao's philosophical thinking was also reported to have guided
a hydrogeological team in the search for subterranean water. "Bourgeois academic authorities" had declared certain areas to be void of
water because they were misled by the 'philosophy of agnosticism."

167

But the team studied Mao's "On Contradiction," in which he taught: "The world outlook of materialist dialectics holds that in order to understand the development of a thing we should study it internally and in its relation with other things; in other words, the development of things should be seen as their internal and necessary self-movement, while each thing in its movement is interrelated with and interacts on the things around it." Enlightened by this easily understood truth, the surveyors examined one "dead cavity" after another and finally struck water.[8] Success in sinking a subterranean well was thus assured by ideological insight.

Other workers and peasants found that their work in constructing a well was put on the right track by their study of Materialism and Empirio-Criticism, in which Lenin taught: "The materialist affirms the existence and knowability of things-in-themselves. The agnostic does not even admit the thought of things-in-themselves and insists that we can know nothing certain about them. Each one of us has observed time without number the simple and obvious transformation of the 'thing-in-itself' into phenomenon, into the thing-for-us. It is precisely this transformation that is cognition."[9]

In the face of long-held belief that oranges are grown in the south and apples in the north, orchard growers in Shanghai experimented with transplanting apple trees to areas south of the Yangtze River. They succeeded, and they attributed their success to the study of Chairman Mao's works, which enabled them "to understand the dialectical relationship between fortuity and certainty."[10]

In another case a production brigade increased the yield of food crops by sowing spring maize earlier than usual. They, too, owed their success to Mao Thought, for Mao taught in his philosophical treatise "On Practice": "The movement of change in the world of objective reality is never-ending and so is man's cognition of truth through practice."[11] From this teaching, they learned that to regard "past experience as flawless and absolutely unalterable . . . is a metaphysical way of thinking" contrary to Marxism-Leninism-Maoism. Thus the planting of maize was politicized into a struggle between the two opposing lines.

With all due recognition of the importance of ideology as a guide to action and the motivating force of Maoism and the Mao cult, one may still wonder what workers and peasants have in mind when they talk about "one divides into two," the "knowability of things-in-themselves," "external causes and internal causes," "materialist dialectics and metaphysics," and so forth. Have they repeated the vocabulary they are taught in the never-ending indoctrination sessions just as pupils used to memorize the classical essays? Or is it their intention to show that they have reached a high level of ideological-political consciousness? Are they merely using a stylish vocabulary to describe their practical experience in order to give it an aura of respectability? Are they using words without really knowing what they mean, thus substituting formalism for genuine understanding? Are they indulging in verbalism?

In education, there are also manifestations of formalism. "Proletarian leadership," "integration of theory and practice," "learning from workers, peasants, and soldiers," "politics in command"—these are sure-fire phrases that are always safe to use and are likely to put the user on the right side of the struggle between two opposing lines. The use of such clichés has often become a ritual. Regardless of the topic under discussion, the speaker or writer always begins with the most commonly used ideological clichés followed by a generous sprinkling of quotations from Mao or Marx or Lenin throughout the speech or writing.

For example, a report on the reeducation of intellectuals in Kiangsu province brought up the problem of intellectuals who after seemingly successful reeducation gradually revert to old attitudes. Further reeducation was necessary, said the report, with emphasis on the "one dividing into two viewpoint." The "one dividing into two viewpoint" must guide the constant analysis of the conditions and problems of reeducating the intellectuals.[12] The puzzling part of the report is that after affirming the importance of the "one divides into two" method, it said nothing about how this abstract idea was to be applied to the concrete problems of intellectuals and how it was related to the solutions proposed. Was the reference to "one dividing into two" a form of ritual or lip service intended to invoke the authority of Chairman Mao for whatever was said or proposed? One of the specific proposals made in the report was that the remolding of outlook is a lifelong process that should never stop. How this proposal is related to the "one divides into two" concept was not made clear.

In another case, cadres in the University of Anhwei were found to be arrogant. To find out the best way to deal with them, the authorities "conducted a 'one divides into two' analysis" on the cadres and were thus enabled to "uncover and resolve contradictions" and understand more clearly the positive as well as negative qualities of the accused cadres.[13] The "one divides into two" concept was also invoked in an article discussing the correct policy for dealing with "old intellectuals." The concept was allegedly used for making a "complete analysis of the class origin and past record" of the intellectuals in order to find out how they could be used while being transformed.[14] To the layman, it would seem that the old formula of "absorb and reform" or that of "use and transform" would be easier to understand than the mystical "one divides into two." But in the current campaign to study Mao's philosophical works, every person feels the need of quoting his philosophical vocabulary. Is this profuse

169

use of stereotyped phrases a form of ritualism? Or is it a form of verbalism?

It is not enough for orchard workers to talk about experimentation with apple growing in terms of irrigation, drainage, and methods of pruning; they must describe their experience in terms of contradictions and their success as the triumph of Chairman Mao's revolutionary line.[15] Whether they are relevant or not, ideological clichés and standard quotations must be interspersed in the discussion. It is possible, of course, to take a favorable view of this process and to argue that Mao Thought is "not studied as a dogma . . . memorized and recited as a panacea for solving problems" but that it is "taken seriously. . . and applied concretely to daily life."[16] Nevertheless, there is ground for skepticism as to whether the workers, peasants, and cadres perceive any actual connection between the big words and ideological concepts they freely quote and the problems they face in daily life.

Formalism is also detectable in the current mode of thinking which attributes all successes of any kind to correct ideological orientation and all difficulties and failures to Liu Shao-ch'i and his fellow revisionists. All problems are reduced to the struggle between "two kinds of philosophy" and "two opposing lines." "Metaphysics," "transcendentalism," "apriorism," and "class enemies at work" are named as culprits whenever anything goes wrong. It is not necessary to go further to find out the roots of the difficulties.

Some cadres have shown a lack of interest in ideological-political study.[17] In dealing with such matters, no attempt is made to find out whether the lack of interest could be due to boredom with the repeated reading of uninteresting materials or to the obscure way in which ideological-political lessons are taught. The easy way is to identify the revisionists and anti-Marxists* as the source of trouble and to conclude that the solution lies in more intensive ideological-political education of the same kind. When urban youths desired to "return to the cities for some relaxation after autumn harvests," the immediate reaction was that they had been poisoned by the revisionist line and "did not have a high degree of consciousness on class struggle, the struggle between lines, and on continuing the revolution."[18] No thought was given to the possibility that the young people might have felt homesick or might have legitimate reasons for wanting to see friends or family in the cities. If they do not perform well on the farm, no effort is made to find out whether the cause is a health

---

*All thought systems other than Maoism are lumped together and labeled as anti-Maoist-Marxist-Leninist. No effort is made to make any distinction between them.

problem or some other difficulty in adjusting to rural life; it is always safe to conclude that the youth in question is weak or confused in ideology and the best way to help him is a stronger dose of ideological-political indoctrination.

It seems that this simple formula of reducing all problems to ideological terms cuts short the thought process and tends to induce a form of intellectual lethargy. It encourages an easy and lazy mode of thinking that accepts Mao Thought as the shortcut to problem solving. It is no longer necessary, it may even be risky, for an individual to seek or propose a solution of his own; the simple and safe way is to find a suitable quotation or directive and let Mao Thought point the way. People all over the country engage in "ideological" study, in revolutionary mass criticism, in struggle-criticism-transformation, in the rectification of the style of work, in the two-line struggle. Through the entire process, they use the same words, the same quotations, the same line of reasoning, in standardized form. How many really know what they are saying? How many mean what they say? This is certainly not what Mao Tse-tung would like to see, but there is a danger that the formalism he detests may be growing rather fast.

It would not be accurate to say that the Communists discourage thinking. As a matter of fact, the educational revolution condemns overuse of the lecture method of teaching and favors group discussion, self-study, and "independent thinking" by students. But all thinking must be within the framework of the Marxist-Leninist-Maoist ideology. Ideological education stresses the "living study and creative application" of Mao Thought, but it is important to note that creativity is to be expressed in the application of Mao Thought, not in a critical examination of its applicability, let alone its relevancy to the problems at hand. Independent thinking is to be exercised in experimenting with ways of achieving socialism, but not in judging the suitability or validity of the socialist system. To guard against overstepping the boundaries, the tendency is to stick closely to the approved formulas, and here arises a danger that the study and application of the creative thought of Mao and Marx and Lenin may degenerate into formalism and verbalism.

Whenever anything goes wrong, the revisionists and the "class enemies" are blamed. If anything goes well, the success is due to the triumph of the Maoist line. When many children drop out of school, when their "bad behavior" creates problems of discipline, or when young people engaged in labor and production are unable to stand hardship, or when they want to marry at an early age, there is no need to go beyond the standard cure of ideological-political study—the same writings and speeches, and the same method of recalling past miseries and the evils of the old society. This is much easier than to attempt to understand the psychology and the interests of individual pupils or

171

to introduce methods of counselling that may discover personal problem or non-ideological and non-political factors contributing to the problems. Here lies the danger of intellectual laziness that may result from the new formalism.

The Problems of Youth

Youths and intellectuals are among the most vexing problems with which the Communist regime must contend. It would seem that with such a comprehensive and intensive program of education and indoctrination, it should not be such a difficult task to mold youth according to Mao's image of revolutionary successors. Many young people have responded to the Communist call for reform and revolution, and they have been among the most active cadres dedicating themselves to the Communist cause. Nevertheless, many still have not responded with enthusiasm, and have become passive, frustrated, unhappy, even rebellious. Even among those who have rallied to the support of the revolution, uncertainty and doubts have weakened capacity for active service.

In a 1965 interview with the then French minister of culture, André Malraux, Mao Tse-tung expressed his deep concern with youth. Youth, he said, after a decade and a half of education and remolding, "is showing dangerous tendencies."[19] Seven years later, after the Cultural Revolution and a half-decade of the educational revolution, the People's Daily published an article on the education of youth which warned that "class enemies at home and abroad" were still plotting for the restoration of capitalism by taking advantage of the "weaknesses of the young people."[20] Another article in the same newspaper called attention to the presence of "extreme leftist ideas" among youth and "bad habits" that presented serious problems for those in charge.[21]

At about the same time, the Red Flag (August 1, 1972) published five articles—actually letters to the editor—on the ideological education of youth, exposing the presence of "anarchistic tendencies" among youths, who rejected discipline and objected to rules and regulations. One of these letters said that anarchism weakened the leadership of the Party and hurt discipline. The wrong ideas of "professional competence first" and "technique first" led to the neglect of politics, but when informed of their error, young people sometimes swung to the other extreme and decided that "technique is useless." Other young people looked upon art and athletics as recreation only and failed to appreciate their political significance. Another letter, written by the secretary of a neighborhood Party branch, concerned young people who were temporarily living in the neighborhood. Some had been assigned for work in the city, others were awaiting assignment, still others were home on account of illness. They tended to think only of their personal problems and were easily swayed by bourgeois ideological infiltration.

In another issue of Red Flag (April 1, 1972), a letter from peasants reports that young people in the rustication program had succumbed to the intrigue of class enemies and were led to think that, having been born and brought up in the new society, they did not need further ideological-political education. They took the view that the class struggle would die out and therefore was not important. They were discouraged because they saw no future for themselves, and they felt that their schooling had been wasted in labor activities that required no academic training. The secretary of a Party branch also complained that many young people were indifferent to the class struggle and did not understand its acute nature. They did not like political study and did not understand Chairman Mao's works. All such reports were made in order to underline the need of continued ideological-political education.

Students' behavior problems reflect their dissatisfaction or disillusionment. Some of the disciplinary problems, attributed by the ideology-minded to "anarchist" ideas spread by class enemies, arose from the effects of the unrestrained freedom of the Red Guards in the most tumultuous years of the Cultural Revolution. Having criticized and accused the teachers, the students could not readily submit to those whom they had charged with ideological-political transgression. Some felt they had been used and discarded, deprived of an active revolutionary role they had just begun to take up. A report on the misbehavior of students mentioned such bad habits as munching beans, peanuts, rice grain, and other irregular snacks. Unwholesome bourgeois influence was seen in the indulgence in such luxuries as wearing wristwatches in school or, in the case of those who did not have wristwatches, painting watches on their wrists.[22]

Children of cadres have proved to be a problem. They are arrogant and act as if they belonged to a privileged class. Some take no interest in ideological-political education because, as children of revolutionary cadres, they feel they are "already Red." This partly explains the reason why Mao Tse-tung, in his directive on reeducation, specifically asked the cadres to send their children to the countryside and thus set a good example for other parents.

Many of the faults identified as misbehavior appear rather harmless to educators in other countries, but they indicate an attitude of defiance that in some cases has found expression in rebellious behavior.

In the countryside, young people have been found to be unenthusiastic about work as well as ideological-political study. They seem deeply moved when they hear poor peasants tell about their past sufferings, but after a while the effects wear off and indifference returns. An interesting story about a gift by Mao sheds some light on the condition of urban youth in the countryside. According to the story, a teacher wrote a letter to Chairman Mao to plead for help in his financial difficulties due to the transfer of his son to the countryside. He had to send money to his son every month because the youth was unable to earn enough to support himself. It had come to the Chairman's attention that the teacher's problem was shared by many other people, so he referred the letter to the regional authorities. To show his sympathy, he sent a gift of 300 yuan (approximately $135) to ease the teacher's financial burden.[23] This incident confirms earlier reports that urban youths unaccustomed to labor do not produce very much; besides being unable to support themselves, the young people are considered a burden to their parents. It also helps to explain why much propaganda and ideological-political education have taken pains to convince the parents that it is their duty to help bring up the revolutionary successors that Chairman Mao has called for.

Another revealing piece of writing is furnished by Wen Hui Pao (July 10, 1967). It lamented an attitude of passivity and noncommitment on the part of young people:

In the cause of the great Cultural Revolution, a number of people have emerged who do not pay attention to state affairs and who stay out of the revolutionary movement. These people are called wanderers. They take an attitude of non-intervention in the struggle between the proletariat and bourgeoisie. Instead of fighting on the battle front, they wander about school campuses, parks and streets; they spend their time in swimming pools and playing chess and cards . . . . Whenever they are required to reveal an attitude they just issue vague statements.[24]

The article added that the "wanderers . . . put self-interest above all else " and "they will become bitter and tough and no longer peaceful." Such an attitude presents a sharp contrast to the adolescent idealism and activism that once made Chinese students the most enthusiastic supporters of reform and revolution. We do not know what percentage of youth belongs to this category, but the open discussion of their attitudes makes us suspect that their number and influence are not negligible. Furthermore, the fact that after so many years of intensive indoctrination there is still a sizable number of young people who resist being drawn into the nation's political life cannot but cast doubt on the effectiveness of the education program, which has stressed above all a positive and definite ideological-political commitment on the part of everyone.

Urban youths who do not accept the fate of long-term settlement in the countryside face a dreary future. They cannot just quit, because all work and living arrangements are assigned by the Party-state and they cannot find employment elsewhere. They are not permitted to go to school for future study. The Party-state controls not only all jobs but also travel and residence permits. Among those who escape, some manage to cross the border to Hong Kong or swim their way into an unknown future. Others merely drift into the cities. Without ration cards, they cannot even get food. They can resort to pilfering and thievery. Street gangs and delinquent youths have appeared on the urban scene. The problem is even more serious for girls. Unable to produce enough to support themselves, they are forced into undesirable marriages or cohabitation in the rural areas, or join the drifting gangs.[25]

An American scholar in Hong Kong made a study of young refugees from the Chinese Mainland, interviewing some 40 persons aged 16 to 25. Erstwhile militant Red Guards, he reported, tended "to be the most disillusioned and psychologically disoriented." Children of former landlords, rich peasants, capitalists, and bourgeois intellectuals had suffered discrimination and humiliation: "No matter how the offspring [of the nonproletarian classes] tried to be a part of the new society, their slightest mistake was linked to parental background." But the refugees did not find happiness in Hong Kong: "All live with the inner contradiction of wanting to go back. . . they dream of returning to China and joyful reunion with their family and friends." Their pathetic situation is well described by some of the young refugees: "I love my country, but my country doesn't love me."[26]

Fresh Air, Cool Breezes

The Chinese-American rapprochement that culminated in President Nixon's visit to China was a dramatic expression of China's new foreign policy. The open diplomacy of today contrasts sharply with the closed-door policy of the Cultural Revolution when China virtually isolated herself from the rest of the world. It is difficult to judge to what extent the liberalization of foreign policy has affected domestic policy. There are mixed trends that defy definite characterization. Even in the area of foreign relations, the hard line persists along with a soft approach; for example, strident attacks on American imperialism still continue on occasions and huge anti-American slogans still adorn two 50-foot pillars on the edge of Peking's Tienanmen Square.[27] Nevertheless, there is no doubt that fruitful contacts are developing between Peking and the rest of the world, and that the atmosphere in China's major cities is more relaxed and less depressing.

Colorful clothes are seen more often in the streets, although the same gray cotton Mao Suit is still the general rule. Books other than the strictly Marxist-Leninist-Maoist works are appearing in the bookstores. A dispatch from Peking reports that "the strains of the Strauss waltz played on an accordian wafted over a park in Central Peking recently. . . . The London and Vienna philharmonic orchestras have performed in Peking. . . and word is out that Western classics can be played again for the first time since the Cultural Revolution."[28]

More Chinese persons are going abroad, although under restrictive conditions, and more foreign visitors are permitted to enter China. Such contacts are bound to bring in fresh ideas and greater knowledge of conditions and practices in other countries. A direct result of contacts with foreign nations and peoples is a restoration of foreign languages in the school curriculum (see Chapter 3). More important is the way foreign languages are taught. A pronounced change was signaled by an article in the July 1, 1972 issue of the Red Flag. Whereas foreign languages previously were studied as "a useful tool in the class struggle,"[29] the article quoted Lenin to the effect that language is mankind's most important means of communication. For this purpose, the materials used in teaching foreign language must be selected with communication needs in view. To be sure, politics must be in command in all subjects of study, but the principle must be clearly understood and fuzzy ideas must be avoided, the article warned; it is wrong to use only political terms and neglect the language of daily use and other types of writing. The article noted that in a text for first-year English, one-half of 648 words appeared only once or twice and such words of daily use as eating, drinking, tea, pen, and room appeared only infrequently. Students learn to say "take the socialist road" but do not know how to say "take a walk." According to the article, students have expressed dissatisfaction with such teaching materials.

In the same spirit of stressing practical use rather than ideological-political formalism is a call for an "improvement in the style of writing." An article on this subject in Red Flag (August 1, 1972) counseled that writing should be in the popular language, easily understood, lively, and vigorous. Absolute affirmation or negation should be avoided. Too often, said the article, today's progress is praised in such a way as to give the impression that yesterday's life was all bad and there is no need for further effort. Such writing, warned the article, commits the very error that Chairman Mao criticized in his 1942 speech opposing Party formalism or stereotyped ("eight-legged") Party writing.

The People's Daily joined the Red Flag in the campaign against stereotyped verbosity. It published articles criticizing newspapers for long-winded articles in dull and dogmatic language.[30] One article by "an old worker who is a Communist Party member" inveighed against "page after page of empty words with no substance at all." Another, written by a group of Chinese language teachers at a middle school, complained that students had been influenced by the long-winded style of the newspapers and were writing drab and dull compositions, monotonous and dry and all following the same stereotyped style. These articles were obviously published with the endorsement of the People's Daily. They were given the headline, "Opposing the new eight-legged writing and new formalism."

As all who try to keep up with Chinese affairs by reading Chinese-language sources well know, the writings are very monotonous, with constant repetition of ideological-political clichés and dogmas. Too many articles follow more or less the same stereotyped pattern, beginning with a note of gratification over the success of the socialist revolution and the consolidation of proletarian leadership. Then follow ideological polemics bolstered by more quotations from the works of Marx, Lenin, and Mao, and finally comes a concluding section exhorting continued struggle against class enemies and their pernicious ideology. Sometimes one has to wade through a deep morass of stereotyped words and phrases in order to glean one or two new ideas. At other times the reader persists to the end without finding anything new. If the current campaign against formalism should succeed in reducing, if not eliminating, the repetitious wordiness and monotonous clichés, Chinese newspapers and journals not only would be more interesting to read but would be more informative than the formalistic and liturgical style that has been current for more than two decades.

Formalism and stereotyped writing, of course, are a creation of revisionists and "swindlers of the Liu Shao-ch'i type." Chairman Mao spoke against them more than 30 years ago. The campaign against formalism, we are told, is really a part of the two-line struggle. Moreover, the "swindlers" are responsible for the "Leftist" error of loading teaching materials with irrelevant political content. Even in mathematics, they present simple problems of applied mathematics amid a plethora of unsuitable political terms.[31] Are we witnessing a new emphasis on regular school studies? The Party branch of a middle school in Tientsin deplores burdening students with too many labor jobs so that they have little time for "socialist cultural studies.[32] The People's Daily published an article stressing the importance of training in penmanship.[33] Criticizing careless writing and poor penmanship of students, the article urges that not only language teachers but teachers of all subjects should demand from students a high standard of writing and that penmanship practice should be made a part of language teaching. Careless penmanship and the omission of the component strokes of written characters should not be tolerated.

Basic Studies

Undue emphasis on politics and labor is now condemned as a

"Leftist" deviation instigated by "swindlers of the Liu Shao-ch'i type." Leftism could even be expressed as excessive stress on practical use to the neglect of "basic studies" not immediately applicable to practice. We now hear more about the need for "fundamental learning" in the elementary school.[34] An article by the Party branch of a middle school in Inner Mongolia may be another straw in the wind. It urged greater attention to the teaching of "basic knowledge and fundamental theories" and warned that one-sided emphasis on ideological-political education, too much time devoted to labor and nonacademic activities, and adventitious attempts to relate teaching to practice have resulted in the teaching and learning of little knowledge.[35]

Moreover, the study of theories is now recognized to have a rightful place in education. Ever wary of being accused of commiting the bourgeois error of teaching "pure knowledge," some teachers have selected only the part of the materials that can be easily linked with practice, skipping the fundamental theories. This is wrong, according to current commentary. In learning knowledge, it is important not only to know the facts but also to understand why they are so. This is certainly a reversal of the position taken by the ideologues in recent years. Again, the problem is put in an ideological context: The error lies in the confusion of thinking in regard to the correct relation between politics and vocation, between theory and practice, between political education and cultural education; the teachers ought to study more carefully the Thought of Mao Tse-tung so that they may understand that the teaching of basic and fundamental theories is different from the "pure knowledge" viewpoint of bourgeois education. Basic study and vocational study must be put under the command of politics and under the guidance of Mao Thought.

These articles in the Red Flag and the People's Daily sound more like the talk of practical schoolmen than that of the ideologues. Needless to say, they could not have appeared in print if the ideas were not officially approved. Are we, then, witnessing another swing of the pendulum toward old-fashioned study in school?

Along the same line is the suggestion that more time, as much as 70 percent, should be given to "cultural studies." Greater emphasis on study is also indicated by the restoration of examinations in schools. Mao once assailed examinations as a means of discriminating against the proletariat and as "surprise attacks against students as enemies." Literal acceptance of his words led to the abolition of examinations during the Cultural Revolution, with students judged according to their labor record and ideological-political awareness. The restoration of examinations may be another small step in the direction of normal schooling and systematic learning. If the time allotment for ideological-political education and for labor and production could be contained within reasonable limits, then time would be released for study and the schools' academic program would be given a healthy impetus.

Greater stress on study has probably been necessitated by the growing realization that the shotgun method of training popularized by the educational revolution has not armed the "proletarian intelligentsia" with the necessary knowledge and capabilities for assuming responsibilities in socialist construction. Workers and peasants who are taught only the bare essentials of production knowledge and skills have proved unequal to the big tasks of proletarian leadership. Now it is realized that without some knowledge of theories, practical skill has definite limitations; the attack on the bourgeois emphasis on technique and theory has gone too far.* The excess is laid at the door of the revisionists, who swing from the extreme Right to the extreme Left and the non-Marxist philosophy of "idealist apriorism." Chairman Mao, we are reminded, taught the unity of theory and action, not action without theory. This means due regard for the study of theory and basic knowledge, but the study should be based on actual practice.[36]

Regardless of ideological polemics, the fact remains that there is a new effort to teach technique based on vocational knowledge. Workers and peasants must "dare to grasp production, management, and technique."[37]

An article on the learning of technique by young workers, in the Red Flag (October 1, 1972), criticizes workers who despise technical work and take the one-sided view that political study is all-important. This is said to be another pernicious idea fostered by the Liu Shao-ch'i "Leftists." Technique is needed for the revolution; it can be learned only by painstaking effort. In another issue of the Red Flag (September 1, 1972), we find a number of articles stressing the need to study theory. One article argues that basic fundamental courses in theoretical science are a necessary prerequisite to specialization. Another suggests that if what is practical in a factory is too narrow in scope, it may be necessary for a school to establish links with several factories so that the breadth of study in the schools may be matched with what is practiced in the factories. Encouraged by the initiative of the noneducators, the universities are making bold to introduce theoretical studies.

Even teachers are asked to pay more attention to their own vocational knowledge. An article by the education bureau of a municipality in Anhwei province pointed out the need to raise the level of

---

*The term technique is used to mean subject matters of vocational importance, beyond the bare essentials required for immediate practice; it also involves some study of the theory needed for the understanding of technique. Technique and theory are both related to the basic academic studies in schooling.

vocational knowledge of teachers.* It advocated that mathematics teachers of "people-run" schools who failed to make students understand their subject matter should be given assistance in getting better teaching materials and visual aids. Not so long ago, the standard remedy would have been more ideological-political study and more rereading of the "Three Great Articles."

Students have been under more effective control and discipline in the post-Cultural Revolution period. Now it is being suggested that they should study hard, to master basic knowledge and fundamental theories. Do these changes add up to a more conservative program of education? It is reported that some universities have even begun to extend the length of study, and Futan University in Shanghai has increased its course to three and one-half years.[38]

A change of attitude toward intellectuals may also be indicative of greater concern for normal study in schools. There is a shift from the criticism of intellectuals and attacks on their bourgeois background to "bold use" of them. The decision to recruit more intellectuals may have been influenced in part by the realization that after all they must be the mainstay of the teaching personnel while the workers-peasants-soldiers can be a supplementary force at best, and in part by the hope that large numbers of intellectuals have been remolded by reeducation and other methods. Be that as it may, the return of more intellectuals to the educational scene will help turn education more in the direction of regular schooling. Likewise, the admission of children of bourgeois background into higher education may have been motivated by economic and political considerations, but it may also signal a modification of the policy of considering class origin and revolutionary record as the chief criteria for admission.[39] Class origin remains of great importance, but ability, political record, and actual performance in production are also to be taken into consideration.

An article on a positive policy of making use of intellectuals, written by the Party committee of a hsien in Honan province, reflects both the new and old points of emphasis.[40] Intellectuals must be made aware of their shortcomings, but it is not wise to dwell only on their negative factors and lose sight of their abilities and talents. They must be "boldly" used in the three great revolutionary movements and as teachers, technicians, accountants, and military cadres. They must be brought into the campaign of criticism-rectification.

---

*Again, the term "vocational" must be understood in its broad sense. It refers to nonpolitical and nonideological studies, sometimes practically synonymous with "cultural studies."

The double-barreled policy of "absorb and reform" is still valid, but where opposition to the domination of bourgeois intellectuals in education once resulted in almost exclusive emphasis on "reform," there is now a new inclination to use and absorb the intellectuals.

It may be premature to speak of trends. It may be overoptimistic to think that a new wave of liberalism has emerged. But these "straws in the wind" are worth noting and watching. In the meantime, one must be aware of many uncertain factors on the political and economic scene, and until we see more clearly the direction of political and economic developments, we would do well to refrain from hasty conclusions.

A Zigzag Course

One difficulty in the assessment of trends arises from the zigzag course of Communist policy. In education, as in economics and politics, Communist policy has often shifted from one direction to another: in the antithesis between rigid control and relative relaxation, between right and left, between the hard line and the "soft" approach, between dogmatism and realism. Such shifts may be due to the ambivalent character and the ever-present "contradiction" inherent in the thinking and ideology of Marxism-Maoism. Intellectual education is bourgeois and book knowledge is useless, but it is wrong to reject knowledge when knowledge is needed for the revolution. Mao Tse-tung himself has on more than one occasion castigated impractical book knowledge, but when young people come to the conclusion that it is useless to study because labor and political activism are what counts, they are told that they must study seriously and earnestly. Intellectuals must be appreciated and absorbed, but they must also be chastised and reformed. Theory without practice is worthless, but practice without theory is ineffective. Communist policy has emphasized one or the other of these opposites at different times. The shifts and pendulum swings may appear rather suddenly, and it is difficult to foretell how long a given course of action will last.

No doubt, the "opposing elements" are present in every situation. The confusing aspect of the Communist position is that when one of the opposites is emphasized, the validity of the other is not conceded and its espousal is treated as a deviation, while when official policy shifts to emphasize the other, what was once advocated now falls into disfavor. The shift is, in most cases, more than a change in relative emphasis; it involves the adoption of a new line of thinking and a reversal of policy. When the official policy shifts, ideological correctness is redefined accordingly. Maoist theory considers these "contradictions" a normal phenomenon and seeks their solution in the "unity of opposites." But for the layman such philosophical distinctions are not easy to understand or to use as guides to action.

In regard to political shifts within the Party during the Cultural Revolution, it was reported that even "leading cadres," that is, members of revolutionary committees, were dismayed that "struggle within the Party had come too abruptly and that it was not easy to understand.[41] Shifts in educational policy have also come about "abruptly," and it is conceivable that educators and intellectuals may be slow in adjusting to new positions. Intellectuals are understandably unsure of the new policy to "use" them, and teachers are hesitant to act too quickly on the suggestion that they can now demand more serious study and higher standards of work from their students. The struggle between two opposing lines is still of crucial importance, but the boundary between the lines shifts. The shift is decreed from above, and the only safe guide to action is to listen carefully to the official pronouncements and follow the new line as enunciated.

In a special issue on the educational revolution, the Red Flag (June 1, 1971) listed ten crucial "relations" that require careful attention. Each of the "relations" contains "contradictions" or opposing lines of thought or action. These relations are:

1. The relation between politics and vocational study. This involves the old "Red and expert" controversy: Which should come first and which should be given greater emphasis. It also involves the relation between ideological-political education and the study of vocational and academic subjects. The latter are now considered important, but there still exists the danger of stressing them to the extent of neglecting politics, for politics must still be in command.

2. The relation between leadership and the masses, between unity and struggle. What does proletarian leadership mean? What relation should there be between the Mao Thought Propaganda Teams and the intellectuals? Which is more important at a given moment: unity or ideological and political struggle?

3. The relation between destruction and construction, between revolutionary mass criticism and compiling new teaching materials. Mass criticism is directed against wrong concepts and objectionable teaching materials. Major targets of criticism have been: "technique first," "theory is basic," and teaching materials based on the revisionist theory of knowledge. After so much repudiation of traditionally accepted thought and practice, what course is open for positive construction and the preparation of new teaching materials?

4. The relation between study, "the main task of the students," and "learning other things," such as industry, agriculture and military affairs. Both are contained in Mao's May 7 (1966) Directive. Which should come first? There are times when "other things" have become the central tasks, but now there is a swing to the "main task" of study.

5. The relation between theory and practice, between book knowledge and practical knowledge.

6. The relation between using and remolding the teaching staff.

7. The relation between popularization and raising standards. The latter has not yet received much attention for it sounds too much like "elitist" education, but the issue is a live one.

8. The relation between self-reliance and external assistance, between local establishment of schools and aid from the state.

9. The relation between classroom and society, between school work and out-of-school activities.

10. The relation between the educational revolution and the revolution on other fronts.

Most of these "relations" involve contradictions that tend to put more emphasis on one aspect or the other. If teachers and the teaching profession were free to examine the opposites and weigh their merits and demerits from the standpoint of education, they might attempt to work out practical programs paying due regard to each and avoiding the pitfall of extreme polarization. Unfortunately, the teaching profession does not take the initiative in policy shifts and does not make recommendations for the resolution of the contradictions. The shifts in education reflect policy changes in economics and politics, and decisions on these changes are made by people outside the schools.

To be more specific, the "fresh breezes" discussed in the previous section could not have appeared without the more relaxed political atmosphere of the post-Cultural Revolution era. The intensity of the campaign for criticism-rectification and revolutionary mass criticism and the amount of time allotted to them depend in large measure on how the authorities of the Party-state view the actual threat of the revisionists and dissident elements. Economically, the need for trained personnel for the manifold tasks of "socialist construction" determines to a large extent the kind of training program the schools are expected to carry on. If the products of the schools prove inadequate for the needs of industry, agriculture, government, and so on, the schools will be called upon to put greater emphasis on technique and vocational training. On the other hand, whenever politics overrules economics, the educational program shifts accordingly to stress politics in command.

Twists and turns and pendulum swings are not new on the Chinese scene in the past two decades. Periods of moderation and relaxation have alternated with periods of harshness and inflexibility. A more "liberal" policy in economics usually goes with such changes as more lenient treatment of intellectuals and more attention to academic study, but the new trends are quickly halted when there are new developments such as the Sino-Soviet split and the ideological rigidity that followed. Taking a more favorable view, one may say that Communist policy is marked by flexibility in adjusting to changing circumstances. Mao has taught that policy-making must be guided by a correct assessment of "objective conditions"; when objective conditions demand a different approach, a new policy is proposed. The goal is constant, but the tactics are subject to constant modification and adjustment, even to abrupt reversals.

Meanwhile, major contradictions remain unsolved, presenting dilemmas that cause confusion and uncertainty. What proportion of school time should be devoted to academic study in relation to ideological-political study? How much time should be allotted to labor and production, to participation in revolutionary movements inside and outside the schools? How much theory should be taught in connection with technical skills? Should scholars engage in research? What kind of research? Even on strictly educational grounds, these are difficult questions for which there are no ready answers. When the questions are laden with ideological and political overtones, the confusion is compounded. The trouble is that it is possible to swing from one opposite to the other and find support all the time in direct quotations from Mao or Marx or Lenin. To denounce "putting technique first" at one time and to stress the importance of technique at another can both be, and are, justified as carrying out the teachings of Mao. It is easy to treat any divergence from the official line at any given moment as ideological-political deviation. The arguments are always presented in ideological-political terms, not on educational grounds.

Teachers and intellectuals ask few questions. Workers-peasants-soldiers who ask how the new attitude toward technique differs from the revisionist policy are given the explanation that technique is now put in the service of the revolution, not to serve the bourgeoisie as previously, and therefore to give it due emphasis under the guidance of Mao Thought is entirely in harmony with the spirit of the educational revolution. An example of the skepticism that greets policy reversals is the report of a technician in a chemical plant who hesitated to join the class organized for technical personnel to raise their technical competence. Although aware of his inadequacy and need for more technical education, the worker was deterred by his fear of committing the revisionist error of "technique first." He had to be guided to study Mao's teachings more carefully in order to overcome his misunderstanding of the distinction between the revisionist and Maoist lines.[42] This kind of report is not unusual. Policy shifts are not readily accepted, partly because they are not understood and also because people are so used to denouncing revisionist ideas and practices that they are afraid of doing the wrong thing. Furthermore, it is also clear from such reports that educational issues cannot be discussed without direct and explicit reference to their ideological-political framework.

Notes

1. See a brief report on the findings of a Japanese survey of the Chinese economy by Peter Grose, in The New York Times, May 19, 1969.

2. See Mao's 1942 speech on "Reform in Learning, the Party, and Literature," translation in Boyd Compton, Mao's China: Party Reform Documents, 1952-54 (Seattle: University of Washington Press, 1951)

3. See Mao's speech on "Opposing Party Formation," in Compton, op. cit.

4. Foreign Broadcast Information Services, Daily Report, Communist China, May 27, 1969, p. B11. (Hereafter cited as FBIS.)

5. Mao Tse-tung, "Fan-tui Tang Pa-ku" (Opposing Party formalism), a speech delivered on February 8, 1942, at a joint meeting of the Propaganda Department and the Bureau of Publication. Boyd Compton, Mao's China: Party Reform Documents, 1942-1944 (Seattle: University of Washington Press, 1952) p. 33.

6. Peking Review, November 6, 1970, p. 10.

7. Peking Review, December 4, 1970, pp. 16-17.

8. Peking Review, December 18, 1970.

9. Peking Review, October 20, 1972, p. 16.

10. Peking Review, November 3, 1972, p. 18.

11. Peking Review, December 8, 1972.

12. Kuang-ming Jih-pao, August 15, 1971.

13. FBIS, September 13, 1971, p. C11.

14. Article on transforming intellectuals in Northwest University, in FBIS, December 30, 1970, p. B1.

15. Hung-ch'i. (Red Flag), October 1, 1972.

16. Janet Goldwassen and Stuart Dowty, "Study Groups: Relating Marx to Daily Life," Understanding China Newsletter (Ann Arbor, Mich.), March-April 1973.

17. FBIS, November 19, 1970, p. H1.

18. FBIS, January 19, 1971, p. B13. Mao Thought is also a part of the treatment prescribed for patients of a psychiatric hospital; see Leigh Kagar, "Report from a Visit to the Tientsin Psychiatric Hospital," China Notes (New York), Fall 1972.

19. André Malraux, Anti-Memoirs (trans. by Terrace Kilmartin; New York: Holt, Rinehart and Winston, 1967), p. 467.

20. Jen-min Jih-pao, December 12, 1972.

21. Article by Party Committee in Anshan Municipality, in Jen-min Jih-pao, July 29, 1972.

22. Jen-min Jih-pao, January 20, 1973, p. 2 (report of a primary school teacher in Shanghai).

23. New York Times, July 23, 1973.
24. Quoted in F. T. Mits, "The Wanderers," Current Scene (Hong Kong), August 15, 1967.
25. "Chinese City Girls Sent To Countryside," New York Times, August 29, 1972.
26. David Raddock, "Innocents in Limbo," Far Eastern Economic Review, April 29, 1972.
27. "In Chinese Game, U. S. Is Still Villian," New York Times, July 30, 1973.

28. Los Angeles Times, June 8, 1973.
29. Diana Lary, "Teaching English in China," China Quarterly, October-December 1965.
30. Jen-min Jih-pao, July 26, 1972; Peking Review, August 4, 1972, pp. 14-16.
31. Jen-min Jih-pao, April 29, 1972.
32. This is a term used for regular school subjects; see Kuang-ming Jih-pao, June 15, 1972.
33. Jen-min Jih-pao, October 29, 1972.
34. Article on teaching materials, in Jen-min Jih-pao, April 29, 1972.
35. Jen-min Jih-pao, October 15, 1972.
36. "Enlivening Studies and Accentuating Student Initiation," Peking Review, February 23, 1973.
37. Current Scene, August 1972, p. 23.
38. New York Times, August 27, 1973.
39. Tillman Durdin, "China's Schools to Readmit Bourgeoisie," New York Times, July 9, 1973.
40. Kuang-ming Jih-pao, January 11, 1973.
41. China News Analysis, no. 905, (January 5, 1973), p. 1.
42. Kuang-ming Jih-pao, November 17, 1972.

9

Any attempt to make an objective and critical evaluation of Maoist education is subject to grave hazards and runs the risk of arousing emotional reactions and contentious arguments. The tendency to take polarized positions makes it difficult to see the achievements and shortcomings in the proper perspective. There is also a tendency to treat any criticism or endorsement of the educational program as rejection or acceptance of Mao's role in other aspects of the Chinese revolution. It should be possible, for instance, to recognize Mao's signal success in elevating China's position in international relations and at the same time to be critical of his educational revolution. It should also be possible to endorse Mao's educational goals but question whether the methods currently used are conducive to the attainment of the goals. Unfortunately, it is not always easy to realize this theoretical possibility.

Even without the emotions arising from resentment of adverse criticism or objection to recognition of positive merits, interpretation and analysis are hampered by the lack of complete knowledge of what is going on, the presence of mixed and confusing trends, and the uncertainty about future developments in the zigzag course of events in Maoist China. Those who visit China see only a few selected areas and aspects of life; those who depend on library resources have access only to sources of information made available to the outside world.

Whatever we hear or read or see can only be a part of the total picture. We are told that the Mao cult is being muted; the red book of quotations, for example, is not obligatory as it was in the heyday of the Cultural Revolution. But the adoration of Mao and Mao Thought is still accorded a central place in all forms of education. Is the cult disappearing or is it assuming new forms? We read that there is a reaction away from overemphasis on ideological-political education, but we note elsewhere that the two-line struggle is still given the highest priority in education and all educational effort must be under the guidance of Mao Thought.

Positive Gains

Despite the confusing picture, Maoist education has beyond doubt made positive gains. Some major achievements were noted in Chapter 8: the expansion of educational opportunity, the wide variety of schools and educational programs outside schools, the close co-operation of school and society. Educational theorists in the West have dreamed of using education as an agency for social change and of a comprehensive program of education that takes into account the total impact of all influences on the human mind and heart. Such a broad concept of education is not merely a dream in Maoist China. Education is, indeed, "coextensive with life," as the educational theorists would say. The "open-door" operation of schools has torn down the walls that used to segregate schools from society. Maoist education has also succeeded in changing the class balance of Chinese society and has contributed directly to the class revolution projected by the Communists. It has effectively raised the status of the prole-tariat and brought down the bourgeoisie from their previous favored position. Education, to use a cliché, is a positive force for remaking society.

At least some measure of success may be claimed for the pro-cess of remolding new citizens for proletarian society. Recent visi-tors to China have been impressed with the response of the people to the new "work ethic," not the hard work of yesteryear aimed at ma-terial benefits for one's self and family but work for the collective good and the glory of the socialist revolution. The campaign against the "feudal" motive of study to become an official and the bourgeois motive of seeking education for the purpose of personal advancement together with the emphasis on serving "the people" and "the revolu-tion" has probably had a positive effect on many people and led to a greater awareness of the social obligations of those who are given the opportunity of education. From all appearances, the common man seems to "have formed a sense of purpose, self-confidence, and dignity."[1] There seems to exist a "sense of national harmony" and high morale and community of purpose."[2] In their conversations with individuals, visitors are impressed with the prevalent adoration of Chairman Mao and the apparent readiness of young and old to obey him and serve the revolution. In some sectors of the population and in some areas, at least, the "new man" seems to be emerging.

Educational theorists may also be fascinated with Maoist in-novations that break boldly with the conventional pattern: new educational methods and content designed to meet the needs of the rural economy, shortening of schooling by elimination of the rigid prerequisites for advanced study, new examination and evaluation methods. They will be pleased to note that there is much experimentation within the framework of Maoist principles and general directives. There is experimentation with different types of schools and different ways of popularizing education among children and adults. Teaching materials are compiled in tentative form and reflect local conditions. Experimentation and local adaptation are, of course, governed by prescribed limits. Major policies are firmly under central direction; such decisions as the relative emphasis on ideological-political indoctrination vis-à-vis the study of vocational or academic or "basic" subjects, the use or remolding of intellectuals and "old" teachers, and the relation between theoretical study and practice are made by the Party-state and applicable to the whole country. But in the implementation of these policies there is room for experimentation with methods and procedures. The result is much variation in practice.

But it would be a mistake to equate this variation with experimental schools as they are understood in the United States and some other countries. Not only is the scope of experimentation circumscribed but there is no assurance of how long the period of experimentation will continue. As more experience accumulates in the implementation of broad guidelines and general principles, the present period of experimentation may give way to more standardization for the whole country. At this juncture, nevertheless, one finds on the educational scene much variation in practice and much room for local initiative in devising practical means of attaining the goals set by the central authorities.

A major gain is the extension of educational opportunity. Schooling is more readily available to the masses and the poor, and there is a wide variety of programs to teach adults as well as children the fundamentals of literacy (including political literacy) and the knowledge and skills applicable to production. Not to be forgotten is the extensive "propaganda network" that brings information and instructions to all parts of the country by a variety of mass media. Not only are the illiterate learning to read and write but villagers who used to have no knowledge or interest in affairs outside their own small community and immediate environment have become aware of the economic plans and political struggles in the nation and the "great revolutionary movements" throughout the land. Liu Shao-ch'i, Lin Piao, Chou En-lai, and many others have become familiar names everywhere. Moreover, people hear about events in the Soviet Union, in faraway Albania and Cuba, and the revolutions in Vietnam, Cambodia, and other foreign lands—events that in previous years would not have entered their thinking at all. To be sure, they are told only what the Party-state wants them to know, and they get no viewpoint other than the current official line, but even strictly controlled information and propaganda cannot fail to widen the horizon of the masses.

The Method of Repetition

Mao Tse-tung makes no distinction between education and propaganda and indoctrination. A principal method of education and propaganda is repetition. In ideological-political education, the words "read and re-read" and "study and re-study" are used repeatedly in connection with the study of Mao's works, his "Three Great Articles" and his directives and instructions. In educational writings, one encounters endless repetitions of the "two-line struggle," memories of the miserable pre-Liberation past, and stereotyped denunciations of feudalism, capitalism, revisionism, Liu Shao-ch'i and his gang of "swindlers," the unworthy motive of studying for personal gain, and so forth. No doubt the method of unceasing repetition is effective to a degree. For some people, at least, it must have a mesmerizing effect, and to that extent it produces changes in thought and action. People who day in and day out chant the title of one of the Three Great Articles, "Serve the People," could be expected to become more aware of this goal.

Psychologically, repetition may be a useful method of emotional conditioning, which is an important task of education. The peasant who goes to an evening class after a day's tiring toil may actually gain strength from the repetition of instructions and pledges that do not require much reflection, and as he stands before the portrait of Chairman Mao he may actually be inspired to greater effort. The repetition of slogans and quotations may be boring and counterproductive for some people, but their mesmerizing effect on many cannot be completely discounted. Those who rebel against the monotony may feel unhappy or may inwardly rebel or even plot to escape, but for the majority who go through the ritualistic process day in and day out, it is quite conceivable that active conditioning and remolding are taking place.

From another point of view, the study and restudy of Mao's works or other ideological writings may serve a useful purpose. The concepts are often difficult to grasp and subject to different interpretations. Restudy accompanied by explanation and discussion may help to bring out the full meaning of dogmas and clichés and their relevance to contemporary problems and issues. Rereading and restudy also afford an opportunity to reinterpret general concepts and principles in the light of shifts in policy and ideological-political emphasis. Although the two-line struggle is constant, its content and points of emphasis often change, and restudy affords an opportunity to apply the general concepts to new situations and to assure the learners that the basic ideological-political teachings remain correct and unchanged, and that any semblance of inconsistency is due to misunderstanding that can be cleared up by a more careful study of the original teachings and instructions.

The Thinking Process

With due recognition of the positive gains made by the Maoist educational revolution, it is still pertinent to raise some questions. One question concerns the effects of the method of repetition on the mentality developed by education. Is there a danger that the repeated study and restudy of the same speeches and writings may contribute to the mental sluggishness that we noted in Chapter 8 in connection with formalism and stereotyped thinking? Is there a possibility that the process may degenerate into mechanical intonation and produce a form of mental numbness that hampers active reflection? Or would diminishing returns result from boredom with monotonous repetition? Is there any validity to a visitor's warning that a mental monotone is being imposed on the nation with "rigid limits" on "the life of the mind"?[3] Or to another visitor's observation to the effect that the individual in China "is enveloped by an Idea, the Thought of Mao Tse-tung" to the extent that there is "near-total control" so pervasive and all-embracing that "people seem to cooperate in their own unfreedom"?[4] If submission and conformity were all that is wanted, it would be unnecessary to heed these questions and critical comments, but if the "new man" is expected to exercise reflective or even independent judgment, then the current method of ideological-political education may prove highly inadequate. Many visitors have been favorably impressed with the oneness of thought and unity of action they observe. The question is whether in the long-range view something important has been left out of the picture.

Even in school subjects other than ideological-political study, visitors have observed much rote learning;[5] students listen passively to the teacher and "recite like scholars."[6] Such observations are contrary to reports of discussion methods and student participation in universities. Conflicting reports may indicate, here as elsewhere, the unresolved contradictions. As long as rote learning is used extensively in the lower schools, there exists the danger of restricting—to use a mild word—the development of the mind. Reference was made earlier to the investigation of a middle school in Hopei province which reported the consensus of workers and peasants that school graduates sent to the countryside were high in political consciousness and good in labor but weak in "scientific and cultural knowledge." According to the report, the students' shortcoming was due to an incorrect understanding of the two lines and a failure to distinguish between the revisionist line of "intellectual education first" and the desired acquisition of knowledge for the use of the revolution; the prescribed cure was none other than more ideological-political study and deeper understanding of the meaning of "politics in command."[7] Do we see a process of thinking that goes around in ideological-political circles? How is mental alertness to be developed by such teaching methods?

That this problem is not just a characteristic of the recent educational revolution but has been a constant one probably rooted in ideology, may be seen from an observer's comment on Yenan education.

> Even in this period one can see the unresolved contradiction between education and indoctrination. . . .
> The Communist position is ambivalent. On the one hand there is recognition of the educational value of discussion and experiment. On the other there is the belief that, on any question where an official Party decision has to be made, only one opinion can honestly be held and no alternative hypothesis can be considered or tested. . . . On the one hand the Communists want people to think; on the other, they are, in certain respects afraid of the possible results of thinking.[8]

The Limits to Remolding

Mention has been made of some measure of success in instilling in the people of China a new motive for hard work and a new spirit of working for the common good. What has been observed and reported in this respect encourages the belief that the Communist dream of a "new man" is being realized, at least in part. At the same time, there is another side of the picture that is not so bright. It shows the tenacious survival of characteristics of the "old type of man" and of unproletarian ideas, customs, and habits that do not disappear so quickly. One may take the optimistic view that it takes time to change deep-rooted habits and customs, and that eventually the new man of the Communist blueprint will emerge to displace the old. On the other hand, one may also raise the question whether some of the unproletarian ideas and habits condemned by the Communists have roots not only in feudal and bourgeois society but in human nature itself, and so may not yield so easily to the remolding of the new education.

Is the desire for physical comfort entirely due to the pernicious influence of bourgeois and revisionist ideology? Can the desire of young people for marriage before the officially approved age of 26 or 28 be explained entirely in ideological terms? Are there human drives and yearnings that cannot be set aside by ideological-political study? The Maoist belief in the power of remolding seems to rest on a few assumptions that may be subject to question: (1) so-called human nature is a product of the environment and can be remolded by the manipulation of the environmental factors;[9] (2) action and thought issue from ideology and the only sure way of changing people is by means of ideological conversion; (3) there is no such thing as universal human nature—recognition of the class nature of man means that the proletarian man must be very different from the man of bourgeois or feudal society.

But, one may ask, does the unrelenting campaign against bourgeois ideology and against selfishness and expectation of material reward indicate the tenacious hold of the unproletarian tradition? Beyond doubt, selfishness and greed are the root of many social evils and much personal unhappiness. Religions have worked toward eliminating these evils, and social reformers have proposed a variety of approaches. But there is a difference between the approach of bourgeois reformers and the Maoist approach. The former usually recognize that there are basic human needs that must be satisfied; these needs, personal and psychological as well as physical, are there regardless of the social order. The Maoists, however, seem to believe that human drives, desires, and needs are all the result of conditioning and can be changed by the process of reconditioning, which is the essence of remolding. Personal ambition, mother love, family relations, and friendship are seen as shaped by environmental factors, above all the nature of the class alignment in society, and therefore subject to reshaping to meet the needs of proletarian society.

It has been emphasized, for example, that human relations, marriage, and personal relations must be reordered in the light of class relations. Cadres have been warned that marriage with a person of bourgeois family may be inimical to the revolutionary cause; personal friendships also must take into account the distinction between class friends and class enemies. Some success seems to have been achieved, for example, in the campaign against superstitions and costly weddings, funerals, and birthday celebrations. But other attitudes and traditions characteristic of a way of life identified with centuries of China's history have proved resistant to change.

Take, for example, the advocacy of cremation in order to make more land available for cultivation. Cremation is increasingly accepted. Related to this change is the effort to convert the Ch'ing Ming Festival, the traditional occasion for visiting and cleaning family tombs, into a Memorial Day for Revolutionary Martyrs. When people tried to honor both the revolutionary martyrs and the deceased members of their families, an "educational campaign" was launched to remold their thinking. Visitors to family tombs found posters giving scientific facts about death, with charts showing the decomposition of the body after burial, the cost of an elaborate funeral and its effects on family finance, the advantages of cremation, and so forth.[10] The campaign was well planned, but it evidently did not take into account the Chinese family traditions and human emotions associated with deceased parents, ancestors, and family elders.

Another facet of the remolding problem is that it is not easy to judge to what extent apparent conformity denotes genuine acceptance of the new way. Through the centuries, the Chinese people have evolved a mode of accommodation with government orders and decrees that has been described as "overt compliance but inward resistance." Whether inward resistance is hidden behind outward conformity and verbal acceptance, only time and the test of changing circumstances will tell. The past two decades have seen more than one instance in which those who made seemingly firm pledges turned out to be opposed to the new order. When reading about the new ideological conversions of today, one may wonder how sincere and lasting they will prove. At the present time, it would be defensible either to see current collective behavior as evidence of genuine conversion or to suspect play-acting; the interpretation varies according to the observer's inclinations.

The Chinese press and broadcasts and the reports of many observers give the image of a nation inspired by a new purpose and working wholeheartedly with a new devotion. Against such claims of successful remolding, it seems fair to note that there does exist a different side of the picture. More than one refugee in Hong Kong has told of successfully feigning absolute loyalty and working hard to win the trust of the cadres, while at the same time plotting to escape. A recent visitor to the Chinese mainland reported that during the campaign against bad books and feudalistic literature he saw a cadre on a train reading a well-known collection of fairy tales and ancient stories of chivalry and romance. After the fierce assault of the Cultural Revolution, "capitalist trends" were reappearing and even Party officials were affected by "a capitalist black wind."[11] With all the effort to popularize the new "revolutionary" opera, the tunes of the old opera are still being hummed by people resting in the park.[12] According to a dispatch from Hong Kong, the officially sponsored birth control program is "severely impaired by widespread resistance in the villages."[13]

These reports are cited to show that the picture is not all clear, that the program of making new men with new minds and new attitudes is neither completely successful nor altogether a failure. At best, there are mixed trends that make appraisal difficult. Even as early as 1966, before the educational revolution gained momentum, the Peking Review (February 19, 1966) editorialized that "a new type of man is emerging in growing numbers." There is no reason to doubt the accuracy of the statement, and one may believe that the numbers of such "new men" have increased with the progress of the educational revolution. At the same time, interviews with young people who have sought refuge in Hong Kong seem to tell another side of the story. At least one told of a double life. His experience was described as follows:

> It was a double life, our young man explained, a life of total subjection, of doing what you were told; everyone obeyed commands with mechanical promptitude . . . not only doing the right things but even saying the right things, exactly what he was expected to say. . . .
> But the other half of [his] ego was not involved in all this. It lay buried below the surface. It lived its own life, not seen, not manifested by any sign.[14]

Elsewhere we read that the old tradition of family ties, personal friendships, and human relations still persists. The old sentiments, the deep-rooted "jen-ch'ing" (amenities and sentiment in human relations) seem to resist the effort to eradicate them. Again, there are two ways of looking at such a situation. One may conclude that the program of remolding is making slow but steady headway and that the persistence of the old way simply underlines the need for continued revolution and continued effort. Or one may deduce that the old traditions have such deep roots in China's ancient culture that they will continue to resist revolutionary change. At least one should recognize that the remolding does not start with a clean slate and that it must contend with strong resistance. A China-born American scholar who revisited China in 1973 wrote:

> I was greatly struck by how much the people we en-
> countered at all levels seemed to behave much as Chinese
> have, in other times and places. Despite two decades of
> revolution, many old patterns of thought and behavior—
> some admirable, others less so—clearly persist. The
> majority of Chinese one meets today still show the same
> curiosity, politeness, and preoccupation with personal
> relationships, as well as matter-of-fact practicality,
> which have long been admired by foreigners, including
> me. The Chinese still impress one as able, proud and
> hard-working, as they always have. They also show
> deep-rooted traditional predisposition to think in terms
> of status and hierarchy, stress protocol, conform to
> orthodoxy and fit into the social roles required of them—

despite the efforts that China's revolutionary leaders have made over the years to change many of their patters.[15]

This is not to say that Communist remolding must fail. It does mean that the Chinese Communists, who have had great success in transforming systems, organizations, institutions, and the material environment, do not find their task so easy when they deal with recalcitrant human beings. If they do eventually succeed and attain their goal by their program of revolutionary education, they will have demonstrated the power of education far beyond the hopes and dreams of educators and educationists of all ages and all lands.

Party Control

The educational revolution has made Party control more firm and complete. Theoretically, responsibility for the administration of education is shared by the school revolutionary committees (and those of communes or factories), the workers-peasants-soldiers who serve on Mao Tse-tung Thought Propaganda Teams (and on revolutionary committees), and the Party branch in the school and in the locality. In practice, the Party organs, which are responsible to the higher Party hierarchy, exercise the controlling authority and all revolutionary committees and Propaganda Teams expressly accept the leadership of the Party (see Chapter 5).

Interlocking personnel in the three bodies further assures the preponderant role of the Party. The Party organs not only lay down the guidelines but take an active part in the daily management of the schools. They exercise "leadership" in all phases of the program: the teaching of nonpolitical subjects as well as ideological-political education, extracurricular activities in school and outside, and the coordination of school work with the family, communes, factories, and other agencies involved in the total educational program. Sometimes a leading Party cadre serves as chairman of the poor peasants committee in charge of the schools. The Party committee of a locality usually designates some of its members to form an "educational leadership" group to look after education in the area. In the school, members of the Party committee visit classes to supervise the teaching of various subjects and to help the teachers compile teaching materials and plan teaching activities.[16] As is to be expected, all ideological-political study and activities are under the direct control of the Party organs. The Party committee of a school passes judgment on the adequacy of the ideological-political remolding of teachers and students.

Party organs keep a watchful eye on the intellectuals, young and old, sent to the countryside for reeducation. They pass on applicants for admission into colleges and universities. They initiate extracurricular activities for youths and ideological-political study classes for adults. They see to it that the revolutionary committees and workers-peasants-soldiers keep up their own ideological-political study while carrying out their educational tasks.

Contradictions and pendulum swings make it necessary to redefine the correct ideological-political line from time to time. Who decides on the correct line? Not the revolutionary committees nor the "three-in-one" teaching force nor the workers-peasants-soldiers who symbolize proletarian leadership. All must listen to the voice of the Party. The Party thus assumes direct control over educational policy and its execution.

The tightening of Party control has gone hand in hand with the termination of the dominant role of bourgeois intellectuals in education. In theory, the control of education by intellectuals has been replaced by proletarian leadership but, as noted, the workers-peasants-soldiers are only a front for the Party. In any case, education has been taken out of the hands of the intellectuals and professional educators. Among the reorganized ministries of the central government there is no ministry to take care of education and culture. The former Ministry of Education, the Ministry of Higher Education, and the Scientific and Technological Commission have apparently been amalgamated and their curtailed functions taken over by the newly created "Science and Education Group" as one of the special agencies of the State Council.

New trends in education are not initiated by the teachers and scholars. Teachers are technicians, at best, under the close supervision of representatives of the Party-state and subject to remolding and rectification. When they speak and write on educational matters, either they do so in support of official policy pronouncements or they merely take advantage of the brief periods of temporary relaxation of control. Prominent scientists have, in 1972 and 1973, expressed themselves on the importance of the study of basic science and theories, but they do so only when noneducators have decreed a pendulum swing away from excessive emphasis on studies that are directly and immediately applicable to practice.

An independent teaching profession does not exist. There is no recognition of educational theory apart from the relation of education to politics and economics. Decisions on such matters as the local management of schools, the relation between decentralization and centralization, and the length of schooling are made on the basis of political and economic considerations, not primarily on educational grounds. An investigation of the educational revolution in the countryside conducted by the People's Daily and the Red Flag advocated the reduction of elementary education from six to five years and of secondary education from six to four years on the ground that the shortened schooling would enable a child to begin schooling at age 6 or 7 and complete secondary education at age 15 or 16, "precisely a suitable age to begin taking part in farm work."[17] Such possible factors as the child's psychological and physical growth have not been mentioned in any of the Chinese writings on this subject.

As a matter of fact, educational psychology and other subjects normally associated with teacher training in other countries have either been dropped or have lost their importance. Teacher training today means two things: (1) acquiring the knowledge needed for teaching school subjects and (2) ideological-political education. The latter is of primary importance, while the former is especially needed for proletarian teachers with insufficient schooling. In-service teacher training consists largely of ideological remolding and the inevitable study and restudy of the works of Mao, Marx, Lenin, and Stalin. An educational conference in Tientsin attended by more than 900 teachers from schools and colleges, including spare-time schools and kindergartens, is typical of such training sessions.[18] Adopting as its central theme the significance of educational work as a means of consolidating the dictatorship of the proletariat, the conference dealt with such topics as the integration of teachers with workers and peasants, the remolding of the world outlook, deep criticism of Liu Shao-ch'i and revisionists, the study of Marxism-Leninism and Mao Thought, reeducation to become both Red and expert, and the strengthening of the sense of responsibility and dedication to educational work. Not included were curriculum matters, teaching methods, and the kind of problems that normally appear on the agenda of professional conferences as understood in the West.

It may be argued, with cogency, that this method of teacher training is consistent with the broad concept of education as inseparable from politics and economics and that it is necessary to stress the economic and political significance of educational work in order to overcome the narrow "purely academic" thinking that characterized the teaching profession in bourgeois society. It may further be stated that diminution of the role of teachers is inevitable in view of the policy of the educational revolution to forbid the domination of education by bourgeois intellectuals. The claim may also be made that the net gain in taking education out of the hands of professional educators is that education is now everybody's business. The public, the masses, the parents, the workers and peasants now take an active interest in the schools; since they support the schools financially and share in running them, they are likely to consider the schools as their own institutions.

At the same time, the absence in China today of any professional organization in which teachers may meet to discuss their problems, and the lack of a professional journal for the specific purpose of stimulating thought and action on educational matters, must be considered a loss. Resigned to a passive role, teachers tend to feel discouraged. A part of the ideological remolding of teachers is directed against the prevalent notion that teaching is an unattractive occupation that offers no future. It has not been easy to recruit new teachers on account of this attitude. The standard remedy is to study Mao's writings in order to understand the contributions that teaching can make to the revolution, but in view of the low salaries, the pressure for ideological reform, and exposure to criticism by students and the "masses," it is difficult to raise the teachers' low morale.

The Question of Standards

The educational revolution rejects "elitist" education and its emphasis on standards of scholarship; since these standards and quality education are associated with elitist education, they tend to be out of favor. Theoretically, it is argued that proletarian education is opposed to the "academic standards" of impractical and effeminate bourgeois education, and that it has its own standards in terms of production ability and devotion to the revolutionary cause. But it is not clear how such standards are applied to student performance in study.

Questions such as the following may not be out of place:

1. Does proletarian society need leaders of broad vision and wide knowledge to be developed by systematic education?

2. Is it possible to develop the desired qualities of leadership by the methods of mass-oriented education that scorns basic fundamentals of knowledge and understanding with no direct and immediate practical value?

3. Should these leaders be selected by a process of systematic advance to higher levels of learning?

4. With due recognition of the evils of elitism, would it be advisable to have a program of leadership education that makes a distinction between the general program for an intelligent proletariat and a program for top leaders of industry, agriculture, education, politics, and all phases of socialist construction? Is there a place in the Maoist scheme of things for "higher intellectuals" to be produced by advanced education requiring as a prerequisite a solid foundation of basic fundamentals? Or for intellectuals, in the stricter sense, who make their contributions in the realm of ideas?

5. Would it be a violation of proletarian principles to demand of future leaders more exacting standards of scholarly achievement than what is sufficient for the masses or for "millions of successors to the revolution"?

6. Granted that the "academic scholarship" of bourgeois society leaves much to be desired, is there a need to develop a new "proletarian scholarship" with due regard to standards apart from political and production performance?

The fact that in the pendulum swings of educational policy Communist leaders have every now and then shown concern for the neglect of study and for insufficient attention to the basic fundamentals of learning shows that they are not unaware of the need for some form of quality education. They also seem to be aware of the problems of leadership education as distinct from those of mass education. At the same time, there is much in the thinking of the educational revolution that militates against proper attention to quality and standards. Some aspects of this thinking that are relevant to the present discussion may be briefly mentioned:

1. The egalitarian ideal, which tends to look askance at any practice that may accentuate the gulf between leaders and followers.[19]

2. Opposition to elitism and education for the development of an intellectual elite.

3. Association of scholarly attainments and standards with elite education.

4. Distrust of intellectuals and their educational ideas.

5. The use of worker-peasant-soldier teachers of limited schooling who have had no experience in intellectual pursuits.

6. Prejudice against systematic study and "regularized" schools and curriculum practices.

7. Commitment to shorter periods of schooling and short-term ad hoc training programs, and a penchant for shortcuts to competence.*

8. The promotion of "indigenous experts," "barefoot doctors," "worker-peasant scientists," and so forth.

9. Popularization versus selectivity on academic grounds.

10. Mao's derogatory statements about bookish study and "useless" knowledge.

---

*One may also note the Communist inclination toward a "guerrilla" type of education rather than a "regular" school system with graded levels of prescribed standards. This may be related to the "guerrilla mode of thinking," which is reflected in the controversy between advocates of the "guerrilla army" and those who want a modernized "regular army."

Anti-Intellectualism

Each of the attitudes noted above may be quite justifiable from the standpoint of the educational revolution. Taken alone, each innovation may be considered a constructive effort to rectify the shortcomings of traditional education in China and the West. But put together, they create an atmosphere unfavorable to quality education and high standards of scholarship. As a matter of fact, it would not be farfetched to say that there is a pronounced anti-intellectual strain in Maoist educational thinking. Distrust of intellectuals carries over to a negative attitude toward their educational background and intellectual achievements. The Maoists may retort that they do not reject intellectual work as such and only object to bourgeois intellectuals. But the term "intellectuals" is used in such a loose way that it loses its original meaning. Glib talk about the intellectual proletariat and proletarian intellectuals tends to dilute the meaning of the "intellectuals" and to equate intellectual work with schooling of any kind. In the reeducation program, middle school and college students as well as scholars, writers, and other professionals are all put in the general category of "intellectuals." "Bourgeois experts" and "authorities" are constantly ridiculed for their ignorance of productive practice and their inability to translate their theories to deal with such practical problems as pest control, operation of machinery, and improvement of farm and factory implements. Numerous instances are cited to show how the unschooled workers and peasants with their practical experience can teach the intellectuals what they never learned from their studies.

The prevalent notion that "study is useless" is in large part fostered by the anti-intellectual climate. Those without schooling do not become targets of reeducation and remolding. On the other hand, unschooled workers and peasants may become teachers and administrators of schools and universities. Moreover, going to school does not necessarily lead to greater opportunities for service because all jobs are assigned by the Party-state and the assigned work may not have any relation to the schooling received. Consequently, there exists a prevalent cynicism in regard to the value of education.

"Science is no mystery" is a popular slogan to show that it is not necessary to devote many years to academic study in order to become a scientist. The glorification of "worker-peasant scientists" is accompanied by the denigration of the scholarly scientists and engineers.[20] Practical experience, in other words, provides shortcuts to knowledge and avoids the wasteful long years that intellectual training traditionally requires. In the same view, the current campaign for the study by the masses of Marxist-Leninist-Maoist philosophical works is supported by the argument that philosophy can

easily be understood and appreciated and that it was the evil design
of bourgeois intellectuals to shroud philosophical study in mystery
in order to keep the masses ignorant of it. Although it may serve a
useful immediate purpose, all this popularization tends to produce a
scornful attitude toward the time-consuming, painstaking study that
characterizes much intellectual work. The result is a watered-down
meaning of "science" and "philosophy," as well as a loose concept
of "intellectuals" and "intellectual work."

"Barefoot doctors" can learn the necessary skills and techniques in a few months; "barefoot journalists" are playing a major
role in the press. An American journalist writes, "peasants, workers
and soldiers are more prominent as writers in the press of Communist China today than professional journalists. The professionals,
whose ranks were thinned by the purges of the Cultural Revolution,
have mostly become anonymous figures working behind the scenes." [21]
Worker-peasant writers have produced plays and written songs,
revolutionary stories and essays. In all cases, the professionals
have lost their former status. The teachers are no exception.

Would it be rash to say that the anti-intellectual climate breeds
mediocrity? A French journalist and writer on the staff of the French
edition of the Peking Review commented: "One discovers on arrival
in Peking. . . the cadres' own mediocrity and their disconcerting
ignorance of the outside world. Those who want to go to Peking are
advised not to have a degree because to have a degree would brand
him as bourgeois, or, in current terminology, a 'poisonous weed.' " [22]
Moreover, the antiprofessional, anti-intellectual attitude contributes
to a narrow program of education that ignores whatever is not of
immediate utilitarian value. Another foreign visitor, who taught in
China for eight years after 1949, wrote as follows:

> The visitor spent a great deal of his China month with
> his two university-educated guides, and was astonished
> to learn that neither knew much of China's pre-Com-
> munist history. Neither could even say whether the
> Ming dynasty came before Ch'ing. He could not obtain
> copies of the old classics, such as the Three Kingdoms
> and the Dynastic Histories. [23]

The two visitors just quoted are not antagonistic to the People's
Republic of China, but their views doubtless reflect their bourgeois
educational background. Nevertheless, they do underscore the neglect
of quality and high standards in contemporary Chinese education.
Their observations on the narrow range of what is taught and learned
are confirmed by an American historian, who reported:

China's people under age 35 are left strikingly unin-
formed. They know nothing about anything outside
their immediate jobs or beyond their own neighborhoods. They ask no questions, have no curiosity and
do not speculate. . . . They know nothing about the
past prior to "liberation" in 1949. The past is one
great big black landlord planted upon a foundation
of feudalism which was gradually transformed into
foreign-aggressive-imperialism-colonialism still
upholding the landlord.[24]

This narrow, simplistic content of learning is bad enough for
the rank and file, but how much worse for the future leaders of the
country, whose higher education must rest on the same shaky foundation. Certainly education as practiced in pre-Communist China and
non-Communist countries leaves much room for improvement. One
may readily agree that the traditional curriculum contains much
deadwood that should be eliminated, and that the removal of deadwood
should make possible the elimination of unnecessary courses of study
and consequently a shortening of the period of schooling. One may
even grant that the proposed program of proletarian education may
produce a new type of man dedicated to the social good and to "serving
the people." But how long can a nation afford to shut its eye to the
needs of the future: the need for professional people who have a broad
knowledge of their fields of competency and understand contemporary
society at home and abroad, for leaders who by virtue of their education are able to view the nation's problems in perspective and may
provide intellectual leadership for a developing nation pressed by the
urgent demand to solve immediate problems in the quickest way?
How are the new leaders of proletarian society to be produced? By
what kind of education?
Granted that Chinese intellectuals in the past remained aloof
from the social, economic, and political struggles of their day and
seem to have spent unproductive years in academic study and research
with little relevance to the acute problems of a revolutionary society,
and that intellectuals of proletarian society could benefit from labor
experience and should learn to relate their work to the problems of the
day, one may still ask whether China—proletarian China—can afford
to squander its intellectual resources by providing for all young
people a leveling type of education that does not go beyond what is
immediately and tangibly useful and does not encourage students to
put forth their best efforts in scholarly attainment. How much can
be actually gained—or lost—by requiring intellectuals to devote long
and regular periods of time to labor and production, to clean latrines
and dig mud for manure, and by requiring university graduates to be

taught and "re-educated" by semiliterate workers and peasants? For those assigned to long-term labor and production, how much is lost in their relinquishing of academic study and their inability to keep up with the rapidly advancing knowledge of the modern age? Is it a wise use of manpower to keep teachers in rural labor and use peasants as teachers, with the resulting phenomenon of clumsy and relatively unproductive teacher-farmers and uneducated peasant-teachers unable to stimulate and nourish student interest in academic work?

If the current policy of stressing mass education rather than leadership education and quantity rather than quality were adopted as a necessary transition from the old to the new, and justified on the basis of priorities and relative urgency, a convincing argument could be made. Unfortunately, there is nothing in official pronouncements to indicate that the current policy is only temporary. On the contrary, the management of schools and universities by workers-peasants-soldiers, the reeducation of intellectuals, and the settlement of educated youths in the countryside for labor and production are announced as long-term policies implementing the basic principles of the educational revolution.

Chinese education in the 1950s resembled Soviet education in its first decade or so, but after the initial revolutionary changes Soviet education moved toward a regularized system in which quality and the teaching of basic subjects were given due attention. In China, after 23 years, education is even more scornful of breadth and quality than it was in the first decade, and there is no indication that a more stable program will be introduced in the near future. True, the Soviet experience reflects a trend toward revisionism and is totally unacceptable to the Maoists. But the Maoists do not seem to have thought of an alternative to the Soviet experience, except to continue the present program which spurns regularization and quality of education. If they should be able to propose a solution compatible with their antirevisionist and antibourgeois stand but providing for some form of quality improvement and intellectual education of proletarian content, if they could devise a program to produce leaders with breadth of knowledge and depth of understanding who are dedicated to "serving the people," they would be making a creative application of Mao Thought and a unique contribution to education in China and elsewhere. So far, there is no inkling that there is any thought of moving beyond the current stage of the educational revolution, except for minor modifications.

It seems certain that there must be some people in the Communist hierarchy—the moderate wing, the less dogmatic ideologues, the intellectuals—who are aware of this gap in the current educational program. They are probably the people behind the current effort to avoid excessive stress on politics in education and to urge more attention to academic study, to technique and theory, and to basic knowl-

edge. Unfortunately, the experience of the recent past fails to give
any assurance that such efforts will be sustained long enough to bear
fruit, and educators and scholars who must shoulder the responsibility
for changes are likely to be deterred by the still-fresh memories of
the charges of revisionism against those who made similar efforts in
the past. Already there are reports that a conflict is raging in China
between those who initiated the recent changes and the Party radicals
who are alarmed by what looks like the beginning of a drift toward
conventional education. Dispatches from Hong Kong speak of "a controversy over who should be eligible to receive a higher education"
and "sharp differences between radicals and conventionalists [that]
reflect discontent with the current trend in education." A heated controversy seems to involve "the qualifications for entering into institutions of higher education. Efforts of educators, possibly backed by
Premier Chou, to upgrade these requirements [in 1973] with regard
to age, health and academic knowledge caused an outburst of criticisms."
The Red Flag has taken the side of the radicals and supports the view
that "students were to be judged from the moral, intellectual and
physical aspects and not on tests of 'how much content of middle
school textbooks they had committed to memory.'" According to the
dispatches, "the Peking reports indicate that the radical view may
prevail."[25] In view of this development, despite the "fresh air, cool
breezes" discussed in Chapter 8, the questions raised here about
standards and intellectual effort are still relevant.

The Faucet Syndrome

Communist confidence in the power of conditioning and remolding by the external environment encourages the belief that the mind
can be wiped clear in order to provide a clean slate for new ideas.
This belief seems to be accompanied by the assumption that emotions
can be engendered to support or oppose any cause if it is properly
presented to the people, and that they can be redirected and re-
channeled by well-planned propaganda and methods of "mobilization."
Having had considerable success in "mobilizing" millions of people
to work on irrigation and construction projects, to join parades and
demonstrations, to respond en masse to the campaign to get rid of
flies and other pests, the Communist leaders believe that they can be
as successful in ordering emotions and that love of the revolution and
the Communist Party can be created as easily as hatred for the bourgeoisie and class enemies. The same persons hailed as heroes yesterday are today castigated as enemies and contemptible scoundrels.
Love of the Soviet Union, once promoted as a symbol of the proletarian
outlook, is replaced by an uncompromising aversion to revisionism
and "social-imperialism."

This is the faucet syndrome, the belief that mass actions and emotions can be turned on and off at will, like water in a faucet. Sometimes the process seems easy. Some years ago, answering the call for the liberation of Taiwan, millions of people demonstrated in the streets to demand immediate liberation by force, but then the propaganda sirens were silenced and the aroused emotions presumably faded away. If some day Taiwan again becomes an urgent issue, an effort may be made to switch on the mass emotions as before.

At other times, it has not been so easy to switch on and off. The Red Guards were turned on to help launch a purge of gigantic scale, but when they became too rambunctious they had to be quelled—turned off. When they did not meekly settle down and return to the classroom, the military was brought in to shut off the steam. But then the military became a dominant force and Mao's long-held policy that the army must be under the Party was endangered. So he had to begin rebuilding the Party and reasserting its authority. When the military refused to be turned off, another crisis was precipitated and another purge became necessary.

The faucet syndrome, the tabula rasa concept of mind, and the abrupt shifts in policy and ideological interpretation are pieces of a puzzle that seem to fit together. In education they lead to a program necessarily different from one that recognizes the mind as an active agent with its own drives and direction that must be taken into account. They are not unrelated to the methods of repetition discussed earlier in this chapter. Mao once said that he wanted revolutionary successors with initiative and a lively spirit. It seems that this goal would call for an educational program based on concepts different from the tabula rasa and the faucet syndrome.

Conclusions

Recognition of the positive accomplishments of Maoist education need not blind us to its problems and difficulties. The past two decades have witnessed the inauguration and phasing out of a succession of "mass campaigns" in which students, teachers, and the population in general were "mobilized" to render active support. From the suppression of counterrevolutionaries and the "3-anti" and "5-anti" campaigns of the early 1950s to the anti-Rightist and antirevisionist campaigns and the Cultural Revolution, each new drive was launched with "fanfare" and strong emotional appeals marshaling all forces to plunge valiantly and courageously into the "life-and-death struggles." Regular school work was often suspended to encourage participation in these campaigns.

It seems that to secure mass support it is necessary to periodically make fresh appeals, to coin new slogans and launch new

campaigns. Strong emotions are evoked to fight against such enemies
as the counterrevolutionary, the hated landlords and rich peasants, the
"bad elements," the traitors and political swindlers, the "demons
and monsters" who plot for the collapse of the revolution. Perhaps
the "continued revolution" calls for continued emotional fervor to be
kept up by a never-ending succession of mass campaigns and "mobilization," but is there a possibility that continued strain and tension may
produce emotional fatigue or emotional insensitivity that diminishes the
the effectiveness of successive appeals? Already we read articles in
the Chinese press complaining that people tend to lapse into apathy
and decline in ideological-political alertness after seemingly successful campaigns. Of the same nature is the often repeated warning that
urban youths and intellectuals who have undergone reeducation and
remolding often revert to old ways and attitudes after their return to
the cities. Does this indicate the tenacious hold of the old culture,
despite the onslaught of the Cultural Revolution? Or does it suggest
the desirability of a different approach in education that may produce
more lasting results?

In education, as in social life and the political-economic area,
it is much easier to agree with Communist criticisms of the old order
than to concur with Communist prescriptions for the cure of recognized evils. Many educators in the West would echo the attack on
examinations and grades, on ivory-tower intellectuals, on artificial
barriers set up by entrance examinations and prerequisites, on elitist
education that bars equal opportunity for the poor and underprivileged.
But the Maoist remedies, attractive as they may sound, are not easily
acceptable to educational reformers in the West. Even if Maoist
education were successful within the framework of Maoist society, it
could not be transplanted into a different type of society elsewhere.
And Maoist education is not an unqualified success.

Superficially, there may be some resemblance between some
American educational reforms and Maoist innovations. On the surface, to relax admission requirements to admit students whose academic deficiency is attributable to inferior environmental and educational background—children of the poor, of certain minority ethnic
groups—may sound a little like measures introduced by the educational
revolution. Quotas set by American universities and professional
schools to recruit students from some minority groups may seem to
parallel the Chinese plan to admit large numbers of worker-peasant
children into the schools and universities. But there are significant
differences. In America, the reforms are adopted as remedial measures and would be labeled by the Chinese Communists as "patchwork" that does not change the basic pattern, whereas in China the
entire apparatus of traditional education is being discarded. In the
admission of students into higher institutions, the Chinese policy is

not only to admit workers and peasants but to exclude or at least seriously curtail opportunities for children of bourgeois background.

But to note these differences is not to deny that Maoist innovations may have stimulated educational experiments along somewhat similar lines elsewhere. It is possible that American proposals for the training of "paramedics" may have been influenced by the system of "barefoot doctors" in China, and that the introduction of "career education" and "action-oriented" courses of study may be departures from the academic-centered education of the past in the same general direction that Maoist education is moving. One may even toy with the idea that when the president of Haverford College near Philadelphia devoted a sabbatical semester in the spring of 1973 to "a variety of hard work experiences. . . as a farmhand in his native Ontario," he may, consciously or unconsciously, have been attracted by Chinese examples. It was reported that he took a variety of jobs in which he "toughened himself" by working successively as ditchdigger, dishwasher, quick-service counter man, and garbage collector. He claimed that the experience gave him a chance to think about American "class consciousness," and that when he took leave of his ditchdigging job one day to preside over the monthly meeting of the board of directors of the Federal Reserve Bank of Philadelphia, he "looked at the other members of the board [and] he could not keep from feeling that there was something unreal about them all."[26] One could not help comparing the adventures of this college president with the purifying experience of thousands of intellectuals in China; yet who would equate his self-chosen experiment in working on low-pay menial jobs with the long-term assignment to labor of Chinese intellectuals? In his own words, "I had a bank account. . . my children's tuition was paid. . . I had a salary and a job waiting for me back in Haverford." This is not the situation that Chinese intellectuals find themselves in, but again this is not to deny that ideas of Maoist education, if not their full practice, may have influenced developments abroad.

Maoist innovations have broken new ground in educational thought and practice, but we should not forget that education is a part of the larger social process and cannot be properly understood or evaluated apart from its social context. As far as Chinese education is concerned it is necessary to bear in mind all the time that "politics is in command" and no phase of the program can be separated from the political goals and ideological tenets of the Party-state.

It is important to point out that the ideological-political commitment central to Maoist education is much more specific and regulatory than the loose expectation that education must serve national ideals. Educational theorists who have often repeated the truism that education everywhere reflects national ideals and contributes to their growth and preservation would be making a serious error if they should equate the supremacy of ideology and politics in Maoist education with the influence of national ideals on education elsewhere. The combination of ideology and politics results in a much more binding "command." True, the ideological-political positions are subject to frequent adjustments and redefinition, but the reinterpretations are made by the authorities in power and laid down as the "line" for all to follow. Failure to bear in mind this all-embracing "command" of ideology-politics may lead to misinterpretation of educational developments in China today.

In China today, no distinction is made between ideology-politics and national ideals, between the Marxist-Maoist proletarian revolution and the yearning of the Chinese people for national greatness and modernization, between Party loyalty and patriotism. An educational program designed to promote broad national ideals and to inculcate patriotism and national consciousness would have almost unlimited possibilities, but it may not necessarily follow the Maoist model of putting ideology-politics in command and schools and universities under proletarian leadership. It might be easier for the Chinese people to support national goals of modernization and regeneration than to understand the concepts of Marxist-Maoist dialectics. As it is, the current program is much more specific in the prescription of content, more narrow in the definition of what is correct and acceptable, and more restrictive in allowing less room for deviation from the approved "line."

What of the future? Much depends on the political situation. We have noted that educational trends follow changes in the political climate. In the zigzag course of the past two decades, periods of political relaxation have been marked by educational liberalism with less rigid control, a more positive role for teachers and scholars, more attention to serious study and basic knowledge, and a more lenient attitude toward intellectuals and their intellectual background. No one dares predict how long the current signs of relaxation will last and whether they only indicate another lull in a continuing storm. In secret documents disclosed in 1970, Mao was quoted to the effect that the Chinese Communist Party had had ten major "line" struggles since its birth in 1921. That makes an average of a major purge every five years. The People's Daily once stated that the Cultural Revolution was the sixth of its kind since 1949. Chiang Ch'ing, Mao's wife, said at the peak of her power in 1967 that the Cultural Revolution should be followed by many more in order to carry on the uninterrupted revolution.

Despite the recent indications of a less dogma-ridden educational policy, a joint editorial of the People's Daily, the Red Flag, and the People's Liberation Army Daily on the twenty-third anniversary of the founding of the People's Republic of China stated: "It is still our cardinal task to deepen education in ideology and political line and do a really good job of criticizing revisionism and rectifying the style of work."[27] And at the beginning of 1973, on January 12, the People's Daily published an article by the Party Committee of Peking University calling for more attention to ideological study and the criticism-rectification campaign. Members of the Party Committee went to the various departments of the university to instigate more energetic efforts to criticize revision: to the law department to study the works of Lenin and Mao on political power, to the history department to repudiate the revisionist interpretation of history that gives credit to the role of heroes, to the economics department to study Marx's Capital, and to all departments to reinforce their criticism of revisionism by the study of family and village histories as told by poor and lower-middle peasants. As long as ideology and politics are in supreme command, the climate is not favorable for liberal reforms.

Prospects After Mao

Mao's death may precipitate a fierce and ruthless power struggle. There are some ominous signs that the power struggle within the Communist Party did not end with the Cultural Revolution. Without Mao's support, the positions of those in power today may not be so secure. But whatever happens, Mao's influence will probably survive his death, at least for some time. Maoism may be replaced by some other symbol or there may emerge a "revised" Maoism.

What will be the characteristics of Maoism without Mao? If the radicals should assume power, the domination of dogma and the harshness of struggle may exceed even the excesses of the Cultural Revolution. Intellectuals and the educated may suffer more humiliation and abuse, and recent efforts to stress the study of technique and theory and to balance the educational program may be nipped in the bud. On the other hand, the more moderate and pragmatic elements may take the reins of government and may develop long-range plans for producing the intelligent citizenry, the trained personnel, and the educated leadership needed for constructive reform, rapid industrialization, agricultural growth, and the building of a united, modernized nation playing an increasingly important role in world affairs.

Would it be possible to popularize education without sacrificing quality and the sure foundation needed for the training of leaders? Would it be possible to promote popular interest and public participation in education without eliminating the positive contributions of scholars and intellectuals? Could educational opportunity be broadly extended to the children of workers, peasants, and soldiers without depriving those from nonproletarian families? Would it be possible to attack the evils of the bourgeois system of education and at the same time recognize that there are some good features worth preserving? Granted that drastic methods are needed to break the stranglehold of outworn traditions, is it wise to throw to the winds all the past experience of other educational systems?

Mao Tse-tung has made extreme statements and taken extreme positions that he later seems to have regretted. He once asked revolutionary youth to "dare to destroy," but he later had to restrain the Red Guards. In secret papers he admitted that the massive smelting of iron and steel he ordered in 1958 "created a great disaster," and he implied that when he gave an affirmative answer to a reporter's question on whether the commune was good, he did not intend to have his offhand answer widely publicized. "Hereafter," he said, 'newspaper reporters should leave me alone."[28] It does not seem to be Mao's intention that every word he ever uttered should be accepted as the gospel truth. If extremism is not necessarily a major characteristic of Mao's thinking, it would seem that his followers may well pursue a moderate program without violating the spirit of his teachings.

Students of comparative education realize that any educational system reflects the social system and philosophy that sustain it. One could readily agree: (1) that neither the American nor the European model of education has met the needs of modern China; (2) that the education of urban, industrialized society is not suitable for a predominantly rural economy; (3) that the Western type of education in China has produced an educated class removed from the masses and ill-equipped to solve the pressing problems of Chinese society; (4) that the elitist education of the past tended to exacerbate the alienation of the educated people from the masses; and (5) that in order to build a new proletarian society it is necessary to devise an educational program fundamentally different from the type that reflects capitalist society and what the Communists call the bourgeois way of life. Maoist education has introduced bold and revolutionary changes in the search for a program better suited to the proletarian revolution. It has made significant contributions, but at the same time the program is weakened by contradictions, dilemmas, one-sided extremism, and an obsession with quick and immediate results at the expense of long-range planning. Many of the criticisms made in the preceding pages arise from the question whether the methods used in Maoist education can achieve the goals Mao projected.

Hopefully, the time will come when Chinese education will be different from what it is today. It may attain maturity, stability, and balance. Overcoming the limitations of one-sided emphasis and a tendency to iconoclasm, it may achieve an integration of the gains and revolutionary contributions of the educational revolution with the heritage distilled from the past and the experience of other lands.

China has a precious educational heritage. Chinese classical education and the civil examination system that preserved and perpetuated the classical tradition served well its age and the society that brought Chinese thought and culture to great heights. But in time it became stagnant and inadequate for modern China, and the old system had to be abandoned and replaced by modern schools. Most people would agree with the Communists in their attack on an educational system that centered on the motive of "study in order to become an official." Yet Chinese classical education left much that is worth preserving in modern China, even in Maoist China. Although condemning classical education in strong language, Mao Tse-tung himself has on many occasions shown a continuing fondness for the classical literature and language.

The new school system adopted at the beginning of the twentieth century rendered significant service in the introduction of modern learning and new knowledge from the fast-growing countries of the West. It produced leaders who shaped the destiny of the young republic in the second and third decades of this century and expressed their intellectual creativity in the epoch-making New Thought Movement and the May Fourth Movement.

Hopefully, history will also draw a balance sheet recording the positive contributions and temporary excesses of Maoist education. It will note that out of the revolutionary changes under Communism the people of China have developed a new civic (not exactly ideological-political) awareness, a wider knowledge of affairs in the nation and abroad, and a sense of social responsibility. They may have left dogmas behind and the class struggle may no longer engross their thinking, but the position and status of workers and peasants will have been significantly enhanced. Educational opportunity will have been extended to all sectors of the population; only lack of ability will stand in the way of advancement. Illiteracy will have been wiped out.

This sounds idyllic, and it may be fanciful daydreaming. But China has a long and glorious past that provides a good foundation for growth and advance. China did not start with a carte blanche in 1949. There is much in China's old traditions to furnish a good foundation on which to build a modern educational system. Respect for learning, to take one example, is certainly an asset for any educational program. It may be recalled that when schooling was made available to the children of workers and peasants in the early 1950s, there was such a rush to attend schools that it was not possible to provide enough schools to meet the rising demand for continued schooling and the government had to launch a campaign to discourage continued schooling and convince young people that they could serve the the revolution best by joining the production front.[29] Later, in a brief period of educational liberalism around 1961-62, when the government recognized the rightful place of academic study and "expert knowledge," there was an astonishing outburst of enthusiasm for book study. An observer reported as follows:

> There are no vacant chairs to be found in the libraries, either by day or in the evening. In some schools the students line up waiting for a seat. Everybody wants to study. . . .
> With the concession of this new freedom, freedom to study, the students have dashed to their books with the same eagerness as students elsewhere—to illicit pleasure or to the playing fields.[30]

The desire for learning has been a tradition in China through the ages. It still exists and may be nurtured and made the basis of a thriving program of education designed not only to fulfill the dreams of ambitious youth but also to "serve the people" and meet the needs of a developing nation. Then it will no longer be necessary to combat the erroneous notion that "study is useless." People will seek education for enlightenment and self-improvement, rather than for ideological remolding.

Hard work, constructiveness, and resourcefulness have long been characteristics of the Chinese people. They accounted for China's past greatness and will be the pillars of the new society to be built. History has shown that in periods of peace and stability the energies and creativity of the Chinese people find expression in culture and the arts as well as in material construction. There is reason to believe that accomplishments of even greater magnitude will be forthcoming with the emergence of more favorable conditions at home and abroad.

Domestically, cheered by political unity and stability, encouraged by success in the country's material development, and enjoying the benefits that accrue from a rising standard of living, people will flock to the schools and universities in unprecedented numbers. Abroad, China will enjoy the highest position in international relations since the beginning of contacts with the West. The world will be ready not only to treat China as an equal and a great power but to accept China as she is, not as a disciple of the West. Education will play a strategic role in this regenerated and revitalized China.

Notes

1. Barbara W. Tuchman in the New York Times, September 4, 1972.

2. David Rockefeller, in the New York Times, August 10, 1972.

3. Tuchman, op. cit.

4. Ross Terrill, "The 300,000,000: Report From China," Atlantic Monthly, November 1971.

5. Rhea M. Whitehead, "Experiments in China's Schools Today," China Notes (New York: National Council of Churches), Spring 1971.

6. Report by Hugh Sidey, in Time, March 6, 1972.

7. Jen-min Jih-pao, October 29, 1972.

8. Michael Lindsay, Notes on Educational Problems in Communist China (New York: Institute of Pacific Relations, 1950), preface.

9. Mao once described the remolding of human nature as follows: "On a blank sheet of paper free from any mark, the freshest and most beautiful characters can be written, the freshest and most beautiful pictures can be painted." Quotations From Chairman Mao Tse-tung, (Peking: Foreign Languages Press, 1966) p. 36.

10. "Burning Issue," Far Eastern Economic Review, April 29, 1966, p. 182.

11. New York Times, November 13, 1969.

12. Report of a Japanese visitor, Central Daily News (Taipei), August 7, 1972.

13. Robert S. Elegant, in the Los Angeles Times, July 1, 1973.

14. China News Analysis, no. 808 (July 17, 1970), p. 6.

15. A. Doak Barnett, "There Are Warts There, Too," New York Times Magazine, April 8, 1973.

16. Kuang-ming Jih-pao, June 15, 1972 (Tientsin), June 17, 1972 (Tibet), and November 18, 1972 (Liaoning).

17. Peking Review, September 27, 1968.

18. Kuang-ming Jih-pao, December 24, 1972.

19. See Donald J. Munro, "Egalitarian Ideal and Educational Fact in Communist China," in John M. H. Lindbeck, ed., China: Management of a Revolutionary Society (Seattle: University of Washington Press, 1971).

20. See report on Shanghai worker-technicians in Peking Review, August 22, 1969.

21. "Amateurs Writing for Red Chinese Press," New York Times, January 31, 1971. See also China News Analysis, no. 828 (January 15, 1971), p. 4.

22. Maurice Cianter, "A Gilded Cage," Far Eastern Economic Review, August 8, 1968.

23. "Traveller's Talks," Far Eastern Economic Review, July 31, 1971.

24. Barbara W. Tuchman, in the Los Angeles Times, September 21, 1972.

25. Dispatches by Tillman Durdin, in the New York Times, August 13 and 19, 1973.

26. Israel Shenker, "College Head's Sabbatical: 2 Months at Menial Jobs," New York Times, June 10, 1973.

27. Peking Review, October 6, 1972.

28. The New York Times, March 1, 1970.

29. Theodore H. E. Chen, "Elementary Education in Communist China," China Quarterly, April-June 1962, pp. 101-104.

30. China News Analysis, no. 407 (February 9, 1962), pp. 2, 4.

1. MAO ON NATURE OF KNOWLEDGE

Excerpted from speech on "Reform in Learning, the
Party, and Literature," February 8, 1942. From Boyd
Compton, Mao's China: Party Reform Documents,
1942-44 (Seattle: University of Washington Press,
1952), pp. 14-17, 21-22.

. . . Our Party School should not be content merely to read the
doctrines of Marxism-Leninism but should be able first to master,
and then to apply them. Application is the sole object of this mastery.
Now that we use percentages to calculate grades, what grade should
you be given if you read ten thousand books a thousand times each but
are completely unable to make application? I would say that not even
one percent should be given. (Laughter) However, if you are able to
apply the concepts of Marxism-Leninism in explaining one or two
actual problems, you should receive commendation and a few percentage points as your grade. The more numerous, the more universal
and profound your explanations, the higher your grade. Our Party
School should now adopt this standard in judging a man's observation
of Chinese problems after he has studied Marxism-Leninism. There
will be some who see clearly, some who do not, some who are able to
see, some who are not; superior and inferior, good and bad, should
be classified according to these distinctions. . . .
   We know that there are many intellectuals who consider themselves very learned and who make a great display of their knowledge,
not realizing that this attitude is harmful and obstructs their progress.
One truth that they should realize is that a great many so-called intellectuals are actually exceedingly unlearned, and that the knowledge
of the workers and peasants is sometimes somewhat greater than
theirs. At this someone may say, "Aha! You're turning this upside
down. It's a mass of confused words!" (Laughter) But, comrades,
don't get excited. What I say is to a certain extent reasonable.
   What is knowledge? From ancient times down to the present,
there have only been two types of knowledge: one type is knowledge
of the struggle in production; the other is knowledge of the class
struggle. Knowledge of the national struggle is also included in these.
What knowledge is there aside from this? There is none. Natural
science and social science are nothing but the crystallization of these

two types of knowledge. Philosophy is then a generalization and summary of natural science and social science. Aside from these, there is no other type of knowledge.

Now let us consider those students who graduate and leave their schools where they have been completely isolated from the practical activities of society. In what position do they find themselves? A man studies through from grade school to university, graduates, and is then considered learned. Yet, in the first place, he cannot till the land; second, he has no trade; third, he cannot fight; fourth, he cannot manage a job—in none of these fields is he experienced nor does he have the least practical knowledge. What he possesses is merely book knowledge. Would it be possible to regard such a man as a complete intellectual? It would be very difficult, and at the most I would consider him a half-intellectual, because his knowledge is still incomplete.

What is comparatively complete knowledge? All comparatively complete knowledge is formed in two stages: the first is that of knowledge through immediate perception; the second is knowledge through reason. Knowledge through reason is a higher stage of development of knowledge through immediate perception. In which category does the book knowledge of students fall? Even if we suppose that their knowledge is correct, it is still theory drawn from the experience of their predecessors in the struggle of production and the class struggle, and not knowledge drawn from their own personal experience. It is absolutely necessary that they obtain this (theoretical) knowledge, but they should realize that, for them, this knowledge is inverted, backward, one-sided; it has been proved by others, but still not verified by the students themselves. They should know that it is not at all difficult to obtain this type of knowledge, that it is even extremely easy. In comparison, the cook's task in preparing a meal is difficult. To create something ready to eat, he must use a combination of wood, rice, oil, salt, sauce, vinegar, and other materials. This is certainly not easy, and to cook a good meal is all the more difficult. If we compare the tasks of the cook at the Northwest Restaurant and the cooks in our homes, we find a great difference. If there is too much fire, the food will burn, too much vinegar, and it will be sour.* (Laughter)

Cooking food and preparing dishes is truly one of the arts. But what about book knowledge? If you do nothing but read, you have only to recognize three to five thousand characters, learn to thumb through a dictionary, hold some book in your hand, and receive millet from

---

*The original text should be translated as ". . . if too much salt, it will taste bitter." See Cheng-fang Wen-hsien (Hong Kong: Hsin Min Chu Ch'u Pan She, 1949), p. 13.

the public. Then you nod your head contentedly and start to read. But books cannot walk, and you can open and close a book at will; this is the easiest thing in the world to do, a great deal easier than it is for the cook to prepare a meal, and much easier than it is for him to slaughter a pig. He has to catch the pig . . . the pig can run . . . (Laughter) he slaughters him . . . the pig squeals. (Laughter) A book placed on a desk cannot run, nor can it squeal. (Laughter) You can dispose of it in any manner you wish. Is there anything easier to do? Therefore, I advise those of you who have only book knowledge and as yet no contact with reality, and those who have had few practical experiences, to realize their own shortcomings and make their attitudes a bit more humble.

How can half-intellectuals be transformed into intellectuals with a title corresponding to reality? There is only one way: to see that those with only book knowledge become practical workers engaged in practical tasks, and see that those doing theoretical work turn to practical research. In this way we can reach our goal. . . .

Our comrades must understand that we do not study Marxism-Leninism because it is pleasing to the eye, or because it has some mystical value, like the doctrines of the Taoist priests who ascend Mao Shan to learn how to subdue devils and evil spirits. Marxism-Leninism has no beauty, nor has it any mystical value. It is only extremely useful. It seems that right up to the present quite a few have regarded Marxism-Leninism as a ready-made panacea: once you have it, you can cure all your ills with little effort. This is a type of childish blindness and we must start a movement to enlighten these people. Those who regard Marxism-Leninism as religious dogma show this type of blind ignorance. We must tell them openly, "Your dogma is of no use," or to use an impolite phrase, "Your dogma is less useful than excrement." We see that dog excrement can fertilize the fields and man's can feed the dog. And dogmas? They can't fertilize the fields, nor can they feed a dog. Of what use are they? (Laughter)

* * * * *

2. MAO'S INSTRUCTION ON THE QUESTION OF "REDNESS AND EXPERTNESS"

(January 31, 1958)

Translation in Current Background, no. 891 (October 8, 1969).

The relationship between redness and expertness, between politics and work, stands for the unity of two opposites. It certainly is necessary to criticize and repudiate the tendency to ignore politics. It is necessary to oppose the armchair politician on the one hand and the practicalist who has gone astray on the other.

There is no question that politics is unified with economics and technique. This is so every year and will forever be so. This is called red and expert. There will still be such a term as politics in the future, but its content will change. The economists and technicians who pay no attention to ideological and political affairs but are busy with work all day long will go astray and this is very dangerous. Ideological work and political work guarantee the accomplishment of economic work and technical work, and they serve the economic foundation. Ideological and political work is the supreme commander as well as the soul. Once we are slack with ideological and political work, economic and technical work will go astray.

Politicians must know their work. It is difficult for them to know too much, and it also won't do for them to know too little, but they must know some of it. Those who know nothing are actually pseudo-red and are armchair politicians. It is necessary to integrate politics with technique, to carry out experiments in the agricultural field, and to lay hold of advanced models and experiment with new technique and the manufacture of new products in industry.

* * * * *

3. MAO'S INSTRUCTION ON PART-WORK, PART-STUDY

(February 1958)

Translation in Current Background, no. 891 (October 8, 1969).

As far as circumstances permit, all secondary vocational schools and skilled workers' schools should tentatively run factories or farms for carrying out production so as to become self-supporting or semi-self-supporting. Students should work as they study. When conditions permit, these schools may enroll some more students but they must not incur greater expenditure to the state.

Apart from carrying out production in their own farms, all agricultural schools may also sign contracts with local agricultural cooperatives for participation in labor, and send teachers to stay in cooperatives for the purpose of integrating theory with reality. Cooperatives should recommend and send some people who meet requirements to agricultural schools.

All middle and primary schools in the countryside should sign contracts with agricultural cooperatives in their places and take part in labor in agricultural and sideline production. Students of the countryside should also utilize their vacations, holidays or after-class hours to return to their own villages to take part in production.

As far as circumstances permit, universities and secondary schools in cities may jointly set up appendant factories or workshops, and they also may sign contracts with factories, worksites or service trades for participation in labor.

All universities, middle schools and primary schools owning land should set up appendant farms. Schools that have no land but are located near suburban areas may go to agricultural cooperatives to participate in labor.

* * * * *

4. INSTRUCTIONS GIVEN AT THE SPRING FESTIVAL CONCERNING EDUCATIONAL WORK

(February 13, 1964)

Translation in Current Background, no. 891 (October 8, 1969).

Chairman Mao said: I want to discuss with you today the question of education. At present some progress has been made in industry and I think that education also should be changed. The existing (education) won't do.

Chairman Mao said: (The period of schooling) may be shortened.

Chairman Mao said: Women detachments may also be formed to enable girls of 16 or 17 years of age to lead an army life for half a year to one year. They also may join the colors when they are 17 years old.

Chairman Mao said: There are too many courses of study at present. They are harmful to people and cause the students of middle and primary schools and universities to lead a strained life every day. Myopia has been on the increase every day because of poor equipment and lighting.

Chairman Mao said: Half of the courses of study may be chopped away. Confucius taught only the six arts—propriety, music, archery, charioteering, poetry and writing—but his teaching brought forth four great men of virtue—Yen, Tseng, Tzu and Meng. It won't do for students to go without cultural recreation, swimming and sports.

Chairman Mao said: To date, no highest graduate of the Hanlin Academy was outstanding. Li Pai and Tu Fu were neither a Chinshih (3rd degree graduate) nor a Hanlin (the highest literary degree). Han Yü and Liu Tsung-yüan were but Chinshih of the second grade. Wang Shih-fu, Kuan Han-ch'ing, Lo Kuan-chung, P'u Sung-ling and Ts'ao Hsüeh-ch'in were also neither Chinshih nor Hanlin. All Chinshih and Hanlin lacked successes.

Only T'ai-tsu and Ch'eng-tsu were the two successful emperors of the Ming Dynasty. One was illiterate and the other was able to read not many characters. Later, when the intellectuals came into power under the reign of Chia-ching, the country was poorly run. Too much education is harmful and one with too much education cannot be a good emperor. Liu Hsiu was a university student, but Liu Pang was an irascible fellow.

Chairman Mao said: Examinations at present are like tackling enemies, not the people. They are surprise attacks, full of catch questions and obscure questions. They are nothing but a method of testing official stereotyped writing. I disapprove of them and advocate wholesale transformation. I advocate that subjects should be made known for the study of students, and books should be read with reference to these subjects. For example, if twenty questions are asked about The Dream of the Red Chamber, and the students can answer ten of them well—among them some are very well answered and contain original ideas—they may score 100 marks. But if their answers are unimaginative and contain no original ideas, even though they are able to give correct answers to all the twenty questions, they are given 50 or 60 marks. The students should be allowed to whisper to each other in an examination or to sit for an examination under the names of other candidates. Since you have given the correct answer, it is a good thing for me to copy it. Whispering to each other or sitting for an examination under the names of other candidates could not be practiced in the open in the past. This can be done now. It is all right for me to copy what you have written because I do not know the answer. We can try this.

The students should be allowed to doze off when lessons are taught by teachers. Since you are unable to teach well, rather than to require others to listen to your tasteless lectures, it is better for them to doze off and take a rest. The students refuse to listen to you when you just make a lot of noise. . . .

Chairman Mao said: It is necessary to drive all opera singers, poets, playwrights and writers from the cities to the countryside. They should be sent stage by stage and group by group to rural areas and factories. They must not stay all the time with their organs since useful things cannot be written in this way. If you do not go to the lower level, you will not be fed. You will be fed when you go to the lower level.

Chairman Mao said: Li Shih-chen of the Ming Dynasty consistently went up the mountains to gather medicinal herbs himself. Tsu Ch'ung-chih also did not go to any middle school or university. Confucius came from a poor family. He also had not gone to a university. He was a musician and he went to homes in mourning to play musical instruments. He had worked as a book-keeper, and was able to play the zither, discharge an arrow from a bow and drive a chariot. He came from among the masses when he was young and he understood the sufferings of the masses. Later, he became an official in the Lu State and heard nothing about the affairs of the masses. Tzu Lu was probably his body-guard who kept the masses away from him. Confucius taught only six branches of learning, and writing probably referred to history. The traditions of Confucius should not be lost. Our policy is correct but the method is wrong. The present schooling system curriculums, and methods of teaching and examination must all be changed because they trample people underfoot.

Chairman Mao said: Gorki received only two years of schooling and he acquired his learning entirely through private study. Franklin of the United States started his life as a newspaper vendor. Watt was a worker but he invented the steam engine. . . .

One cannot read too many books. Marxist books should be studied, but we also cannot read too many of them, and it will do to read a few dozen of them. Should one read too many of them, one would proceed to the negative side and become a bookworm, a dogmatist or a revisionist.

* * * * *

5. MAO'S TALK WITH THE NEPALESE EDUCATIONAL DELEGATION ON EDUCATIONAL PROBLEMS

(1964)

Translation in Current Background, no. 891 (October 8, 1969).

There are many problems in our education, and the most important one is dogmatism. We are in the process of reforming the educational system. The present period of schooling is too long, there

222

are too many courses of study, and many of the teaching methods are not good enough. The textbooks and concepts studied by the students remain to be textbooks and concepts, and the students know nothing else. They do not make diligent use of their limbs and they are unable to distinguish the five kinds of cereal from each other. Many students do not know what are cattle, horses, sheep, chickens, dogs and pigs, nor can they tell rice, sorghum, maize, wheat, panicled millet and glutinous, panicled millet from one another. A student cannot graduate from a university until he is more than 20 years old. The period of schooling is too long and there are too many courses of study. The method adopted is the feeding type and is not the spontaneous one. The method of examination tackles the students like enemies and launches surprise attacks against them (laughter). Therefore, I advise against your having blind faith in China's educational system. Don't regard it as good. There are still plenty of difficulties for us to carry out too many reforms at the present. Many people are against this. At present, few people are for the new method, and more people are against it. This may be pouring cold water on you. You hope to see what is good, but I just tell you what is bad (laughter).

But this also does not mean that not a bit is good. For example, let us talk about geology in the industrial field. The old society left us only 200 geologists and technical personnel, but there are now more than 200,000 personnel of this type.

Broadly speaking, the intellectuals of the industrial field are better because they are in contact with reality. Those in the scientific field, that is in the field of pure science, are poorer, but they are somewhat better than those dealing with arts. Those who are most divorced from reality are the ones in departments of arts be they students of history, philosophy or economics. They are so divorced from reality that they know nothing about world affairs.

I have said that we are great in no respect except that we have learned something from the common people. To be sure, we also have learned some Marxism-Leninism, but it also won't do just to learn Marxism-Leninism. It is necessary to proceed from the characteristics and facts of China to study the problems of China. We Chinese people—people like me for example—at first had not much understanding of conditions in China. We knew that we should oppose imperialism and its lackeys, but we did not know how to oppose them. This required us to study things in China—in the same way as you study things in your country. It took us a very long time—a solid 28 years from the formation of the Communist Party of China to the liberation of the whole country—to formulate gradually a set of policies suited to China.

Strength comes from the masses. Without reflecting the demands of the masses, nobody is equal to his job. One should learn knowledge from the masses, lay down policies, and after that go back to educate the masses. Therefore, in order to be a teacher, one should first be a pupil. No teacher is not a pupil first. Furthermore, after becoming a teacher, one also must learn from the masses in order to understand how he stands in his own studies. That is why there are two branches of science—psychology and education—in the science of education. Those who have no knowledge of reality will be unable to apply what they have learned.

Tsinghua University has its workshops, and it is a plant of science and engineering. It won't do for its students to acquire only knowledge from books without working. However, it is infeasible to set up workshops in a college of arts, and it is infeasible to run workshops for literature, history, economics or novels. The faculty of arts should take the whole society as its own workshop. Its students should contact the peasants and urban workers, industry and agriculture. Otherwise, they are of not much use on graduation. For example, the students of law cannot study law successfully if they do not go to society to study criminology. There cannot be any workshop for law, and society should be regarded as the workshop.

Therefore, comparatively speaking, China's faculty of arts is most backward because there is too little contact with reality. This applies both to the student and teachers. Lessons are taught in the classroom, and philosophy is taught from textbooks. If one does not go to society or among the masses of the people or to Mother Nature to learn philosophy, the philosophy learned is of no use, and only the concepts are known. The same also applies to logic. One may read the general textbooks but will not learn much. Things can be understood gradually in the course of application. I did not understand logic very well when I studied, but I gradually understand it in the course of application.

* * * * *

6. PEKING STUDENTS WRITE TO PARTY CENTRAL
COMMITTEE AND CHAIRMAN MAO STRONGLY URGING
ABOLITION OF OLD COLLEGE ENTRANCE
EXAMINATION SYSTEM

(June 6, 1966)

Translation in Peking Review, June 24, 1966.

The fourth class of the senior third grade at Peking No. 1 Girls'
Middle School in a letter sent on June 6 to the Central Committee of
the Communist Party of China and Chairman Mao Tse-tung, has proposed that senior middle school graduates go straight into the midst
of the workers, peasants and soldiers, to integrate themselves with
the masses, temper themselves and grow in the storms of the three
great revolutionary movements and in the first place get "ideological
diplomas" from the working class and the poor and lower-middle peasants. The letter also proposed that the Party select the best from
among the fine sons and daughters of the proletariat, young people
who truly serve the broad masses of the workers, peasants and soldiers, and send them to study in the higher educational institutions.
The text of the letter follows:

Dear Central Committee of the Chinese Communist Party,
Dear Chairman Mao,

We are senior graduating students of the Peking No. 1 Girls'
Middle School. With powerful revolutionary sentiments filling our
hearts, we are writing to you to express our determination to stand
for a thorough revolution, for the thorough destruction of the old educational system in its entirety.

With the advance of the world revolution and the steady deepening
of the great socialist cultural revolution in our country, we feel increasingly that the young people of our generation are definitely a key
generation in the Chinese and world revolution to carry on what has
been achieved and to press ahead to the future. The history of the
proletarian revolution has pushed us into the arena of the world revolution, has turned Peking into the center of the world revolution and our
respected and beloved Chairman Mao has become the great Standard-

bearer of the contemporary world revolution; the Chinese people have become the main force of the world revolution and China has become its red base. It demands that we defend the red political power won at the cost of the blood and lives of countless revolutionary martyrs and predecessors; inherit the spirit of our predecessors in carrying on the revolution resolutely through to the end; shoulder the heavy task of carrying China's socialist revolution through to the end, wiping out imperialism, revisionism and the reactionaries of all countries and carrying the world revolution through to the end. It demands that we take over Mao Tse-tung's thought which is great, correct and invincible, and pass it on to the coming generations. This generation of ours is truly a most crucial generation!

Dear Central Committee of the Party and dear Chairman Mao, you place boundless hopes on us. You have said: "The world is as much yours as ours but ultimately it is yours. You young people are full of vitality and at a stage of vigorous growth; you are like the sun at eight or nine in the morning. We put our hopes on you. . . . The world belongs to you and the future of China belongs to you."

Dear Central Committee of the Party and dear Chairman Mao, we are students who will soon graduate from senior middle school. In this great cultural revolution, the responsibility falls first of all on our shoulders to smash the old college entrance examination system. We wish to express our views on the existing system of admittance to higher schools.

We hold that the existing system of admittance to higher schools is a continuation of the old feudal examination system dating back thousands of years. It is a most backward and reactionary educational system. It runs counter to the educational policy laid down by Chairman Mao. Chairman Mao says that education must serve the politics of the proletariat and be integrated with productive labour. "Our educational policy must enable everyone who gets an education, to develop morally, intellectually and physically and become a cultured, socialist-minded worker." But the existing educational system is not set up in accordance with this directive of Chairman Mao. In fact it is extending and prolonging the three major differences—between manual and mental labour, between worker and peasant and between town and country. Concretely, we make the following charges against it:

1. Many young people are led not to study for the revolution but to immerse themselves in books for the university entrance examination to pay no heed to politics. Quite a number of students have been indoctrinated with such gravely reactionary ideas of the exploiting classes as that "book learning stands above all else," or "achieving fame," "becoming experts," "making one's own way," "taking the road of becoming bourgeois specialists," and so on. The present examination system helps the spread of these ideas.

2. It makes many schools chase one-sidedly after a high rate in the number of their students who will be admitted to higher schools and as a result many become "special" and "major" schools which specially enroll "outstanding students." These schools have opened the gates wide to those who completely immerse themselves in books and pay no attention to politics and have shut out large numbers of outstanding children of workers, peasants, and revolutionary cadres.

3. It seriously hampers students from developing morally, intellectually and physically and particularly morally. This system fundamentally ignores the ideological revolutionization of the youth. It is, in essence, exactly what is preached by the sinister Teng To gang: "teaching one in accordance with his ability" and "using one in accordance with his ability."

Therefore, this system of admittance to higher schools serves a capitalist restoration; it is a tool for cultivating new bourgeois elements and revisionists. No wonder the sinister Teng To anti-Party gang regards it as its finest treasure and that the U.S. imperialists gleefully place their hopes of "peaceful evolution" on China's "bureaucrats in the field of technology" and "experts in the field of ideology."

Respected and beloved Chairman Mao, you have repeatedly taught us that "we should support whatever the enemy opposes and oppose whatever the enemy supports." As the enemy claps his hands and applauds the old system so desperately, can we allow it to continue to exist? No! Not for a single day! Today, in this great and unprecedented cultural revolution, we must join the workers, peasants and soldiers in smashing it thoroughly. We suggest in concrete terms that:

1. Beginning this year, we abolish the old system of enrolling students to the higher schools.

2. Graduates from senior middle schools should go straight into the midst of the workers, peasants and soldiers and integrate themselves with the masses.

We think that at a time when their world outlook is being formed, young people of seventeen or eighteen years old should be tempered and nurtured in the storms of the three great revolutionary movements [of class struggle, the struggle for production and scientific experiment—Ed.]. They should first of all get "ideological diplomas" from the working class and the poor and lower-middle peasants. The Party will select the best from among the fine sons and daughters of the proletariat, young people who truly serve the broad masses of workers, peasants and soldiers, and send them on to higher schools. We absolutely do not agree that one should go among the workers, peasants and soldiers, after one's graduation from college because at that time one's world outlook will have basically been formed, and any remolding will have become difficult. Moreover, some persons who have acquired "knowledge" think that they have got the "capital" to bargain with the Party and the people.

3. If a number of students must be admitted to institutions of higher learning this year, we request the Party to select them directly from among the graduates of the senior middle schools. Everything we have belongs to the Party and the people, we have no right to bargain whatsoever. We will go with firm determination to any place we are asked to go to by the Party and wherever we go, we must take root, germinate, blossom and bear fruit there.

We are young people armed with Mao Tse-tung's thought; we have been imbued with a revolutionary consciousness. The old system of entrance examination can only repress our demand for revolution. If we smash it, we will study even more consciously for the revolution.

We hold that by acting in this way we will not only save a great deal of manpower and material resources for the socialist construction of our country, but, what is still more important, we will uproot the poisonous revisionist source of "bureaucrats in the field of technology" and "experts in the field of ideology" and do away with an important condition which engenders ideas of "achieving fame and fortune," of "making one's own way" and "following the road of becoming bourgeois specialists." It is a great revolution in the education circle.

Of course, we know that to thoroughly smash the existing entrance examination system of enrolling students to higher schools needs time and experience. It calls even more for the heightening of the people's level of political consciousness. But anyway, our proletarian revolution will not allow it to exist any longer. If a change of the entrance examination system throughout the whole country is unfeasible at the moment, then we ask that it be done experimentally here in Peking. If this cannot be carried out for the time being in all Peking's schools, then we ask determinedly that it be experimented with in our class. In the present great socialist cultural revolution, our whole class has furthermore come to understand that we must be staunch, dependable successors to the proletarian revolution, that we can never allow Mao Tse-tung's great thought to be lost in our generation, that we can never let the proletarian revolution, both of China and the world, cease to continue in our generation. We have also come to understand that the present great cultural revolution is a great revolution that touches the people to their very souls, a great creation in world history! We know that the road we are going to take is an untrodden road. But we are the youth of the Mao Tse-tung era. The Chinese revolution as well as the world revolution call on us to be the revolutionary vanguard of the world's youth. We must be those who dare to think, to speak, to do, to break through and to make revolution. We know the road we are going to take is a new road, a new road that leads to communism. We must and can tread out our proletarian road. Of course, we will still meet many "tigers" on the road of revolution. But can revolutionary youth be frightened by them? We regard the obstacles put up by backward ideologies, by our families, and by public opinion as nothing. We are determined to cleave through and to over-power the ill winds and evil forces! What we need is the dauntless, heroic spirit of a revolutionary who "knows there are tigers on the mountain, but insists on taking that road."

Dear Central Committee of the Party, dear Chairman Mao, please rest assured! We are fully prepared to wipe out all the tigers on our way! We have a most extremely powerful weapon—Mao Tse-tung's great thought. With that weapon in our hands we will fear nothing, neither heaven nor earth, nor any monsters. With that weapon in our hands, we can follow this road to its end. No one will lag behind. Dear Communist Party, respected and beloved Chairman Mao, the youth here by Chairman Mao's side should be sent to the most difficult places. Please rest assured, Chairman Mao; we are standing by, awaiting your instructions!

Dear Central Committee of the Party, dear Chairman Mao, please rest assured: Our generation is a generation that persists in the revolution, in thorough revolution. We will assuredly take over the great red banner of Mao Tse-tung's thought, and hand it down from generation to generation!

We hope, if it is agreed by the Party's Central Committee and Chairman Mao, that this letter be sent as a proposal to all senior middle school graduates this year and to the teachers and students of all schools in Peking.

Long live our dearest and most respected leader Chairman Mao!

The Fourth class of the Senior Third Grade
at Peking No. 1 Girls' Middle School
June 6, 1966

* * * * *

7. DECISION OF CCP CENTRAL COMMITTEE
AND STATE COUNCIL ON REFORM OF ENTRANCE
EXAMINATION AND ENROLLMENT IN HIGHER
EDUCATIONAL INSTITUTIONS

(June 13, 1966)

Translation in Peking Review, June 24, 1966.

The Central Committee of the Chinese Communist Party and the State Council issued a notice on June 13 announcing that, to ensure

229

the successful carrying out of the cultural revolution to the end, and to effect a thorough reform of the educational system, a decision had been made to change the old system of entrance examination and enrollment of students in higher educational institutions and to postpone this year's enrollment of new students for colleges and universities for half a year.

The full text of the notice follows:

Considering that the great cultural revolution is only now developing in the colleges, universities and senior middle schools, a certain period of time will be needed in order to carry this movement through thoroughly and successfully. Bourgeois domination is still deeply rooted and the struggle between the proletariat and the bourgeoisie is very acute in quite a number of universities, colleges and middle schools. A thoroughgoing cultural revolution movement in the higher educational institutions and senior middle schools will have most far-reaching effects on school education in the future. Meanwhile, though it has been constantly improved since liberation, the method of examination and enrollment for the higher educational institutions has failed, in the main, to free itself from the set pattern of the bourgeois system of examination; and such a method is harmful to the implementation of the guiding policy on education formulated by the Central Committee of the Party and Chairman Mao, and to absorption into the higher educational institutions of a still greater number of revolutionary young people from among the workers, peasants and soldiers. This system of examination must be completely reformed. Therefore, time is also needed to study and work out new methods of enrollment.

In view of the above-mentioned situation, the Central Committee of the Chinese Communist Party and the State Council have decided to postpone for half a year the 1966 enrollment into the higher educational institutions so that, on the one hand, they and the senior middle schools will have enough time to carry out the cultural revolution thoroughly and successfully and, on the other hand, there will be adequate time for making all preparations for the implementation of a new method of enrollment.

In order that enrollment and the opening of a new semester in the senior middle schools shall not be affected, the students graduating from senior middle school this term in schools where the cultural revolution is still under way should be properly accommodated and their time-table arranged by the school authorities so that the movement may be carried out thoroughly and successfully; in the case of students in schools where the movement is completed before enrollment into the higher educational institutions has begun, their schools should organize them to participate in productive labour in the country-side or in the factories.

* * * * *

230

8. STUDENTS PROPOSE NEW EDUCATIONAL SYSTEM IN ARTS FACULTIES

This letter from seven students of the China People's University was published by Jen-min Jih-pao on July 12, 1966. Translation in Peking Review, July 22, 1966.

... We are students of the China People's University and also victims of the old educational system.

For many years now your every directive on educational work has had an immediate response in our hearts. But in a hundred and one ways those lordly "authorities" have raised up all kinds of barriers and restrictions to oppose those directives. They have neither carried out Chairman Mao's instructions from above nor listened to the voice of the masses from below. Their treacherous aim is a vain attempt to ensure that the cause initiated by our revolutionary forbears will have no successors and that our proletariat will have no sons and grandsons to carry on its revolutionary work; they are attempting to turn us young people into instruments for the restoration of capitalism. Now we want to sternly tell these lordly bourgeois "authorities": your pipe dream will never come true. While you do not, we will follow Chairman Mao's teachings; while you do not, we will fulfill Chairman Mao's directives.

Respected and beloved Party Central Committee and respected and beloved Chairman Mao: We are revolutionary youth, born amidst the gunfire of revolution, nurtured in our growth by the Party and advancing in the brilliant sunshine of Mao Tse-tung's thought. Some people say that we always smell strongly of gunpowder. Yes, during this great cultural revolution, we will act in accordance with your instructions and, together with the masses of the workers, peasants and soldiers, resolutely, thoroughly and swiftly, smash the old educational system and open fierce fire on the lordly bourgeois "authorities."

We consider that under the existing system education lasts too long and it also has many criminal defects. Therefore, it must be shortened.

Its criminal defects are as follows:

One. This system runs completely counter to Chairman Mao's theory of knowledge; it treasures book knowledge as all-important, despises practical work, isolates students from the workers and peasants and divorces them from the three great revolutionary movements of class struggle, the struggle for production, and scientific experiment. It leads inevitably to the emergence of revisionism or dogmatism.

Two. The present system widens the gaps between the workers and peasants, between town and countryside and between physical and mental labour and trains successors for the bourgeoisie. Those lordly bourgeois "authorities" have only one worry: that the young people will stay for too short a period in college, will read too few books, will not be deeply enough influenced by the bourgeoisie and thus will not become its filial sons and grandsons.

Three. The existing educational system stipulates six years for primary school, six years for middle school and in general five years for college and university. One first enters school at the age of seven or eight and at graduation from college one is 25 or 26 years old. Studying in school and college takes up the most valuable period in one's life. Seventeen years of hard academic study really wastes one's youth and leads the young generation astray.

Four. The teachers and students in the schools bury themselves in books every day, study like bookworms, showing no interest in politics and ignoring the wide world outside.

Five. The students now in college live in tall buildings, eat polished rice and fine flour, read ancient and foreign "masterpieces"; and, with ideas of seeking fame and material gain instilled in their minds, they think of gaining individual distinction and academic achievements and advance along the road to becoming specialists without a socialist consciousness. If they keep on in this way, how can the children of workers and poor and lower-middle peasants prevent themselves from forgetting their origins?

Six. The system puts too much stress on so-called systematic knowledge. In reality it spreads dogmatism, metaphysics and scholasticism.

Seven. The content of the study material is diffuse and repetitive. As a result, the longer students study the more muddle-headed they become. Teachers indulge in trifling textual research and use the cramming method of teaching. Students bury themselves in ancient books every day of every month throughout the year. Consequently the young people lose their bearings and are physically weak and often ill.

Eight. The country needs trained people urgently but the time students take to complete their courses is very long. As the educational system requires too many years of schooling, the rate at which graduates are turned out and new students admitted is extremely low. It can neither satisfy the needs of the country in the quickest way nor enable great numbers of children of workers, and of poor and lower-middle peasants and large numbers of demobilized armymen to enter colleges.

Nine. There is a waste of teachers and manpower. If the period of education were shortened by half, teachers would be able to teach twice as many students as they are teaching now.

Ten. Because of their long isolation from practical work and from class struggle, many students build up a whole bourgeois outlook on life while at school and this is difficult to change. As a result, college students on whose training the state has spent so much money are not welcome. They are inferior to the functionaries in the basic units whose formal educational level is no higher than that of primary or junior middle schools but who have tempered themselves in the struggle for production or other practical work. They are still more inferior to the veteran revolutionaries who may have had only a few days' schooling or even none at all but who have seasoned themselves in protracted revolutionary struggles and practical work. And they are by far still more inferior to such outstanding people as Lei Feng, Wang Chieh, Ouyang Hai, Mai Hsien-teh, Chen Yung-kuei, Wang, "the Man of Iron," and Li Su-wen. It is obvious that real revolutionaries are not trained in schools and real heroes do not come from the classroom.

Therefore, we propose:

One. As soon as the great cultural revolution ends, all those students who have done at least two years in the arts faculties should be graduated ahead of time and be assigned to take part in the three great revolutionary movements of class struggle, the struggle for production, and scientific experiment and should for a long time unconditionally integrate themselves with the workers, peasants and soldiers.

Two. The arts faculties must use Mao Tse-tung's works as teaching material and take class struggle as the main subject of study.

* * * * *

9. "THE MAY 7 DIRECTIVE"

(May 7, 1966)

Translation in Current Background, no. 885 (July 31, 1969).

The People's Liberation Army should be a great school. In this great school our armymen should learn politics, military affairs and agriculture. They can also engage in agricultural production and side occupations, run some medium and small factories and manufacture a number of products to meet their own needs or exchange with the state at equal values. They can also do mass work and take part in the socialist education movement in the factories and villages. After the socialist education movement, they can always find mass work to do, in order to insure that the army is always as one with the masses. They should also participate in each struggle of the cultural revolution as it occurs to criticize the bourgeoisie. In this way, the army can concurrently study, engage in agriculture, run factories and do mass work. Of course, these tasks should be properly coordinated, and a difference should be made between the primary and secondary tasks. Each army unit should engage in one or two of the three tasks of agriculture, industry and mass work, but not in all three at the same time. In this way, our army of several million will be able to play a very great role indeed.

While the main task of the workers is in industry, they should also study military affairs, politics and culture. They, too, should take part in the socialist education movement and in the criticizing of the bourgeoisie. Where conditions permit, they should also engage in agricultural production and side occupations, as is done at the Tach'ing oilfield.

While the main task of the peasants in the communes is agriculture (including forestry, animal husbandry, side occupations and fishery), they should at the same time study military affairs, politics and culture. Where conditions permit, they should collectively run small plants. They should also criticize the bourgeoisie.

This holds good for students too. While their main task is to study, they should, in addition to their studies, learn other things, that is, industrial work, farming and military affairs. They should also criticize the bourgeoisie. The school term should be shortened, education should be revolutionized, and the domination of our schools by bourgeois intellectuals should not be allowed to continue.

Where conditions permit those working in commerce, in the service trades and in Party and government organizations should do the same.

* * * * *

10. THE "16-POINT DECISION"

Decision of the Central Committee of the Chinese
Communist Party Concerning the Great Proletarian
Cultural Revolution, Adopted on August 9, 1966 (Excerpts)

Peking Review, August 12, 1966.

1. A New Stage in the Socialist Revolution

The great proletarian cultural revolution now unfolding is a great revolution that touches people to their very souls and constitutes a new stage in the development of the socialist revolution in our country, a deeper and more extensive stage.

At the Tenth Plenary Session of the Eighth Central Committee of the Party, Comrade Mao Tse-tung said: To overthrow a political power, it is always necessary, first of all, to create public opinion, to do work in the ideological sphere. This is true for the revolutionary class as well as for the counter-revolutionary class. This thesis of Comrade Mao Tse-tung's has been proved entirely correct in practice.

Although the bourgeoisie has been overthrown, it is still trying to use the old ideas, culture, customs and habits of the exploiting classes to corrupt the masses, capture their minds and endeavour to stage a come-back. The proletariat must do just the opposite: it must meet head-on every challenge of the bourgeoisie in the ideological field and use the new ideas, culture, customs and habits of the proletariat to change the mental outlook of the whole of society. At present, our objective is to struggle against and crush those persons in authority who are taking the capitalist road, to criticize and repudiate the reactionary bourgeois academic "authorities" and the ideology of the bourgeoisie and all other exploiting classes and to transform education, literature and art and all other parts of the super-structure that does not correspond to the socialist economic base, so as to facilitate the consolidation and development of the socialist system.

2. The Main Current and the Zigzags

The masses of the workers, peasants, soldiers, revolutionary intellectuals and revolutionary cadres form the main force in this great cultural revolution. Large numbers of revolutionary young people, previously unknown, have become courageous and daring pathbreakers. They are vigorous in action and intelligent. Through the media of big-character posters and great debates, they argue things out, expose and criticize thoroughly, and launch resolute attacks on the open and hidden representatives of the bourgeoisie. In such a great revolutionary movement, it is hardly avoidable that they should show shortcomings of one kind or another, but their main revolutionary orientation has been correct from the beginning. This is the main current in the great proletarian cultural revolution. It is the main direction along which the great proletarian cultural revolution continues to advance. . . .

4. Let the Masses Educate Themselves in the Movement

In the great proletarian cultural revolution, the only method is for the masses to liberate themselves, and any method of doing things on their behalf must not be used.

Trust the masses, rely on them and respect their initiative. Cast out fear. Don't be afraid of disorder. Chairman Mao has often told us that revolution cannot be so very refined, so gentle, so temperate, kind, courteous, restrained and magnanimous. Let the masses educate themselves in this great revolutionary movement and learn to distinguish between right and wrong and between correct and incorrect ways of doing things.

Make the fullest use of big-character posters and great debates to argue matters out, so that the masses can clarify the correct views, criticize the wrong views and expose all the ghosts and monsters. In this way the masses will be able to raise their political consciousness in the course of the struggle, enhance their abilities and talents, distinguish right from wrong and draw a clear line between the enemy and ourselves. . . .

10. Educational Reform

In the great proletarian cultural revolution a most important task is to transform the old educational system and the old principles and methods of teaching.

In this great cultural revolution, the phenomenon of our schools being dominated by bourgeois intellectuals must be completely changed.

In every kind of school we must apply thoroughly the policy advanced by Comrade Mao Tse-tung, of education serving proletarian politics and education being combined with productive labour, so as to enable those receiving an education to develop morally, intellectually and physically and to become labourers with socialist consciousness and culture.

The period of schooling should be shortened. Courses should be fewer and better. The teaching material should be thoroughly transformed, in some cases beginning with simplifying complicated material. While their main task is to study, students should also learn other things. That is to say, in addition to their studies they should also learn industrial work, farming and military affairs, and take part in the struggles of the cultural revolution as they occur to criticize the bourgeoisie. . . .

12. Policy Towards Scientists, Technicians and Ordinary Members of Working Staffs

As regard scientists, technicians and ordinary members of working staffs, as long as they are patriotic, work energetically, are not against the Party and socialism, and maintain no illicit relations with any foreign country, we should in the present movement continue to apply the policy of "unity, criticism, unity." Special care should be taken of those scientists and scientific and technical personnel who have made contributions. Efforts should be made to help them gradually transform their world outlook and their style of work. . . .

16. Mao Tse-tung's Thought Is the Guide for Action in the Great Proletarian Cultural Revolution

In the great proletarian cultural revolution, it is imperative to hold aloft the great red banner of Mao Tse-tung's thought and put proletarian politics in command. The movement for the creative study and application of Chairman Mao Tse-tung's works should be carried forward among the masses of the workers, peasants and soldiers, the cadres and the intellectuals, and Mao Tse-tung's thought should be taken as the guide for action in the cultural revolution.

In this complex great cultural revolution, Party committees at all levels must study and apply Chairman Mao's works all the more conscientiously and in a creative way. In particular, they must study over and over again Chairman Mao's writings on the cultural revolution and on the Party's methods of leadership. . . .

* * * * *

11. REOPEN SCHOOL TO MAKE REVOLUTION—
TO PRIMARY SCHOOL REVOLUTIONARY
TEACHERS AND STUDENTS

Wen-hui Pao Editorial. From Peking Kuang-ming Jih-
pao, February 18, 1967. Translation in Current Background, no. 846 (February 8, 1968).

. . . In reopening school to make revolution, it is first necessary
to resume the lesson of class struggle and to carry out the great cultural revolution in schools to a further extent. This makes it necessary for teachers and students to return to their schools to participate in the historically significant, earth-shaking, all-round and
thorough struggle to seize power. This also makes it necessary for
the revolutionary teachers and staff members and the revolutionary
students to form an alliance to a further extent to win over and unite
with the revolutionary leading cadres to seize power. In the course
of the revolutionary struggle, it is necessary, through discussion by
the masses, to set up cultural revolution committees and cultural
revolution groups of the schools, to improve and re-elect the administrative groups of the schools, to take good care of the life of teachers
and students, and to put all power of the school firmly in the hands of
the revolutionary rebels who faithfully follow Chairman Mao's revolutionary line.

To seize power in school, in the final analysis, is to seize the
power of educating the students, and to use the thought of Mao Tse-
tung to arm the students' minds and occupy all educational fronts.
Therefore, the purpose of seizing power in school is not only to defeat
the handful of power-holders within the Party who take the capitalist
road and sweep away the landlords, rich peasants, counter-revolutionaries, bad elements, and rightists (this does not refer to family background) among the teachers and staff members who stubbornly take
the reactionary stand. At the same time, we must thoroughly smash
the old, revisionist educational system, exactly implement Chairman
Mao's educational line, establish a brand new educational system of
the proletariat. This also is an important part of the "struggle, criticism and transformation" in schools. . . .

At present, after their reopening, some primary schools first
organize Young Red Fighters among their students and teach them to
defend Chairman Mao even though they have to sacrifice themselves—

this is an excellent organizational measure for implementing Chairman Mao's educational guideline and bringing up a younger generation that is loyal to Chairman Mao and the thought of Mao Tse-tung. The schools must totally smash the outmoded content and form of teaching, so that the thought of Mao Tse-tung may penetrate the curriculum. The students should, in conjunction with the great cultural revolution, study Quotations from Chairman Mao Tse-tung, the "three good old articles," and the 16-Point Decision of the CCP Central Committee on the great proletarian cultural revolution, and learn to sing revolutionary songs. This also is an effective measure for smashing the outmoded content of teaching. During the great cultural revolution, primary school students, of course, must also study some arithmetic and scientific knowledge appropriately, and the junior students must learn to read more characters. Only by perseveringly making this series of innovations can we smash totally the content of teaching that is filled with viruses of the bourgeoisie, and promote effectively the "struggle, criticism and transformation" in schools. . . .

* * * * *

12. MIDDLE AND PRIMARY SCHOOLS REOPEN CLASSES AND MAKE REVOLUTION

Jen-min Jih-pao Editorial. From Peking Jen-min Jih-pao, March 7, 1967. Translation in Current Background, no. 846 (February 8, 1968).

. . . Primary and secondary schools (including specialist middle schools, part-work and part-farm part-study schools) constitute an important battlefront of the great proletarian cultural revolution and an important battlefront on which the proletariat and the bourgeoisie struggle for possession of the younger generation. Chairman Mao has said: "The period of schooling must be shortened, education must be revolutionized, and the domination of our schools by bourgeois intellectuals must not be allowed to continue any longer." Revolutionary pupils and teachers of primary and secondary schools must resolutely carry out the great task set out by Chairman Mao, carry the great proletarian cultural revolution in primary and secondary schools through to the end, thoroughly reform the old system of education and temper themselves in the fire of the acute and complex class struggle, so as to make themselves successors to the proletarian revolutionary cause and good students of Chairman Mao Tse-tung. . . .

To re-open classes and make revolution means re-opening classes in Mao Tse-tung's thought and in the great proletarian cultural revolution. In keeping with the spirit of the great proletarian cultural revolution, the lessons will consist mainly of the conscientious study of Chairman Mao's works and of his quotations, of documents related to the great proletarian cultural revolution and the criticism and repudiation of bourgeois teaching material and method. Meanwhile, in secondary schools the necessary time should be devoted to revising some of the work previously done in mathematics, physics, foreign languages and basic general knowledge of various kinds, and, in primary schools, to learning some arithmetic and general scientific knowledge. . . .

Re-opening classes and making revolution in primary and secondary schools is another test for the revolutionary teachers and pupils. All revolutionary pupils, teachers and administrative and auxiliary staff must get rid of all selfish ideas, ignore personal considerations and shoulder the glorious task of re-opening classes and making revolution.

Revolutionary youngsters in middle and primary schools: Our great leader Chairman Mao has said: "The world is yours, as well as ours, but in the last analysis, it is yours. You young people, full of vigor and vitality, are in the bloom of life, like the sun at eight or nine in the morning. Our hope is placed on you." "The world belongs to you. China's future belongs to you." In this great proletarian cultural revolution without parallel in history, you have already made many contributions. Now, you should respond to the Party Central Committee's great call to re-open classes and make revolution, raise high the great red banner of the thought of Mao Tse-tung, forge ahead by exploiting past successes and win new victories!

* * * * *

13. CIRCULAR OF THE CCP CENTRAL COMMITTEE,
THE STATE COUNCIL, THE CENTRAL MILITARY
COMMISSION AND THE CENTRAL CULTURAL RE-
VOLUTION GROUP CONCERNING THE
RESUMPTION OF CLASSES AND REVOLUTION OF
UNIVERSITIES, SECONDARY AND PRIMARY SCHOOLS

(October 14, 1967)

From Union Research Institute, CCP Documents of the Great Proletarian Cultural Revolution, 1966-67 (Hong Kong, 1968), pp. 566-67.

240

All provincial, municipal and autonomous region revolutionary committees (preparatory groups), military control committees, all military regions and provincial military districts, and for transmission to all mass organizations:

1. Universities, secondary and primary schools in all places are to commence classes immediately without exception.

2. All schools must seriously carry out Chairman Mao's directive concerning the combat against self-interest and the repudiation of revisionism.

3. All universities and secondary and primary schools are to carry on teaching and study, while carrying on at the same time reforms. In the practice of teaching and study, Chairman Mao's thought of educational revolution should be thoroughly applied, and revolutionary plans for teaching and study systems and teaching and study contents should be proposed step by step.

4. All the schools should obey Chairman Mao's directive of March 7, 1967, and should realize the revolutionary great alliance, and establish the leadership of revolutionary three-in-one combination, under the principle of revolution and according to the systems of classes, grades and departments.

5. Teachers and cadres of all the schools, for the most part, are good or relatively good. Except for landlords, rich peasants, counter-revolutionaries, bad elements and Rightist elements, those who committed mistakes in the past, if only they can recognize and correct their mistakes, should be allowed to step up and continue to work.

6. All universities and secondary and primary schools should start immediately to prepare for the recruitment of new students.

The CCP Central Committee
The State Council
The Central Cultural Revolution Group
The Central Military Commission
Oct. 14, 1967
(This document is to be posted in all schools.)

* * * * *

14. CCP CENTRAL COMMITTEE'S NOTIFICATION
(DRAFT) CONCERNING THE GREAT PROLETARIAN
CULTURAL REVOLUTION IN PRIMARY SCHOOLS
(FOR DISCUSSION AND TRIAL ENFORCEMENT)

(February 4, 1967)

Translation in Current Background, no. 852 (May 6, 1968).

1. Primary schools form an important front in the great proletarian cultural revolution. They must firmly carry out the proletarian
revolutionary line represented by Chairman Mao and thoroughly criticize and repudiate the bourgeois reactionary line. They must act
according to the "Decision of the CCP Central Committee Concerning
the Great Proletarian Cultural Revolution."
2. Primary schools in all places shall resume classes after the
Spring Festival. Primary school teachers and pupils who have gone
to other places to exchange revolutionary experience should return
to their own schools to play an active part in the great proletarian
cultural revolution, to carry out struggle-criticism-transformation
and to organize studies for the pupils.
3. Primary school pupils may organize Red Little Soldiers.
Those in the 5th and 6th year classes and graduates of 1966 should,
in conjunction with the great cultural revolution, study quotations from
Chairman Mao, the three most widely studied articles, the three main
rules of discipline and the eight points for attention, and the sixteen
articles of the cultural revolution, and learn to sing revolutionary
songs.
Those in the last, 2nd, 3rd and 4th year classes should be organized to study quotations from Chairman Mao and learn to read characters and sing revolutionary songs with the revolutionary teachers
and pupils in senior classes acting as their supervising personnel.
During the period of the great cultural revolution, primary
school pupils must also be taught some general arithmetic and scientific knowledge.
4. Cultural revolution committees and cultural revolution groups
in primary schools shall be brought into being by teachers and pupils
in senior classes through democratic elections. Revolutionary teachers

and pupils in senior classes should form the main body in these organizations.

School administration should be strengthened or re-elected through mass discussion to take good care of the life of teachers and pupils.

5. In the great cultural revolution, no leaders shall be permitted to adopt various means to hit back in revenge on the ground that the masses have criticized them or exposed their problems. Revolutionary teachers and pupils who have been branded as "counterrevolutionaries," "pseudo-leftists but genuine rightists," "little monsters and demons," etc., in the great cultural revolution must be vindicated.

6. A handful of Party persons in authority taking the capitalist road should mainly be attacked in the great cultural revolution. Meanwhile, those landlords, rich peasants, counterrevolutionaries, bad elements and rightists (not referring to their family background) among the teachers and staff members who firmly cling to the reactionary stand should be purged, and the educational organs should arrange for their reform through labor in their own places.

This notification may be posted in urban and rural basic-level units and primary schools throughout the country.

* * * * *

15. MAO'S "MARCH 7 DIRECTIVE" CONCERNING THE
    GREAT STRATEGIC PLAN FOR THE GREAT
    PROLETARIAN CULTURAL REVOLUTION

(March 7, 1967)

Peking Review, March 15, 1968.

Comrades Lin Piao, En-lai and the Comrades of the Cultural Revolution Group:

This document should be distributed to the whole country to be acted upon accordingly. The army should give political and military training in the universities, middle schools and the higher classes of primary schools, stage by stage and group by group. It should help in re-opening school classes, strengthening organization, setting up the leading bodies on the principle of the "three-in-one" combination and carrying out the task of "struggle-criticism-transformation." It should first make experiments at selected points and acquire experience and then popularize it step by step. And the students should be persuaded to implement the teaching of Marx that only by emancipating all mankind can the proletariat achieve its own final emancipation,

243

and in military and political training, they should not exclude those teachers and cadres who have made mistakes. Apart from the aged and the sick, these people should be allowed to take part so as to facilitate their remolding. Provided all this is done conscientiously, it is not difficult to solve the problems.

Mao Tse-tung
March 7, 1967

* * * * *

16. DRAFT PROGRAM FOR PRIMARY AND MIDDLE SCHOOLS IN CHINESE COUNTRYSIDE

NCNA (New China News Agency) -English Peking, May 13, 1969. In Survey of China Mainland Press, no. 4418 (May 19, 1969).

Programme for Primary and Middle School Education in the Rural Areas (Draft, for General Discussion).

Chapter One: General Programme

. . . The primary and middle schools must meet the demand of the children of the poor and lower-middle peasants for schooling, open their doors wide to such children and truly serve the interests of the poor and lower-middle peasants and other commune members.

The aim of education in the countryside is to "enable everyone who receives an education to develop morally, intellectually and physically and become a worker with both socialist consciousness and culture." It should enable the young people to temper themselves in the three great revolutionary movements of class struggle, the struggle for production and scientific experiment and become reliable successors to the cause of the proletarian revolution loyal to the great leader Chairman Mao, to Mao Tse-tung Thought and to Chairman Mao's revolutionary line and whole-heartedly serving the great majority of the people of China and the world.

Chapter Two: Leadership

Article 1. In accordance with Chairman Mao's teaching "In the countryside, schools and colleges should be managed by the poor and lower-middle peasants—the most reliable ally of the working class,"

the middle school should establish "three-in-one" revolutionary committee which comprise poor and lower-middle peasants, who are the
mainstay, commune and brigade cadres and representatives of the
revolutionary teachers and students. Such committee should be placed
under the leadership of the party organizations and revolutionary committees of the commune and the production brigade. The primary
school should be placed under the unified leadership of the brigade's
leading group in charge of education. Representatives of the school
who are members of the leading group are in charge of the routine
work of the schools.

(Some comrades think that the commune revolutionary committee
should establish a committee for the revolution in education, but some
other comrades hold that such a committee is unnecessary.)

Article 2. Following are the main tasks of the poor and lower-
middle peasants in managing the schools: ensure that Chairman Mao's
proletarian line and principles on education and his proletarian policies
are carried out to the letter; do a good job in the school's struggle-
criticism-transformation by depending on "The masses of revolutionary
students, teachers and workers in the schools and colleges and on the
activists among them"; bring about the ideological revolutionization
of the teachers; and decide upon and review the expenditures of the
schools.

Article 3. In managing schools the poor and lower-middle peasants should apply the principle of democratic centralism, exercise
political leadership over the schools and hear reports on the work at
regular intervals. The representatives of the poor and lower-middle
peasants should constantly supervise and review the work of the
schools. They should study the important questions in the schools
and take decisions on them. Under ordinary circumstances, they
should fulfil their duty in their spare time.

Chapter Three: Ideological and Political Work

Article 4. Politics is the commander, the soul in everything.
The fundamental task in the ideological and political work of these
schools is to ensure that Mao Tse-tung Thought take firm root in all
positions of education and that the living study and application of Mao
Tse-tung Thought is put in first place in all the work of the schools.

Article 5. Arm the teachers and students with Chairman Mao's
theory of continuing the revolution under the dictatorship of the proletariat, constantly familiarize them with the situation and tasks and
the principles and policies of the Party and raise their consciousness
of class struggle and the struggle between the two lines. Teach the
students to have a clear aim in studying and to take the revolutionary

road of integrating themselves with the workers, peasants and soldiers.

(Some comrades suggest that "educate the students always to maintain the fine qualities of the poor and lower-middle peasants" should be added to the ideological and political work.)

Article 6. Learn from the Liberation Army, give prominence to proletarian politics, persist in the "four firsts" (foot note one) and energetically foster the "three-eight" working style (foot note two).

Article 7. A new-type, proletarian relationship between the teachers and students should be established in the rural primary and middle schools: they should encourage each other politically, help each other ideologically, learn from each other in teaching and study and care for each other's welfare.

Article 8. Education by the school, society and the family should be combined, and the three sides should jointly shoulder their responsibility for doing good ideological and political work among the students.

Article 9. Bring into full play the exemplary and vanguard role of the Communist Youth League members and Red Guards in the schools and enable them to help the Party organizations and school revolutionary committees to do a good job in ideological and political work. They should actively propagate Mao Tse-tung Thought, take part in extracurricular public activities and strengthen their revolutionary spirit, scientific approach and sense of organization and discipline.

(Some comrades suggest adding "consolidate the Little Red Soldier organizations.")

Chapter Four: Distribution of Schools and
Length of Schooling

Article 10. All irrational rules and regulations in the old schools should be abolished. Necessary proletarian rules and regulations

----

Foot note 1: "four firsts" means: 1. As between man and weapons, give first place to man; 2. as between political and other work; 3. as between ideological and routine tasks in political work, give first place to ideological work; 4. in ideological work, as between ideas in books and the living ideas currently in people's minds, give first place to the living ideas currently in people's mind.

Foot note 2: the "three-eight" working style: the "three" refers to a firm and correct political orientation, an industrious and simple style of work, and flexible strategy and tactics; the "eight" refers to the eight characters which mean unity, alertness, earnestness and liveliness.

should be instituted in accordance with specific conditions and a revolutionary new order established.

Article 11. In setting up such primary and middle schools, the principle of "make it convenient for peasants' children to go to nearby schools" should be followed and the confines of administrative areas should be broken.

The primary school should be run by the production brigade. The middle school should be run by the commune, or branches of it set up in several villages, or run jointly by brigades, or run solely by a brigade where conditions permit. The commune or the brigades will cover the school expenses, plus state aid.

Article 12. There should be an uninterrupted nine-year system, and the division into stages can be made according to local needs and conditions.

Article 13. In accordance with the specific needs of local agricultural development, counties and communes may run some agricultural technical schools enrolling students who come from and will return to their communes after graduation so as to popularize agrotechnique and train agro-technicians.

Article 14. Eliminate age restrictions for enrollment, which were enforced by the counter-revolutionary revisionist line. Abolish the old systems for examination and leaving students in the same class without promotion. Allow those students who excel politically, ideologically and in their studies to jump a grade.

The enrollment for middle schools should be both by recommendation and selection, giving priority to the children of workers, poor and lower-middle peasants, revolutionary martyrs and armymen.

(As regards the proper age to start primary school, some think it should be at age six while others think it should be at age seven.)

Article 15. The school year in general should start in the spring so as to facilitate over-all unified state planning.

Article 16. Those who complete rural primary and middle schools should mainly work in the countryside; they should take part in the three great revolutionary movements of class struggle, the struggle for production and scientific experiment, and work for socialist construction.

Chapter Five: Teachers

Article 17. "In the problem of transforming education it is the teachers who are the main problem." The rural primary and middle schools should strive to build up their ranks of proletarian teachers.

Article 18. Conscientiously purify and strengthen the ranks of teachers in accordance with Chairman Mao's policy of uniting with,

247

educating and remolding intellectuals. Encourage the present teachers to serve the poor and lower-middle peasants. Clear out class enemies who sneaked into the ranks of the teachers. In strengthening the ranks of the teachers, recommend poor and lower-middle peasants, demobilized soldiers, and educated young people having been tempered in manual labour for a certain period, who hold aloft the great red banner of Mao Tse-tung Thought and are qualified to teach. The appointment and dismissal of teachers should be discussed by the poor and lower-middle peasants, proposed by the revolutionary committee of the production brigade for endorsement by the revolutionary committee of the commune, and reported to the revolutionary committee of the county.

Article 19. Recommend poor and lower-middle peasants with practical experience, revolutionary cadres, and militiamen who are activists in the living study and application of Mao Tse-tung Thought, to be part-time teachers or to form lecturers' group.

Article 20. In line with Chairman Mao's teaching that "being educators and teachers, they themselves must first be educated," the teachers should take an active part in the three great revolutionary movements, and, by taking part in labour in the production teams at regular intervals and in other ways, consciously accept re-education by the poor and lower-middle peasants so as to remold their world outlook.

Arrangements should be made to ensure that the teachers have adequate time needed to raise their educational level and study problems related to their work. Help the teachers, constantly raise their professional competence by making arrangements for them to study at their posts or get special full-time training in rotation.

Article 21. The production brigade should take over the management of state-run primary schools in the rural areas. The teachers should be paid instead by the brigade on the work-point system, supplemented by state subsidies. In general, this new wage system should not lower the present living standards of the teachers. The work points received are to be reckoned annually. Men and women teachers are to receive equal pay for equal work.

(With regard to the pay of middle school teachers, one view is that they should be paid according to the work-point system plus a state subsidy; another view is that the methods should be fixed after further study and that the work-point system should not be adopted.)

Article 22. Before the promulgation of new regulations, the existing regulations should be carried on with regard to sick leave and maternity leave for teachers, free medical care for them with the cost borne by the state, and burial expenses. For teachers who have not been transferred to work in the production brigades where their homes are, leave should be granted for them to visit their families.

Article 23. The appropriate number of students in each class in the rural primary and middle schools should be between 30 and 50. As for the size of the teaching staff, on the average there should be 2.5 teachers to each middle school class (the exact number can be fixed by the commune or production brigade according to the school grade), and 1.3 teachers to each primary school class.

Chapter Six: Teaching

Article 24. In arranging the curriculum, adhere to the principles of giving prominence to proletarian politics, of combining theory with practice and of making the courses fewer and better. This is in line with Chairman Mao's teachings that "Courses should be fewer and better. The teaching material should be thoroughly transformed, in some cases beginning with simplifying complicated material," and "While their main task is to study, students should also learn other things."

Five courses are to be given in primary school: Politics and language, arithmetic, revolutionary literature and art, military training and physical culture, and productive labour.

Five courses are to be given in middle school: Education in Mao Tse-tung Thought (including modern Chinese history, contemporary Chinese history and the history of the struggle between the two lines within the party), basic knowledge for agriculture (including mathematics, physics, chemistry and economic geography), revolutionary literature and art (including language), military training and physical culture (including the study of Chairman Mao's concepts on people's war, strengthening the idea of preparedness against war, and activities in military training and physical culture), and productive labour.

(Another view on the middle school curriculum is that it should include: education in Mao Tse-tung Thought, general knowledge about agriculture, mathematics, physics, chemistry, language, revolutionary literature and art and military training and physical culture.)

With regard to the importance of the various courses, politics is of primary importance and should be put first in order, relative to productive labour and general knowledge and culture. But in arranging time, more periods should be given to courses in general knowledge and culture. It is appropriate for these courses to account for about 60 percent of the periods for study in middle school and not less than 70 percent in primary school.

Article 25. With regard to arranging teaching time for the whole school year, schools should open classes for about forty weeks of the year (including the time taken up by courses in productive labour) and the students given about 35 days of leave during the busy farming seasons. The length of time can be increased or reduced in accordance with the specific conditions in the locality and the age of the students.

(Some poor and lower-middle peasants proposed that one and a half to two months' leave is needed during the busy farming seasons.)

The school should give about 35 days of winter and summer vacations, according to local climate.

(Some comrades suggest that this should be decided by areas in line with local climate.)

Article 26. In accordance with Chairman Mao's instruction "Teaching material should have local character. Some material on the locality and the villages should be included," aside from the teaching material compiled by the state, localities should organize workers, peasants and soldiers and revolutionary teachers and students to compile teaching material on the area as supplementary teaching material.

Article 27. In teaching, theory should be combined with practice. Chairman Mao's "ten teaching methods" should be applied by encouraging the students to investigate for themselves, relating what is near to what is far and what is elementary to what is advanced so that the initiative of the students is stimulated for study.

The method of teachers and students teaching each other and commenting on their teaching and study should be followed. The methods of combining teaching both in the classroom and on the spot and teaching by both full-time and part-time teachers should be used so as to link study closely with practice.

In the upper grades of the primary schools and in middle schools, students should be encouraged to undertake self-study and discussion, and to learn to use Mao Tse-tung Thought to distinguish fragrant flowers from poisonous weeds. Students should be given time to read, think, analyse, criticize and study problems.

Article 28. A reasonable amount of homework should be assigned to students and a certain number of tests and examinations should be given. Open book texts and practical skills are methods to be used in raising and testing the students' ability in analysing and solving problems. The teachers should conscientiously mark and correct the homework and text papers of the students.

Chapter Seven: Run Schools on a Part-time Work, Part-time Study Basis

Article 29. The road of relying on our own efforts should be firmly followed and diligence and frugality should be practised in running schools so as to lighten the burden on the poor and lower-middle peasants. Extravagance and waste and the tendency to seek grandeur and what is bourgeois should be opposed.

Where conditions permit, the primary and middle schools should set up bases for production and labour in agriculture, forestry, animal husbandry, fishery and side-line occupations. Where circumstances allow, scientific research should be conducted.

Article 30. Follow Chairman Mao's teaching "rural students should make use of their vacations, week-ends and holidays and spare time to return to their own villages to take part in production." The primary way is for the students to participate in production in the people's commune, the production brigade and the production team, while their participation in labour arranged by the schools is supplementary. The main form of participation in production conducted by schools should be productive labour classes.

All income from such production should be taken care of by the people's communes and production brigades.

* * * * *

17. PUT MAO TSE-TUNG THOUGHT IN COMMAND OF CULTURAL COURSES

By the Revolutionary Committee of the
Peking No. 31 Middle School

Peking Review, September 25, 1970.

Formulated under the personal direction of Chairman Mao, the Decision of the Central Committee of the Chinese Communist Party Concerning the Great Proletarian Cultural Revolution pointed out: "In the Great Proletarian Cultural Revolution a most important task is to transform the old educational system and the old principles and methods of teaching." How to give prominence to proletarian politics and occupy the positions of the cultural courses is an urgent question which must now be solved in the educational revolution.

The cultural courses account for the largest proportion of their time in all the students' school activities. (Cultural courses in our school include politics, Chinese, history, geography, mathematics, physics, chemistry, music, drawing, physical training and foreign languages.) Moreover, the subjects are varied and exert a great influence on the formation of the students' world outlook. But for a long time in the past, the principle of "giving first place to intellectual education" was followed in the old educational system, with the result that feudal, bourgeois and revisionist influences were deep-seated in the cultural courses. It is imperative, therefore, to occupy the

251

important positions of the cultural courses in order to exercise the dictatorship of the proletariat over the bourgeoisie in the field of teaching and study and carry out the series of instructions by Chairman Mao on proletarian educational revolution. Ignoring these positions means ignoring the educational revolution, and giving up these positions means giving up the educational revolution. Led by the workers' and P.L.A. men's Mao Tse-tung Thought propaganda team, the revolutionary teachers and students in our school have always regarded the occupying of these important positions as a battle in which arduous and unremitting efforts must be made.

Some people used to say that in the cultural courses the students obtain cultural knowledge and that it is a question of the students receiving an education to develop intellectually. To these people, giving prominence to proletarian politics is solely the task of the political course, while in other cultural courses, especially mathematics, physics and chemistry, it is neither necessary nor possible to give prominence to politics. Such a view is extremely wrong. Chairman Mao teaches us: "In all its work the school should aim at transforming the student's ideology." Not only are political activities and labour in the schools for transforming the students' ideology, but all the cultural courses, including mathematics, physics and chemistry, are without exception primarily for transforming their ideology. In fact, there is no such thing as "pure" cultural courses divorced from politics. In every course and in every class, there is bound to be a guiding thought which plays the leading role. It is simply a case of giving prominence either to proletarian politics or to bourgeois politics. It must be one or the other. When the revisionist educational line prevailed, the cultural courses advocated "giving first place to intellectual education" and "seeking fame and position," and peddled large quantities of feudal, bourgeois and revisionist trash. This meant giving prominence to bourgeois politics and served the purpose of restoring capitalism. In our socialist cultural courses, we must put Mao Tse-tung Thought in command and give prominence to proletarian politics, the purpose being the transformation of the students' ideology and fostering their proletarian world outlook. Herein lies the basic difference between the old and the new cultural courses. . . .

Through the living study and application of Chairman Mao's thinking on the educational revolution and by carrying on revolutionary mass criticism in a deep-going and sustained way, the revolutionary teachers in our school have raised their consciousness of giving prominence to politics and made further efforts to correctly handle the relationship between politics and knowledge. They conscientiously pay attention to putting Mao Tse-tung Thought in command of the cultural courses, using one of Chairman Mao's concepts to command a class and organically and repeatedly using this concept to explain what is taught. In this way, the teachers have not only given prominence to politics in this course but also have given the students knowledge in a thoroughgoing way.

In giving a lesson on "ignition and fire extinguishing," a chemistry teacher guided the students to study again and again Chairman Mao's teaching that "external causes are the condition of change and internal causes are the basis of change, and that external causes become operative through internal causes." As a result of the reconstruction done by the workers in our school in connection with the boiler for boiling drinking water, coal rocks are used instead of coal as fuel. Using this example, she asked the students: "Why can coal rocks burn? Why can't ordinary rocks burn under normal conditions?"

The students' reply was: "Because there are coal ingredients in the coal rocks. So they have the internal causes for catching fire, while ordinary rocks don't have them."

"Why then was it not possible to use coal rocks as fuel before reconstruction?" she asked again.

"That was because the question of external causes was not solved," replied the students. "The oven was too small, so there wasn't enough draught and oxygen to make the coal rocks burn."

Then the teacher made three experiments. The first was with a piece of paper which she daubed with phosphorus. The paper spontaneously burst into flame in the air. The second experiment was with some petrol which immediately caught fire when ignited with a match. Then she experimented with some turpentine which could not be set ablaze with a match, but was ignited only by increasing the heat. After the experiments, she led the students to study Chairman Mao's teaching: "Qualitatively different contradictions can only be resolved by qualitatively different methods." The students were thus helped to understand better the relationship between different internal causes and different external causes. The lecture then naturally went on from ignition to fire extinguishing. Since certain conditions, namely, external causes, are needed for any material to catch fire, it would not be possible, therefore, for this material to burst into flame if these external causes were removed.

After explaining how to use the fire extinguisher, she asked: "If U.S. imperialism or social-imperialism launches a war of aggression against our country and state property is set on fire, what should we do in case we have no fire extinguisher at hand?" When she got the right answer, she summed up the lecture and said: "Now we use coal rocks as fuel to boil water after the workers in our school have done some reconstruction on the boiler by their own efforts. This saves the state more than 3,000 jin of coal every month. Some heroes have put out fires with their own bodies and saved state property. What does all this show? It tells us that there are conditions for both

ignition and extinguishing fire, but people are the primary factor."
Finally, the teacher led the students to study Chairman Mao's teaching:
"Of all things in the world, people are the most precious. Under the
leadership of the Communist Party, as long as there are people, every
kind of miracle can be performed." Thus the students were helped to
get a still deeper understanding of this teaching of Chairman Mao's.
We consider that prominence was given to proletarian politics in this
lecture while at the same time knowledge was taught to the students.
The lecture was conducted in such a way that Mao Tse-tung Thought
was put in command, and the teacher handled the relationship between
politics and knowledge well. . . .

In his lectures to the students on the concept of positive and
negative, one of the teachers cites by way of example the fact that
China is a country without external or internal debts. With the relevant data he has gathered, he shows that revenue exceeds expenditure
in our country's budget. The surplus is positive, and is denoted by
a "+" sign. U.S. imperialism, on the other hand, carries out suppression at home and aggression abroad, with the result that it has external
and internal debts running to several hundred thousand million U.S.
dollars. The excess of expenditure over revenue is marked in red in
accounting. This is called a deficit, as we often read in the newspapers, and is negative and denoted by a "-" sign. Making a comparison by drawing charts on the blackboard, the teacher has helped the
students quickly master the concept of positive and negative and get
a more profound understanding of Chairman Mao's infinitely brilliant
thesis: "The enemy rots with every passing day, while for us things
are getting better daily." In this way the students realize in a more
concrete way the superiority of the socialist system. . . .

Take military and physical training in our school as an example.
At first, we remained at the stage of political agitation. Later, through
the living study and application of Chairman Mao's works, the teacher
in this course further raised his consciousness of giving prominence
to proletarian politics and conscientiously paid attention in class to
grasping living ideas that might at any time crop up in the students'
minds. Once during training, one student carelessly threw the dummy
hand-grenade only a few metres away. The teacher immediately picked
it up and hurled it some distance. Then he asked the students: "Sup-
posing we're fighting in a war and the enemy troops are only 30 metres
away, what will happen if a hand-grenade is thrown only a few metres
away from us?"

"It would mean disaster for our own men," the students replied,
"and enemy troops would seize the opportunity to rush up."

After quoting Chairman Mao's instruction "Go all out and be
sure to destroy the enemy intruders," the teacher said: "If anything
should happen as it did just now, it would mean casualties for our

class brothers. More important, we would fail to kill the enemy troops, who would rush towards us. And, you should know, losing our positions is no small matter. Now think, what would the Liberation Army men do when faced with such a situation?"

"Fighters of the Liberation Army fear neither hardship nor death," said the students. "In order to annihilate the enemy troops and protect their comrades-in-arms, they would surely pick up the grenade even at the risk of their own lives and hurl it at the enemy. The newspapers have reported many heroic deeds of this kind." It was in this way that the teacher paid serious attention to grasping living ideas in class to educate the students and give prominence to proletarian politics from beginning to end. As a result, the students not only improved their physiques and obtained military knowledge, but also further strengthened their sense of organization and discipline and got a better idea of actual combat.

Promote Teachers' Ideological Revolutionization

Chairman Mao has taught us: "In the problem of transforming education it is the teachers who are the main problem." To give prominence to politics in the cultural courses, it is necessary first and foremost that those giving these courses give prominence to politics; in order that the cultural courses will help transform the students' ideology, it is necessary first and foremost that those giving these courses strive to transform their own ideology and do well in revolutionizing their own ideology. . . .

* * * * *

18. THE "MAY 7" CADRE SCHOOL

Peking Review, May 12, 1972.

A new thing born in the Great Cultural Revolution, "May 7" cadre schools are all over China. Every province, municipality and autonomous region as well as many special administrative regions, counties and cities, all have this type of school. More than a hundred belong to the departments under the Central Committee of the Chinese Communist Party and the State Council.

Those who have been sent to the school include veteran cadres who went through the Long March, the War of Resistance Against Japan or the War of Liberation; cadres who joined the revolution after liberation; those who went from their homes to schools and from there to government offices and who were lacking in practical experience; and young cadres who had been Red Guards. While at cadre school, they get their regular wages and the same welfare facilities as when they are on the job. The term generally is for a year or so, the least six months, the most two to three years.

Versatile Activities

Regardless of seniority or how high a post held, everyone is an ordinary student, a "May 7" fighter. At the Chingkou "May 7" Cadre School in Kirin Province, the former director of the agriculture bureau becomes a pig-breeder, the former secretary of the city Party Committee a carpenter, a department head a cart driver and a county head a cook.

Students' lives are many-sided. They do productive manual labour as well as study. They criticize the bourgeoisie and do mass work. The school also organizes militia training and cultural and sports activities. Some schools set aside time for students to study their vocations or raise their general educational level.

The "May 7" cadre school is a school for training cadres at their posts in rotation.

How does the school accomplish its tasks? How do students study? It can be generalized as follows:

Studying Marxist-Leninist Works

In the light of the revolutionary struggle and their ideology, the students study the works of Marx, Engels, Lenin and Stalin and Chairman Mao's works to raise their level of Marxism and their consciousness of the struggle between the two lines, thereby raising their ability to distinguish between genuine and sham Marxists.

The students at the Huangho "May 7" Cadre School in Hunan spend half a day studying and the other half doing manual labour. In the busy farming season, they work during the day, studying in the morning or evening. Last year they studied the Manifesto of the Communist Party, Critique of the Gotha Programme and The State and Revolution as well as On Practice and On Contradiction. They pay special attention to linking theory with practice and often organize group discussions and criticism meetings.

Participating in Class Struggle

Students at cadre schools take part in class struggle and in criticizing the bourgeoisie to temper themselves. They often link

256

their work and ideological problems with their mass criticism of swindlers like Liu Shao-chi, of the theory of the dying out of class struggle, the bourgeois theory of human nature, the theory of productive forces, idealist apriorism, the theory that doing manual labour is a punishment and the theory of going to school in order to get an official post. Some cadre schools carry out various political movements in step with the movements in the units they belong to. Some have sent students to rural people's communes to take part in or help local people carry out a political campaign like attacking active counter-revolutionaries, campaigns against embezzlement and theft, extravagance and waste and speculation.

Taking Part in Productive Labour

Cadre schools devote themselves mainly to agricultural production. Where conditions allow, they branch out into forestry, animal husbandry, side-occupations and fisheries. At the same time they go in for small industries, such as machine-repairing, manufacturing of chemical fertilizers, insecticides, paper- and brick-making, and sugar refining.

Every cadre school has cultivated land—much was once wasteland—ranging from hundreds to thousands of mu, parts of which are reclaimed tracts along sea coasts or lakeshores and on barren hillsides and alkaline slopes. Inner Mongolia's Ikh Chao League cadre school converted much sandy land into fertile fields by covering the sand with layers of mud.

"Plain living and hard struggle" and "self-reliance" is the motto of all the cadre schools.

The object of students taking part in industrial or agricultural productive labour is not only to create material wealth for the country but mainly to better their ideology and to transform their subjective world as they transform the objective world.

Cadres of the General Office of the Chinese Communist Party's Central Committee turned the building of their school into a process of edifying their thought. Instead of choosing a ready-made site, they preferred to build it from scratch. They turned 5,000 mu of lakeshore and other wasteland into fields, and built dormitories and factories on their own. They dug canals, wading knee-deep in mud. They went into icy streams to get sand and braved eye-stinging smoke to burn limestone in the kilns. They fought floods to save people's lives and property. They met all these trials head-on in the revolutionary spirit of "fearing neither hardship nor death."

Going Among Workers and Peasants

Students often leave their schools for short stays in nearby people's communes or factories. Living, eating and working alongside workers or peasants, they learn from them and carry out social investigations among them at the same time. They also do mass work, such as organizing workers and peasants to study philosophy, helping them get some general education and aiding local Party organizations carry out Party rectification and Party building. All these activities aim at raising their ideological level and reforming their world outlook.

Transforming Man

Cadres come to the schools in turns. They go back to their original posts after "graduation," or are transferred to new work. Practice has shown that their stay at cadre schools, brief as it is, is excellent training. The great majority of students come out of the schools changed in outlook in more ways than one.

One artist at the Kuantang Cadre School in Hunan Province who had joined revolutionary work straight from school had not liked to draw peasants because he considered their weatherbeaten faces no objects for art. After entering the cadre school, he had a chance to live and eat with peasants, and made some social investigations into their lives. He found out the tragic histories of many peasant families in the old society under the exploitation of the landlord class. His sentiments changed, and he began to have a great compassion for the once-downtrodden peasants. He said: "Before, I looked at things according to bourgeois aesthetic standards; the more I drew, the farther from the labouring people I got. Now, the more I draw peasants, the closer I feel to them."

Lin Hsiang-wei, vice-director and chief engineer at a designing institute in Hunan, had designed a highway bridge which wasted tons of bricks because he wanted it fancy. The workers criticized him, without convincing him he was wrong. After going to the Kuantang Cadre School, he happened to be working at a brick-kiln. A rush assignment in summer had him drenched in sweat and covered with dirt in the sweltering heat day after day. Only then did he fully realize what it meant to make one brick. He said with genuine feeling: "It's only after you've taken part in labour that you get to feel akin to the workers and peasants." During a fierce rainstorm, Lin ran to the kiln and covered up the clay molds, though he got soaking wet. He often expresses his determination to continue to make revolution and thoroughly transform his old ideas, to become an intellectual welcomed by the workers, peasants and soldiers.

Veteran cadres with much revolutionary experience also gain a great deal from going to cadre school. It puts them back in the war years and helps them get rid of bureaucratic airs and the inactivity that crept up on them in peace time. It rejuvenates them. . . .

Origin of Cadre Schools

"May 7" cadre schools were set up in all parts of the country according to Chairman Mao's May 7, 1966 Directive.

In 1968, when the Proletarian Cultural Revolution was developing in depth, the question of how to carry forward the cadres' ideological revolutionization and revolutionize government institutions was discussed on a wide scale. In October that year Chairman Mao issued the call: "Going down to do manual labour gives vast numbers of cadres an excellent opportunity to study once again; this should be done by all cadres except those who are old, weak, ill or disabled. Cadres at their posts should also go down in turn to do manual labour."

Cadres at every level all over the country enthusiastically responded to this call and asked to go to the most difficult places to do manual labour and to "study once again." The "May 7" cadre schools were set up to meet these needs, and in the single month of October alone new ones appeared almost every day.

* * * * *

19. MAO'S DIRECTIVE ON WORKING CLASS
LEADERSHIP

Peking Review, August 30, 1968.

In carrying out the proletarian revolution in education it is essential to have working-class leadership; it is essential for the masses
of workers to take part and, in co-operation with Liberation Army
fighters, bring about a revolutionary "three-in-one" combination, together with the activists among the students, teachers and workers
in the schools who are determined to carry the proletarian revolution
through to the end. The workers' propaganda teams should stay permanently in the schools and take part in fulfilling all the tasks of struggle-
criticism-transformation in the schools, and they will always lead the
schools. In the countryside, the schools should be managed by the
poor and lower-middle peasants—the most reliable ally of the working
class.

* * * * *

20. THE WORKING CLASS MUST EXERCISE
LEADERSHIP IN EVERYTHING

By Yao Wen-yuan

Translation in Peking Review, August 30, 1968.

A great high tide of struggle-criticism-transformation is coming.
The publication of Chairman Mao's latest instructions and the systematic entry, under leadership, of the mighty army of industrial workers
into schools and all other units where struggle-criticism-transformation has not been carried out well are signals of the coming high tide.
This high tide follows the work on a number of tasks, including the
establishment of revolutionary committees in provinces, municipalities
and autonomous regions, mass criticism and repudiation and the purifying of the class ranks. It will bring about profound changes in all
fields, fiercely storm all those parts of the superstructure which do

not conform to the socialist economic base, educate the masses, smash the hidden reactionaries, carry the great proletarian cultural revolution forward to all-round victory and greatly stimulate the development of the social productive forces.

The important task now confronting the revolutionary committees at all levels is to do the work of struggle-criticism-transformation conscientiously and well, and without losing any time. In order to accomplish this task, it is imperative to persist in leadership by the working class and to "bring into full play the leading role of the working class in the great cultural revolution and in all fields of work". . . .

The workers' propaganda teams are entering the field of education. This is an earth-shaking event. Schools were the monopoly of the exploiting classes and their children from ancient times. Conditions improved somewhat after liberation, but in the main the schools were still monopolized by bourgeois intellectuals. Some students from these schools have been able for various reasons to integrate themselves with the workers, peasants and soldiers and serve them (generally speaking, because they themselves or their teachers are comparatively good or because of the influence of their families, relatives or friends, but chiefly because of the influence of society). Some others have not. In a state of the dictatorship of the proletariat, there is a serious situation—the bourgeoisie contends with the proletariat for leadership. When the young Red Guard fighters rose in rebellion against the handful of capitalist roaders within the Party during the current great proletarian cultural revolution, the reactionary bourgeois forces in the schools for a while got hard blows. But shortly afterwards, certain people were again active in secret. They incited the masses to struggle against each other, and set themselves to sabotage the great cultural revolution, disrupt struggle-criticism-transformation, undermine the great alliance and the revolutionary "three-in-one" combination and obstruct the work of purifying the class ranks and of Party rectification. All this has aroused dissatisfaction among the masses. The facts show us that under such circumstances it is impossible for the students and intellectuals by themselves alone to fulfil the task of struggle-criticism-transformation and a whole number of other tasks on the educational front, workers and People's Liberation Army fighters must take part, and it is essential to have strong leadership by the working class. . . .

The working class has rich practical experience in the three great revolutionary movements of class struggle, the struggle for production and scientific experiment. It most bitterly hates all counter-revolutionary words and deeds against socialism and against Mao Tsetung's thought. It utterly hates the old educational system which served the exploiting classes. It most strongly opposes the "civil war" activities of certain intellectuals in damaging state property and

261

obstructing struggle-criticism-transformation. It thoroughly detests the habit of empty talk and the practice of double-dealing, where words and actions do not match. Therefore, when they combine with fighters of the Chinese People's Liberation Army—the main pillar of the dictatorship of the proletariat—the masses of the working class will be most powerful in stopping all erroneous tendencies contrary to Chairman Mao's revolutionary line and most effective in resolving all kinds of problems which have been described as long-standing, big and difficult. Contradictions that the intellectuals have been quarrelling over without end and unable to resolve are quickly settled when the workers arrive. As regards the handful of villains who have been hiding behind the scenes and inciting the masses to struggle against each other, only when the workers and Liberation Army fighters take a hand in this matter is it possible to lay their counter-revolutionary features completely bare.

"It's quite enough for the workers to run factories." This is an anti-Marxist viewpoint. The working class understands that it can achieve its own final emancipation only by emancipating all mankind. Without carrying the proletarian revolution in education in the schools through to the end and without rooting out revisionism, the working class cannot achieve its final emancipation, and the danger of capitalist restoration and of the working class being again exploited and oppressed will still exist. It is the bounden duty of the politically conscious working class to take an active part in the great cultural revolution in all fields and to ensure that Mao Tse-tung's thought occupies every front in culture and education. . . .

"Workers don't understand education." So say some so-called high-ranking intellectuals. Away with your ugly, bourgeois intellectual airs! There are two kinds of education: bourgeois education and proletarian education. What you "understand" is the pseudo-knowledge of the bourgeoisie. Those who teach science and engineering do not know how to operate or repair machines; those who teach literature do not know how to write essays; those who teach agricultural chemistry do not know how to use fertilizer. Aren't such laughing-stocks to be found everywhere? The proletarian educational system under which theory and practice accord with each other can be gradually brought into being only if the proletariat takes a direct part. You are utterly ignorant of this.

"The workers don't know the situation in the schools and the history of the struggle between the two lines." Don't worry, comrades. The workers will get to know them. Compared with those short-sighted intellectuals who see only their small mountain-strongholds, the working class stands on a far higher eminence. The workers will not stay in the schools for just a few days; they will keep on working there permanently and always occupy the school front and lead the schools.

Everything that exists objectively can be known. The working class will deepen its recognition of the world through its own revolutionary practice and remake the world in its own image.

* * * * *

21. IT IS ESSENTIAL TO RELY ON THE POOR AND LOWER-MIDDLE PEASANTS IN THE EDUCATIONAL REVOLUTION IN THE COUNTRYSIDE

Report of an Investigation into the Experience Gained by the Shuiyuan Commune in Yingkou County in Carrying out the Revolution in Education

By Jen-min Jih-pao and Hung-ch'i Investigators. From Hung-ch'i, no. 3, 1968. Translation in Peking Review, September 27, 1968.

The revolution in education which has been taking place in schools of the Shuiyuan Commune in Yingkou County, Liaoning Province, is rather remarkable. The most important experience lies in the fact that the revolutionary teachers and students in the schools have integrated themselves with the poor and lower-middle peasants and closely relied on them in launching a mass movement for revolutionizing education; the schools are managed by the poor and lower-middle peasants, who are the main force, in combination with the revolutionary teachers and students.

Going Beyond the Narrow Confines of Schools

At first, because of their ideas belittling the workers and peasants, the leadership and teachers of the schools did not sufficiently understand the role of the poor and lower-middle peasants as the main force in the educational revolution in the countryside. Some said: "The poor and lower-middle peasants have had no schooling. What can they do?" Others said: "Since we ourselves are of poor or lower-middle peasant origin and live all the time with the poor and lower-middle peasants, we have already integrated with them." As a result, the movement was carried out in the schools behind closed doors and mass criticism and repudiation was not thoroughgoing. As far as educational reform was concerned, this was confined to working out plans, studying the curricula, selecting and editing teaching material, improving teaching methods, and so forth. Hard as they worked at all this, they could not break out of the old circle. While carrying on the revolution, they resumed school classes in March 1967, but made little progress in the year that followed and did not produce any significant results.

Taking the above-mentioned conditions into account, the commune revolutionary committee and the Mao Tse-tung's thought propaganda team from a Liberation Army unit last March ran Mao Tse-tung's thought study classes for the revolutionary teachers and students. They all studied Chairman Mao's instructions on the revolution in education and the experience gained in educational revolution by the Dengshahe Commune in Chinhsien County. On the basis, they summed up the experience and lessons of the previous stage as follows: First, the educational reform was carried out behind closed doors and was therefore divorced from the poor and lower-middle peasants; second, the reform was restricted to the content and methods of teaching and the system as a whole was not revolutionized; and third, they did not understand that without first revolutionizing ideology, the revolution in education could not be carried out well. The revolutionary teachers and students came to realize that, in order to solve these problems, it was imperative to go out of the schools, to go among the masses, integrate themselves with the poor and lower-middle peasants and learn from them, and launch a vigorous mass movement for revolution in education. . . .

Based on their own experience, the poor and lower-middle peasants condemned the old educational system for its crimes on several such fundamental questions as for whom the doors of the schools are opened, what kind of people are to be trained, and who should be relied on in running a school. They pointed out that the revisionist educational line put up a host of barriers regarding schooling for the children of poor and lower-middle peasants. These included: entrance examinations, the practice of making a student continue in the same class for another year if he failed in exams, compelling a student to drop out of school for one reason or another and regulations on promoting a student to a higher class. Furthermore, schools were irrationally distributed, and children of the poor and lower-middle peasants were thus unable to go to schools near their homes. A poor peasant member of the "August 1st" Production Brigade said: "There are 29 households in our brigade. Of the three graduates from the senior middle school, only one belongs to the 28 families of us poor and lower-middle peasants, while the other two belong to a rich peasant and capitalist family. For whom after all are the doors of the schools opened?" Many children of the poor and lower-middle peasants got inferior marks because they had to help their parents work after classes instead of being helped by their parents in reviewing their lessons at home. A class in the Qunli Primary School had an initial enrollment of 38, but in the course of six years, 33 pupils were left behind in the same class for another year's study or compelled to drop out of school. All were children of the poor and lower-middle peasants, and only five pupils were left at the time of graduation.

The poor and lower-middle peasants pointed out that in the past what the schools practised was the principle that "intellectual training comes first" and "marks come first." This meant "recognizing marks only but not persons, recognizing persons but not the social classes they belong to." Many pupils were thus spoiled and became "preoccupied with marks while reading their books." In school, they strove for marks, and when working in the brigade they strove for "marks" too, that is, work points. Their minds were taken up with "marks, marks, marks," and as a result the revolution was completely discarded.

The poor and lower-middle peasants made this trenchant criticism: Many students trained by the schools in the past set their hearts on going to the cities and did not want to strike roots in the countryside. They described some of the senior middle school students as follows: "The first year they are still country folk; the next year they become different, and the third year they look down on their parents." Apart from not putting Mao Tse-tung's thought to the fore at all, the textbooks contained a lot of feudal, bourgeois and revisionist junk, such as "Szuma Kuang Breaks the Large Jar," "Kung Offers the Larger Pear to Others" and China's Khrushchev allegedly "had plenty of courage" when he was in Anyuan. The textbooks also advocated "the growing of pumpkins and beans in the front and back yards." The poor and lower-middle peasants declared angrily: "This rot was China's Khrushchev's 'san zi yi bao' (the extension of plots for private use and of free markets, the increase in the number of small enterprises with sole responsibility for their own profits or losses, and the fixing of output quotas based on the household) which we completely repudiated and discredited long ago. What's the use of reading such books!" Since such things were taught in the schools, self-interest filled many students' minds and they looked down upon the workers and peasants. There was a junior middle school graduate who had gone back to the "August 1st" Brigade to take part in production. When the poor and lower-middle peasants elected him accountant, he went so far as to say: "Do I still have to do such a job after studying for eight or nine years!" Comparing the Liberation Army with the schools, the poor and lower-middle peasants said that the Liberation Army was really a great school of Mao Tse-tung's thought. Within a short time, it had brought up large numbers of heroes of the Lei Feng, Wang Chieh, Liu Ying-chun, Li Wen-chung and Men Ho type. On the other hand, the schools, which took up sixteen to seventeen years from primary schools to university, trained large numbers of intellectuals who look down upon the workers and peasants and were divorced from reality and did not put proletarian politics to the fore.

Facts have proved that the poor and lower-middle peasants cherish the deepest class feeling for Chairman Mao, have the most incisive understanding of the poisonous effects of the revisionist line in education and have the greatest say in criticizing and repudiating the old educational system. Speaking of their own experience, the teachers and students of the schools in the Shuiyuan Commune said: "Chairman Mao has shown us the way forward and the poor and lower-middle peasants have opened our eyes."

Relying on the Poor and Lower-Middle Peasants in
Building a New Educational System

Who should hold power is the basic question in the revolution in education. Chairman Mao has recently pointed out: "In the country-side, schools and colleges should be managed by the poor and lower-middle peasants—the most reliable ally of the working class." Should the poor and lower-middle peasants have power over education or not? In the Shuiyuan Commune, there were previously differences of opinion on this question. Some members of the revolutionary committee said: "The best educated member of our revolutionary committee hadn't even graduated from junior middle school. We are bound to become a laughing-stock if we exercise power over culture!" After studying Chairman Mao's May 7 directive and other relevant documents, the members of the revolutionary committee realized the importance of exercising power over culture and understood that if the workers and peasants did not exercise power over education, domination of the schools by bourgeois intellectuals couldn't be ended. Consequently, they unanimously expressed their determination to exercise power over education [as] well.

After holding repeated discussions and soliciting the poor and lower-middle peasants' opinions, the commune revolutionary committee decided to abolish the former system of giving the school principal sole responsibility, and to set up in each school a committee for the educational revolution, consisting of representatives both of the poor and lower-middle peasants and of the revolutionary teachers and students. The educational revolution committee in a school works under the leadership of the commune's or production brigade's revolutionary committee and exercises unified leadership. The vice-chairman of the production brigade's revolutionary committee is concurrently vice-chairman of the school's committee for educational revolution; the chairman of the school's committee for educational revolution takes part in the work of the production brigade's revolutionary committee.

In accordance with Chairman Mao's teaching, "it is essential to shorten the length of schooling," the revolutionary teachers and

266

students of the Shuiyuan Commune have changed the primary school's
six-year period to a five-year period. The middle school's six-year
period—three junior grades and three senior grades—was changed to
a four-year period—two junior grades and two senior grades. They
have given full play to the spirit of diligence and frugality in running
the schools. Without adding personnel or equipment or increasing
the burden on the masses, they have established 20 schools, including
five-year primary schools, schools of a seven-year period which goes
from primary school through junior middle school and schools of a
nine-year period which goes from primary school through junior and
senior middle school. Virtually every production brigade has its own
school. Students can study in a junior middle school within the confines of the production brigade and they can study in a senior middle
school within the confines of the people's commune. As all students
live at home, this cuts down on costs for school buildings and the poor
and lower-middle peasants can also afford to let their children study
in such schools. Entering school at the age of six or seven, a child
is only 15 or 16 years old at the time of graduation from senior middle
school after nine years. This is precisely a suitable age to begin taking
part in farm work. After doing farm work for a few years and gaining
practical experience, some can be selected to go to university. Relatively speaking, such a period of schooling conforms to actual conditions in the countryside, it facilitates universal education and is greatly
welcomed by the poor and lower-middle peasants.

New Changes and New Atmosphere

The creative study and application of Mao Tse-tung's thought
has now become a prevailing trend among the revolutionary teachers
and students in the schools of Shuiyuan Commune. The new school
system based on the new periods of tuition has been popularized in the
commune. School enrollment of the children is one hundred per cent.
Those who formerly dropped out of school mid-way or did not have a
chance to study are now in school. Taking the commune as a whole,
there has been an increase of 26 classes and more than 1,100 students.
Since they have really exercised power over education, the poor
and lower-middle peasants have changed their old way of looking on
the schools. The former relationship between the school and the production brigade was: "I do my teaching; you do your farm work."
When speaking of a school, the poor and lower-middle peasants used
to say: "Your school . . ." Now they always talk about "our school."
The relationship between the school and the commune and production
brigade and between the teachers and the peasants has radically changed.
The teachers and students "go out among the peasants and invite the
peasants to the schools." On the one hand, they take part in the three

great revolutionary movements in the commune and the production brigade, propagate Mao Tse-tung's thought and carry out investigations into social conditions; on the other hand, the poor and lower-middle peasants, who suffered endless misery in the old days and have a deep hatred for the exploiting classes, are invited to the schools to talk about their family and village histories, and, together with the teachers and students, contrast their pre-liberation sufferings with their present happiness. The schools also invite the production brigade's security committee chairman to give lectures on class struggle and ask the militia's company leader to lecture on military training and veteran peasants and agro-technicians to lecture on productive skills. Many commune members also understand that educating children is not only the duty of the school but also that of the family. They must educate their children to guard against revisionism. Thus school education, social education and family education are combined.

Because the teachers have made big strides in revolutionizing their thinking, the relationship between them and the students has greatly changed. Many teachers realize that in the past they and the students were not on good terms, the main responsibility lay in their incorrect attitude towards the young fighters' revolutionary rebel spirit. This is not a question of method, but of basic attitude. Therefore, they take the initiative in examining their own mistakes before the students, fight self-interest and identify themselves with the students, and together they study, engage in revolutionary criticism and repudiation, do productive labour and take part in military drill and recreational activities. As a result, the few mischievous students have also examined their own shortcomings and errors. A new relationship has thus been established between teachers and students. Teachers teach students, students teach teachers and students teach one another. Teaching and studying supplement each other and standards are raised together. A lively atmosphere now prevails in the schools.

* * * * *

22. PROMOTE DILIGENCE, FRUGALITY AND
ECONOMY, OPPOSE PUTTING UNDUE EMPHASIS
ON BIGNESS AND MODERNNESS

By The Workers' Propaganda Team and the PLA
Propaganda Team Stationed at Lanchow University,
and the Revolutionary Committee of Lanchow University

Translation in Current Background, no. 916 (October 6, 1970).

The great leader Chairman Mao teaches us: "It is imperative to promote diligence and frugality." "It is imperative to adhere to the principle of diligence and frugality in everything." Institutions of higher learning should also firmly and consistently adhere to this instruction. However, because the pernicious influence of renegade, hidden traitor and scab Liu Shao-ch'i's counterrevolutionary revisionist line has not been completely eradicated, there are still various erroneous ideas that impede our firmly adhering to Chairman Mao's instruction.

Some hold this view: "Whether or not the scientific instruments and equipment for teachers are large in quantity, modern, complete and good reflects the high or low level of an institution of higher learning." In the view of the bourgeoisie and some people seriously affected by bourgeois ideas, the more modern, the more complete and the larger in quantity the scientific instruments and equipment for teaching are, the higher is the "standard" of the school. This was promoted on a large scale by renegade, hidden traitor and scab Liu Shao-ch'i and his agents in our school in the past. The proletariat is of the view that the principle of diligence, frugality and economy must be firmly adhered to in operating socialist universities, and that blind worship of modernness is bourgeois thinking and the philosophy of the foreign slave.

Under the rule of the counterrevolutionary revisionist line, the former Lanchow University might buy books, scientific instruments and equipment not in accordance with the actual need of the socialist revolution and socialist construction and of teaching and scientific research, but for the purpose of "erecting the temple according to the deity" and serving the bourgeois intellectuals everywhere. When a professor made various requests in the desire to "form" his own so-called "school," the former Lanchow University readily compiled with all of them and bought for him a profusion of scientific instruments and equipment. The laboratories, scientific instruments and equipment of the university all laid undue emphasis on bigness, modernness and completeness. So long as a scientific instrument was imported, it was considered to be good and up to "standard." When a certain department learned that a micro-milli-second oscilloscope had been imported, it ran around and devised all ways and means to buy it. Actually, the performance and index of this scientific instrument are inferior to certain oscilloscopes produced in China. . . .

23. THE WORKER-PEASANT-SOLDIER TEACHERS ARE A MOST DYNAMIC REVOLUTIONARY FORCE: CHAIRMAN MAO TELLS US TO MOUNT THE UNIVERSITY ROSTRUM

By a Teacher of Poor-and-Lower-Middle-Peasant
Origin of the "May 7" Experimental Class of the
Northwest Agricultural College

Peking Jen-min Jih-pao, December 28, 1970. Translation in Current Background, no. 933 (June 4, 1971).

Last year, in accordance with the great leader Chairman Mao's teaching that "in the countryside, the schools should be managed by the poor and lower-middle peasants—the most reliable ally of the working class," we were invited to serve as teachers of the "May 7" experimental class of the Northwest Agricultural College.

Under the rule of the revisionist line in education, the former Northwest Agricultural College did not open its door to us poor and lower-middle peasants. The few children of poor and lower-middle peasants who had been admitted were either thrust aside and attacked or corrupted with bourgeois ideas disseminated from the rostrum. Seeing this situation, we poor and lower-middle peasants were most indignant. Today, after the great proletarian cultural revolution and under the guiding light of Mao Tse-tung thought, we poor and lower-middle peasants have come to the socialist college, mounted the rostru and used Mao Tse-tung thought to occupy and transform this school front. This is a glorious task entrusted us by Chairman Mao.

The mounting of the university rostrum by poor and lower-middle peasants is an unprecedented event. Like other new things, it was opposed by the old force of habit right from beginning. A few bourgeois intellectuals wanted to see us making a "farce" of ourselves and certain individuals sarcastically remarked that we teachers of poor-and-lower-middle peasant origin "need very little capital to do big business." In the beginning, some comrades among us were faint-hearted. We therefore ran study courses in Mao Tse-tung thought to study Chairman Mao's teaching that "education should be revolutionize and the domination of our schools by bourgeois intellectuals should by no means be allowed to continue," thus raising the political conscious-ness of the majority. We realized that the mounting of the university rostrum by poor and lower-middle peasants was for the purpose of carrying out to the letter Chairman Mao's proletarian revolutionary line and implementing all-round dictatorship over the bourgeoisie in the sphere of the superstructure, and no matter how great the diffi-culties were, we also must overcome them. . . .

We poor and lower-middle peasants play a direct part in the three great revolutionary movements in the countryside to fight against nature, the soil and the class enemy, and brave year in and year out the stormy class struggle and struggle for production. As far as the two courses of class struggle and struggle for production are concerned, we poor and lower-middle peasants have the greatest right to speak. We are capable of using Mao Tse-tung Thought to train successors for the proletarian revolutionary cause, and our rich practical experience to contribute strength to the revolution in education in agricultural colleges and schools.

In the practice of revolution in education in the past year, we attached importance to grasping the following two things:

Chairman Mao taught us: "All work in a school is for the purpose of transforming the thought of the students." As we poor and lower-middle peasants mounted the rostrum, we first energetically grasped revolutionary mass criticism and at all times gave first place to the education of the students in making living study and application of Chairman Mao's writings and to the ideological transformation of the students. We ate together, lived together and did manual work together with the students. When living ideas were discovered, we studied Chairman Mao's writings together, and recalled the bitter past and thought of the happy present together. When the students came to our team, we invited the poor and lower-middle peasants who knew bitterness and hate to recall their bitter past and tell their happy present, and to prepare for them meals for recalling the bitter past. We used what we had gone through in person to acquaint the students with the heroic spirit of the broad masses of poor and lower-middle peasants in making living study and application of Chairman Mao's works and in fighting against nature and the soil. We inspired the students to raise incessantly their level of consciousness in the class struggle and the struggle in line, and establish the thought of studying and tilling land for the revolution and of wholeheartedly serving the people.

In accordance with Chairman Mao's teaching that "there is in the world only one kind of genuine theory which is drawn from objective reality and is also testified in objective reality," we firmly opposed the tendency to divorce theory from reality in the practice of revolution in education, tightly grasped the important problems found in production, recommended the experience accumulated over a long time by us in actual production, put forward measures for the solution of these problems, and discussed and studied things together with the students. Because theory was closely linked with reality and the practical problems of our locality were discussed, the students felt that the discussion was useful for solving problems.

As we taught in the past year, we studied and worked together with the former teachers. We helped each other, overcame one's weaknesses by acquiring other's strong points, continuously reinforced the content of teaching and improved the teaching method. This not only was advantageous to transforming their ideology and style of work, but also raised the level of our theoretical knowledge and stimulated us to make a greater success of scientific experiment and teaching work.

* * * * *

24. MAO'S DIRECTIVE ON
RE-EDUCATION OF INTELLECTUALS

Peking Review, December 6, 1968.

The majority or the vast majority of the students trained in the old schools and colleges can integrate themselves with the workers, peasants and soldiers, and some have made inventions or innovations; they must, however, be re-educated by the workers, peasants and soldiers under the guidance of the correct line, and thoroughly change their old ideology. Such intellectuals will be welcomed by the workers, peasants and soldiers.

* * * * *

25. MAO'S "LATEST INSTRUCTION"
ON RE-EDUCATION

Jen-min Jih-pao, December 22, 1968.

It is necessary for educated youth to go to the countryside to be re-educated by lower and lower-middle peasants. It is important to persuade the cadres and other people in the cities to send their own children to the countryside upon graduation from the junior middle school, and senior middle school, or the university. The comrades in the countryside should be mobilized to welcome the young people to their midst.

* * * * *

26. ON THE RE-EDUCATION OF INTELLECTUALS

By Jen-min Jih-pao and Hung-ch'i Commentators. From Jen-min Jih-pao, September 12, 1968. Translation in Peking Review, September 20, 1968.

When the working class enters cultural and educational institutions, its work is primarily directed towards the intellectuals. Correct grasp of the Party's policy towards intellectuals is therefore an important guarantee for victory in the struggle. . . .

The great leader Chairman Mao teaches us that throughout the whole course of the socialist revolution and socialist construction, the remolding of the intellectuals is a question of major significance. After seizing political power, the proletariat should remold the intellectuals in accordance with its own outlook and train a contingent of proletarian intellectuals which serves it.

. . . This involves not only the schools, but also the vast number of intellectuals on our cultural and educational front and in the ranks of our cadres. Why is it called re-education? Because what they received in the past was bourgeois education and the education they are receiving now is proletarian. This is one meaning. Another is that in the past, under the pernicious influence of the revisionist line of China's Khrushchev, they received education from bourgeois intellectuals, whereas now, under the guidance of Chairman Mao's proletarian revolutionary line, they are being re-educated by the workers, peasants and soldiers. The remolding of one's world outlook is something fundamental. We should educate the intellectuals according to the proletarian world outlook so that they can change the bourgeois ideas they formerly received from bourgeois education. Such is the content of this re-education. The fundamental road in this re-education is for them to take the road of integrating themselves with the workers, peasants and soldiers and serving them.

In conducting re-education, it is necessary to bring the positive factors into full play. The question of line is the fundamental issue. The line that is followed produces the kind of people that are trained. We should concentrate our hatred on the handful of top capitalist roaders in the Party and their agents since it is their counter-revolutionary revisionist line in education that poisoned the youth. The thorough repudiation of this reactionary line will impel people to make further efforts to carry out Chairman Mao's proletarian educational line. In socialist new China, the majority or the vast majority of the students trained in the old schools will, when educated in Mao Tse-tung's thought, be able gradually to integrate themselves with the workers, peasants and soldiers. In the course of this, there will inevitably be wavering and reversals. But provided these people do follow and advance along Chairman Mao's proletarian revolutionary line and accept re-education by the workers, peasants and soldiers, and thoroughly repudiate and continuously change the old bourgeois ideas they brought along from home and school, they will be able to contribute their share in serving the workers, peasants and soldiers. The workers, peasants and soldiers welcome such intellectuals. While there are indeed counter-revolutionaries and diehards, they are very few in number. The vast number of intellectuals are willing to remold themselves with the workers, peasants and soldiers, and they have bright prospects under the socialist system. The editor's

274

note pointed out: "Some of them are sure to make a success of this integration and achieve something in regard to inventions and innovations. Mention should be made of these people as encouragement." This means to encourage and in a positive way urge the great number of intellectuals to take firmly the road of integrating themselves with the workers, peasants and soldiers. People who have made a success of this integration and have made inventions and innovations are to be found everywhere. Their example should be cited to educate those intellectuals who have already gone to working posts, or are going. . . .

* * * * *

27. HOOLIGANS AND TEDDY BOYS ARE NOT ALLOWED TO DISRUPT FARM PRODUCTION

Shanghai Wen-hui Pao, August 4, 1968. Translation in Survey of China Mainland Press, no. 4251 (September 5, 1968).

Comrade Editor:

The nearer the great proletarian cultural revolution is approaching an all-round victory, the more desperate the struggle the class enemies will wage against us. In our Peits'ai area live a group of hooligans and Teddy boys, who for some time have collaborated with ghosts and monsters in society in fights and looting, using such weapons as leather straps, slings, and clubs. They have seriously damaged State property and incurred the wrath of the poor and lower-middle peasants.

This group of hooligans and Teddy boys, in defiance of the decrees, orders, notifications and notices published successively by the proletarian headquarters, frequently go in groups to the production teams where they, besides damaging the farm crops, encircle and attack the poor and lower-middle peasants. Using daggers, they damaged more than 400 catties of melons and wrecked many chili fields. A farm plot measuring more than 10 mow owned by a production team was so trampled underfoot that it didn't look like a farm plot any more.

One day these gangsters were heading for a nearby production team when they were stopped and advised to turn back by an old poor peasant. He was brutally assaulted. Some poor and lower-middle peasants were bitterly beaten up because they criticized the misbehavior of these gangsters, who threatened to "burn XXX production brigade in fire, flatten the XX production team, and catch the production team leader alive." They have really become lawless.

Recently, the proletarian headquarters issued a new combat order. It is being strictly enforced by the broad masses of poor and lower-middle peasants and the revolutionary masses. We are extremely indignant at the criminal activities of this gang of hooligans and Teddy boys defying the combat order of the proletarian headquarters. We will wage an uncompromising struggle against them, puncture their reactionary arrogance, and impose proletarian dictatorship on them. As for those youngsters who merely followed them in doing bad things, we advise them to turn back and dissociate themselves from the bad people. They should promptly wake up, expose the bad people who pull the strings behind them, launch a counterattack on them, and return to the correct road.

> A number of poor and lower-middle peasants
> of Peits'ai commune, Ch'uansha hsien
> A number of revolutionary masses in
> Peits'ai chen, Ch'uansha hsien

* * * * *

28. WIPE OUT ALL VERMIN

From Shanghai Wen-hui Pao, August 4, 1968. Translation in Survey of China Mainland Press, no. 4251 (September 5, 1968).

The following comment and the three letters from readers of Wen-hui Pao that follow it condemn the "hooligans and Teddy boys" in Shanghai who are said to be sabotaging production, obstructing "resumption of classes to make revolution," stealing State property, and committing other crimes.
                                        —SCMP Editor

Shanghai is under the control of proletarian revolutionaries. Its revolutionary situation, like that in other parts of the country, is exceedingly fine. A small handful of class enemies, sensing their impending doom, are waging a death-bed struggle.

A small band of hooligans and Teddy boys, a reactionary partisan force of the class enemy, are meeting the needs of the small handful of traitors, special agents, and diehard capitalist-roaders represented by China's Khrushchev, as well as unreformed landlords, rich peasants, counter-revolutionaries, bad people, and rightists, by doing a large number of bad things. They sabotage production, impede the "resumption of school classes to make revolution," steal State property, and commit armed robberies. They insult women and instigate teenagers to commit crimes. They are nothing but a heap of dog's dung spurned by man.

Chairman Mao teaches us: "Dictatorship must also be imposed on thieves, swindlers, murderers, arsonists, gangs, and all kinds of bad elements who gravely upset social order."

Recently, the proletarian headquarters headed by Chairman Mao with Vice Chairman Lin as the deputy issued a new combat call to us. By attacking a small handful of bad eggs, we shall go a long way toward promoting the revolutionary justice of the proletariat and holding the evil atmosphere of the bourgeoisie in check. By attacking this small handful of bad eggs, we shall accord the best protection to the masses of the people.

The law of class struggle has proved once again: "Everything reactionary is the same; if you don't hit it, it won't fall. This is also like sweeping the floor; as a rule, where the broom does not reach, the dust will not vanish of itself." Reactionary things will be swept away only where the revolutionary forces can reach. The fact is exactly so. Those bad eggs may start trouble here and there and act like bullies, but once the proletarian revolutionaries stretch out their iron fists and resolutely take revolutionary action against this pack of bad eggs, all vermin will fall into the net.

We must impose proletarian dictatorship on all bad eggs who dare to counter the proletarian dictatorship. As for those teenagers imbued with hooliganism, we hope that they will immediately turn back and start a new life. Our policy has always been this: Those who confess frankly shall be dealt with leniently, those who resist shall be dealt with harshly, ring-leaders shall be punished; those who are forced to commit crimes shall not be punished, those who are hoodwinked are guiltless, and those who redeem themselves by turning round to strike at the evil-doers shall be considered as meritorious.

As in the case of wiping out of the four pests, we must attack the hooligans and Teddy boys continually. The elimination of four pests is a regular task. As for the hooligans and Teddy boys, they should be wiped out where they are found, and several campaigns against them should be conducted in a year. Once these bad eggs raise their heads, we shall sweep them away in no time. If they raise their heads again, we shall sweep them away again.

"Sweep away all vermin and we are peerless."

* * * * *

29. MAO'S INSTRUCTION GIVEN ON AN INSPECTION
TOUR OF TIENTSIN UNIVERSITY (EXCERPTS)

(August 13, 1958)

Current Background, no. 891 (October 8, 1969).

From now on, schools should run factories and factories should run schools.

Teachers should also take part in labor, and they cannot just give lip service to the matter without giving a hand to it.

Institutions of higher learning should lay hold of three things: first, the leadership of the Party committee; second, the mass line; third, the integration of education with productive labor.

＊ ＊ ＊ ＊ ＊

30. SOME TENTATIVE PROGRAMMES FOR
REVOLUTIONIZING EDUCATION

Peking Review, November 17, 1967.

Tongji University's Proposals for Transforming
Education

In accordance with Chairman Mao's May 7, 1966 instruction, Shanghai's Tongji University sent more than 100 people in groups to factories and construction sites in August and September this year to make investigations and study the question of transforming education. Bold proposals have been worked out for the reorganization of the university.

It is proposed to transform Tongji University into the "May 7th" Commune consisting of a tuitional unit, a designing unit and a building unit, an integrated whole having three-fold function of tuition, designing and building. This will change the present phenomenon of education being divorced from production.

The "May 7th" Commune will abolish existing departments and teaching research groups and set up in their place a number of

278

specialized committees each composed of personnel from the tuitional unit, the designing unit and the production unit. Each committee will have a number of classes under its direction with teachers, students, workers, engineering and technical personnel organized along military lines.

The commune will implement two types of "three-in-one" combination: one is the "three-in-one" combination of revolutionary leading cadres, and leaders of the revolutionary mass organizations and the militia; the other is the combination of tuition, designing and building.

The commune will operate a rotation system whereby a part of its teaching staff will be enabled to be tempered and remolded by practical participation in production at fixed intervals.

The "May 7th" Commune will set up political work departments in its organizations at all levels. Every specialized committee will be provided with political instructors and each class with political workers.

The period of schooling will be shortened to three years. Apart from courses in Mao Tse-tung's thought and military affairs, the time allocated to specialized theoretical subjects will be proportionally increased each year. All students in each academic year will be required to take part in productive labor. In the first year, half the time will be assigned to building and engineering work. In the second year, two-thirds of the time will be used for learning the basic knowledge about designing through practical work under the guidance of technical workers or teachers. In the third year, stress will be put on the study of specialized courses while the student continues to spend part of his time in productive labor. . . .

* * * * *

31. TONGJI UNIVERSITY'S PROGRAMME FOR REVOLUTIONIZING EDUCATION: SIX MONTHS' PRACTICE

Peking Review, May 17, 1968.

It is already six months since Shanghai's Tongji University began putting into practice its tentative programme for revolutionizing education drawn up in accordance with Chairman Mao's well-known May 7, 1966 directive. . . .

Tongji is a university specializing in civil engineering. Last August, revolutionary teachers and students there studied this new directive of Chairman Mao and launched into criticism and repudiation of the old revisionist educational line. They also went to the factories and work-sites and sought the workers' opinions. After this, they decided that they would transform Tongji into a great school of Mao Tse-tung's thought combining tuition with designing and building. Only then, could it train "workers with both socialist consciousness and culture" as stipulated by the Chinese Communist Party's educational policy. . . .

Ending the Domination of Schools by Bourgeois Intellectuals

Power in the May 7 Commune belongs to the revolutionary teachers and students and revolutionary workers and technicians. This is in vivid contrast to the past, when bourgeois intellectuals dominated the university in all respects. The commune leaders elected by the members are people with very high proletarian consciousness and political levels. They are loyal to the fundamental orientation charted by Chairman Mao of "education serving proletarian politics and education being combined with productive labor." The commune revolutionaries, under their leadership, have found through practice an entirely new educational road.

In accordance with Chairman Mao's teaching "to learn warfare through warfare," Tonji's revolutionary teachers and students, in addition to necessary classroom studies, also take part in designing and building together with the workers and designers, learning as they work. Following Chairman Mao's instruction that "officers teach soldiers, soldiers teach officers and soldiers teach each other," not only the teachers, but workers and designers as well as students give lectures. This has fundamentally changed the previous state of affairs when bourgeois intellectuals monopolized the teaching platform. The curriculum has been greatly simplified. Teaching is carried out in architectural and structural designing and building, and this is now integrated with actual construction work. Formerly, the curriculum included over 30 subjects taking five years to complete; now, it has been cut by half and takes only three years. Teaching material has also been revised, some being taken from former textbooks and simplified, and some being newly written by the collective in the course of practice.

Criticizing the Bourgeoisie

The realization of this programme is a great revolutionary transformation involving the complete revolutionizing of the old educational system and principles and methods of teaching. Naturally, it met with resistance from the handful of capitalist roaders in the

Party and the bourgeois reactionary academic "authorities" under their wing. At the same time, it met with obstruction from the old forces of habit. In the last half year, the commune revolutionaries have waged sharp struggle against all this.

At first, the capitalist roaders and bourgeois reactionary academic "authorities" tried to strangle the new-born commune in its cradle, attacking it as "utopian communism" and saying that, under it, "the quality of teaching will inevitably suffer." When the revolutionaries insisted on carrying out their programme, a handful of class enemies, in an attempt to exclude the workers who had most practical experience from taking part in the teaching, slandered them as "good for nothing except mixing mortar." The revolutionaries, however, did not waver in the materialist view that knowledge comes from practice and clearly saw through the class enemies' scheme to speak for the bourgeois intellectuals, who were divorced from social practice, and let them continue to dominate the school. They persisted in going forward. Then a few bourgeois intellectuals who had wormed their way into the commune covertly spread fallacies in favour of giving prominence to professional work and technique, so that the revolutionary teachers and students should continue to take the revisionist road of being divorced from proletarian politics. Others tried to lead the commune on to the wrong path from the ultra "Left."

The commune revolutionaries waged a tit-for-tat struggle against the class enemies. Bearing firmly in mind Chairman Mao's words that "before a brand-new social system can be built on the site of the old, the site must first be swept clean," they unfolded a big revolutionary mass criticism and repudiation campaign to eliminate the poisonous influence of the counter-revolutionary revisionist educational line of China's Khrushchev. The revolutionary teachers, students, workers and technicians, on the work-sites, criticized and struggled against the handful of capitalist roaders in the Party and some bourgeois reactionary academic "authorities" from the university and the associated building and designing units. They also exposed bad elements hidden in the commune. At the same time, they held a succession of Mao Tse-tung's thought study classes. . . .

The half year of practice has made them understand particularly profoundly this teaching of Chairman Mao's: "Class struggle, the struggle for production and scientific experiment are the three great revolutionary movements for building a mighty socialist country. These movements are a sure guarantee that Communists will be free from bureaucracy and immune against revisionism and dogmatism, and will for ever remain invincible." They said that the commune has closely integrated the three great revolutionary movements, and this has tempered them as well as the workers. The commune is a school for tempering and bringing up successors for the revolutionary cause of the proletariat.

The past six months of practice is only a beginning. The revolutionary teachers and students firmly believe that running education this way conforms in the main to Chairman Mao's May 7 directive, which advocates the orientation of turning every field of work into a great school of communism. They are determined to advance in accordance with Chairman Mao's teachings with great strides and to carry through to the end of the proletarian revolution in education.

* * * * *

32. THE ROAD FOR TRAINING ENGINEERING AND TECHNICAL PERSONNEL INDICATED BY THE SHANGHAI MACHINE TOOLS PLANT

Report of an investigation, written by Wen-hui Pao and Hsin-hua correspondents and published in Jen-min Jih-pao, July 22, 1968. Translation in Peking Review, August 2, 1968.

Profound Changes Brought About by the Great Proletarian Cultural Revolution

The Shanghai Machine Tools Plant is a large factory famous for its production of precision grinding machines. It has a technical force of more than 600 engineers and technicians which is made up of people from three sources: 45 percent of them are from the ranks of the workers, 50 percent are post-liberation college graduates and the remainder are old technicians trained before liberation. The tempest of the great proletarian cultural revolution has brought about a profound change in the ranks of the technicians who work at the plant.

This great revolutionary change manifests itself mainly in the following ways:

First, the proletarian revolutionaries have truly taken into their hands the leadership in the factory, including power over technical matters; the reactionary bourgeois technical "authorities" who formerly controlled the leadership in this field have been overthrown. Many technicians of worker origin, revolutionary young technicians and revolutionary cadres are now the masters in scientific research and technical designing. They are proletarian revolutionary fighters with deep class feelings for Chairman Mao and the Communist Party. . . .

282

Third, relations between the workers and technicians have changed. . . . During the great cultural revolution, a "three-in-one" combination of workers, revolutionary technicians and revolutionary cadres was introduced in the plant. The rank-and-file workers now take part in designing and the technicians go to operate machines in the first line of production, closely linking theory with practice. As a result there is a big improvement in relations between workers and technicians.

Road for Training Engineering and Technical Personnel

The young technicians up to 35 years of age at the plant come from two sources: college graduates (numbering some 350, of whom one-tenth are post-graduates or graduates of colleges abroad) and technical personnel promoted from among the workers (numbering around 250, a few of them having studied for several years at secondary technical schools). The facts show that the latter are better than the former. Generally speaking, the former have a great number of backward ideas and are less competent in practical work, while the latter are more advanced ideologically and are more competent in practical work. At present, the overwhelming majority of the technical personnel of worker origin have become the technological backbone of the plant and about one-tenth of them are capable of independently designing high-grade, precision and advanced new products. The chief designers of six of the ten new precision grinding machines success-fully trial-produced in the first half of this year are technical personnel of worker origin.

Selecting technical personnel from among the workers is the road for training proletarian engineers and technicians. . . .

The contrast between technicians of worker origin and the old bourgeois intellectuals who were deeply poisoned by the desire for personal fame and gain is even more striking. One bourgeois "expert" spent eight years trying to design a grinder and wasted a large amount of state funds, without succeeding; but he accumulated considerable "data" as capital for his own reputation and gain. The workers say: How can we expect such a person to have the slightest feeling for our new society?

* * * * *

33. CHAIRMAN MAO TSE-TUNG'S LATEST DIRECTIVE

Peking Review, August 2, 1968.

It is still necessary to have universities; here I refer mainly to colleges of science and engineering. However, it is essential to shorten the length of schooling, revolutionize education, put proletarian politics in command and take the road of the Shanghai Machine Tools Plant in training technicians from among the workers. Students should be selected from among workers and peasants with practical experience, and they should return to production after a few years' study.

* * * * *

34. THE WISHES OF WORKERS, PEASANTS AND SOLDIERS IN THEIR HUNDREDS OF MILLIONS HAVE COME TRUE!—HAILING THE WORKERS, PEASANTS AND SOLDIERS ENTERING THE NEW-TYPE SOCIALIST UNIVERSITIES

Peking Review, September 30, 1970.

With the solicitude of our great leader Chairman Mao, worker, peasant and soldier university students chosen by China's hundreds of millions of workers, peasants and soldiers themselves, have marched confidently and in high spirits into two new-type socialist universities—Tsinghua and Peking Universities—during the Great Proletarian Cultural Revolution's struggle-criticism-transformation movement.

China's first workers' Mao Tse-tung Thought propaganda team entered the Tsinghua University in Peking on July 27, 1968. Since then, the working class has mounted the political stage of struggle-criticism-transformation in the superstructure. Following Chairman Mao's great teaching "Take the road of the Shanghai Machine Tools Plant in training technicians from among the workers. Students should be selected from among workers and peasants with practical experience," Tsinghua and Peking Universities have selected students group by group from among the workers, peasants and soldiers and set up various specialized classes on a trial basis, while carrying on a deep-going revolution in education. Furthermore, both universities have chosen over 4,000 worker, peasant and soldier university students from different parts of the country since the beginning of this year. These students were recommended by the workers, peasants and soldiers and examined and approved by the leadership of the revolutionary committees at various levels. The method adopted by the universities in choosing students from among the workers, peasants and soldiers having practical experience is a great creation in putting Chairman Mao's thinking on educational revolution into practice. . . .

Winning Honor for Chairman Mao

On the morning of August 27, 1970, a "long march contingent" made up of worker, peasant and soldier university students arrived at Tien An Men Square in the capital, full of vigour and vitality. They had marched more than 300 li for four days from Tientsin.

Carrying red banners and with packs on their backs, these students held high their red-covered copies of Quotations From Chairman Mao Tse-tung as they greeted the morning sun rising from the east. Looking up at the brilliant portrait of our great leader Chairman Mao, they made a solemn pledge in the square:

"Chairman Mao, dear Chairman Mao! We 221 workers, peasants and soldiers, have come to Peking where you live to study in the universities. We owe this greatest happiness to you. We are determined to win honor for you and for our great socialist motherland! We pledge that though our work posts have changed, our consciousness of continuing the revolution will not change; though our environment has changed, our quality as working people will not change; though our tasks have changed, our style of hard struggle will not change. Whatever changes may take place, our loyalty to you will never change!" . . .

Carrying Forward the Revolutionary Tradition

These workers, peasants, and soldiers have brought with them to the universities the glorious tradition of the People's Liberation Army and the revolutionary spirit of hard struggle shown by the working people. Some have brought their shovels, hoes and sickles, others had hair-cutting instruments and needle and thread boxes in their knapsacks. Since their arrival at the universities, they often take part in reclaiming and cultivating land, fertilizing the fields, going to factories and countryside to do a stint of labor or working in university-run factories. They repair broken windows at the universities, mend their own clothes or shoes and help cut each other's hair.

Sons and daughters from the Chingkang Mountains, a sacred place of the revolution, wore the kind of straw-sandals veteran Red Army men used to wear and had bamboo rainhats on their backs when they came to Peking to study in the universities.

The fact that they wore straw-sandals when they came shows that they are determined to always follow the revolutionary road pointed out by Chairman Mao. And the fact that they had brought their bamboo rainhats shows that they have made up their minds to always follow Chairman Mao in facing the world and braving the storms.

It was late at night on the eve of her departure for Peking that Tsou Cheng-hsiang, a poor-peasant commune member of the Teaching Production Brigade of the Chingkangshan Commune, sat with members of her family before a portrait of Chairman Mao. Her father once again told her about their miserable family history and how their family had been liberated. He gave her four precious gifts: a volume of Selected Works of Mao Tse-tung, a copy of the family history, two pairs of straw-sandals tied with red ribbons and a bag of red rice such as the Red Army men used to eat. When Cheng-hsiang was about to leave, the village's poor and lower-middle peasants all came to see her off. Her grandfather Tsou Wen-kai, leader of the insurrection corps of the Red Army, once again led her to pay respects to Chairman Mao's former residence so that she would firmly keep in mind the glorious history of how Chairman Mao had led the Chingkang Mountain people in making revolution. Holding Cheng-hsiang's hands, many elderly poor peasants, with tears in their eyes, urged her: You're the first poor-peasant university student we poor and lower-middle peasants in the Chingkang Mountains have selected in following out Chairman Mao's instruction and you must never fall short of the expectations of Chairman Mao who is so concerned for the people in the Chingkang Mountains. When you get to Peking and see Chairman Mao, you must never fail to shout "Long live Chairman Mao!" over and over again for us.

Entering the new-type socialist university with her was P.L.A. fighter Liu Chi-ying, the younger brother of the heroine and revolutionary martyr Liu Hu-lan. He was a "five-good" fighter and an activist in the living study and application of Mao Tse-tung Thought when he served in a P.L.A. unit, the great school of Mao Tse-tung Thought. With profound proletarian feelings of boundless loyalty to our great leader Chairman Mao, Liu Chi-ying pledged: "I'll never forget class struggle and will do my part to make the new-type socialist university a success."

Exercise Power Over Education for the Proletariat

A veteran coal-miner and a Communist Party member from Inner Mongolia Sun Teh-yu also came to attend university in Peking where Chairman Mao lives and works. None of the Suns, who had been coal-miners for generations, could read or write. Sun Teh-yu's mother died of illness when he was nine. His younger sister became a child-bride and he himself was forced to work for a capitalist in order to pay the family debts. There were tears in his eyes when he arrived at Tsinghua University and he said with feeling: "We workers were crushed by the three big mountains—imperialism, feudalism and bureaucrat-capitalism—in the old society. How could we have the right to study at a university! Before the Great Cultural Revolution, we workers were still barred from the university doors by Liu Shao-chi's counter-revolutionary revisionist line. I'll never forget that it is our great leader Chairman Mao who has given me the right to go to a university today!" . . .

These educated young people coming from all over the mother-land to attend universities in Peking have brought many precious gifts from the poor and lower-middle peasants. These include the red treasured books by Chairman Mao and a quilt used by three genera-tions, a kerosene lamp the poor and lower-middle peasants had used when they studied Chairman Mao's works with them, and a sewing kit knitted by an elderly aunt who was a poor peasant. . . . The fervent hopes the poor and lower-middle peasants place on them always in-spire them to use Mao Tse-tung Thought to remold their world out-look and to master skills for the revolution, encourage them to always take the road of integrating with the workers, peasants and soldiers and train themselves into new-type proletarian intellectuals.

Inspired by the Communiqué of the Second Plenary Session of the Ninth Central Committee of the Communist Party of China and led by the workers' and P.L.A. men's Mao Tse-tung Thought prop-aganda team and the universities' Party committees, students of worker, peasant and soldier origin in Tsinghua and Peking Universities are filled with the lofty aspiration to play their part as taught in the quotation from Chairman Mao "China ought to make a greater con-tribution to humanity." They are intensifying their efforts to study and apply Mao Tse-tung Thought in a living way and working hard to help make the new-type socialist universities a success.

* * * * *

35. TAKING ALL SOCIETY AS THEIR FACTORY—
PEKING UNIVERSITY'S ACHIEVEMENTS IN
EDUCATIONAL REVOLUTION IN THE LIBERAL ARTS

Peking Review, February 2, 1973.

Having gone through the Great Proletarian Cultural Revolution, Peking University is developing into a new-type socialist university. It has 17 departments embracing over 60 specialities and a teaching staff of more than 2,000. Since August 1970, it has enrolled some 4,000 students from among young workers, peasants and soldiers with practical experience all over the country. This is something unheard of in the old-type universities.

The liberal arts in Peking University, which is located in the northwestern suburbs of the capital, include Chinese, history, philosophy, political economy, international politics, law and library science departments. Chairman Mao has pointed out: "The liberal arts should take all society as their factory." Like the science and engineering colleges which have their own factories or establish contacts with local plants to enable teachers and students to link study with actual production, the liberal arts teachers and students, apart from class work, devote some time every year to taking part in class struggle and productive labor in factories, people's communes, P.L.A. units and shops and making social investigations, stressing theoretical study based on practice. Good results have thus been obtained in educational revolution.

Prior to the Great Cultural Revolution, Chairman Mao time and again called on the liberal arts teachers and students to go among the workers and peasants and learn how to make revolution by taking part in class struggle. He clearly pointed out: "Education must serve proletarian politics and be combined with productive labor." However, Liu Shao-chi and his agents in the field of education pushed a revisionist line in a futile bid to lead teachers and students astray, making them divorce themselves from proletarian politics, the worker and peasant masses and productive labor.

Profound Changes

Repudiation of this counter-revolutionary revisionist line in education during the Cultural Revolution has enabled the students and teachers in the college of liberal arts to embark on the road of taking all society as their factory, thereby drastically changing the teaching system.

Since two years ago, they have incorporated their study in and out of the university. While attending classes, students concentrate their time and energy in systematically studying the basic knowledge of the various subjects they major in. Together with their teachers, they are out in society four months a year, applying what they have learnt to practice. In this way, the old bookish way of studying has been done away with and the students' ability to use Marxist theory to analyze and solve problems has been raised.

In 1971, the students in the Chinese department specializing in literature and their teachers went to a production brigade in Miyun County on Peking's outskirts to do some investigation work. The heroic deeds of Liu Mao-ching, the brigade's late Party branch secretary who had led the peasants in building a socialist new countryside, inspired them to do creative writing. While tutoring students in such writing, the teachers lectured on the relevant parts of such courses as the Marxist theory of literature and art, writing methods, analysis of classical and modern literary works and grammar and rhetoric, and organized the students to conscientiously study Chairman Mao's Talks at the Yenan Forum on Literature and Art and other works. The result was the students wrote a collection of revolutionary stories.

In co-operation with the Peking Historical Relics Administration, teachers and students in archaeology under the history department unearthed a Western Chou Dynasty (c. 1066-771 B.C.) village and discovered 3,000-year-old houses, kitchen ranges, pottery and other things. This initial training in field excavation helped extend their knowledge of what had been learnt in the classroom.

The Ming Tombs in Changping County on Peking's northwestern outskirts, where thirteen Ming emperors are buried, became lecture rooms on the history of the Ming Dynasty (1368-1644 A.D.) and Ching Dynasty (1644-1911 A.D.) Teachers and students read historical data, visited the luxurious underground mausoleum of a Ming emperor and his wife, and investigated the family histories of the peasants living in the locality for generations. What they found spoke volumes for the harsh exploitation and oppression of the peasants by the feudal rulers and the former's resistance and struggle. This was very conducive to grasping Marxist historical materialism and using the theory of class struggle to study historical problems and criticize the idealist concept of history.

From Abstract Concepts to Weapons of Struggle

Before the Great Cultural Revolution began, the philosophy department did not regard philosophy as a subject in which the students study theory to carry out class struggle and serve proletarian politics. Instead, it confined philosophy to textbooks and the classroom and asked the students to learn only some philosophical concepts from books. The situation has now fundamentally changed.

In conjunction with the study of the basic theories of historical materialism, 150 teachers and students of the philosophy department in the third year not long ago spent one and a half months carrying out social investigations in several factories, shops and schools and among the inhabitants in the capital's western district. They put the stress on investigating the management system of industrial enterprises, class struggle in commercial departments, education among children and youngsters, and other questions. In the course of which the students raised many practical and theoretical questions, such as the law of class struggle in the period of socialism, the features and law of struggle between the proletariat and the bourgeoisie in influencing and winning over the younger generation. With the teachers' guidance, they read and studied hard and strove to use the Marxist stand, viewpoint and method to answer these questions. In addition to over 60 fact-finding reports and study notes by individuals, they joined efforts to write more than 30 investigation reports.

To gain a deeper understanding of the Marxist theory of knowledge, a group of teachers and students from the same department visited the Yungting Machinery Plant where experienced workers had through collective efforts created a new-type drill bit. Their aim was to analyse, in the light of this technical innovation, such reactionary fallacies as idealist apriorism spread by Liu Shao-chi and other political swindlers and to find out typical examples of workers' applying the materialist theory of reflection in practice. On the basis of investigations, the students carried out mass revolutionary criticism together with the workers. Meanwhile, they earnestly restudied Theses on Feuerbach, Ludwig Feuerbach and the End of Classical German Philosophy, some chapters of Anti-Duhring and Materialism and Empirio-Criticism and other works by Marx, Engels, Lenin and Stalin and Chairman Mao's works like On Practice and Where Do Man's Correct Ideas Come From? . . .

Lively Pedagogic Activities

When studying the road of development for socialist agriculture, the students in the political-economy department read Engels' The Peasant Question in France and Germany, Lenin's On Co-operation and Chairman Mao's works on agricultural co-operation. Afterwards the teachers took them to several people's communes with different characteristics to carry out social surveys. While in Hsipu Production Brigade of the Chienming People's Commune in Hopei Province's Tsunhua County, a brigade commended by Chairman Mao during the movement for agricultural co-operation, they learnt about the entire course of agricultural collectivization from old poor peasants and cadres. When the co-operative which later developed into the present brigade had been set up, it was very poor and owned only three-fourths of a donkey, the sole draught animal shared by a number of peasant households of which one-fourth did not join the co-op. Today farming in this brigade is being mechanized. After reading and collecting a large amount of data coupled with serious study of Marxist works in the course of investigation, the teachers and students gained a deeper understanding of the Marxist-Leninist theory of co-operation.

Some teachers and students in the international politics department had their lessons on Lenin's Imperialism, the Highest Stage of Capitalism in the Mentoukou Coal-Mine, the iron-smelting mill of the Shoutu Iron and Steel Company and the Shihchingshan Power Plant

290

on Peking's western outskirts. All had been victims of imperialist plunder. While extensively investigating the history of savage imperialist plunder, the teachers and students held forums with veteran workers who accused the imperialists of barbarous exploitation and raised many questions on the current international class struggle. This was an impetus to the teachers and students in their theoretical study and research work. With the help of the teachers, the students extensively read relevant material and at the same time studied Lenin's work. As a result, they arrived at a deep understanding of Lenin's thesis that export of capital is a major characteristic of imperialism. These lively pedagogic activities enabled the students to write four fact-finding reports, including "Plunder of the Mentoukou Coal-Mine by the Imperialist Powers," "An Investigation on Imperialist Capital Export in the Shihchingshan Tube Casting Mill" and "Imperialist Control and Plunder of the Shihchingshan Power Plant."

Taking all society and their factory has brought marked improvement in the quality of teaching to the liberal arts. Speaking of his own experience, a young philosophy teacher said: "I studied philosophy for five years in the old Peking University. When I wrote year-end and graduate theses, I often copied abstract concepts and philosophical jargon. Now with only a little over a year's study, students have begun to use Marxist theory to criticize the bourgeoisie and write articles with clear-cut views and rich contents. This is a striking contrast between the two lines in education and the results produced."

* * * * *

Adult education, 10-11, 22, 32, 75-
76, 78
American influence, 20-21, 23, 122
Agricultural school, 30, 52, 150-51,
220
Anti-intellectualism, 217, 222,
251-52, 283
Anti-Rightist Campaign, 30, 122,
138

Barefoot doctors, 119, 150-51,
203, 209
Book knowledge, 6, 117, 133, 138,
143, 159, 181, 218-19, 225
Bourgeois education, 164, 178, 231,
234, 262, 274
Bourgeois ideology, 59-60, 122-23,
127, 194, 228

Cadres, 32, 118-19, 238, 242, 245;
training, 8-11, 96-97; (see May
7 Cadre School)
Chinese People's University, 16,
231
Chou En-lai, 32, 122-23, 189
Class education, 33, 47, 60, 65-66,
154
Class consciousness, 48-49, 60,
72, 122; class love, 125
Class enemies, 48, 56, 72, 107,
120, 124, 172, 248, 276, 281
Class struggle, 3, 34, 60, 63, 118-
19, 122, 124, 152, 173, 217, 233
238, 247, 256-57, 261, 268, 277,
286, 289
Classical education, 20, 34, 165-66,
212, 221
Collective learning, 15, 116
Communist Youth League, 44, 61,

70-73, 79, 103, 155, 246
Confucius, 34-35, 222
Control of education, 5-6, 109, 196
Criticism-rectification, 72-73, 117,
183, 210
Cultural courses, 2, 54, 131, 251
Curriculum, 6, 42, 52-55, 117,
203, 239, 242, 249, 280 (see
Teaching materials)

Decentralization, 11-12, 45 (see
Local management)
Directives: March 7; 243, May 7,
113-14, 233, 259, proletarian
leadership, 90, 260; reeducation of
intellectuals, 95, 273; part-work,
part-study, 219; sixteen-point
decision, 234-35; factories and
schools, 278; universities, 283-
84
Discussion method, 11, 62, 116, 250

Education: broad concept, 2, 104,
162, 188; World War II, 23
Educated youth, 52, 95, 174, 273
Educational revolution, 1, 4-7, 13,
30, 38-39, 42, 137-39, 142, 149,
160, 182-83, 187, 191, 194-96,
204, 239, 252, 260-63
Educators, 55, 197-98
Elementary education, 11-12, 48,
50, 242
Elitist education, 26-28, 39, 88,
124-25, 137-39, 154, 199-200
Emotions (feelings), 2, 48, 75, 129,
142, 194, 205-206
European influence, 22-23
Examinations, 44, 139, 143, 178,
221, 223, 229-30, 250

Exhibits, 10, 48, 64-65, 76, 103
Extracurricular activities, 62,
    67-69, 163, 246

Factories and schools, 46, 81-82
Fame and personal gain, 29, 34,
    56, 99, 122-23, 125, 130, 150,
    188, 226
Family education (home; parents),
    46-48, 50, 101-102, 246, 248
Flexibility, 50, 183
Foreign languages, 54, 176; English,
    55; Japanese, 55; Russian, 24,
    55
Formalism, 165, 169-71, 176, 191
Freedom, 21-22, 122, 148
Futan University, 90, 92, 149, 154,
    180

Girl students (Women), 99-100,
    108, 116-17, 220

Higher education, 10, 17, 24, 45,
    137, 154; admissions, 5, 139-41,
    162, 180, 205, 228; closed, 4,
    138-39, 230; problems, 156,
    205; science and engineering,
    141, 283, 287 (see Liberal arts,
    Shanghai Machine Tools Plant
    Universities)
Histories, three or four, 33, 64,
    129, 165
Human nature, theory of, 34, 61,
    64, 117, 192
"Hundred flowers" Campaign,
    30, 122

Ideological remolding, 8, 15, 32,
    59-60, 115, 124-26, 151-52,
    192-93, 243; long process, 106,
    127, 152
Immediate needs, 12, 52, 202
Intellectuals, 96, 123, 216, 218,
    223, 262, 273-74; absorb and
    reform, 87, 93, 121, 122, 131,

169, 181, 273; bourgeois, 25-29,
    87, 160-61, 163, 280-81; down-
    graded, 127-28, 153, 156, 248;
    remolding, 8, 87, 92, 99, 121,
    123, 125-26, 128, 153, unclean,
    98; use of, 123, 128-29, 169, 180

Kang Ta, 8-10; spirit of, 50, 53
Knowledge, Mao's theory, 35, 62,
    131, 181, 216, 231-32
Kuomintang education, 15, 20-22,
    25, 27-28

Labor, 27-28, 35, 80-81, 115, 117,
    120, 151, 164, 226, 236, 249,
    251 (see Production)
Language reform, 17, 76
Liberal arts college, 27, 137, 141,
    145, 224, 288
Line education, 34, 47, 51, 63-66,
    68, 79
Line struggle, 44, 61, 103, 118,
    121, 131, 142, 145, 156, 167, 171,
    182, 188, 245
Literacy, 11, 17, 75-77, 161
Literature and art, 53, 68, 77,
    123, 146-47, 155, 235
Liu Shao-ch'i, 26, 30, 74, 117, 155,
    177, 189, 269
Local management, 11-13, 44-45,
    163, 183, 189

Mao Tse-tung, 1, 6, 42, 48, 50, 55,
    285; educational line, 29-30, 35,
    63, 66, 159-60, 226; portrait,
    190, 285-86; quotations, 1, 42, 48,
    50, 55, 62, 285; Thought, 44, 53,
    62-63, 67, 74, 91, 132-33, 142,
    144, 146, 148, 154, 163-64, 167,
    191, 248; works, 6-7, 63, 140,
    233, 237, 242-43, 286
May 4 Movement, 21, 27, 148, 212
May 7 Cadre School, 113, 255-59;
    directive, 113, 144, 233; problems,
    120

Marxism-Leninism, works, 15,
62, 117, 153, 165, 256
Medical education, 53, 119, 149-50
(see Barefoot doctors)
Military, role of, 82, 100, 113, 234
Military training, 42, 51, 53, 116,
139, 144, 220, 234, 236, 249, 279
Missionary education, 21, 24, 155

New man, 3-4,29, 73-74, 188, 191-
92, 194-95, 203, 258
New Thought Movement, 21, 27,
148, 212

Open-door schools, 46, 116, 118,
149, 163, 188

Party leadership, 46, 53, 69, 71,
94, 103-104, 109, 131, 155, 196
Past miseries, present happiness,
33, 47, 64-66, 154-55, 171, 271;
bitterness meals, 65, 92, 155,
271
Peasant, poor and lower-middle,
44, 48, 52, 89, 102-103, 118, 149
225, 232, 244-45, 260, 263-68,
271
Peking University, 28, 31, 141,
147-48, 153, 155, 284, 287
Philosophy, study of, 62, 77, 117,
145, 147, 156, 167, 169, 217, 224
Political education, 6, 15, 42, 51,
61-62, 77, 79, 144, 152, 245-46,
249, 252; political consciousness, 75, 78, 134, 142, 151, 219,
228; politics in command, 44, 52,
59, 124, 133-34, 219, 249, 252
Preschool education, 47
Private education, 22-24, 45-46
Production, 6, 16, 35, 45, 60, 80,
119, 220 (see Labor)
Proletarian intelligentsia, 16, 35,
141, 144, 154-56, 179
Proletarian leadership, 5, 88, 164,
182, 260

Propaganda team, Mao Tse-tung
Thought, 5, 68, 83, 89-91, 142,
146, 153, 155, 163, 260; problems
92

Rectification campaign, 1, 7, 13,
32, 61, 66, 104, 122
Red and expert, 30, 51, 75, 80,
138-39, 182, 218-19
Red Guards, 3, 40-41, 42, 44, 70-
71, 91, 97, 105, 175, 246, 261
Red Little Soldiers, 42, 48, 70-72,
242
Reeducation of intellectuals, 6, 52,
94, 109, 114, 125, 273; results,
104; problems, 106
Refugees, 107, 175
Repetition, method of, 62-63, 117,
148, 163, 190
Revolutionary Committee, 44-45,
94, 109, 115, 148, 155, 196-97,
245, 261, 264
Revisionism, 13, 26-27, 34, 48-49,
56, 99, 124, 137, 160, 182
Revolutionary mass criticism, 35,
52, 63, 120, 146, 148-50, 153,
182-83, 263

School programs, 42-44
Schools, regular, 12-14, 16-17, 26,
31, 38-39, 200, 204
Schools, reopened, 4, 40-41, 83,
238-40, 242-43
School system, 17, 20, 22, 31, 38-
39, 42, 44, 222, 231-33, 235, 239,
251, 261, 264; modern, 20-21;
Kuomintang, 32
School and society, 46, 68, 146,
162-63, 183, 188, 224 (see
Family education;Extracurricular
activities)
Secondary education, 11, 51
Self-criticsm, 94, 122-23, 125
Self-interest (vs. selflessness),
74-75, 99, 125, 188, 193, 241

Serve the people (or revolution), 74-75, 114, 150, 188, 203
Shanghai Machine Tools Plant, 141, 282, 284
Shifts and reversals, 16, 181, 183
Shortened schooling, 9, 12, 35, 42, 220, 222, 231-32, 236, 239, 266-67
"Sixteen Points", 42, 64, 234, 242
Social investigation, 65, 147, 149-50, 153, 163, 165, 258, 289
Socialist education movement, 31, 113, 234
Songs, 42, 53, 70, 100, 242
Soviet influence, 20, 24, 137, 204-05, Kairov, 34-35
Spare-time education, 16-17, 24, 78-79, 131, 137, 161
Standards, scholarship, 23, 26-27, 143, 149, 161, 183, 199
Struggle-criticism-transformation, 44, 64, 91, 101, 119, 130, 139, 142, 238, 242-43, 245, 260-61
Study, academic, 53, 177-79, 183, 212-13 (see Cultural studies)
Study, ideological-political, 61, 71, 78, 118, 121
Successors to revolution, 26-27, 31-32, 73, 103, 138-39, 172, 228, 231, 239, 244

Tabula rasa, 206
Teachers, 129-30, 153, 221, 243, 247-48; morale, 133, 199; old, 93, 130-31, 132, 154, 165, 248; problems, 132; remolding, 44, 51, 129, 248, 255; shortage, 130-31, 159; training, 129, 131, 198 (see Educators)
Teaching materials, 55-56, 146, 148, 156, 163, 165, 176, 182, 233, 249-50; bad books, 68
Teaching methods, 222-23, 232, 236, 250-51, 264 (see Repetition)
Technicians, 6, 141, 219, 236, 282
Technical schools, 51

Technique, importance of, 11, 51 172, 179, 182, 184, 219
Textbooks (see Teaching materials)
Theory and practice, 17, 35, 121, 124, 144-45, 147, 150, 178-79 181-82, 201, 218, 249-50, 271
Three Great Articles, 41-42, 50, 52, 62-63, 150, 166, 190
Three Great Revolutionary Movements, 44, 52-53, 105, 117, 142, 146, 149-51, 225, 227, 231, 244, 248, 261, 281
Three-in-one combination, 55, 241, 243, 260, 279; teachers, 143, 154 (see Revolutionary Committee)
Thrift and economy, 9, 45, 47, 51, 115, 117, 151, 250, 268
Tsinghua University, 5, 28, 90-91, 114, 126, 139, 141-42, 147, 224, 284
T'ung-chi University, 141, 144, 154, 278-80

Universities, 5, 10, 16, 27, 137, 220, 222, 225, 230, 232, 284; Christian, 21, 155 (see Higher education)

Variations, 47, 50, 68, 82, 183, 189
Vacations, 68, 103
Verbalism, 169-71

Work-study plan, 17, 30, 51, 161, 250
Worker-peasant schools, 16-17, 24, 38-39, 78-79, 88, 161, 284
Workers-peasants-soldiers, 5, 83, 87-88, 102-03, 118, 120, 130, 139, 149, 161, 163, 197, 225, 227, 235, 237, 273, 284; integration with, 99, 115, 118, 120, 273
Yenan education, 7-10, 12, 160, 192
Youth, 104, 275-77 (see Educated youth)
Youth organizations, 68, 70, 103; rectification, 72

THEODORE HSI-EN CHEN is Professor of International Education at the University of Southern California, where he has also served as chairman of the department of Asian Studies and director of the East Asian Studies Center. He is the former Dean and President of Fukien Christian University of Foochow, China, and organized Tunghai University in Taiwan as a representative of the United Board of Christian Higher Education in Asia.

The author of seven books and over 100 articles, Dr. Chen has written widely on Chinese education.

Dr. Chen received his B.A. from Fukien Christian University, his M.A. from Columbia University, and his Ph.D. from the University of Southern California.

RELATED TITLES
Published by
Praeger Special Studies

CHINA AND THE QUESTION OF TAIWAN:
Documents and Analysis
edited by Hungdah Chiu

LAND REFORM IN THE PEOPLE'S REPUBLIC
OF CHINA: Institutional Transformation in
Agriculture
John Wong

THE MILITARY AND POLITICAL POWER IN
CHINA IN THE 1970s
edited by William W. Whitson

THE ORGANIZATION AND SUPPORT OF
SCIENTIFIC RESEARCH AND DEVELOPMENT
IN MAINLAND CHINA
Yuan-li Wu and Robert B. Sheeks

RENEWALS 691-4574

D